Managing the UK Economy
Current Controversies

Edited by

Grahame Thompson, Vivienne Brown
and Rosalind Levačić

Polity Press

This book is based on the Open University Social Sciences course D210 Introduction to Economics, first presented in 1985, Material is reproduced by Permission of the Open University.

First published in 1987 by Polity Press in association with Basil Blackwell.

Editorial Office: Polity Press, Dales Brewery, Gwydir Street, Cambridge CB1 2LJ, UK

Basil Blackwell Ltd, 108 Cowley Road, Oxford OX4 1JF, UK

British Library Cataloguing in Publication Data
Thompson, Grahame
   Managing the UK economy: current controversies.
   1. Great Britain—Economic conditions—20th century   I. Title
   II. Brown, Vivienne   III. Levačić, Rosalind   IV. Introduction to economics
   330.941′085   HC256

ISBN 0-7456-0316-5
ISBN 0-7456-0317-3 Pbk

Library of Congress Cataloging-in-Publication Data
Thompson, Grahame.
   Managing the UK economy.
   Includes bibliographies and index.
1. Great Britain—Economic policy—1945-
2. Unemployment—Great Britain—Effect of inflation on.
3. Keynesian economics.   4. Chicago school of economics.
I. Brown, Vivienne.   II. Levačić, Rosalind.   III. Title.
HC256.5.T48   1987   338.941   86-26860

ISBN 0-7456-0316-5
ISBN 0-7456-0317-3 (pbk.)

Phototypeset in 10 on 12pt Dutch Old Style
by Dobbie Typesetting Service, Plymouth, Devon
Printed in Great Britain by T. J. Press, Padstow

Contents

Notes on the Authors

Vivienne Brown is a Lecturer in Economics at The Open University.

David Cobham has been a Lecturer in Economics at The University of St Andrews since 1976.

Rosalind Levačić is a Lecturer in Economics at The Open University.

Grahame Thompson is a Senior Lecturer in Economics at The Open University.

Preface

This book has its origins in the Open University course D210 *Introduction to Economics*. The essays in this book are based on sections of the course dealing with central issues of macroeconomic regulation. Open University courses are designed to meet the needs of large numbers of non-specialist students, and so are frequently directed towards a problem-solving and policy-orientated approach, and this approach is reflected here in the way the chapters of this book have been prepared. Empirically-grounded policy issues provide the context for presenting theoretical problems and the more abstract analysis. The result is a set of linked but independent chapters dealing with the main areas of macro policy and macroeconomic analysis. A common analytical theme is the exploration and extension of the aggregate demand and supply model, but different chapters are written from different theoretical perspectives, illustrating the range of policies and theories that economists are currently debating.

We would like to thank the original course team members for the comments they made on the original material, and also Betty Atkinson, Iris Manzi and Janet Vroone for preparing the manuscript.

We would like to thank the following for permission to reproduce material in this book:

Basil Blackwell for tables drawn from Roger Backhouse, *Macroeconomics and the British Economy*

The Controller of Her Majesty's Stationery Office for material drawn from p. 14 of *Economic Trends Annual Supplement 1985*; figures from *British Industrial Performance*; extracts from *The Government's Expenditure Plan 1980-1 to 1983-4*; and from *Memorandum on Monetary Policy* (HCSCT & S, 1979-80, vol. 2, p. 9)

W. H. Freeman and Co. for adaptation of a table from W. W. Leontief, 'The Distribution of Work and Income', *Scientific American*, September, 1982

OECD for charts and tables drawn from *Role of the Public Sector*

The Royal Economic Society and Macmillan, London and Basingstoke, for a quote from a letter by J. M. Keynes to George Bernard Shaw

Introduction

GRAHAME THOMPSON

Managing the UK economy has become one of the most problematical tasks besetting any government. The relative decline of the economy during the post-war period became acutely focused with the onset of the deep depression in the 1970s. This heralded a renewed politicization of debates and discussion about the economy. As a result the UK now has one of the most fiercely contested economic policy environments amongst all the advanced industrialized countries. This has largely become polarized around monetarist versus Keynesian positions in an often entrenched, antagonistic and highly rhetorical manner. At least at the level of popular discussion it is these two approaches to economic policy-making that have dominated, and which tend to provide the framework for debate and controversy. In this book we examine these in some detail, but at the same time show how a range of intermediate positions, and indeed alternative ones, are also worthy of serious consideration. Thus one of the aims of the book is to present as clearly as possible the differences between various approaches to managing the national economy that have arisen within the UK debate over the past 10 years or so. In a moment we come back to the nature of these positions and their wider implications, but first it will be useful to sketch in some of the historical background to that emergence.

One of the main points of contemporary controversy concerns the legitimate role of the government as an actor in the economy. This issue has arisen primarily as a result of the growing involvement of state intervention and regulation of capitalist economies since the war. An indication of such involvement is given by figure 1, which shows the increasing importance of general government revenues and expenditures as a percentage of GDP for a number of countries. This helped propel the issue of the trends in government expenditure to the forefront of political and ideological discussion, particularly in the UK. But the UK by no means displays unusual or extreme growth of such involvement, as measured in these terms. A number of countries, perhaps best exemplified by Sweden in figure 1, have experienced faster government expenditure growth rates than in the UK over the post-war period. As figure 2 demonstrates, the UK was very close to the OECD average in terms of government revenues and expenditure as a percentage of GDP

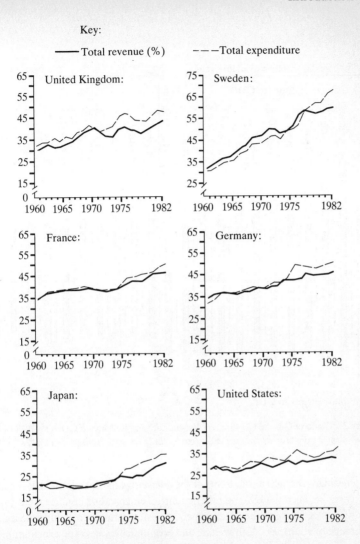

Key:

———Total revenue (%)   – – –Total expenditure

Figure 1. *Trends in General Government Expenditure and Revenue Shares of GDP* (%, 1960–82).
Source: Adapted from 'The role of the public sector' *OECD Economic Studies* 4, Spring 1985,
OECD, Paris, Chart 2, pp. 32–5.

in 1982 – eleven countries had higher proportions of government expenditures, while ten has lower. Nor should the UK's 48 per cent be taken exactly at face value, since in terms of general governments' share of final consumption this was only 25 per cent of GDP in 1982, the same as in 1960, again very much lower than a number of other countries (OECD, *Economic Studies* 4, Spring 1985, Table 11, p. 59).

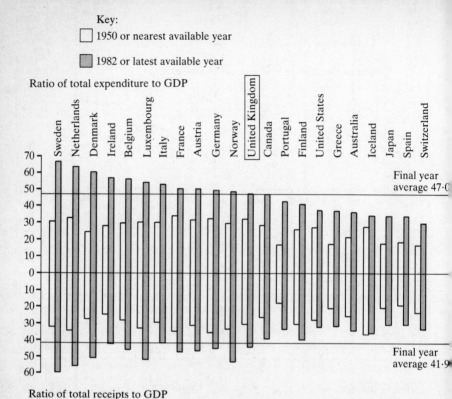

Key:
☐ 1950 or nearest available year
▨ 1982 or latest available year

Figure 2. Ratio of General Government Expenditure and Revenue to GDP (1960 and 1982) *Source:* adapted from 'The role of the public sector', *OECD Economic Studies*, 4, Spring 1985, OECD Paris, chart 2, p. 30.

Interestingly enough, it is in terms of the *composition* of expenditure that the main differences between the UK and other countries emerge. For instance table 1 gives the differences between the mean expenditures on a number of functional areas for a range of countries. With welfare and economic services type expenditure the UK consistently falls below the OECD mean, despite the emphasis in popular political debate given to the supposed undesirable consequences of the growth of the welfare state and economic support for industry in the UK. It is on defence expenditure and the cost of the administrative apparatus that the UK demonstrates higher than mean scores.

Another economic issue to re-emerge as important over this period was the inflation rate. Figure 3 shows indexes of inflation for the period 1914–84. During and after the First World War inflation escalated, but through the 1920s and early 1930s prices were falling. They climbed a little in the late 1930s, remaining

Table 1. Ratio of general government functional expenditure components to GDP[a] (percentage point deviations from sample mean)

	Defence	Education	Health	Social security	Economic services	General administration[b]
Sample mean	2.9	6.2	5.2	15.3	5.7	7.0
Australia	−0.4	−0.2	−0.5	−7.0	−1.9	−1.5
Belgium	−0.1	1.4	−0.1	8.9	1.4	2.4
Denmark	−0.4	1.8	0.5	5.8	−0.8	1.6
France	0.6	−0.4	0.8	3.4	−2.1	0.3
Germany	0.0	−1.1	1.2	4.3	−0.4	−1.1
Ireland	−1.1	−0.2	1.4	−5.2	5.2	1.0
Italy	−1.0	−0.7	0.7	0.3	2.0	−0.9
Japan	−2.0	−1.3	−0.6	−8.0	0.3	−0.8
Netherlands	0.3	1.1	—	5.8	—	—
United Kingdom	1.8	−0.3	−0.6	−3.2	−1.3	1.5
United States	2.3	−0.2	−2.8	−5.1	−2.4	−2.4

[a] Average of latest available five years; to 1982.
[b] Including the category 'Other'.
— Not available.
Source: 'The role of the public sector', *OECD Economic Studies*, 4, Spring 1985, table 4, p. 47.

Table 2. UK unemployment rates

Period	Mean	Maximum	Minimum
1851–1920	4.4	11.9	0.4
1921–40	14.0	22.5	10.9
1941–70	1.5	2.4	0.4
1971–80	4.0	5.8	2.3
1981–5	11.2	13.1	9.1

Source: D. Morris and P. Sinclair, 'The employment problem in the 1980s', *Oxford Review of Economic Policy*, 1(2), Summer 1985, table 1, p. 2.

remarkably stable during the Second World War and after. For some 30 years the UK experienced very low inflation – which helped to establish this as the accepted pattern of economic behaviour. This expected pattern was dramatically broken in the early 1970s, as figure 3 shows.

The issue of inflation has become intimately intertwined with that of unemployment in economic policy debates. The possibility of a trade-off between inflation and unemployment, promoted strongly by the conventional economic wisdom of the 1950s and 1960s, was increasingly challenged in the 1970s and 1980s (see chapters 1–4 and 6, below, in particular). As table 2 shows, UK unemployment rates escalated in the early 1980s, virtually reaching the levels experienced during the inter-war depression.

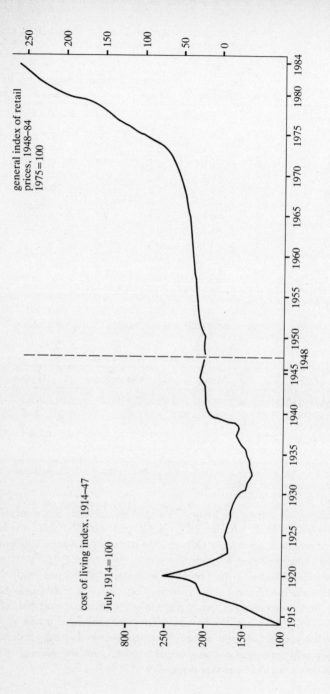

Figure 3. Inflation, 1914–84. *Sources: Cost of living index 1914–47 from Retail Prices: Indices 1914–1983*, Department of Employment, HMSO, 1984, p. 77. General index of retail prices 1948–84 from *Economic Trends, Annual Supplement: 1986 edition*, CSO, HMSO, 1986.

Despite differences amongst economists on many aspects of theory and policy, there is increasing concern with the high levels of unemployment experienced in the 1970s and 1980s. This is widely recognized to represent a major economic problem but one that shows little sign of being easily resolved. In this book we pay particular attention to different explanations of why unemployment reappeared in this period, and to proposed remedies in a policy context to ameliorate it. Three chapters (3, 4 and 5) are explicitly devoted to analysing these problems, each written from a slightly different perspective. Chapter 3 pursues an essentially neo-classical approach to unemployment, chapter 4 looks at Keynesian explanations, and chapter 5 introduces the idea of 'long waves' and technological innovation as the cause of unemployment. However, these are also designed to engage with others' arguments, and thus represent a complementary set of discussions about unemployment, rather than strictly antagonistic ones.

Perhaps the main change to have occurred in the UK economic policy environment over recent years concerns the relative importance attributed to fiscal and monetary policy. It is probably fair to suggest that until the mid-1970s fiscal policy dominated all UK governments' management strategies, with monetary policy assigned a very secondary importance. In the post-1970s period, however, this relative importance has for all intents and purposes been reversed, with monetary policy dominating fiscal policy. It is this reversal of priorities that also helps sustain the Keynesian versus monetarist character of economic debates.

One of the most obvious manifestations of the reversal is the way control over the rate of growth of the money supply virtually became the sole instrument that a government might use to discharge its responsibilities for the level of prices and aggregate demand in major industrialized economies, at least for a while in the early 1980s. Current conventional wisdom has perhaps softened a little from this extreme position, but in the UK the Conservatives' medium-term financial strategy still sees fiscal policy objectives as dependent upon the need to achieve a given outcome for the growth of the money supply, at least in its explicit announcements (see chapter 7, very recently this may have changed however).

Nevertheless, we should be careful not to reduce all economic policy debates simply to questions of fiscal or monetary policy and their relationship. For instance, there has remained a continued interest in industrial policy broadly conceived, involving various institutional initiatives and government-backed fiscal and subsidy measures. In addition the importance of balance-of-payments considerations and attendant exchange rate issues should not be underestimated. Indeed, as is argued in a number of chapters (1, 8 and 9 in particular), the international position of the economy has increasingly come to dominate domestic policy initiatives, particularly after the demise of the Bretton Woods fixed (but managed) exchange rate system in 1973 when the world economy adopted a flexible exchange rate regime. The death knell for the fixed-rate system was in fact sounded 2 years earlier when the US dollar ceased to be convertible against gold – a recognition once and for all of the domination of international credit money as the major means of world payments. Thus behind some of the domestic-oriented debates lay increasing structural changes at the level of the world economy itself.

One further consequence of the increasing internationalization and integration of economic activity has been a revival of interest in what might be termed 'managing the world economy' rather than the traditional focus on managing individual economies within it. Historically the first identifiable approach to managing a world economic system was the gold standard period which lasted roughly from 1860 to 1930. This is discussed in chapter 1. There it is pointed out that even during the 'classical' period of the gold standard (1880–1914) the system never operated as a totally efficient and quasi-automatic mechanism for co-ordinating the actions of national monetary authorities. The rules of the gold standard game were often 'massaged' by central banks intent on neutralizing rather than accommodating or reinforcing the effects of other economies on them (Eichengreen, 1985a,b).

The Bretton Woods system, inaugurated in 1946 and referred to above, probably represented the high point of international policy co-ordination so far achieved at a world level. Along with the IMF and GATT it set up a framework of institutional mechanisms for the relatively successful alignment (and at times realignment) of domestic and international economic conditions. Above all else this approach was designed to maintain monetary stability and effective world aggregate demand, both at the same time. Those countries with (temporary) balance of payments surpluses would take expansionary domestic action, and those with deficits would take restrictive domestic action, while administrative means were deployed to arrange 'fixed' (and sometimes re-fixed) exchange rates in the context of world demand and inflationary conditions.

But if the gold standard regime turned out to have a deflationary bias built into its mechanism (Eichengreen, 1985a), then in retrospect the Bretton Woods system seems to have had an inflationary bias built into its operation. The relative monetary stability of the 1950s and 1960s collapsed as international inflation escalated in the early 1970s, and with it fixed exchange rates dissolved. The reasons for this collapse are various, and a number are discussed in the chapters that follow. But with floating rates, and a renewed emphasis on the efficacy of market processes, international co-ordination of economic policies suffered a severe setback. Even the remaining international institutions of economic management appeared to be under suspicion, if not direct threat (Marris, 1984).

Again the idea of government intervention as a cause of problems, rather than being part of the solution to problems, gained momentum. In this context, with more severe domestic and international inflation, a deflationary bias once again entered into world economic mechanisms, but now in a rather unco-ordinated manner. Competitive strategies of deflation emerged in which each country set its monetary and fiscal policy with the objective of moving the exchange rate in its favour. This involved contracting the domestic money supply for the disinflationary benefits of an exchange rate appreciation, thereby passing any possible current account deficits on to partner countries. But with symmetric policies of this kind, no one country can achieve such an appreciation. Rather all suffer a real output contraction instead (Buiter and Marston, 1985).

In the face of these kinds of responses attempts at restimulating some form of co-ordinated economic effort to adjust the world economy out of depression have hesitatingly re-emerged. These have not met with any great success, however. For instance, the multilateral initiatives taken after the Bonn summit of 1978 are generally thought to have failed. In addition the attempt by any small individual country to singly 'demand manage' its way out of depression is now no longer possible, as the experience of France's effort to do this in 1980–81 testifies. External constraints severely limit the effectiveness of such moves. Calls have been made, however, for co-ordinated European-wide efforts to reflate all the economies of the EEC (e.g. by Layard *et al.*, 1984). This would involve a temporary fiscal expansion by the Federal Republic of Germany and the UK in particular, together with accommodating monetary policy to prevent a rise in interest rates and exchange rates. The inflationary dangers of such a package would be taken care of under this proposal by some form of tax-based incomes policy. In addition, it has been shown that modest Pareto gains can be made by internationally co-ordinated macroeconomic management – particularly if this were led by the United States, Germany and Japan (Oudiz and Sachs, 1984).

Other approaches to co-ordinated economic policy on a European-wide basis, involving the UK in particular, have centred on the European Monetary System. This mechanism is one designed to generate exchange rate stability within the EEC, though Britain is not a full member. Whether sterling should join the 'snake' – whereby exchange rates are kept within certain determinate bands – and thus relinquish at least some control over domestic monetary policy to the EEC, remains an open political and economic issue (Pando Schippa, 1985).

The difficulty with any policy co-ordination along these lines is clearly a political one. Economic policy co-ordination requires as a prerequisite under contemporary conditions a political commitment, which is generally lacking. This raises once again the acute politicization of economic policy debates. The main alternatives to such co-ordination at present are either a continuation of the deregulation and liberalization of international economic relations – i.e. a further freeing of markets and possibly the undermining of international institutions associated with economic management – or a return to some form of widespread protectionism. Only if the 'danger' associated with either of these two alternative developments becomes so great is the co-ordination option likely to take serious hold. In the European context such a coincidence of political commitment amongst the disparate governments involved looks unlikely in the immediate future. In fact one condition that seems necessary for any summit dealing with policy co-ordination to be successful is for there to be substantial disagreements *within* governments, rather than between governments.

This enables the formation of coalitions across government lines, and amongst various parties within each government, to pursue and achieve a particular line. By contrast when governments have gone to summits with well-defined and hardened positions, agreement has been much more difficult to achieve (Putnam and Bayne, 1984). What is clear, however, is that the likelihood of any single European government, divided or otherwise, successfully managing itself out of a depressed situation, whether this be led by fiscal or monetary policy, is difficult to envisage.

Returning now to the more central focus of this book it is also the case that domestic-orientated policy debates are thoroughly imbued with political disputes (Tomlinson, 1986). Further, it should be noted that there is no clear coincidence between political positions taken within such debates and the theoretical underpinnings that inform the policy proposals made. Whilst it is true that by and large some form of Keynesianism is favoured by the left of the political spectrum, and monetarism by the right, this distinction itself, as far as UK macroeconomic debates are concerned, has recently been questioned (Cobham, 1984). The argument here is that there has been a convergence between Keynesianism and monetarism in recent years, where elements of each position are being re-articulated into a more common approach. Some Keynesians are beginning to accept the importance of monetary factors in the determination of real economic activity and for the primary need to control the money supply, while some monetarists accept the need for fiscal policy and do not see the economy as 'naturally' reaching a full employment level in the context of perfect market clearing. On the Keynesian side there has also been some recognition of real wage resistance in the labour market, giving rise to formulations accepting the absence of money illusion. Thus it is accepted that labour may bargain on the basis of the real wage rather than the money wage. At the same time on the monetarist side important short-term cost push effects on the price level have been recognized (e.g. sharp oil price rises).

One important area where such theoretical convergence is tending to emerge concerns 'buffer stock monetarism' or 'disequilibrium money' (Goodhart, 1984; Laidler, 1984; Bain and McGregory, 1985). This explains money holding in terms of a 'buffer' held to absorb unexpected shocks to the financial system and unforeseen fluctuations in income and expenditure. Thus monetarists can find in this analysis at emphasis on money as central to the level of economic activity, and Keynesians can accept the implication that markets do not continuously clear (if markets clear continuously and prices adjust instantaneously there is no need for buffer stocks).

But while there may be a convergence between *some* Keynesians and *some* monetarists along these lines other positions more closely associated with the traditional separation also continue to exist. Thus economists such as Kaldor have clung to the more conventional Keynesian formulations, where money is thought to have no autonomous impact on the conditions of economic activity, and have carried out a sustained critique of all monetarisms and their policy implications

(Kaldor, 1982). In addition, the post-Keynesian school associated most closely with Joan Robinson has stood by the Keynesian-inspired wage bargaining model as being conducted in money terms rather than in real terms (the monetarist assumption) and developed its analysis of other markets in terms of imperfect competition and oligopoly (Kregel, 1975).

On the other hand the new-classical form of monetarism has not embraced the 'buffer stock' approach but has instead pressed ahead with the idea of rigorous market clearing and the near-instantaneous adjustment of markets via the notion of rational expectations (Minford, 1980). Nor should this position be confused with strict 'supply side economics' or the Neo-Austrianism of Hayek and his supporters (see Thompson, 1986, chapter 4).

By and large these later Keynesian and monetarist positions are not directly addressed as such in this book, other than where they impinge on the mainstream Keynesian and monetarist analysis, or where they have been of particular importance in contemporary policy debates. We have focused the analysis in the chapters below on those positions which have been of central importance to the UK macroeconomic controversies over the past 10 years or so. This is not to suggest that these other positions are unimportant or not worthy of consideration; only that they have not played a central role in such contemporary policy debates. By and large they have offered a critical assessment of those debates rather than being instrumental in organizing them. This also goes for contemporary Marxism, though again this is introduced peripherally in some of the chapters. Marxism does not appear to have anything distinctive to say about managing a capitalist national economy. Indeed it would argue that such a project is misplaced. Rather Marxism begins from quite different premises. It stresses structural features of capitalism underpinned by a sharp and enduring conflict between capital and labour. Longer cycles of economic change, involving successive booms and slumps, require a restructuring of the economy to allow renewed cycles of accumulation. This theory would focus on a different set of economic variables for critical assessement, notably the rate of profit. For this position weaknesses in the UK economy are not analysed in terms of the usual macro-economic aggregates but around the axis of class struggle. The relative performance of the economy has to do with the orientation of UK capital – involving the institutional and political dominance of financial over industrial interests. Clearly a different set of policy issues to those hinted at so far in this Introduction, and indeed to those discussed in the chapters below, arises in this context. The labour market for instance would be seen as above all else an arena for exploitation rather than one involving the more or less rapid adjustment of wages (though here the labour market and its mode of operation under capitalism is still a crucial site of Marxist interest). Given the focus of this book however, which accepts that more traditional conceptions of economic management of capitalist economies are at least possible, we do not consider Marxism at any length.

Where these other positions arise most acutely in the chapters below involves the discussion of the manner in which the aggregate demand and supply (AD/AS) model deployed in the book has itself shifted the terms of the debate between Keynesianism and monetarism, and possibly in the latter's favour. It is in chapter 10 that the issue of 'convergence' between positions, at least in terms of the manner of conducting policy debates, is located and discussed. Here it is the very terms of the debate that are questioned rather than the particularities of the formulations adopted by either Keynesians or monetarists.

It now remains to say something about the overall objectives of this book, the approaches adopted within it, and the role of individual chapters. As should be clear by now, we have designed the chapters so that they bring out differing approaches, both theoretically and in terms of policy implications, towards managing the economy. This has been our overriding aim. To do this we have adopted the AD/AS model as the most efficient way of representing these differences. This model is set up early in the book (chapter 2) and then used as the organizing framework around which the analyses of the subsequent chapters are developed. Thus although these chapters are written with very different objectives in mind, and often from quite divergent theoretical premises, they are co-ordinated in terms of the AD/AS model as far as is possible.

In addition the book is designed to provide a series of secondary readings that might accompany a more traditional textbook treatment of the issues raised. Thus the chapters also stand individually in their own right. They are self-contained analyses of a definite issue or problem but share this common framework. Clearly while such an approach has obvious advantages in terms of organizational continuity and pedagogic clarity, it also suffers from a number of disadvantages. To begin with not everything there is to say about managing the economy can easily be fitted into such a framework. For instance we have somewhat neglected the interaction of the real economy and monetary sectors that IS-LM analysis or budget-constrained models deal with. In addition the level at which the model is developed does not allow a full integration of the open economy into the analysis. This accounts for the way chapter 8 develops its discussion relatively independently, though even here the model still provides the analytical basis of the material presented. Thirdly, this framework is itself not necessarily neutral in terms of the different approaches presented to managing the economy. While the AD/AS model is increasingly being deployed in textbook expositions of macroeconomic theory – because of its usefulness in highlighting the basic differences between traditional Keynesian and monetarist approaches with respect to the supply side of the economy – it makes non-equilibriating analyses of economic management more difficult to explain. To try and open up this issue more clearly the final chapter of the book provides a critique of the AD/AS model deployed within the rest of the book. It is thus important to note that differences of opinion with respect to the legitimacy and usefulness of the AD/AS model are represented within chapters 2 and 10, which are themselves written by two of the editors of the book.

The second main aim of the book is to develop the chapters very much in terms of historical and empirical examples. What theory is taught in this book is done in the context of concrete policy problems that have appeared in connection with managing the UK economy over the post-war period in the main. We have already tried to give a flavour of this approach within the earlier part of this introduction. But because the chapters stand as independent analyses in their own right, and are informed by historical and empirical problems, there are times when the separate analyses overlap a little. As far as possible, however, each chapter develops a distinct area or approach and any overlap is minimized.

Another feature of this book we feel worth drawing attention to is the emphasis given to supply-side management. The supply side has become a popular policy arena over the past 10 years or so, and debates that have gone on around it are particularly focused in chapters 3, 4 and 5 with respect to labour market conditions, and in chapter 9 with respect to capital inputs and productivity. As will become apparent on reading these chapters, a concern with the supply side is not necessarily confined to any one particular economic position, though it has tended to become associated with arguments for deregulation and the restimulation of market mechanisms in recent years.

In general we have tried to develop the analytical material in this book discursively and with as little resort to mathematical notation as possible. The AS/AD model is itself largely presented graphically without much formal derivation, other than the use of simple equation notation. By and large this is the way other chapters are also arranged. Our aim has been to make the book accessible to non-specialist economists and others interested in policy problems, but also to provide an interesting and slightly more specialist grounding for first- or second-year under-graduate economists at the same time. This is the type of audience that the Open University attracts to its economic courses, and these chapters were originally developed as part of a course providing such an introductory approach.

The plan of the rest of the book is as follows:

Chapter 1: Objective and instruments of economic management. This chapter provides an overview of the changing ways in which economic objectives have appeared in macroeconomic management, and of the instruments developed by governments to try and steer the economy along a more desirable trajectory. It looks in detail at the historical emergence of economic problems, at the way different hierarchies of objectives have been formulated, and at the constraints and policy instruments devised to try to circumvent problems and to achieve the policy objectives set. In doing this the conflicts inherent in any macroeconomic policy regime are highlighted, and points of direction indicated to where these are more thoroughly treated in later chapters.

Chapter 2: The analysis of economic management: the aggregate demand and supply model. This serves a double purpose. In the first place it develops the main analytical apparatus used in the subsequent chapters of the book. This involves detailing the relationship between the goods and money market to derive the aggregate demand schedule, and looking at the labour market and aggregate production function relationship to derive the aggregate supply schedule. These are then put together to depict the characteristic Keynesian and monetarist analysis of short-run macro-management problems. Secondly, this framework is used to preliminarily specify how the economy was actually managed over the post-war period, and to point to the changing theoretical underpinning of economic management that developed during the 1970s. These two aspects are interwoven in the chapter.

Chapter 3: The determinants of the natural rate of unemployment. This is the first of the chapters dealing with unemployment. It presents a largely neo-classical analysis of the aggregate labour market with particular emphasis on the determinants of the supply of labour and on the role of the concept of a market clearing real wage rate. The concept of the natural rate of unemployment is examined, together with the main variables thought to determine it (e.g. trade union activity, employment legislation, replacement ratio). Supply-side policies aimed at reducing the natural rate of unemployment are then considered.

Chapter 4: Demand-deficient unemployment. This chapter offers a Keynesian approach to unemployment and recession. It argues that the mistakenly short-run charter of the AD/AS model has weakened Keynesian arguments for promoting policy initiatives for non-inflationary increases in aggregate demand and output. The chapter argues that the effect of changes in capital use (including the effects of changes in investment demand) on the supply side of the economy should be taken into account in the AD/AS model, and that this interaction of the demand and supply sides strengthens the traditional Keynesian emphasis on the importance of deficiences in aggregate demand in causing unemployment. In addition the chapter cautions against a real wage cut as the only means of restoring employment equilibrium.

Chapter 5: Unemployment and technology. This completes the three chapters dealing with unemployment by focusing on the technological causes of unemployment. The chapter is designed to try and determine whether at least some part of unemployment can be identified which is not the result either of a real wage rate which is too high, or of the lack of aggregate demand, but of technological and other structural changes in the economy. It does this by reviewing a number of approaches to issues of input combination in the production process, and by looking at empirical research directed at the consequences of technological change.

Chapter 6: Inflation and unemployment. This chapter uses the AD/AS model to present typical Keynesian and monetarist views on the causes of inflation and appropriate policies for tackling it. The chapter then examines the nature of the relationship between inflation and unemployment, and investigates the question of whether there is a trade-off between them. As there are different answers to this question, the chapter concludes by discussing various policies proposed for coping with the interconnected problems of unemployment and inflation.

Chapter 7: Controlling the money supply. This deals with the important policy change in the post-war period already alluded to above – that is the increased emphasis given to monetary policy and, within monetary policy, to controlling the money supply rather than influencing general liquidity or the interest rate structure. It examines the problems experienced by the monetary authorities in pursuing their monetary targets, and discusses the main alternative method of monetary control which has been proposed, namely monetary base control.

Chapter 8: Managing the open economy. This chapter examines how the conduct of economic policy in a country such as the UK is affected by its integration into the world economy. It shows how the openness of an economy constrains the pursuit of domestic reflation under fixed exchange rates, and analyses whether changing or floating the exchange rate gets rid of this constraint. The main conclusion drawn is that policy problems are more complex in an open economy than in a closed one, but there are advantages as well as disadvantages to openness and the balance between the two is not obvious *a priori.*

Chapter 9: The supply side and industrial policy. This chapter pursues the non-labour market aspects of the supply side of the economy, which has attracted a great deal of attention since the mid-1970s. It looks at the reasons for concern about the supply side of the UK economy, particularly in terms of its loss of international competitiveness, and then at various arguments, strategies and policies that have been developed to try and affect this.

Chapter 10: Some reflections on the AD/As model. This presents both a critical review of the model used to provide the framework for the previous chapters and a pointer to areas of economic analysis that this framework does not address. It argues that the AD/AS model is not a neutral technical device but rather biases analysis in the direction of monetarist conclusions, broadly speaking. The chapter traces the history of the development of the model and then points to certain of the positions that it tends to marginalize or eliminate from focus. This latter discussion may strike the reader as something unnecessary from the point of view of a book on macro-economic policy. However the objective here is to open up policy analysis a little and point to what other than the mainstream positions suggest in this respect.

In particular it is argued that those traditions which emphasize a non-equilibrating framework or which stress long-term structural trends and conflicts in the economy offer interesting and useful insights into how capitalist economies are run. Thus this chapter serves to highlight the range of economic analysis available in anticipation that it might stimulate further enquiry. The book concludes therefore on a somewhat theoretical note, but one designed to open up issues rather than to close them off.

Finally, as mentioned above, these chapters were originally developed as part of the course material for the Open University second level course D210: Introduction to Economics. We would like to thank all the members of the original course team for what was really a collective effort in formulating the approach adopted in that course, and in commenting on the various drafts of the material as it later emerged. Economists at the Open University display a wide range of theoretical and political approaches to their subject, and getting agreement on the content of course material has not always proved easy. However, we have managed to develop a co-operative approach despite deep and continuing differences between us. Some of these differences are registered in the chapters printed below. The editors have not seen eye to eye on everything, as a reading of the chapters should indicate, but we share a common open commitment to encouraging debate and controversy. This also has the advantage of allowing a presentation of different and related perspectives on a common set of issues. It is hoped that this experience, as registered below, will prove useful to others faced with similar problems and with similar commitments.

References

Bain, A. D. and McGregor, P. G. (1985) 'Buffer-stock monetarism and the theory of financial buffers', *The Manchester School*, 4, December, pp. 385–403.

Buiter, W. H. and Marston, R. C. (eds) (1985) *International Policy Co-ordinating*. Cambridge University Press, London.

Cobham, D. (1984) 'Convergence, divergence and realignment in British macroeconomics', *Banca Nazionale del Lavoro Quarterly Review*, 149 June, pp. 159–76.

Eichengreen, B. (1985a) 'International policy co-ordination in historical perspective: a view from the interwar years', in Buiter, W. H. and Marston, R. C. (eds), *International Economic Policy Co-ordination*. Cambridge University Press, London.

Eichengreen, B. (ed) (1985b) *The Gold Standard in Theory and History*. Methuen, London.

Goodhart, C. E. (1984) 'Disequilibrium money – a note', *Monetary Theory and Practice: The U.K. Experience*. Macmillan, London.

Kaldor, N. (1982) *The Scourge of Monetarism*. Oxford University Press, Oxford.

Kregel, J. (1975) *The Reconstruction of Political Economy: An Introduction to Post-Keynesian Economics*. Macmillan, London.

Laidler, D (1984) '"The buffer-stock" notion of monetary economics', *Economic Journal*, 94 (Suppl.), 7–34.

Layard, R., Basfri, G., Blanchard, O., Buiter, W. and Dornbusch, R. (1984) 'Europe: the case for unsustainable growth', *Centre for European Policy Studies*, paper 8/9.

Marris, R. (1984) Managing the world economy: will we ever learn?, *Essays in International Finance*, 155, Princeton University, NJ.

Minford, D. P. (1980) 'A rational expectations model of the U.K. under fixed and floating exchange rates', *Carnegie-Rochester Conference Series in Public Policy*, 12.

Oudiz, G. and Sachs, J. (1984) 'Macroeconomic policy co-ordination among the industrialised economies', *Brookings papers on Economic Activity*, 1, 1-75.

Pando Schippa, T. (1985) 'Policy co-operation and the EMS experience', in Buiter, W. F. and Marston, R. C. (eds), *International Policy Co-ordination*, Cambridge University Press, London.

Putnam, R. D. and Bayne, N. (1984) *Hanging Together: The Seven-Power Summits*. Harvard University Press, Cambridge, Mass.

Thompson, G. F. (1986) *The Conservative's Economic Policy*. Croom Helm, London.

Tomlinson, J. (1986) *Monetarism: Is there an Alternative?* Basil Blackwell, Oxford.

1

Objectives and Instruments of Economic Management

GRAHAME THOMPSON

1. Introduction

The issue of what are the legitimate and pertinent objectives and instruments of government-backed macroeconomic policy remain controversial and unsettled. While most economists would agree with the idea of promoting general economic welfare as an ultimate objective, when it comes to narrowing this down to something more explicit and concrete, opinions begin to diverge. For instance will general economic welfare be better promoted by controlling inflation and setting this as the main objective, or by setting a target for employment as the main objective? Even if the main objective is agreed to be the control of inflation, will this be better tackled by using money supply control or an incomes policy as the main instrument to affect it? We might also point to the way the balance of payments, or the existing or proposed level of government borrowing, could be thought to operate as a constraint on desirable economic policy, or not, as the case may be. For instance, the level of domestic activity may have to be kept below the full employment level because the balance of payments would go into deficit if such activity were expanded or if an increase in public expenditure would create inflationary pressures that were deemed unacceptable. It is these kinds of controversies that beset the management of economies at an aggregate level, and which form the focus of this chapter.

The chapter introduces the notion of 'managing an economy' and lays out some of the ideas that will be taken up in more detail in later chapters. An overview approach is adopted to chart the changing ways in which different economic objectives, instruments and constraints have developed, mainly over the post-war period, and the problems associated with their reconciliation.

The focus is upon the historical constitution of 'problems' in managing the economy, where 'problem' has a range of meanings and implications. For instance 'unemployment' has been variously perceived as a problem in the UK context; in the first place because of the cost it involves in terms of government expenditure on relief measures; or because of the 'burden' it places on an economy as a whole;

1

or in terms of the underemployment of available resources. But it has also been seen as a problem in that it is a cause of pauperism, and of moral and physical degradation. In addition it has been characterized as a cause of political unrest or of violence and other crime. Furthermore, it has been seen as a sign of uncompetitiveness, or of impending national decline. At different times during this century one or other of these features has predominated in government thinking on unemployment. What is true of unemployment is also true of other issues in economic policy, as will be shown later.

An important adjunct to this issue of problems is to recognize from the start that, just because certain economic ills may beset an economy, it does not *necessarily* imply that these will form recognized 'problems' for government or state agencies, so that they proceed to develop policy proposals and instruments to tackle them. One of the aims of this chapter is to specify the way, and under what conditions, particular economic issues have become policy problems. The general point here is not to take any economic policy objectives for granted, or regard them as though they had simply fallen out of thin air into the laps of policy-makers. Rather it is to try to establish their historical credentials more fully, and to plot the changing relationships between them. In other words it is to make the constitution of economic policy itself problematical.

2.   Objectives, Instruments and their Relationship

It is generally recognized that four main objectives have preoccupied government policy-making in the post-war period (Streeten, 1966; Kaldor, 1971). These are:

(a) *The maintenance of full employment*. Whilst there is difficulty in specifying exactly what 'full employment' means, it is generally recognized that despite the ambiguity it has constituted a major objective for government policy in the post-Second World War period. The White Paper of May 1944 on *Employment Policy* (Cmd 6527) first spelt out this objective in the UK context. It is usually discussed in terms of an average percentage of unemployment which is not expected to be exceeded. Much of the subsequent discussion in this chapter deals with the developments and problems associated first with the establishment, and then with the demise, of this objective in the UK.

(b) *Price stability*. The question of inflation and its effects has concerned government economic policy-making since at least the seventeenth century, but it has become a sustained focus for macroeconomic policy during the present century and especially since the Second World War. As will be seen, 'price stability' has not meant so much a zero rate of inflation but rather a low level of inflation and an attempt to keep it within fairly stable limits. This objective could thus be specified in terms of a target percentage increase or decrease in the average price level in any period.

(c) *Equilibrium on the balance of payments.* This objective could be specified in a number of slightly different ways. In general the attempt has been to maintain a 'reasonable' balance on the overall account over a period of years. Alternatively the objective might be specified in terms of a surplus on current or capital account of so many millions of pounds in any one year.

(d) *Economic growth.* Perhaps the major rationale for government-induced attempts to manage economies overall has been in the interests of growth. Thus targets involving a percentage increase in GNP could be specified. It is perhaps in centrally planned economies where this kind of objective is more predominantly deployed. In economies like the UK, where economic growth is clearly an objective of economic management, it is less often explicitly specified in terms of a particular growth rate per year. Rather it is more vaguely specified as something that should emerge as a result of getting all the other targets and management instruments to work correctly. I return to this issue later in the chapter.

As they stand, these objectives are not always clearly defined. They can simply express rather vague sentiments, though from time to time more precise targets come to the fore in official deliberations and pronouncements. They are also not exclusive; other objectives have arisen in post-war policy-making, but those outlined above are the four concentrated on in this chapter.

Having raised the question of the *objectives* of government agencies in the field of macroeconomic management it now remains to explain what is meant by the *instruments* of such regulation. Following Morris (1979), these can be divided into three broad types:

(a) *Fiscal policy.* This involves control over taxation and expenditure, sometimes summed up as the 'power of the purse'. Thus to try and influence the course of economic activity the government can change the levels of its taxation or its expenditure. There are two main forms of taxation; direct taxation involves taxes on income, while indirect taxation refers to taxes on goods and services. Government expenditure can either take the form of the government's direct purchases of goods and services for current use, or it can involve exenditure on investment, or it can take the form of transfer payments to individuals, firms or other organizations. Clearly there is a relationship between the revenue raised by the government and its expenditure.

Its income is predominantly in the form of taxation revenue, but this will also include the payments made for the consumption of government-provided goods and services, and any borrowing that the government engages in. If, in any period, its expenditure is exactly matched by its non-borrowed income (i.e. by taxes and payments to it) then the budget is said to be balanced. Unbalancing the budget is the traditional Keynesian way in which the government is said to affect aggregate demand in the economy and hence to attempt to regulate it. If the government takes an *expansionary fiscal stance*, it will spend more than it is raising in the form of taxes and payments. This, according to Keynesian theory, will stimulate economic activity by injecting autonomous expenditure into the system. It increases aggregate demand in the first instance and this itself results in an expansion of aggregate supply. On the other hand, if the government raises more taxes and revenue from payments than it spends, it will be taking a *restrictive fiscal stance*, which will withdrawn spending power from the economy and hence dampen down economic activity. This is the basic Keynesian way in which fiscal policy works in the context of regulating mixed economies of the UK type. Fiscal policy is an instrument, or set of instruments, of economic policy intended to affect output and employment.

(b) *Monetary policy*. This instrument arises from the fact that it is the government, via the central bank, that has a monopoly over the provision of legal tender. This enables it to influence the quantity of credit or money in the economy and its price, in terms of interest rates. It is generally agreed that such a policy is designed to produce reactions in the portfolios of economic agents such as banks, other financial institutions, companies and households which induce them to change their demand for real assets. (A portfolio is a range of assets held by an economic agent.) Thus the objective of monetary policy is to affect the real economy in some way. It does this either by altering a given set of interest rates on a spectrum of financial assets or by altering the flow of money within the economy more directly. Thus, broadly speaking, if the government takes up an *expansionary monetary stance*, it is trying to reduce the level of interest rates in the economy to encourage economic agents to borrow and thus to spend, and/or it will borrow more itself by selling bonds to the banking system. The banking system will in turn use those bonds as assets upon which the banks involved can create deposits for their customers and hence increase the level of credit in the economy. This will further stimulate economic activity. On the other hand, to dampen down economic activity, the government should take a *restrictive or 'tight' monetary stance*. This would involve reversing the measures outlined above in an attempt to cut back on the amount of money circulating in the economy and/or to force up interest rates and restrict credit.

In addition to this domestic side of monetary policy, the central bank, on behalf of the government, also manages the country's foreign exchange reserves. As a result it can regulate foreign exchange transactions and influence the exchange rate. Thus monetary policy has an international dimension, the exchange rate being an important policy instrument in connection with the balance of payments position and in terms of the level of domestic economic activity that can be prudently run.

(c) *Legal and administrative powers and policies*. Under this heading we can include a heterogeneous group of direct and indirect controls. Direct controls arise in the context of nationalization and regulatory bodies like the Monopolies and Mergers Commission. Indirect controls arise in the context of the legal framework of business and commerce. Wages and incomes controls can also be included under this general heading, although these are important enough for some to suggest that wages and incomes policies should be treated as a separate instrument in their own right.

Bearing these distinctions between objectives and instruments in mind, it can be shown in a formal sense that within any model set up to characterize the policy-making process as a whole, there must be the same number of instruments in the system as there are objectives, if all the objectives are to be simultaneously achieved. This is sometimes known as the 'Tinbergen rule' after the Dutch economist who was the first to analyse these relationships in the 1950s (Tinbergen, 1952). Thus if we take the four objectives of economic policy outlined above, we need four separate instruments of policy if the system is to be sure of approaching and achieving these objectives. The reasons for this are set out below.

It is not usually possible to control one objective with just one policy instrument, because the effect of a particular instrument on the *other* objectives has to be taken into account. This problem of interdependence between objectives and instruments is further complicated when an instrument *positively* affects one objective while it also *negatively* affects another. For instance, when discussing the objective of full employment in a situation of less-than-full employment we might suggest that fiscal policy be brought to bear to increase aggregate demand and hence stimulate economic activity. The government would then take up an expansionary fiscal stance, mentioned above. But as a result of this the budget is unbalanced, and to pay for its added expenditures the government needs to borrow from the financial markets. Thus the government's monetary policy is affected as well; if to achieve this borrowing the government needs to sell more debt to the banking system, such a policy might lead to an expansionary monetary position as the banks create credit in the economy. In turn this expansionary fiscal and monetary position could have the consequence of higher inflation and thus come into conflict with one of the other objectives of the government, namely that of price stability. In addition, the balance of payments could be affected negatively, and economic growth impaired.

Alternatively we might consider the consequences of the initial increase in government borrowing caused by fiscal policy on the instrument of monetary policy itself. While the argument above assumed that there was no problem for the government to borrow, with the consequence that the money supply and credit increased, in fact there could be a constraint on this. To induce any such holding of its debt by the private sector, the government might have to increase the return on it by forcing up interest rates. This could have the opposite effect to that assumed above by depressing the demand for loans and thus dampening down economic activity.

On the one hand, then, the use of the fiscal policy instrument increases economic activity via its effect on monetary policy, but on the other hand it could depress it. Equally it could have a positive effect on employment but a negative effect upon price stability. Thus there is a *conflict* in how the objectives are affected in this instance and hence a conflict over exactly how (or even if) the economy can be managed effectively to meet the objectives set.

In an ideal world policy-makers would have an accurate and fully specified model of the economy that would enable them to simultaneously calculate the values needed for the policy instruments (for example, a tax increase of n pounds, or an increase in the interest rate of m per cent) in order to achieve the desired values for the objectives. Thus the values needed for all four instruments would be simultaneously determined once the policy-makers has fed into their model the desired values for all their objectives.

In practice such accurate models of the economy are not available, so it is not possible to work out in advance the simultaneous determination of the instruments, given the desired value of the objectives. Instead policy-makers have to be much more pragmatic and adopt a trial-and-error approach which involves relating a particular instrument to one particular objective and then seeing how the objective variables behave. The instruments are then adjusted in the light of what happens to the targets. The problem is knowing which instrument relates to which objective; this is known as the assignment problem. In general the idea here is to assign the instruments to the objectives in such a manner that minimizes, or at most eliminates altogether, the contradictory possibility of the instruments positively affecting one objective while negatively affecting another. Herein lies the major problem of economic policy-making in this area.

What this discussion illustrates is the dependent character of the relationship between objectives and instruments on different conceptions or 'models' of the economy. Keynesian, monetarist or any other model of the economy will not only promote different objectives and instruments, they will also differentially assign the objectives to the instruments in an attempt to technically manage the policy problems highlighted. This relates to a further important general issue. It is not absolutely clear whether any hard-and-fast distinction can be maintained between objectives and instruments. Might not nationalization, investment or monetary growth at times become objectives in their own right, rather than being seen as instruments? The exchange rate could become an objective rather than an instrument for balance of payments equilibrium. In a similar way, price stability might become an instrument for the objective of greater equality. Thus additional objectives can get built into the system, thereby rendering objectives in other circumstances into instruments. If we bring in the constraints issue again, things can get even more complicated, since the balance of payments is often treated as constraint on other desirable policy objectives rather than (or indeed as well as) a desirable objective in its own right.

Bearing these reservations and qualifications in mind we can now turn to the actual way in which objectives, instruments and constraints have been mobilized in attempting to manage the UK economy. The analysis begins with the immediate pre-Second World War conditions; it then briefly refers to some important war-time developments, and this is followed by a more sustained discussion of post-war changes.

3.   The Immediate Pre-war Conditions

Any discussion of the immediate pre-war economic management in the UK cannot but be concerned with the effects of the gold standard and its demise. Britain was forced off the gold standard in 1931 and the exchange rate allowed to float downwards. In the purely British context the reasons for this were complex, but one of the most immediate concerned the long-run decline in the international competitiveness of British exports. This put the City's pre-eminent position as manager of the gold-standard under increasing strain (Eichengreen, 1985). Internal costs and prices proved more inflexible downwards than the maintenance of a relatively high exchange rate demanded. In effect the maintenance of the exchange rate would have required a more severe internal deflationary stance than could be adopted by the governments at the time. As concern with the possible unemployment consequences of this mounted during the 1920s, so a conflict was perceived between the interests of the domestic economy and that of its international position. Promoting industrial expansion at home was hampered by high interest rates and the high exchange rate. The Liberal Party/Keynes proposals to relieve widespread unemployment floated during the 1929 election campaign (*We can conquer unemployment*) – suggesting government-funded public works to induce added aggregate demand, i.e. a reflation – foundered on the difficulties of borrowing under the prevailing circumstances, *constrained* in the main by the international position of the economy. This resulted in a conflict of objectives, involving important differences between the Bank of England and the Treasury in the conduct of economic management.

The Treasury was against any increase in government expenditure because this would have had to be financed by borrowing. At the time the Treasury felt itself severely constrained in terms of its attempts to manage the government debt, largely as a result of forcing sterling back on to the gold standard in 1925. This has meant the pursuit of a high interest rate policy in London to try and strengthen the exchange position. The First World War was financed in the UK largely by credit – the government borrowed from the financial system to finance the expenditures rather than simply resorting to the 'printing press' to create money, as had been the case in Germany and other countries. This meant that there was a great deal of outstanding government debt within the financial system which had to be funded by the Treasury.

Before the war the London money market was dominated by commercial paper ('commercial bills', involved with the finance of trade in the main). After the war it was the Treasury bill that began to dominate: prior to 1914 the value of the annual issue of these bills rarely exceeded £30 million, whereas throughout the 1920s they fluctuated from £600 to £800 millions, consistently exceeding the value of commercial paper. This made monetary control difficult; it was rendered even more difficult by the liquidation of between £200 and £300 millions worth of short-term assets in London to help finance the war effort. Largely as a result of this, debt service charges (the cost to the government mainly made up of interest payments required to service the national debt) rose for the Treasury from 11 per cent of central government spending in 1913 to 24 per cent in 1920 and to as high as 40 per cent by 1930. The principal objective of the Treasury during this period was the conversion of the 5 per cent government loans of 1917 to a lower interest rate to reduce the cost of debt servicing (Cairncross and Eichengreen, 1983). This put it into conflict with the Bank of England, which wanted to keep long-term interest rates high so as to secure the exchange rate at $4.86. Thus serious conflict arose between the Bank and the Treasury during this period, since both had different objectives in mind in the conduct of economic policy.

It is interesting to note that there was also a difference of opinion over the *type of instrument* to employ to remedy the situation. Keynes, for instance, strongly advocated tariff controls as an alternative to devaluation, combined with a 'great National Treaty amongst ourselves' to reduce the general level of wages and production costs, and 'rationalization' of the productive structure in the form of subsidies to domestic industry for exports. He continued to press for tariffs as the single most viable alternative right up to the time of the devaluation in September 1931.

The devaluation initiated what became known as the 'cheap money policy' of the 1930s. When the constraint of the exchange rate was removed, interest rates dropped, as the Bank of England no longer had to worry to the same extent about attracting capital funds and keeping them in London. This cheap money policy stimulated domestic production; investment in housing and in the industrial structure increased significantly and the economy entered a sustained growth phase, right up to the outbreak of war in 1939. Thus the break with the gold standard enabled a new form of *monetary policy* to be pursued. While in the early 1920s the prevailing view of monetary policy was neither controversial nor considered to be connected with unemployment, by 1936 it was subject to significant dispute in the context of debates about unemployment. With the demise of the gold standard a range of new features of the economy began to become the object of government policy. It became necessary to think seriously about policies for the 'national economy'. A number of these were emerging in the mid-1930s, among which were the Liberal Party/Keynes proposals. In particular a flexible exchange rate made a domestic *monetary* policy possible (the 'cheap money' policy of the 1930s being the dominant example at the time) and it meant that the exchange rate and budgetary position of the government were also open for a new kind of calculation and policy formation. It is in this context that employment policy took a new turn after the Second World War, and indeed in which macroeconomics as we know it, and which forms the focus of this book, could be conceived.

Besides the issue of the demise of the gold standard, a further set of conditions were necessary before attempts to manipulate the government budget in the interests of the objective of 'full employment' could be mounted (Tomlinson, 1981a). In particular the government budget itself must be of a sufficient size for its use to have any real impact on the economy. Additionally (a) such a budget must be under the control of the central authorities so that local or regional state fiscal policy does not offset the direction of its use, and (b) the constituents of the budget must be open to manipulation.

By and large these conditions were met with the advent of the post-Second World War period. For instance, UK general government expenditure (local and central government current expenditure, but excluding public corporations) as a percentage of GDP at factor cost was 10.5% in 1930, 15.1% in 1938, rose to 56.1% in 1944 and was back to 18.9% in 1950, rising to 25% in 1980. In 1950 total public expenditure, which is the government expenditure figure plus government investment, debt interest and the expenditure of the public corporations, was over 41% of GDP, whereas it had been below 28% in 1930 and only 21% in 1910 (*Economic Outlook*, June 1981, Table 3, p. 32). This growth reflects the increasing involvement of state intervention to organize and regulate the UK economy.

There was also a centralization of economic decision-making with respect to expenditures, although a high proportion of actual expenditures were still made (and still continue to be made) at local level. In addition the budget was amenable to relatively quick changes in that the PAYE system was introduced in 1946. This expanded direct taxation after the war and enabled changes in tax rates and conditions of taxation to have a relatively swift impact on consumption and investment decisions in the private economy.

The final point to make here concerns the need for an elaborated system of national accounts before any serious regulation of the economy becomes a possibility. These were developing in the USA and in the UK during the 1930s, although it is generally agreed that the first time they were employed in any serious way to look at the macro character of the economy in the UK context was in the famous 1941 budget calculations, which were stimulated by Keynes himself in 'How to pay for the war' (Keynes, 1978). In fact these developments had their genesis well before Keynes began to write the *General Theory*, and they were essentially pre-Keynesian in character, stressing factor costs and rewards, market prices as expressing values of production cost, etc. They had for a long while been associated with the analysis of the US business cycle and depressions (Carson, 1975). However, they were elaborated into a *system* and fused with Keynesian theory after the Second World War. This system of accounts provided the crucial information about the hypothesized macro-relations between aggregated aspects and sectors of economic activity. It enabled the government to apply the Keynesian theory to think out and calculate the effects of changing their policy stance and of manipulating aggregates. It also enabled the different instruments of policy at hand to be assessed with respect to their likely impact.

4.   The Role of the Second World War

There are two further important elements associated with the War period that set the context for a fully fledged 'full employment' policy objective to emerge in 1945. Both of these are less economic in character but they nonetheless provide important adjuncts to the development of that particular policy (Tomlinson, 1985, chapter 1).

In the first place the great bulk of the population supported the objectives of the war. Part of the way of gaining this support was to initiate policies for social and economic reform during the war years, particularly as it was drawing to a close. These emerged as quite radical in character. William Beveridge, for instance, proposed a comprehensive scheme for social insurance, which was enthusiastically received by the population. After the war this formed a part of the basis for the construction of a 'welfare state'. In addition the famous White Paper on employment policy of 1944 (Cmd 6527) declared, 'The Government accepts as one of their primary aims and responsibilities the maintenance of a high and stable level of employment after the war' (HMSO, 1944).

These proposed schemes proved realistic in tapping popular sentiment. The enthusiastic reception of the Beveridge Report stemmed from an undoubted radicalization of the population that took place during the war. This was seized on after the war was over by the Labour Party, which provided a feasible electoral strategy for widespread social reform and for full employment. In turn this latter aspect became not simply an adjunct of social policy, but an important objective in its own right. Indeed, it was one that was shared across the political spectrum, with the Conservative and Liberal Parties also adopting it as an objective. Such a consensus on a central aspect of social and economic existence marked a very considerable consequence of the war. This was not something confined to the UK. In the USA it was embodied in the Employment Act of 1946. Other European countries adopted similar objectives, and table 1.1 shows the results of this in the immediate post-war period. Clearly some countries adopted tighter definitions and objectives than others. Britain in particular shows very low levels of overall unemployment during the period to the early 1960s.

A second important consequence of the war was the consolidation of a 'rationalistic' and 'technicist' ideology that was developing during the inter-war

Table 1.1. Percentage of civilian labour force unemployed in selected European countries and the United States, 1950–62

Year	Belgium	France	Germany (Fed. Rep.)	Italy	Nether- lands	Sweden	United Kingdom	United States
1950	4.9	—	7.2	—	2.0	2.2	1.2	5.2
1951	4.3	—	6.4	—	2.4	1.8	0.9	3.2
1952	5.0	—	6.1	—	3.5	2.3	1.4	2.9
1953	5.3	—	5.5	—	2.5	2.8	1.3	2.8
1954	5.0	1.6	5.2	8.7	1.8	2.6	1.0	5.3
1955	3.8	1.4	3.9	7.5	1.3	2.5	0.8	4.2
1956	2.8	1.1	3.1	9.3	0.9	1.7	0.9	4.0
1957	2.3	0.8	2.7	7.4	1.2	1.9	1.1	4.2
1958	3.3	0.9	2.7	6.4	2.3	2.5	1.7	6.6
1959	3.9	1.3	1.9	5.4	1.8	2.0	1.7	5.3
1960	3.3	1.2 (1.9)	0.9 (1.0)	4.0 (4.3)	1.1	1.8	1.3 (2.4)	5.4
1961	2.6	1.1 (1.7)	0.6 (0.5)	3.4 (3.7)	0.8	1.7 (1.5)	1.1 (2.2)	6.5
1962	2.0	1.2 (1.8)	0.5	2.9 (3.2)	—	1.5 (1.5)	1.6 (2.8)	5.4

Note: Figures in parentheses show unemployment rates revised to correspond with American definitions.
Source: Gordon, 1967, table 1.1, p. 27.

period. The war brought to the fore a cadre of scientifically trained technocrats imbued with a rationalistic ideology. These had set about winning the war using their technical knowledge and their status was enhanced when it was over. Combined with ideas about an administrative elite, this developed into a comprehensive ideology. Problems, any problems almost, were subject to a rational dissection and an engineered solution. Planning was simply a matter of the correct application of brainpower. The solution to social and economic problems was to be found in the use of 'scientific' analysis and could be left largely to technocrats to decide. When this was fused with Keynesian theoretical deliberations and the other conditions mentioned above, it might have seemed that most of the economy's problems were over. Sadly, perhaps, this was not to be the case.

5. Economic Objectives from the 1950s to the 1970s

5.1. *The fate of 'full employment'*

While the post-war 'boom' may now only linger as a fading memory in our economic thinking, we should not forget the character of this 'never had it so good' era. It provided one of the major conditions on which a full employment policy

Table 1.2.   Government budgets, 1952–80

Date	(1) Current account surplus (£m)	(2) Public investment (£m)		(3) Nominal PSBR (£m)		(4) PSBR as percentage of GDP	(5) PSBR as percentage of total government expenditure
1952	604		1168		771	4.9	11.9
1953	507		1445		591	3.5	8.8
1954	549		1232		367	2.0	5.5
1955	777		1475		469	2.4	6.7
1956	743		1541		564	2.7	7.5
1957	894		1667		486	2.2	6.1
1958	935		1632		491	2.1	5.9
1959	874		1768		571	2.3	6.5
1960	745		1863		710	2.8	7.6
1961	905		2152		704	2.6	6.8
1962	1272		2222		546	2.0	5.0
1963	1079		2366		842	2.8	7.2
1964	1444		2944		986	3.0	7.8
1965	1834		3296		1205	3.4	8.5
1966	2103		3621		961	2.5	6.3
1967	2148		4353		1863	4.6	10.6
1968	2891		4736		1278	2.9	6.7
1969	4214		4704		−466	−1.0	—
1970	5007	**4139**	5216	**3271**	−17	0	—
1971	4542	**3651**	5841	**3528**	1372	2.4	5.6
1972	3102	**2026**	5843	**3598**	2047	3.2	7.5
1973	2965	**1929**	7706	**4689**	4168	5.6	12.9
1974	2312	**1435**	10328	**5439**	6422	7.5	15.1
1975	1423	**619**	12552	**6190**	10160	9.9	19.3
1976		**−127**		**6852**	8938	7.5	16.3
1977		**847**		**6410**	5478	3.9	9.3
1978		**−1473**		**6732**	8461	5.0	12.2
1979		**−427**		**7014**	12671	6.4	16.1
1980		**−1475**		**7831**	11817	5.1	11.4

Note: In 1977 definitions were changed, so that except in the financial accounts nationalized industries were excluded and a category of 'general government' introduced embracing just central and local government. Recalculations on this basis are shown in bold figures.
Source: National Income and Expenditure of the UK (Blue Books), various years; Tomlinson (1981a), table 1, p. 388.

was built. During the early post-war years, and in fact through into the late 1960s, 'full employment' was the central objective of government policy.

Matthews (1968) has argued that it was just this boom that enabled full employment to become a realizable objective for governments, as well as a desirable one. He suggests that the buoyant levels of private investment and the rapid expansion in post-war trade meant that the regulation of employment could be undertaken within very narrow limits conditioned by this growing world and domestic economy. Although Britain's relative position may have been deteriorating during this period it too shared in the generally buoyant character of the world economy, and this delayed the emergence of underlying weaknesses in the economy.

Over the period of the 1950s and 1960s the government's general stance towards the economy was somewhat deflationary. This is shown in table 1.2, which gives the financial position of the UK government sector between 1952 and 1980. The budget current account position (column 1) was in surplus throughout the period until the late 1970s, although a small deficit was shown in 1976.

Of course government investment can also act as an 'autonomous' generator of aggregate demand. The public component of this is shown in column 2. Clearly this expenditure outweighed the surplus on current account, leading to a small public sector borrowing requirement (PSBR) or deficit, which is shown in column 3. The PSBR is the difference between overall public revenues and public expenditures. In column 4 its percentage of GDP is shown, and in column 5 its significance with respect to the overall government budget is given.

The significance of the surplus on current account is that running a deficit here is one of the ways in which a Keynesian demand management policy is supposed to operate in times of weakening demand by pumping 'autonomous' expenditure into the economy through running its own deficit. In fact governments ran a surplus here. Current government expenditure was less than tax revenues, and the small overall size of the government deficit did not exert a major expansionary force. Matthews argues that the government-induced net investment contribution to autonomous expenditure should not be ignored but that it was less important than the levels of *private* investment in stimulating the buoyant level of economic activity over the post-Second World War period.

From columns 4 and 5 it should be clear that net public expenditure was not a significant 'problem' for the economy during the 1950s and 1960s. It was small in absolute terms, and low and 'under control' as a proportion of both total public expenditure and of GDP. It was in the early 1970s, when this position changed, that it began to appear as a 'problem'. Indeed as Peacock and Shaw (1981, p. 9) note the term PSBR appears to have been unknown before the 1970s.

Thus it was the underlying high levels of *private* investment and activity that stimulated the economy and enabled a government budgetary policy to emerge which guided the economy along a path of more or less full employment. There was, of course, short-term cyclical activity in the economy, but this generally implied only temporary unemployment. Most of those laid off in the short-term slumps were able to find work again when the upturn came. Here budgetary policy, but in a rather limited sense, was used to 'iron out' these fluctuations. This was aided by so-called 'automatic stabilizers' that are built into governments' expenditure and revenue patterns (see chapters 2 and 7).

In a sense, then, there was little 'problem' of the long-term unemployed, as had been the case during the formative period of Keynes's ideas and the general Keynesian system in the 1930s. This provided the essential political conditions for the acceptance of full employment across the mainstream political spectrum. It 'cost' little in political terms to hold to this policy in the post-war period because it also 'cost' little to hold to it in economic terms. It as only when this 'cost' to the government began to mount in the mid-1970s that the policy came under pressure and rapidly began to collapse. We return to this below.

5.2. *The balance of payments*

Of course, it should not be thought that government budgetary policy was ever *unconditionally* subordinate to the levels of employment during this period. In particular it was often conditionally subordinate to the balance of payments position. A continuing feature of the UK economy in the post-war period has been its difficulty in responding quickly to an increase in demand and consumer spending. The UK economy is particularly sluggish on the 'supply side', i.e. in terms of producing goods and services rapidly enough to meet any extra demand. As a result, when aggregate demand has risen for one reason or another, this usually manifests itself in a balance of payments deficit on current account, sometimes accompanied by runs on sterling and exchange rate difficulties. Any increase in domestic demand has been met by increased imports, whether of raw materials, capital goods or increasingly of consumer goods themselves (see chapter 9).

Here, then, we encounter once again an issue of a *conflict* in objectives. The balance of payments has been an objective of governments in the post-war period, too. Indeed, I would suggest that it only really became such an objective after the war. Balance of payments accounts as such only started to be constructed in the late 1930s, and were only systematically integrated into general macro-accounts in the late 1940s. This provided the necessary informational base on which to conduct calculations and formulate policy with respect to the balance of payments overall. Clearly this is not to suggest that aspects of the external position of the UK economy were not a policy issue before this time. The exchange rate became a dominant 'problem' at times, particularly in the inter-war period.

At this stage it will be useful to discuss briefly the changing manner in which the exchange rate and the balance of payments have been conceived in economics over the longer period since the turn of the century. In doing this we shall also be able to give a more formal exposition of the conflict in objectives with respect to the internal and external balance of the economy that came to the fore in the 1950s and 1960s in the UK, and which was subsequently eclipsed in the 1970s and 1980s as conditions changed.

5.2.1. *Balance of payments adjusted under the gold standard*

The gold standard was a system that relied upon a number of 'ideal' rules and conditions:

(a) In each country the appropriate authorities would establish *once and for all* the gold value of its national currency.
(b) The free movement of gold between countries must be guaranteed.
(c) The persistent movement of gold either into or out of a country must be permitted to influence the domestic money supply in each country.
(d) In each country there should be wage and price/cost flexibility.

This latter condition is the one that, in theory, allowed the mechanism of adjustment to operate. Put briefly, it implied the following. A country with a balance of payments surplus would experience an inflow of gold. The consequent expansion of the money supply would create an excess demand for goods and services and hence also for labour, which would cause money prices and wage rates to rise. As wage rates rose the forces of competition would induce a further rise in the prices of the surplus country's goods. There would be opposite effects on the money wages and prices in the deficit country. Given the rise in prices of the surplus country's products, there would be a shift of demand in both countries on to the now relatively cheaper products of the deficit country and a corresponding re-allocation of resources between the two countries. The balance of payments would therefore adjust as imports rose relative to exports in the surplus country and the converse took place in the deficit country.

But this supposed 'automatic' adjustment process, involving wages and price flexibility, took place very much in terms of overt domestic policy initiatives. It was thus 'non-automatic', relying instead on explicit policy changes. Countries relied upon domestic *expenditure-reducing* policies to influence their current accounts, and interest rate policies to influence their capital accounts. They tended therefore to resort to domestic-orientated adjustments rather than allowing their exchange rates to fluctuate with respect to gold. This was because of the first condition pointed out above, namely the fixed character of the domestic currency's value with respect to gold, which underpinned the gold standard. It also meant that the authorities had to produce, or try to produce, the 'flexibility' in wages and prices that was rather presumed a condition for the analysis to take place and adjustment mechanism to work. In addition, given the fixed character of the gold/exchange rate, any expenditure-reducing policies were a forced consequence of balance of payments maladjustments rather than a calculated element in the context of possible exchange rate adjustments. Some of the consequences of this were pointed out above in section 3, when discussing the inter-war conflict in objectives over economic policy.

The point to recognize from the discussion is the way that, as a consequence of this mechanism, the 'balance of payments' was conceived very much in terms of *purchasing power parity* (PPP) issues. The problem for the authorities was to look towards, and where necessary to adjust (or try to adjust), the domestic purchasing power parity of their currencies, in order to keep these in balance. Purchasing power, or, which amounts to the same thing, the comparative price and cost structures as between countries, was the dominant framework in which such adjustments were conceived. If such comparative purchasing power of currencies could be adjusted by internal expenditure policies and the gold parity of the domestic currency maintained, then the balance of payments would right itself as a result and would not form the object of policy as such via gold/exchange rate re-adjustments.

5.2.2. *Balance of payments adjustments in the 1950s and 1960s*

After the Second World War and the demise of the gold standard, the Bretton Woods system of fixed but managed exchange rates was established. Officially inaugurated in 1944, the Bretton Woods system – at least the fixed exchange rate element of it – lasted until the early 1970s. (The system also involved the establishment of the IMF, the function of which still continues.)

With the 1931 devaluation of the pound, many economists turned from the PPP approach, which had assumed a fixed exchange rate in terms of gold, to embrace what subsequently came to be known as the elasticities approach. This focused upon relative prices as a way of gauging the expenditure-switching potential of exchange rate changes. In calculating the effects of the 1931 devaluation, estimates were made of the size of the relevant demand elasticities, thus emphasizing the tendency of a lower exchange rate to raise the relative price of Britain's imports and reduce the relative price of its exports to potential foreign customers.

After the war, at the time of the 1949 devaluation of sterling, this elasticities approach (expenditure-switching) was still the dominant mode of analysing the consequences of balance of payments disequilibrium, although it was now supplemented by a growing awareness of the importance of possible income effects. Britain was running a very high level of activity, near full employment, and it became a concern whether under these circumstances devaluation would succeed *by itself* in reducing the internal demand for traded goods, or whether additional measures to lower domestic demand would be needed to restore the external balance. Here, then, emerged an explicit concern with expenditure-reducing issues and the 'absorption approach'. As pointed out above when discussing the gold standard adjustment mechanism, expenditure-reducing activity had arisen under this system in an *ex post* manner but it was now recognized as an *ex ante* concern, so calculations were made before exchange rate devaluations or adjustments were initiated.

The 1949 devaluation marked an important event in post-war economic development. The US authorities encouraged the UK to return to convertibility in 1947. But for reasons associated with the demand for US goods, capital account speculation emerged against sterling in order to convert sterling balances into US dollars. The authorities found it impossible to defend the parity, and in September 1949 Britain undertook a huge 30 per cent devaluation (from $4.03 to $2.80). This was followed by twenty-five other important trading countries to varying degrees. Such a large devaluation, by so many countries, had significant effects on the balance of payments current accounts of all members of the IMF for the next twenty-five years. The European economies were effectively transformed into export economies by this drastic exchange rate realignment, which itself helped to provide another important condition for the subsequent post-war boom. Significant structural adjustments to European currencies were thereby ruled out by this move (until the early 1970s) with the subsequent establishment of strong exporters' lobbies in all the European countries concerned (De Cecco, 1979, p. 60).

Within this general context the problem for the managers of the economy in the subsequent period was to achieve an 'internal balance' and an 'external balance' for the economy, i.e. 'full employment' internally and 'balance of payments equilibrium' externally, broadly speaking. This then is to stress the relationship between these two potentially conflicting objectives. In fact by and large full employment was sacrificed as an objective in the interests of the balance of payments in the UK over the post-war period up to the late 1970s.

When the balance of payments threatened to get out of control, or when the exchange rate came under pressure, full employment was temporarily sacrificed in the interests of 're-balancing' the international position. Thus the simultaneous achievement of both an internal and an external balance proved somewhat problematic. Domestic activity was dampened down by various means and unemployment allowed to appear above trends levels. In this sense, then, the balance of payments position (and its attendant exchange rate issue) had by and large dominated the full employment objective. But this should be viewed in the context of the underlying buoyant position of the economy during this period which allowed the economy to be run at near full capacity despite these temporary 'stop–go' cycles. Thus unemployment levels were quite low throughout this period. Very severe conflicts between these objectives did not emerge until around 1967 when, in effect, the economy found itself facing both internal inflation, i.e. over-full employment, and an external deficit.

The response was to devalue the currency in an attempt to reach an external balance and move to retrench on government expenditure to approach an internal balance in true Keynesian style. Soon after this devaluation, however, the system of fixed the managed exchange rates collapsed, on which a good deal of the above analysis depended. This shifted the focus of concern with respect to balance of payments and exchange rate policy, as will be shown below.

One further persistent problem that emerged during the later 1960s and early 1970s in an attempt to achieve an overall balance (internal and external) was the coincidence of persistent inflation *and* unemployment. One approach here would have been to recognize that there were now three targets, with the 'internal balance' bifurcated into 'full employment' and 'price stability'. This would have required an additional instrument to achieve the two domestic objectives plus the external balance. Countries such as the UK did move towards this kind of strategy in experimenting with incomes policies and other devices to curb inflation through channels other than reducing aggregate demand. This we return to in section 6, when looking at the objective of price stability for government to help achieve 'internal' balance, but first it is necessary to round off the discussion of balance of payments issues by considering briefly the emergence of the so-called 'monetary approaches to the balance of payments' (MAB). It is this approach that developed in the late 1970s and early 1980s.

5.2.3.   *Monetary approaches to the balance of payments*

In the analysis of section 5.2.2 the emphasis was on the current account. While the analysis could have been extended to include issues of capital movements in the context of an 'internal' monetary policy associated with changes in interest rates, for simplicity this was excluded. However, this exclusion also reflects the relative unimportance attributed to capital flows in the type of analysis conducted in section 5.2.2. Most countries maintained some controls on the capital flows into and out of their countries during the 1950s and 1960s, so capital movements were subject to a different set of determinations and constraints, set within the framework of such controls. In addition the prevailing (Keynesian) thinking stressed the 'real' determinants of the balance of payments – the flows of traded goods and services were thought to provide the basis upon which capital flows would subsequently follow, if in a lagged or tenuated relationship.

However, with the advent of floating exchange rates, the growth of new forms of international monetary instruments (like Eurocurrencies), the progressive integration of money and capital markets on a world scale, and with the development of a large OPEC surplus, *capital movements* within the international economy began once again to dominate balance of payments and exchange rate considerations. Speculative capital movements on a very large scale began to undermine systems of capital control and individual economies found it increasingly difficult to resist pressures for decontrol. Added to this was a growing awareness of inflation as a significant and entrenched 'problem' for individual countries, which itself affected their ability to withstand speculative pressures and capital movements into and out of their currencies.

This provided the context in which monetarist economic thinking was to emerge and become effective (I return to this in the next section). But in the rather more specific context of balance of payments considerations, it helped stimulate a change in emphasis towards recognizing the monetary determinants of this account. Now instead of the balance of payments being fundamentally determined (or 'caused') by 'real' considerations, it began increasingly to be thought of as being determined by 'monetary' flows and considerations. The whole Keynesian analysis was also criticized for effectively ignoring stock equilibrium conditions. It allowed the goods market to be in equilibrium despite balance of payments imbalance. Some monetary adjustments would be called for under these circumstances which in turn would feed back into the goods market and disturb the balance there. The full implications of this change in the style of thinking about the balance of payments are discussed further in chapters 2 and 8 below, but here I introduce one of the main ways in which this shift in concern has been registered.

If we look at the way in which the money supply is related to its 'credit counterparts' derived from the balance sheet items (assets and liabilities) of the banking system as a whole, this appears as an identity as follows:

$$1 \qquad\qquad \Delta M^S \equiv DCE + \Delta FA$$

where ΔM^S equals change in the money supply, DCE equals domestic credit expansion and ΔFA equals the change in the bank's holdings of gold and foreign exchange reserves. (See chapter 7 for a derivation and further discussion of this identity.)

The equation forms the basis of the monetary approach to the balance of payments. As it stands this is an identity which follows from the accounting relationships between the assets and liabilities of the financial system as a whole and does not express any *causal* connection between the variables involved. But this has been used in connection with the development of such causal relationships, which in turn requires a theory of how the behavioural elements expressed by the identity are linked and determined. For instance, if we assume that the money market is in equilibrium or gets to an equilibrium quickly, then the money market clears and the supply of money (M^S) will equal the demand for money (M^D). If $M^S = M^D$ we can rearrange **1** as follows:

$$2 \qquad\qquad \Delta FA = \Delta M^D - DCE$$

The MAB develops an argument to suggest that it is changes in the foreign exchange reserves (FA), or, which amounts to the same thing, the balance of payments, that are equal to and *determined by* changes in the demand for money (M^D) less the increase in domestic credit expansion (DCE). So, for example, if DCE exceeds ΔM^D, ΔFA will be negative, i.e. the balance of payments will be in deficit. Thus the balance of payments is caused solely by monetary factors, in the first instance. Instead of the typical 'Keynesian' suggestion that the balance of payments (a 'monetary' phenomenon) is caused by 'real' factors such as the flows of imports and exports as analysed in section 5.2.2, this approach suggests that the causality is reversed. It is now monetary factors that determine the balance of payments, which itself in turn affects the real variables in the economy. It is approaches based upon equation 2 that have tended to dominate in the late 1970s and early 1980s.

6.   Inflation and Wage Bargaining

When discussing the balance of payments, above, the issue of inflation already appeared as an element, if a rather implicit one, in the debate and issues associated with internal balance and also in the context of monetary approaches to the balance of payments. In this section I look at the importance of a stable price level in its own right as an objective of governments.

Different conceptions of the role of money in the economy have different implications for what are believed to be the reasons for inflation. Inflation has to do with the value of money (the store of value function), and this in turn has significant implications for 'confidence' in the economic mechanism as a whole, i.e. in its ability to fulfil the other functions of money and particularly to act as the means of exchange and the standard for prices.

We can point to two important ways in which money and price formation might be linked by reference to the so-called 'quantity equation'. This equation is an identity (i.e. it must hold by definition):

3 $$MV \equiv Py$$

Here M is the money stock and Py is national income at current prices. It is made up of real output y times the price level P. The income velocity of circulation V expresses the rapidity with which the money stock circulates in any time period. This would have to be determined statistically by dividing national income at current prices by the money stock. Hence with this simple formulation of the relationship between money and prices.

4 $$V \equiv \frac{Py}{M}$$

Since V is determined in this manner, equation 3 is an identity. This equation is often used to determine the demand for money equation. The amount of money required as a proportion of income is the reciprocal of the velocity of circulation $(1/V)$. This can be seen by transposing equation 4 so that $M^D = 1/V Py$. This derivation, its importance and implications are further developed in chapter 6. As it stands, equation 3 has no causal implications. All it states is that there must be an equality between the stock of money times its velocity of circulation, and the real output of an economy times the price of goods and services. However, some theorists have gone further than this and have attributed a *causal* connection between these two sides, setting up a relationship of determination between them.

Suppose we interpret equation **3** in the form of a causal connection so that the right-hand side determines the left-hand side. In this case $Py{\rightarrow}MV$ (where $\rightarrow$ means 'causes') and it is the quantity of goods and services (expressed in money terms) that determines the amount of money in the economy (holding P and V constant for convenience). This direction of causality appears in the post-war Keynesian approach (though this is complicated by the fact that some Keynesian reject the constancy of V) and it can be seen that it also emphasizes the 'real' over the 'monetary' in terms of the causality mechanism (i.e. real output determines the stock of money).

On the other hand, suppose we reverse the mode of causality, thus making $MV{\rightarrow}Py$. Under these circumstances (now holding V and y constant for convenience) it is the quantity of money that determines the price level. This direction of causality typifies the 'monetarist' approach and it gives rise to this theory's characteristic emphasis on controlling the money supply to control the aggregate price level. In addition it emphasizes the 'monetary' factors over the 'real' factors in the determination of prices. Later in this section I come back to the importance of this position.

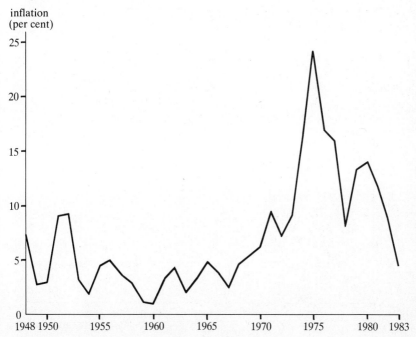

Figure 1.1. UK inflation rate, 1948-83. *Source: Retail Prices: Indices 1914-1983*, Department of Employment, 1984.

During the Second World War a range of policies and restrictions were implemented to control inflation. Experience during and immediately after the First World War, when prices rose by nearly 150 per cent between 1914 and 1920 (see the Introduction, p. xvi), taught the authorities to pay close attention to the possible inflationary impact of war. By and large the measures taken were relatively successful, since there was only 5 per cent inflation on average during the Second World War. But equally important were the low levels of inflation after the war. Ignoring the Korean War period, figure 1.1 shows that inflation did not rise above 5 per cent until after 1968. Given that the economy was working at or near full employment capacity over much of this period, how can the absence of any sustained inflation be explained? A full answer to this question cannot be offered here. Indeed any explanation would be highly controversial. While it is possible to point once again to the high level of economic activity associated with the boom in the post-war economy, exactly why this provided the conditions for a relatively high level of employment (of resources in general, but of labour in particular) combined

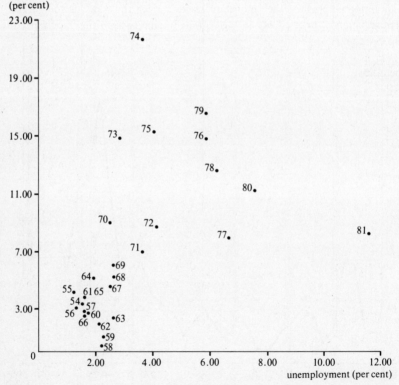

Figure 1.2.   UK inflation against unemployment, annual data, 1954–81. *Source:* adapted from 'Britain's economy under strain', *The Economist*, 1982, p. 14, plus author's own figures.

with a relatively low level of inflation, is open to dispute. Some of the elements of this dispute are discussed in other chapters of the book (chapters 2, 3, 4 and 6 in particular). Here I mention *one* of the features associated with this, namely the possible trade-off between inflation and employment as embodied in the so-called Phillips curve.

The Phillips curve was based upon empirical observations of the relationship between inflation rates and unemployment rates for the UK economy over the period from the 1860s through to the first half of the twentieth century (Phillips, 1958). Figure 1.2 plots the range of such observations over the period 1954–81.

The Phillips curve, derived from these figures, was subsequently used in the 1950s and 1960s to suggest a mechanism for achieving an 'internal balance' between the objectives of price stability and near-full employment. The general character of the relationship between unemployment and inflation is stylized in figure 1.3. A curve such as AA 'summarizes' in a reasonably accurate way the position of the variables for the mid-1950s to the mid-1960s as shown in figure 1.2. It is based upon the idea that money wages rise faster the lower the level of unemployment, and vice-versa, and shows the possible trade-off between unemployment and inflation thought to be embodied in the Phillips curve.

At an inflation rate of approximately 3 per cent, for instance, unemployment would be about 2½ per cent. If the unemployment rate were *lower*, then inflation would have to be higher, and vice-versa. Here, then, is a further case where there is at least a trade-off between two 'desirable' economic objectives. A zero rate of inflation could not be achieved with a zero rate of unemployment. However, if the government could move the Phillips curve to the *left*, i.e. shift the whole

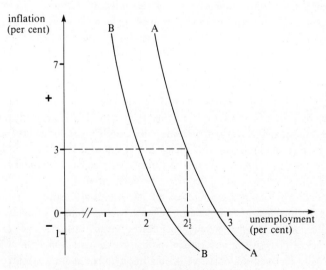

Figure 1.3.   A stylized Phillips curve trade-off

schedule with the aid of an 'incomes policy' say to position BB, then it might be possible to achieve zero inflation with 2¼ per cent unemployment rather than with a 7 per cent inflation as before. An incomes policy reformulates the character of the labour market, redefining the relationship between unemployment levels and inflation. In the 1960s and 1970s it seemed to offer a mechanism by which the tendency to push the schedule out to the right as inflation gained momentum could be resisted. In this case the incomes policy would form a particular *instrument* or means to achieve a more desirable combination of objectives. Here, then, is a case of trade-off or conflict between objectives and the role that a particular instrument might play in at least overcoming that conflict. Even in the absence of this particular instrument, general fiscal and monetary policy (i.e. demand management) could be employed to keep the relationship between unemployment and inflation within reasonable limits because of the trade-off thought to be involved.

This mechanism can also be used to point to the way the idea of a constraint may be added into the analysis. One of the problems of trying to organize an incomes policy or any other form of wage restraint is that trade unions are traditionally committed to 'free collective bargaining' in their wage negotiations. Free collective bargaining refers to the manner in which employers and employees bargain about wages without any government interference or fixed legislative framework. Traditionally the unions have demonstrated a strong adherence to such free collective bargaining largely because it seemed to provide increased wages in the relatively prosperous years of the post-war boom. In the face of this the organization of an incomes policy was *highly constrained*. An incomes policy implies that free collective bargaining by individual unions with employers is itself partly undermined. It becomes conditional upon some more generally agreed or legally instituted maximum wage rate increase. This practice of free collective bargaining to which the trade unions strongly adhered restricted the use and usefulness of an *instrument* like incomes policies to affect what might be a more desirable combination of economic *objectives*.

Referring back to figure 1.2, it can be seen that the Phillips curve derived from observations for the 1950s and 1960s seemed to completely break down in the 1970s. The relationship became an unstable one, and this coincided with the fairly rapid increase in inflation shown in figure 1.1 for the 1970s and early 1980s. (In chapter 6 this rather 'Keynesian' example of the possible relationship between wages, unemployment and inflation is challenged: it is argued that the relationship needs to be 'augmented' with an expectations variable and that this undermines *any* trade-off since the Phillips 'curve' becomes a vertical line.)

The dramatic UK inflation rates of the late 1960s and early 1970s shown in figure 1.1 propelled the 'problem' of inflation to the forefront of public concern. The reduction of the inflation rate, which reached over 25 per cent in 1975, became the principal objective of government policy in the period after the mid-1970s. It gradually replaced the objective of full employment as the central concern of government policy.

In addition, during this period a change in the way that unemployment was conceived can be discerned. Its existence was increasingly thought to be more the responsibility of the trade unions or ultimately of people's personal preferences and calculations with respect to their work/leisure trade-offs than being the responsibility of governments. People's financial position in employment as opposed to taking unemployment benefit and other social welfare benefits was increasingly emphasized here. This was part of a wider theoretical shift in terms of the economic and political debate but it was also a very controversial one that was disputed strongly by many economists. There was no longer thought to be a *trade-off* between inflation and unemployment. Inflation was now thought to be solely caused by monetary growth and to have little if anything to do with the levels of unemployment as such.

In connection with this change in emphasis in the 'hierarchy of objectives' there was a change in emphasis with respect to the means or *instruments* to be brought to bear on the objectives. With the demise of full employment and with the argument about unemployment being more a matter of trade union or personal responsibility gaining currency, went the demise of any incomes policies as legitimate instruments of government intervention. As inflation became perceived as the main economic problem, so a new range of instruments emerged to affect this, mainly involving issues of 'monetary growth'. A range of *intermediate objectives* was set up based on the control of the money supply in an attempt to gain control over the *primary objective*, inflation.

These mechanisms are more fully discussed in chapter 7, but here we look at how this change in objectives was registered with respect to the role of government expenditure and the money supply.

In connection with table 1.2 it was pointed out that net government borrowing only began to rise significantly as a percentage of overall government expenditure and as a percentage of GDP in the early to mid-1970s. In addition public expenditure itself peaked as a percentage of GDP in 1975 at over 45 per cent (figure 1, Introduction). This growth in the importance of public expenditure in the economy was partly responsible for it appearing as a major 'problem' in the mid-1970s. It became a 'problem' when it became difficult to finance (just as it had become a 'problem' in the 1920s under similar circumstances). Increasingly, governments have had to pay close attention to the 'confidence' of the private financial markets in their economic policies. During this period the level of the PSBR became a central indicator of such confidence. As the level of the PSBR grew, so did the amount of gilts and Treasury bills (the two major instruments the government uses to borrow from the financial markets) and with these interest rates rose as well. Figure 1.4 shows the Treasury bill rate – a measure of short-term interest rates – between 1972 and 1979. In the autumn of 1976 the government was forced to increase this rate to nearly 15 per cent to 'encourage' participants in the financial markets to hold its short-term debt (Treasury bills), thus adding to the cost of financing its

Treasury
bill rate
(per cent)

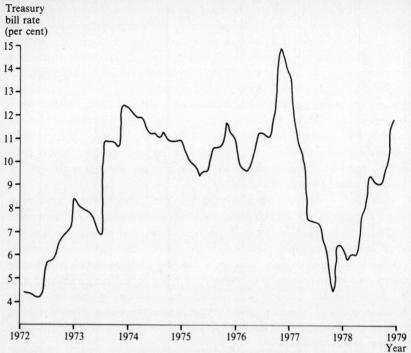

Figure 1.4. Short-term interest rates, 1972–9. *Source: Bank of England Quarterly Review,*
various issues.

expenditures. The financial markets are thus a major *constraint* on the ability of
governments to run up budget deficits (Keegan and Pennant-Rea, 1979, p. 133).

The PSBR was also shown to be linked to the growth of the money supply
at this time. The relationship here can be generated by expanding the credit
counterpart identity (equation 1) discussed in section 5.2.3. Domestic credit
expansion is made up of three separate items. Any change in the money supply
is a product of the PSBR minus the change in the non-bank private sector's lending
to the public sector (ΔG_p), plus any change in the banks' lending to the non-bank
private sector (ΔL_p). These, combined with any 'external financing' (*EF*), i.e.
borrowing or lending abroad, gives the extended credit counterpart identity as
follows:

$$5 \qquad \Delta M^S \equiv \text{PSBR} - \Delta G_p + \Delta L_p + \text{EF}$$

The PSBR is one of the counterparts of the money supply shown in this equation.
Now there are four basic ways in which government expenditure can be financed.
These are via taxation, via charges for the use of publicly provided goods and services,

via borrowing and thus going into debt, and finally via printing money (which is really a sub-variant of going into debt, since the government could simply issue notes or coin to finance its expenditure). The basic point here is that if the first three of these sources of finance are constrained, then the only way the government can finance its expenditure is via directly increasing the money supply. The relationships are expressed by equation 5. As concern developed with controlling inflation, and as this was increasingly theoretically linked to the control of the money supply, equation 5 offered a link between controlling inflation and controlling the PSBR. In turn this implied putting downward pressure on those items contributing to the PSBR, notably public expenditure itself. Thus the level of public expenditure emerged as a prime 'cause' of inflation, if indirectly via its link to the PSBR and the money supply.

From the point of view of the money supply it is important to know exactly how the government finances the PSBR. The complicated relationship between the PSBR and the money supply is discussed more fully in chapter 7, but at this stage it is important to note that the *more* the government can 'fund' its debt by selling it to the non-banking private sector, the *less* this is likely to increase the money supply. This is because if the government sells its debt to private non-bank agents these will have to draw on their own bank accounts to pay for it, which in turn will decrease the net deposit in the banking system and decrease the money supply (other things remaining equal). On the other hand, if the government sells its debt to the banking system, this can then act as an asset within the banking system. Such assets could then form the basis for an expansion of credit or money supply as the banking system creates liabilities, in the form of deposits, to match its increase in assets. Thus in this latter case the money supply would expand.

Finally, we can point to another consequence of this analysis. Arguments were advanced for the idea that public expenditure 'crowded out' private expenditure. To show formally how this works we can refer once again to equation 5. Suppose we argue that the external position is constrained so that we hold EF constant. In addition let us assume that the negative item in the equation, G_p is also held constant, i.e. that changes in the private sector lending to the public sector is also constrained in the short run. Holding both of these constant we can interpret equation 5 as:

6
$$\Delta M^S = PSBR + L_p$$

In this case, if we want to control the money supply, ΔM^S, by maintaining it at a constant level, for instance, then the PSBR and L_p (bank lending to the non-bank private sector) are substitutes for one another. To *increase* the PSBR is to *decrease* lending to the private sector. Thus the PSBR 'crowds out' lending to the private sector under these circumstances. A reduction in the PSBR will allow more bank lending to the private sector while still maintaining the money supply constant and under control. Attached to this was a further consideration, namely that public expenditure was less productive than private expenditure. Thus it was an 'unproductive' (public) expenditure that was crowding out or displacing a more productive (private) expenditure, and this was argued to be one of the causes for the poor performance of the economy.

This question of 'crowding out' has implications for the effectiveness of fiscal policy. As we have seen, such a policy involves the generation of 'autonomous' expenditure on the part of the government, which, other things being equal, will itself generate a budget deficit that has to be financed from government bonds floated on the capital markets. In figure 1.5 the supply and demand for investment capital is shown. The demand for funds D_0D_0, arises from both the public and the private sector, which are presumed aggregated into this market demand curve. The market is in an initial equilibrium with the real rate of interest at r_0 and the quantity of funds at Q_0. After the fiscal policy injection, the government's increased demand for funds pushes the curve out to D_1D_1. The real interest rate rises to r_1. However, at this higher rate planned private sector investment projects are no longer profitable. This is equivalent to saying that with reference to the original demand curve D_0D_0 and at the now higher interest rate r_1, private sector planned investment is cut back by Q_0 minus Q_2 (assuming that only the private sector reacts to the higher interest rate). Overall investment rises, however, to Q_1. Hence the public sector increases investment by Q_2Q_1, of which Q_2Q_0 was 'crowded out' private investment, giving a net increase of Q_0Q_1 in investment.

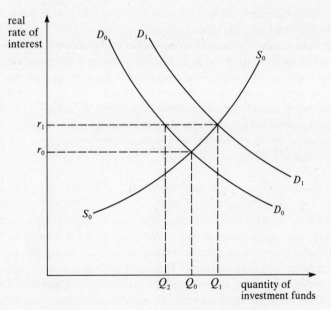

Figure 1.5.   Fiscal policy and 'crowding out'

However, there can be yet another round of effects, since the newly issued government debt creates some 'wealth effects'. It increases the wealth of those holding it and can thus stimulate higher levels of consumption out of a given flow of income. This could shift the supply curve up to the left, since in effect it reduces the supply of savings (which lies behind the supply of investable funds). In addition this greater wealth could also have some effects on the demand side by increasing the demand for money and bonds at any level of income and interest rate. This would force the demand curve out even further to the right. Exactly which of these two effects dominates the other is an empirical (and conjunctural) matter. In principal fiscal policy overall could be effective, inflationary or have no impact at all (Blinder and Solow, 1973).

7. Economic Growth

The growth performance of the UK economy has for a long time been the subject of debate, and at times even of despair. The relative decline of the British economy has been evident since the latter part of the nineteenth century but became increasingly evident in the decades following the Second World War. While over the long run real national output has grown, the UK economy has performed relatively worse than other comparable advanced industrial economies. This is shown in figure 1.6. One thing that stands out clearly from this figure is that the UK's growth rate in the post-war period has been consistently lower than the other OECD countries. When a country has relatively low economic growth, then although its standard of living as measured by real GDP per capita may rise absolutely over time, it falls relative to faster growing countries. This is shown in figure 1.7, from which it can be seen that between 1968 and 1978 living standards in the UK were overtaken by those of France and Japan.

The problem of Britain's relatively slow growth rate has been exacerbated by the fall in growth rates experienced by most economies since the mid-1970s. For most countries the graph of real GDP per head over time rises less steeply after 1973, and in some cases actually declines after 1979, indicating the effects of the most recent recession. These slower growth rates of the decade 1973–83 had much to do with the two world recessions in 1974–5 and 1980–2, which were much more severe than earlier post-war recessions. Both recessions were associated with marked increases in the price of oil. This worsened the terms of trade for oil-importing countries and so reduced real incomes in these countries since a given quantity of their exports could buy less oil. The fall in real incomes reduced aggregate demand both for domestically produced goods and for the exports of other countries. Also, the increase in the price of intermediate goods relative to labour can reduce the demand for labour and so lead to a rise in unemployment. (Further analysis of these supply-side shocks can be found in chapter 9.)

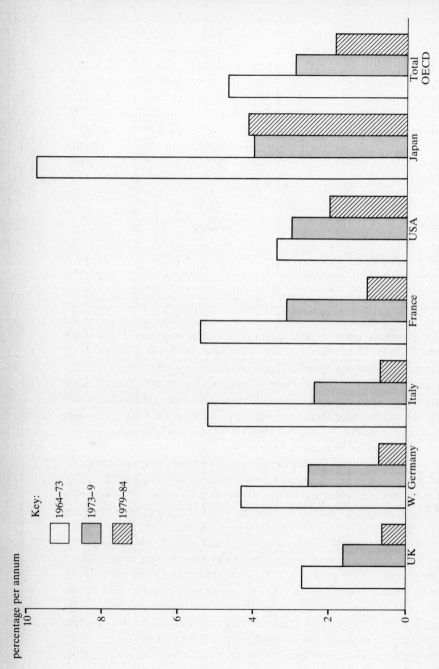

Figure 1.6. Growth: average annual increase in real GDP (constant 1975 prices). *Source:* House of Lords: *Report from the Committee on Overseas Trade*, vol. 1, figure 3.1, p. 24 (HLP 238–1), 1984–85. HMSO, London.

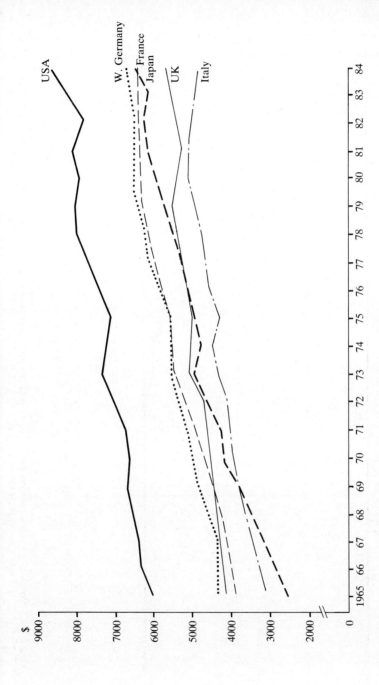

Figure 1.7. Standard of living: real GDP per head (constant 1975 $ prices, purchasing power parity basis). *Source*: NEDO, British Industrial Performance, 1984.

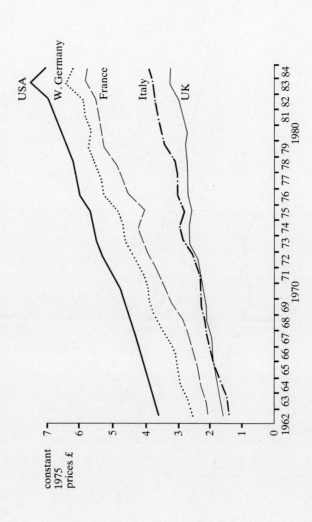

Figure 1.8. Productivity: manufacturing output per man hour (gross value added per man-hour) in UK £. *Source:* House of Lords: *Report from the Committee on Overseas Trade*, vol. 1, figure 3.5, p. 33 (HLP 238–1), 1984–85. HMSO, London.

In addition to this weak overall growth performance the UK has also shown low relative growth rates of labour productivity as shown in Figure 1.8.

Productivity growth is not only important from the point of view of its impact on income per person at any particular time, but it is also important in terms of cumulative competitive advantage. Productivity plays an important part in determining the efficiency of the productive system and hence in fixing the relative costs of output produced. As a result, countries with low productivity growth can rapidly fall behind those with higher rates in international competitiveness.

As mentioned in the introductory remarks to this chapter, economic growth as such has perhaps been the objective that has been least satisfactorily analysed, both theoretically and in a policy context. This is not to say that a great deal of academic analysis has not been directed towards the problem of economic growth: it has. But very few conclusive answers have emerged as to why it happens more satisfactorily in one country than another, and whether anything worthwhile can be drawn from this, and said about the comparative reasons for economic growth. In the context of the analysis of this chapter the emphasis has been upon getting the other macroeconomic objectives and instruments consistent and to work properly, with the expectation or presumption that economic growth will emerge as a result. By and large the emphasis has been on policy action directed towards organizing for the other economic objectives, rather than an emphasis on the growth process itself.

There have, however, been a number of occasions when economic growth as a specific object of government policy has emerged in post-war Britain. The first of these was immediately after the war when the 1945–50 Labour government began with a strong rhetoric in favour of planning the economy. This was embodied in successive versions of the *Economic Survey* which began in 1947 (Budd, 1978, chapter 4). These surveys were concerned almost entirely with output and manpower needs. There were three main official working parties associated with them – one on manpower, one on investment, and one on imports and the balance of payments. They produced trial balance sheets designed to indicate gaps between resources and demand, and it was envisaged that 'planning' would close these gaps 'in the way most advantageous to the national interest'. In fact the macro-pressures on the economy soon came to dominate the objectives set by the surveys. The external balance became the prime problem; in particular the perceived need to restore the balance of payments, especially with the dollar area. In addition, inflationary pressures were seen to present a severe risk to this. The 1949 devaluation brought this phase of growth planning to an end.

The second attempt at promoting growth above all other objectives also occurred during a Labour administration, that of 1964–7. Here an attempt was made to establish a new framework for economic planning via the Department of Economic Affairs (DAE), The National Plan and the use of the National Economic Development Council. This was the highpoint of the era of 'corporatist planning', involving tripartite negotiation about the possible course of the economy between the government, industry and the unions. The National Plan envisaged 25 per cent growth between 1964 and 1970, but it had to be cruelly aborted after only 3 years with, once again, a balance of payments crisis, this time in 1967. Treasury/DAE rivalry, and a lack of any enforcement mechanism for the plan targets, also contributed to its demise.

A third effort at growth involved the Conservative administration's 'dash for growth', engineered during the so-called Barber Boom of 1972–3 (named after the then Chancellor of the Exchequer, Anthony Barber). Although the Conservatives had engineered a mini pre-election boom preceding the 1964–7 Labour 'corporatist planning' exercise, this was not a focused policy. Their effort of 1972–3, however, was a definite political programme for growth (Tomlinson, 1985, p. 186). It involved a massive 'go' for the economy engineered by demand management and monetary policy (involving the ending of 'competition and credit control' amongst other things). For the first time the exchange rate was also to be subordinate to growth given the decision to float the pound in 1972. However, once again this attempt was decisively interrupted by an exchange rate crisis (in 1976) demonstrating the continued international constraint on the UK economy.

With the demise of this particular 'thrust for growth' so government's explicit policy efforts to promote growth as an overriding policy objective also failed. Not even the radical reforming Labour administration of the late 1970s could promote growth as its main objective, given the onset of the depression and the other macroeconomic problems it soon began to face in the context of this. For all intents and purposes 'growth' was thus abandoned for more immediate and pressing economic objectives.

If we return to some of the underlying reasons put forward to account for the inability of the economy to 'spontaneously' generate its own growth independently of changing government initiatives, a great deal of emphasis has been placed on the UK's investment record. Here, however, we again enter a rather complex area, since the exact relevance of various measures of investment and capital formation to economic growth is open to dispute.

Table 1.3 shows that in terms of gross capital formation the UK has consistently invested less of its GDP that other comparable countries, except the USA. Thus the argument is that too much of GDP is devoted to consumption and not enough

Table 1.3.   Gross fixed capital formation as a percentage of GDP, 1960, 1970 and 1980

Year	UK	USA	Japan	France	W Germany	Italy	Netherlands	Belgium
1960	16	18	30	20	24	22	24	19
1970	19	17	35	23	26	21	26	22
1980	18	19	32	22	24	20	21	21

Source: United Nations, *Statistical Yearbook*, 1981.

to investment in the UK, which has had adverse effects on the growth rate of the economy. However, these percentages only differ by a few points between most countries. In addition, from the point of view of economic growth, the particular type of investment is important. It might be argued that investment in manufacturing only is the most relevant form here. This is shown in table 1.4, and the UK's position, while slightly better than the USA's, now seems to be more significantly worse than the other countries shown.

The figures in tables 1.3 and 1.4 are gross data. They do not show the *net* capital formation as a percentage of GDP, which allows for depreciation of the capital stock. Nor are they converted to a capital formation per worker basis. In fact neither of these two adjustments seemed to affect the relative position of the UK during the 1970s, other than to enhance the USA's position relative to that of the UK's (Brown and Sheriff, 1979, p. 247; Smith, 1984, chapter 10).

A further point in this consideration of the type of investment concerns the relative emphasis on research and development expenditure in different countries. International comparisons of this are notoriously difficult to generate but the data in table 1.5, for what they are worth, confirm once again the UK's weak position in this vital area of activity.

But there are some even more important objections to the figures and explanations given so far. In the first place these tables show the amount of investment made per year. They are *flow*-based. But of some importance would be the *stocks* of already accumulated investment and its age structure. There is some evidence to suggest

Table 1.4   Gross capital formation in manufacturing industries as a percentage of GDP

Year	UK	USA	Japan	France	W. Germany
1960	2.5	2.1	10.8	5.9	na
1965	4.0	2.7	6.0	6.8	5.9
1970	3.6	2.4	17.4	7.6	6.8
1975	3.4	2.6	11.1	na	3.9

na = Not available.
Source: compiled from *UN Yearbook of National Account Statistics* (various years).

Table 1.5.   International comparison of growth of R & D spending (percentages)

	Period	Total R & D	Industry financed	Industry performed
UK	1964–78	2.1	2.3	2.2
France	1963–79	5.5	7.7	6.8
W. Germany	1964–79	6.9	6.2	7.1
Japan	1963–79	11.0	na	11.2
USA	1964–79	1.7	4.6	1.8

Source: House of Lords, *Report from the Committee on Overseas Trade, vol. III (238-III), table 8, p. 23.*

that the UK economy is less disadvantaged than might be thought if its stock of investment is looked at. This is taken up again in chapter 9. Secondly, and perhaps more important, there is the issue of the *quality* of investment, in terms of how the capital equipment is used and what productive results arise from this. One of the UK's problems has been that the return on investment – in terms of output per unit of capital input or in terms of the profitability of investment – seems to have been particularly low. This raises a third objection, since it is precisely the low quality of the investment that needs to be explained. The fact that Britain has low levels of investment explains nothing. Rather low investment is the problem to be explained: low investment may be an effect rather than a cause of low growth.

8. Conclusions

The two recessions of the past decade cannot be attributed solely to the supply-side shock of the rise in oil prices. Another factor is that governments have been reluctant to use the Keynesian technique of expanding aggregate demand to reduce unemployment when faced simultaneously with the problem of accelerating inflation. In the 1970s countries in general experienced higher rates of inflation than in the 1950s and 1960s. The UK shared this problem with other countries, but has also performed relatively poorly in maintaining price stability, compared to them. As we have seen, it performed particularly badly in the area of maintaining full employment. While unemployment rose in the period in all OECD countries, the UK moved from a position of relatively low unemployment to one of relatively high unemployment.

It is in relation to these statistical indices of the UK's economic performance that the heart of the issue raised in this chapter and pursued in the rest of this book lies. How can economies be managed so as to achieve simultaneously the desirable economic objectives outlined in the introduction to the chapter? Indeed, as the analysis has proceeded this question has changed somewhat. In the early post-war period both economists and politicians were optimistic about their ability to achieve simultaneously all the objectives in a reasonably satisfactory manner, but from the mid-1970s, with the advent of recession, the question became 'is it *possible* to achieve these objectives' rather than 'how can they be achieved?' The ability to manage an economy along a trajectory of stable growth, with low levels of unemployment, low inflation and an acceptable balance of payments position became increasingly uncertain. Fundamental disputes arose concerning the character of the economy itself and the viable trade-offs between desirable economic outcomes (e.g. unemployment against inflation, growth against balance of payments equilibrium). Indeed, the very possibility of there being viable trade-offs between desirable economic objectives was itself challenge with the advent of monetarism. It is these disputes about the character of the macroeconomy and the policy options available in the light of this that are taken up in more detail in the following chapters. Here, as we shall see, it is conflicts between economic objectives that have given rise to the characteristic problems of managing an economy.

References

Blinder, A. S. and Solow, R. W. (1973) 'Does fiscal policy matter?', *Journal of Public Economics*, 2, 319–37.

Brown, C. J. F. and Sheriff, T. P. (1979) 'De-industrialization: a background paper'. In Blackaby, F. (ed.), *De-industrialization*. Heinemann, London.

Budd, A. (1978) *The Politics of Planning*. Manchester University Press, Manchester.

Cairncross, A. and Eichengreen, B. (1983) *Sterling in Decline*. Blackwell, Oxford.

Carson, C. S. (1975) 'The history of US national income and product accounts: the development of an analytical tool', *Review of Income and Wealth*, series 21, no. 2, pp. 153–81.

De Cecco, M. (1979) 'Origins of the post-war payments system', *Cambridge Journal of Economics*, 3, 49–61.

Eichengreen, B. (ed.) (1985) *The Gold Standard in Theory and History*. Methuen, London.

Gordon, R. A. (1967) 'Full employment as a policy goal'. In Ross, A. M. (ed.), *Employment Policy and the Labour Market*. University of California Press.

HMSO (1944): *Employment Policy*. Cmd 6527, London.

Kaldor, N. (1971) 'Conflicts in national objectives', *Economic Journal*, 81, 1–16.

Keegan, W. and Pennant-Rea, R. (1979) *Who Runs the Economy?* Temple Smith, London.

Keynes, J. M. (1978) *Collected Writings*, vol XXII, Activities 1939–1945; Internal, War Finance. Macmillan/Royal Economic Society, London.

Matthews, R. C. O. (1968) 'Why has Britain had full employment since the war?', *Economic Journal*, 78, 556–69.

Morris, D. (ed.) (1979) *The Economic System in the UK*. Oxford University Press, London.

Peacock, A. and Shaw, G. K. (1981) 'The public sector borrowing requirement', *University College at Buckingham, Occasional Papers*, no. 1.

Phillips, A. W. (1958) 'The relation between unemployment and the rate of change of money wages in the United Kingdom, 1861–1957', *Economica*, 25, 283–99.

Smith, K. (1984) *The British Economic Crisis*. Penguin, Harmondsworth.

Streeten, P. (1966) 'The objectives of economic policy', in Henderson, P. D. (ed.), *Economic Growth in Britain*. Weidenfeld & Nicolson, London.

Tingergen, J. (1952) *The Theory of Economic Policy*. North Holland, Amsterdam.

Tomlinson, J. (1981a) 'The "Economics of Politics" and public expenditure, a critique', *Economy and Society*, 10(4), 381–402.

Tomlinson, J. (1981b) *Problems of British Economic Policy, 1870–1945*. Methuen, London.

Tomlinson, J. (1985) *British Macro-economic Policy since 1940*. Croom Helm, London.

2

The Analysis of Economic Management: the aggregate demand and supply model

ROSALIND LEVAČIĆ

The concept of the managed economy was born out of Keynes's great work, the *General Theory of Employment, Interest and Money*. The overriding influence this book had on post-war macroeconomic policy up till the mid-1970s has already been considered in chapter 1, together with an account of its demise in favour of monetarism. The purpose of this chapter is to set out an analytical framework for studying the different conceptions of how government should go about its task of managing the economy. These conceptions have changed over time as macroeconomists have responded to developments in the UK economy and its links with the world economy, and as policy-makers have themselves, in turn, responded to these developments. The main aim of this chapter is to present the aggregate demand and supply model of the economy with its main variants – in order to provide a theoretical rationale for the way the practice of economic management has mutated over the post-war period. It also provides a framework for understanding current controversies in macroeconomics which are reflected in the contrasting policies for managing the economy in the 1980s advocated by the Alliance and Labour Parties on the one hand, and pursued by the Thatcher Government on the other.

1. Introducing the Aggregate Demand and Supply Model

The purpose of a macroeconomic model is to capture the essential features of how an economy works. Such a model is essential in analysing macroeconomic behaviour because it enables us to study the interrelationships between variables and how these mesh together. For policy purposes a macroeconomic model suggests what are the likely trade-offs between economic objectives, what are feasible values for these target variables, and which other variables can be used as policy instruments by the government and in what ways they can be applied. The strength of a macroeconomic model is that it encompasses the workings of a whole economy and its linkages with the world economy via the balance of payments and the exchange rate. But this can only be done at some cost: economic relationships have to be studied at a high level of aggregation. This is particularly true of a teaching model which can be explained using only words, diagrams and symbols.

The aggregate demand and supply model, or AD/AS for short, is the most basic model which can adequately represent current controversies on how the macroeconomy functions. Although it is highly aggregated and contains just a few relationships, nevertheless it has the same basic framework as the larger and more complex econometric forecasting models, run on computers, used by such bodies as the Treasury, the Bank of England, the National Institute of Economic & Social Research, the London Business School and the Cambridge Economic Policy Group. All these models, including the AD/AS variant, developed out of Keynes's *General Theory of Employment, Interest and Money*, and the ensuing post-war developments in macroeconomics. As the AD/AS model provides the analytical framework for this book, the purpose of this chapter is to explain how the AD/AS model is derived and how it is used for analysing macroeconomic policy. As is well known, the earlier Keynesian consensus on macroeconomic policy has now broken down. The theoretical basis for the divergent views as to how macroeconomic policy should be conducted can be readily explicated within the AD/AS framework. It shows how the contrasting policy scenarios are underpinned by different conceptions about how the economy works, which can be represented by different formulations of the aggregate demand and aggregate supply functions. Because the epicentre of current disagreement relates to the behaviour of the supply side of the economy, models which neglect aggregate supply (as did the Keynesian models of the 1950s and 1960s which still linger on in the textbooks) are incapable of explaining the issues over which controversy currently rages.

The explanation of the AD/AS model given in this chapter assumes the reader already has some knowledge of basic microeconomic theory – demand and supply, the theory of costs, the marginal productivity theory of the demand for labour, and the theory of the supply of labour.

The first thing to note about the AD/AS model is that it is a short-run model: it does not take account of longer-term developments in an economy. This reflects the short- to medium-term focus of economic management, concerned as it is with inflation, unemployment and the balance of payments. As indicated in chapter 1, economic growth has been largely perceived as contingent upon appropriate fiscal, monetary and exchange rate policies, rather than as an objective to be directly secured by government manipulation of its policy instruments. Thus the AD/AS model assumes a given amount of productive capacity, i.e. a given capital stock, a given population of working age and a given state of technology as embodied in the existing capital stock, the skills of the labour force and in current methods of organizing production. The focus of the model is on short-term economic cycles caused by exogenous shocks, and on whether stabilizing government policy measures can be devised. The model abstracts from economic growth in order to simplify. It concentrates on the main issues of short-term economic management that it is explicitly designed to deal with.

The AD/AS model disaggregates the economy into three separate markets – or sectors – the goods and services market, the money market, and the labour market. It analyses how the three markets interact with each other to determine the level of real output, the level of employment, and the price level. These are the three main endogenous variables upon which the model focuses. The open economy version of the model incorporates a fourth market – the foreign sector – and so includes balance of payments variables and the exchange rate. Thus the AD/AS model analyses the determination of the four basic objectives of economic policy, otherwise known as target variables, namely real output, employment, inflation (changes in the price level), and the balance of payments. The model shows how these target variables are affected by government action to change those variables that are instruments of economic policy, such as government spending, taxes, and the money supply. Thus the model provides a formal framework for analysing the relationship between the objectives and instruments of economic policy.

The major economic relationships which constitute the model are distilled into two functions – the aggregate demand function and the aggregate supply function – and so can be represented by a single diagram. Whether an increase in aggregate demand results in an increase in the volume of output produced by private sector firms depends on the specification of the aggregate supply function.

The chapter proceeds by deriving the aggregate demand function, and then the aggregate supply function. They are put together and used to obtain different variants of the AD/AS model which represent Keynesian, monetarist, and new classical views on how the economy should – or should not – be managed.

2. Aggregate Demand

In Keynesian macro models aggregate demand plays the major role in determining the amount of real national output produced in the domestic economy. In the simple Keynesian model, taught for several decades by Keynes's disciples as representing the essence of his ideas, the supply of real national output is entirely demand-determined up to the point at which all resources are fully utilized – called full-employment output, by Keynesians. The strong policy conclusion of the Keynesian approach is that the government can, and should, manage the economy by managing the level of aggregate demand. It does this by operating on variables which affect the level of aggregate demand.

2.1.   *The goods market*

So what is aggregate demand? It is the amount people wish to spend on the output of the domestic economy. There are two crucial things here. First, aggregate demand is what people *wish* to spend: it is their desired or planned level of spending. This may differ from the actual amount of national expenditure. So if aggregate demand exceeds actual national expenditure, then some would-be purchasers remain unsatisfied. Aggregate demand could be less than actual national expenditure, in which case some firms would end up with unsold golds on their hands. This means that firms undertake unintended inventory investment which counts as part of actual national expenditure. The second crucial aspect of the definition of aggregate demand is that it is the demand *for* output produced in the domestic economy on the part of *domestic* and *foreign* residents. That is, it includes exports and excludes imports. Thus aggregate demand is not the total amount *domestic* residents want to spend, as this latter amount includes imports which are part of the national output of foreign countries.

Aggregate demand is subdivided into four major components; these are households' consumption, private sector firms' investment, government expenditure, and exports. As all these include imported goods and services, imports are subtracted from the total to arrive at domestic aggregate demand.

The conventional classification of the major components of aggregate demand is shown in table 2.1, together with the symbols we are using in the book to denote their real values. The components of aggregate demand make up the goods market. By definition they sum to total aggregate demand, hence the identity sign $\equiv$ in table 2.1.

The goods market is also concerned with the determination of the components of aggregate demand. Consumption is the largest component. Its major determinant is the level of disposable national income – what people have available to spend after paying tax. Consumption also depends on the amount of wealth. The wealthier people are, the higher their consumption is likely to be. The more liquid wealth is, i.e. the easier it is to convert into money without fear of loss, the greater its

Table 2.1.   The components of aggregate demand

Components of aggregate demand	Symbol for real value of the variable
Consumption	c
Investment	i
Government expenditure	g
Exports	x
Minus imports	$-h$
Aggregate demand	$e \equiv c + i + g + (x - h)$

likely impact of consumption. Thus the quantity of money balances exerts a positive impact on consumption. As the analysis is conducted in real terms, what matters is *real* money balances – that is nominal money balances deflated by an index of the price level. Another variable thought to have some impact on consumption is the rate of interest. The higher the rate of interest the lower is consumption, because saving is more attractive and borrowing to finance consumption more expensive. Hence consumption in the AD/AS model is assumed to vary directly with real disposable income and real money balances, and inversely with the rate of interest. The consumption function is set out below.

Consumption function

$$c = f\left(yd, \frac{M}{P}, r\right)$$

where yd = real disposable national income
  M = nominal money supply, i.e. the number of pounds held as cash and bank deposits
  P = price level of all goods and services
  M/P = real money balances
  r = interest rate

Disposable national income is national income, y, minus the amount paid in tax. For the purposes of the model we assume a single rate of income tax, t. Hence disposable income, yd, is $y - ty = (1 - t)y$. The tax rate is exogenous as it is a policy instrument fixed by the government. The nominal money supply, M, is the number of pounds held as cash or as bank deposits, and is also assumed fixed in the AD/AS model.

The investment function in the AD/AS model has a relatively simple specification. Investment is assumed to depend inversely on the rate of interest – the higher the rate of interest the greater the opportunity cost of using capital and hence the lower the volume of investment, given the expected future profitability of such investment. Such expectations are assumed exogenous, but liable to change. So if expected future profitability rises, there will be an increased desire to invest at the current rate of interest. The investment function is expressed algebraically as:

Investment function

$$i = f(r, \text{expectations})$$

where i = real investment in capital goods
a fall in r leads to a rise in i
a rise in r leads to a fall in i

Government expenditure is easily explained in the model – it is just assumed exogenous! Exports are assumed to depend on the exchange rate – a lower exchange rate increases exports – and on the domestic price level. Given the exchange rate, a fall in the UK price level relative to price levels abroad will improve the competitiveness of British goods and so increase exports. Conversely, imports are assumed higher the greater the value of the exchange rate and the higher the UK relative price level. Imports are also assumed to vary directly with UK national income. Thus the current account balance is expressed as:

Current account balance of payments

$$(x-b) = f(y, er, P)$$

where er = sterling exchange rate; $(x-b)$ rises if y, er or P falls

---

In this chapter the exchange rate will be assumed fixed. The implications of exchange rate behaviour for macroeconomic policy are discussed in chapter 8.

Adding together the consumption, investment, government expenditure, and current account balance of payments functions we get an expression for total aggregate demand. The variables with bars are assumed exogenous in the AD/AS model:

Aggregate demand

$$e = c\left(y(1-\bar{t}),\ \frac{\bar{M}}{P},\ r\right) + \bar{g} + (x-b)(y, \bar{er}, P)$$

This expression for aggregate demand contains three endogenous variables – national output (y), the price level (P) and the interest rate (r). National income and the price level are the two endogenous variables of prime interest for the AD/AS model: we are building up the model in order to solve for them. So I will put them to one side for the moment and turn to the rate of interest. To understand how the interest rate is determined we need to bring in the money market or financial sector.

2.2.   *The money market*

The AD/AS model has a very simple financial sector which consists of just two financial assets – an interest-bearing bond, which can be issued by the government or firms in order to borrow resources saved by households, and money. The money supply consists of cash in circulation and held as bank reserves, plus bank deposits. This is equivalent to the £M3 measure of the money supply. (Money supply determination is discussed much more fully in chapter 7.) The AD/AS model can only be in equilibrium if all its constituent markets are also in equilibrium. The money market is in equilibrium when the amount of money people wish to hold – the demand for money – equals the stock of money supplied by the government. If the whole model is in equilibrium, and the money market is in equilibrium, then it must be true that the bond market is also in equilibrium. Hence it is only necessary to consider the money market and the condition required for it to equilibrate.

These are two main reasons for wanting to hold money – to use it as a medium of exchange for financing transactions and to enjoy the advantages of holding the most liquid asset there is. The demand for money depends on the level of national income. The higher the quantity of national output the greater the volume of transactions there are to finance and hence the higher the demand for money. But there is an opportunity cost to holding money: this is the rate of return that could have been obtained from holding other assets. In the AD/AS model the opportunity cost of holding money is the rate of interest on bonds. Hence the higher the rate of interest the lower is the demand for real money balances. Thus the demand for money function is written algebraically as:

Demand for money function

$$m^D = f(y, r)$$

where $m^D = (M/P)^D =$ quantity of real money balances demanded
$y =$ real national income or output
$r =$ rate of interest

There are other factors that affect the demand for money, such as the characteristics of the payments system – how often people get paid wages, in what form, the use of credit cards, and so on. All these factors are assumed exogenous in the AD/AS model.

In figure 2.1 I have depicted the demand and supply of money with the rate of interest on the vertical axis. This diagram can only show how the demand for money varies as the interest rate changes, holding all the other determinants of the demand for money, in particular national income, constant along any one demand for money curve. So the demand for money curve in figure 2.1 shows how the demand for real money balances rises as the interest rate falls, given a constant level of real national income of y_1. If the national income were to rise, then there would be an increase in the demand for money which would cause an upward shift to the right in the demand schedule. At every value of the interest rate more money would be demanded.

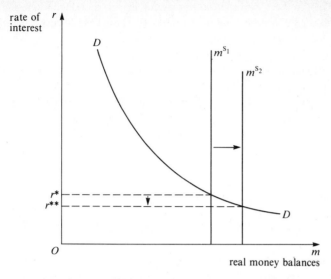

Figure 2.1. A downward-sloping aggregate demand schedule

The supply of real money balances in figure 2.1 is shown as a vertical line because the model assumes that the supply of nominal money is exogenous: it is not determined within the model under consideration and does not vary with the rate of interest or national income. You need to bear in mind that figure 2.1 depicts the supply of *real* money balances, which is the stock of nominal money balances, i.e. the amount of £s held as cash and in bank accounts, deflated by the price level. For the time being we assume in the AD/AS model that the nominal quantity of money is under the complete control of the monetary authorities, i.e. the government and the central bank. We make this assumption so that we can treat the nominal money supply as exogenous (indicated by a bar over the symbol in the equation below). The problems the monetary authorities actually have in controlling the supply of nominal money balances are investigated in chapter 7.

The money market is in equilibrium when the demand for real money balances equals the real supply (or stock) of money. This is expressed algebraically as:

Money market equilibrium

$$m^D = (M/P)^D = f(y, r) \quad \text{demand for money}$$
$$m^S = \bar{M}^S/P \quad \text{supply of money}$$

where $\bar{M}^S$ indicates that the nominal money supply is exogenous

$$m^D = f(y, r) = \bar{M}^S/P \quad \text{equilibrium condition}$$

In figure 2.1 the equilibrium in the money market is shown where the demand for and supply of money schedules intersect. If the level of real national income is y_1, then the rate of interest at which the money market is in equilibrium is r^*. An increase in the supply of real money balances is shown as a shift to the right in the money supply schedule. To induce people to hold the increased quantity of real money balances at an unchanged real level of national income, y_1, the interest rate has to fall to r^{**}. *Thus an increase in the supply of real money balances reduces the rate of interest, while a decrease in the supply of real money balances has the opposite effect and increases the rate of interest.* The quantity of real money balances can be increased in two ways: by an increase in the nominal quantity of money (i.e. the number of £s) or by a decrease in the price level. An increase in the price level, or decrease in nominal money balances, reduces the volume of real money balances.

The goods and money markets are interconnected, since developments in one affect the other. For instance changes in the demand and supply of money alter the rate of interest, and this in turn affects aggregate demand, via its influence on consumption and investment. An increase in aggregate demand, which increases real output, the price level, or both, affects the demand for money. Hence in figure 2.1 any increase in real money balances will, if it results in higher real output, shift the demand for money function up to the right. The interest rate rises, causing some contraction of aggregate demand. Thus following any change there are a series of repercussions as all endogenous variables adjust towards a new equilibrium. The new equilibrium that results can be deduced by deriving the aggregate demand and supply functions.

2.3. *Deriving the aggregate demand function*

We are now in a position to derive the aggregate demand function or schedule. The aggregate demand function in the AD/AS model is the relationship between the amount of aggregate demand and the price level. In the general version of the AD/AS model aggregate demand increases as the price level falls. This happens because a fall in the price level increases the quantity of real money balances, given an unchanged nominal money stock. This rise in the quantity of real money balances has two channels or transmission mechanisms whereby it has a positive impact on aggregate demand.

The first is due to the *direct* relationship between the quantity of real balances and the level of consumption. The larger the quantity of real money balances the greater is consumption, because consumers have more wealth to spend. This effect is called the *real balance effect*.

The second channel is *indirect*. An increase in the quantity of real money balances lowers the rate of interest and this increases investment and consumption.

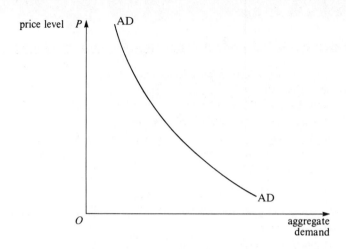

Figure 2.2.   A downward-sloping aggregate demand schedule

This relationship between aggregate demand and the price level is shown in figure 2.2. The lower the price level the higher is aggregate demand. One important point to note is that all along this aggregate demand schedule the goods and money markets are in equilibrium. Money market equilibrium has already been defined. The goods market is in equilibrium when national income equals aggregate demand, i.e. when the level of national income is such that it determines a level of aggregate demand which is the same as the level of national income. As national income and national output are identical, we can use them interchangeably. So we get:

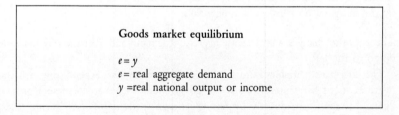

Goods market equilibrium

$e = y$
e = real aggregate demand
y = real national output or income

Hence we relate the amount of national output demanded, y, to the price level along the aggregate demand schedule in figure 2.2. You can now appreciate that in order to determine values for real national output and the price level we need to add an aggregate supply schedule. But before we do that, let us first review the changes in the exogenous variables of the AD/AS model which shift the entire AD schedule up or down.

2.4. *Shifts in the AD function*

The exogenous variables included in the goods and money market specifications are:

(a) the tax rate which affects disposable income
(b) government expenditure
(c) the nominal stock of money
(d) the exchange rate – which affects imports and exports
(e) the marginal propensity to consume: this is the increase in consumption that results from an increase in income and appears as the b coefficient in a linear consumption function like this one:

$$c = a + b(1-t)y$$

(*a* is also exogenous)
(f) expectations about the future profitability of investment
(g) the marginal propensity to import: this is the increase in imports due to an increase in national income.

There will be an increase in aggregate demand, i.e. the AD schedule will shift up to the right, if

(a) the tax rate falls, increasing disposable income and consumption
(b) government expenditure rises
(c) the nominal money stock increases
(d) the exchange rate depreciates
(e) the marginal propensity to consume increases
(f) the expected future profitability of investment increases
(g) the marginal propensity to import falls.

The opposite changes will decrease aggregate demand and shift the AD schedule down to the left.

The first two variables, the tax rate and government expenditure, are the instruments of fiscal policy. So if the government wishes to increase aggregate demand it can do so directly by raising its own spending or by reducing taxes, thereby increasing disposable income and so consumption. The third is the instrument of monetary policy. An increase in the money supply increases aggregate demand, both directly via the real balance effect and indirectly via lower interest rates stimulating investment and consumption. The government can also alter the exchange rate, but has to tailor its other instruments to achieve its target exchange rate, and so is relatively constrained within a range of feasible values. The problems of managing an open economy are discussed much more fully in chapter 8.

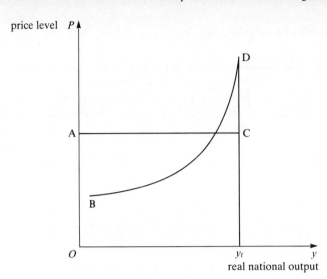

Figure 2.3   Three possible shapes for the aggregate supply function

3.   The Aggregate Supply Function

However, whether an increase in aggregate demand will actually induce domestic firms to produce more real output, rather than raise their prices, depends on the nature of the aggregate supply relationship. Whereas aggregate demand is the amount domestic and foreign residents wish to spend on the national product of a country, aggregate supply is the amount of national output domestic firms wish to produce. An aggregate supply function indicates how much national output firms wish to produce in relation to the aggregate price level, given that they can only vary the quantity of labour and raw materials they employ. As noted before, the AD/AS model is a short-run model in which the capital stock, the state of technology, and the population of working age are assumed fixed. At the heart of current disagreements about the extent to which unemployment can be reduced by the government expanding aggregate demand, are different assumptions about the relationship between aggregate supply and the price level. There are three distinct possibilities, illustrated in figure 2.3.

(a) The aggregate supply schedule is horizontal, i.e. it is perfectly elastic with respect to the current price level up to full capacity where it becomes vertical, like ACD in figure 2.3.

(b) The aggregate supply schedule slopes upwards, as does BD: firms will only produce more real output when aggregate demand increases if the price level rises as well.

(c) The aggregate supply schedule is vertical, like Dy_f: y_f real output is produced irrespective of the price level.

Nowadays the first type of AS schedule is assumed in radical Keynesian analysis, typified by the Cambridge Economic Policy Group; the second encompasses a wide spectrum of moderate Keynesian and of the monetarist opinion, while the view that the AS schedule is always vertical is propounded by new classical economists.

3.1.   *The relationship between aggregate supply and costs*

The purpose of section 3 is to explain the theoretical assumptions which underlie these three propositions about the aggregate supply schedule. The first thing to appreciate is that the shape of the aggregate supply schedule depends on how firms' average and marginal short-run costs behave as they expand real output. There are three possibilities:

(a) The aggregate supply schedule is AC in figure 2.3 if average and marginal costs are constant in the short run as output is expanded, so long as firms have underutilized capacity.
(b) Average and marginal costs rise in the short run as output is increased to give the upward-sloping AS schedule BD.
(c) Firms are operating at full capacity, at which point average and marginal costs rise very steeply (i.e. tend to infinity) to give a vertical aggregate supply schedule.

Under perfect competition a firm's marginal cost curve is its supply function. But we can still relate the shape of the aggregate supply function to the shape of the aggregate cost function if firms are modelled as oligopolists who set their prices as a mark-up on average cost. Constant unit costs will result in a horizontal aggregate supply schedule, while rising marginal and average costs will probably give rise to an upward-sloping aggregate supply function.

Having established the direct connection between the aggregate supply function and the behaviour of average and marginal costs as output varies in the short run, we need to consider briefly the determinants of short-run production costs. These determinants are of two kinds:

(a) This is related to the physical aspects of the production process as expressed in the production function. Of prime concern here is how the marginal product of labour behaves as output is increased in the short run. Is the marginal product of labour constant as output expands, does it decline or does it rise?
(b) The other determinant of the short-run average and marginal cost of output in the money wage rate. How marginal and average costs vary as output is

expanded depends also on whether the money wage rate stays constant or rises as more labour is employed. This in turn depends on the shape of the aggregate supply of labour function. If it is horizontal (i.e. perfectly elastic with respect to the money wage rate) then firms can increase employment (i.e. demand more labour) at an unchanged money wage rate. If the supply of labour slopes upwards with respect to the wage rate, then firms can only get more labour if they increase wages.

Given labour is the only variable factor of production, then the relationship between the short-run average cost of output and the average product of labour and the money wage rate is:

$$\text{Short-run average cost} = \frac{\text{Money wage rate}}{\text{Average product of labour}}$$

If the average and marginal product of labour are constant and the money wage rate remains unchanged as output expands, then the average and marginal cost of output curve and the aggregate supply curve will be horizontal. Many Keynesians have argued that the marginal product of labour in fact increases in the short run when firms start expanding output after a recession. This is because they are initially operating their fixed plant at below its optimum level of utilization as well as underemploying their labour force. So as output expands from its recession level, the average and marginal product of labour expands. If this is the case, then money wages can rise to some extent, while average costs still remain constant. This argument is less plausible than it used to be because manufacturing firms since the 1980/81 recession shed labour rapidly and productivity grew while output declined. But if the marginal product of labour declines when output expands, or the money wage rate rises as the demand for labour increases, then short-run average and marginal costs will also rise.

3.2. *The inverted L-shaped aggregate supply function*

An inverted L-shaped AS schedule underlies the simple Keynesian model, containing just a goods market, which has dominated the textbooks since the 1940s. It was originally devised by Keynes's disciples to popularize *The General Theory*, which is itself a complex and difficult book, still subject to different interpretations. The simple Keynesian model became very widely used – even for policy purposes. Up to the mid-1970s the Treasury model was a highly disaggregated, multi-equation version of the simple Keynesian model with no explicit supply side at all. Demand management, as practised in the 1950s, was an application of the economic principles embodied in the simple Keynesian model. This model was taught (and still is) entirely in terms of aggregate demand. The assumption of an inverted L-shaped aggregate

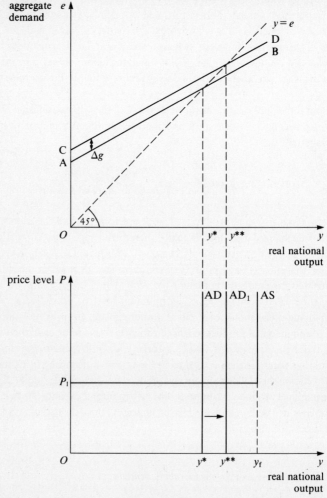

Figure 2.4.   A radical Keynesian AD/AS model

supply function, which is required to complete the model, is still not usually made explicit in elementary textbooks. The significance of assuming an inverted L-shaped AS schedule is illustrated in figure 2.4. The top half shows the much used diagrammatic representation of the simple goods-market Keynesian model. (As the inverted L-shaped AS function is nowadays only held to by radical Keynesians, not orthodox ones, I have called figure 2.4 the radical Keynesian model. A fully fledged radical Keynesian model has a monetary sector and a foreign trade sector, as in Godley and Cripps, 1983.) AB is an aggregate demand or expenditure function with respect to income: it shows how desired expenditure on the national output rises with national income, which is the only endogenous variable in the model. The 45° line indicates all co-ordinate points at which aggregate demand, e equals real national output, y. The goods market is in equilibrium at the point where the expenditure function, AB, intersects the 45° line. At this point the level of aggregate demand called forth by the level of real national output, y^*, is the same as the level of output; hence there is equilibrium.

The bottom half of figure 2.4 is usually omitted. It makes explicit the supply-side assumptions underlying the radical Keynesian model. This is that aggregate supply up to full employment is perfectly elastic at the current price level, P_1: whatever is demanded is supplied by firms. In a simple Keynesian model with just a goods market and no money market, aggregate demand depends only on income and not on the price level: hence the AD schedule is vertical. So if y^* output is demanded at the current price level, this is the amount produced. As y^* is less than the full employment level of output, there is deficient aggregate demand and – by definition – involuntary unemployment. Given this representation of the economy, the appropriate response by government is to increase aggregate demand. It can do this by means of fiscal policy: raising its own spending or reducing taxation and so raising disposable income and thereby increasing consumption. This will shift up the expenditure function in the top half of figure 2.4, thus shifting the AD function to the right in the bottom half of the diagram. To achieve full employment the AD function has to be shifted outwards until it coincides with the amount of output firms can produce when utilizing their capacity fully.

Thus Keynesian analysis pinpoints the cause of unemployment as deficient aggregate demand, the remedy for which is government action to increase demand. Raising government spending and/or lowering taxes implies an increase in the government's budget deficit. Keynesians have thus always regarded increased budget deficits as a wholly appropriate response by government to recession. They have always been highly critical of the Treasury view, held by the authorities in the 1930s, that the prudent conduct of the public finances requires balanced budgets. For Keynesians, government attempts to balance its budget in a recession are totally counterproductive. Certain 'automatic stabilizers' cause the budget to move further into deficit in a recession: tax revenues decline because incomes and expenditure fall, while government expenditure on welfare benefits rises. To attempt to maintain a balanced budget over a recession would require increased tax rates and reduced government expenditure: both would worsen the recession by reducing aggregate demand still further.

In a boom aggregate demand exceeds full employment output. As a result the price level rises and the balance of payments is likely to move into deficit because imports rise and export fall as domestic firms divert their goods to the home market. The appropriate policy response is now a reduction in aggregate demand: increased tax revenues and reduced government expenditure lower the budget deficit. Thus the budget deficit should move countercyclically – rising in a recession and falling in a boom.

In the 1950s demand management was used in an attempt to secure both internal balance (low inflation and unemployment) and external balance. The technique of raising aggregate demand a bit when the economy moved into recession, and lowering it when the economy became overheated, was known as fine-tuning. A popular analogy compared demand management to steering a car along a twisting road, applying a touch of the brake at one point and the accelerator at another.

The main instrument of Keynesian demand management was fiscal policy. Early Keynesianism held that monetary policy was ineffective, especially in a recession. It was believed that any increase in the money supply would be held and not spent on other assets or goods: there was no real balance effect and interest rates would not fall. 'Pushing on a string' was a popular analogy to describe the ineffectiveness of monetary policy in a recession. Furthermore, it was held that consumption and investment depended on the general degree of liquidity in the economy, not on the money supply or on interest rates directly. Liquidity is a somewhat amorphous concept that embraces the ease of obtaining credit and the risks attached to it. These ideas were embodied in the influential Radcliffe Report on the Working of the Monetary System (1959). Given this attitude to monetary policy, the absence of a monetary sector in the simple Keynesian model or the Treasury's version of it was not regarded as a critical neglect until the late 1960s. A vertical AD function reflects these views.

This does not mean that monetary policy was not used. It was; but it played second fiddle to fiscal policy. In contrast to the concern with monetary targets in the years since 1976, monetary policy prior to this focused on liquidity. It involved changes in interest rates – signalled by changes in Bank Rate and measures to alter the availability of credit. So a restrictionary monetary policy involved higher interest rates, tighter hire purchase terms and quantitative restrictions on bank lending. (All this is discussed more fully in chapter 7.) Often changes in monetary policy were introduced as part of a 'package' which included fiscal measures as well.

Not only did fiscal policy carry the main burden of demand management, but within it, taxation assumed a much more important role than government expenditure. The latter proved unsuited to quick and fine adjustment by central government. Much of government spending is predicated on specific expenditure programmes – health, education, defence, administration, social security, etc. To raise and lower spending on these disrupts the provision of these services. Cuts in current expenditure mean staff reductions or lower welfare benefits. Increases are difficult to claw back later as more public servants have been hired, while the beneficiaries have become accustomed to better services or higher real benefits. Thus cuts in government expenditure are resisted both by the bureaucrats who administer them and the citizens who benefit from them. On the whole, capital expenditure has proved easier to cut than current expenditure, since it has less effect on the jobs of currently employed public sector workers or on current services. Thus public sector investment, which averaged around 11 per cent of government expenditure in the 1960s and early 1970s, has fallen since then to around 4 per cent over the years of continued restraint on public spending. The problem with using *changes* in government capital expenditure as a means of fine-tuning is that it makes public sector investment planning difficult to operate. Planned projects get cancelled after some resources have already been committed, or extra capacity is acquired which is then underutilized because of inadequate demand, as in electricity generation where capital projects were brought forward. Thus the

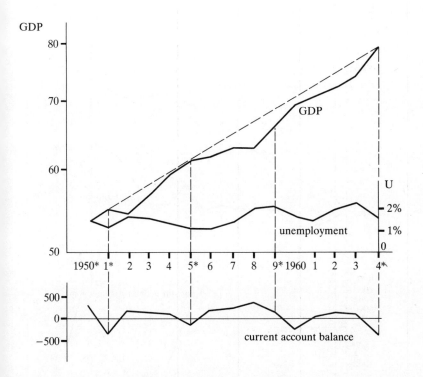

Figure 2.5. Stop-go, 1950–64.
General election years are marked with an asterisk. Note that GDP is plotted on a logarithmic scale. This means that a straight line corresponds to a constant percentage growth rate. The broken line is thus the level of GDP that would have occurred if GDP had grown at a constant rate between 1951 and 1964: it gives an approximate value for full employment or full capacity GDP. *Source:* Backhouse (1983)

main instruments of the fine-tuning type of demand management were changes in income tax rates and thresholds, in indirect taxes and the cost and availability of credit.

In theory, fine-tuning should have stabilized the economy by counteracting fluctuations in aggregate demand emanating from the private sector, both at home and abroad. For instance, an exogenous shock, such as a fall in private sector investment, would be prevented from causing a depression by countervailing fiscal and monetary policies. However the actual practice of demand management came to be increasingly criticized for creating instability (e.g. Dow, 1964). Demand would be stimulated, unemployment fall to around 1.5 per cent and the balance of payments would consequently move into deficit. The government would then deflate

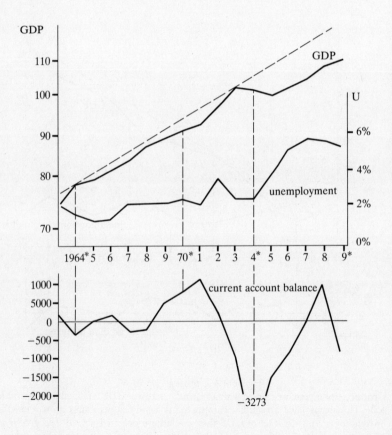

Figure 2.6.   Stop-go, 1964–79. *Source:* Backhouse (1983).

aggregate demand to restore balance of payments equilibrium. The existence of this policy behaviour, called 'stop-go' is clearly evident in figure 2.5.

Determined efforts were made to break out of the stop-go cycle by the Labour Government under Harold Wilson, which came to power in 1964. This was aborted by a severe balance of payments crisis in 1967 to which the government responded by devaluation plus restrictive fiscal and monetary policies. The 1971-2 Barber 'dash for growth' met a similar fate (see chapter 1, p. 34 for more details). Thus 'stop-go' continued into the 1970s, as shown in figure 2.6. The advent of oil has eased the balance of payments constraint – at least for a while.

Apart from the balance of payments constraint on demand management, inflation – a related problem – emerged in the 1950s. From 1953 to 1962 inflation averaged 2.5 per cent. Though low by today's standards, it was in marked contrast to the inter-war years of stable or slightly falling prices. The early forebodings (expressed by Keynes and the 1944 White Paper on Employment Policy) that full employment would carry with it the associated cost of inflation, had been borne out. Highly influential research by Phillips, published in 1958, showed a trade-off between unemployment and inflation. (This was referred to in chapter 1 and will be discussed in detail in chapter 6.) Thus the assumption of the simple Keynesian model that the price level remains constant right up to full employment, became increasingly unrealistic.

3.3.   *An upward-sloping aggregate supply schedule*

But in the *General Theory*, Keynes had made no such assumption. He had worked with an upward-sloping aggregate supply schedule, not an inverted L-shaped one. However, a model with an upward-sloping aggregate supply schedule is inherently more complex than the simple Keynesian model which could get away with having no explicit supply side. To derive an aggregate supply function we need to include in the model the labour market and the economy's production function. I now wish to consider how such an upward-sloping aggregate supply schedule can be derived, following Keynes's own exposition.

First, Keynes accepted the neo-classical view that the marginal product of labour declines in the short run as employment is increased but the capital stock and state of technology are fixed. He therefore accepted that the demand for labour is inversely related to the real wage. This theory is derived from the assumption that firms are profit-maximizers. A firm will hire labour until it has reached the profit-maximizing level of employment. If the firm operates in perfectly competitive product and labour markets the profit-maximizing output level is that one at which the marginal product of labour equals the real wage rate. If a firm employed any more labour the marginal product of labour would decline, while the real wage stayed unchanged, so that profits would decline. Given an unchanged production function the firm will only demand more labour if the real wage falls. Thus the demand for labour depends inversely on the real wage rate. Its algebraic form is given below. (The assumption of monopolistic product and/or labour markets alters the profit-maximizing rule but not the conclusion that the demand for labour depends on the real wage rate. However, the demand for labour now depends on the elasticity of demand for the firm's output as well.)

The demand for labour

$$l^D = f\left(\frac{W}{P}\right)$$

As the real wage falls, the demand for labour rises.
$l^D =$ demand for labour
$W =$ money wage rate
$P =$ price level
$W/P = w =$ real wage rate

While Keynes accepted the neo-classical theory of the demand for labour, he laid great stress on his rejection of the neo-classical formulation of the supply of labour function. He rejected the neo-classical view that the amount of labour supplied to the economy was always a positive function of the real wage, even in a recession. He argued that the neo-classical labour supply function did not operate where there is excess capacity. According to Keynes, unemployed workers are willing to work at a real wage lower than that currently in existence, and this was his definition of involuntary unemployment.

But although many workers are willing to take a job at a lower real wage, they are not prepared to accept a cut in real wages that comes about via a reduction in the money wage. They are only willing to accept a cut in their real wage if this is brought about by a rise in the price level. The reason Keynes gave for this asymmetry is that a cut in money wages is resisted by individual groups of workers because it implies a reduction in their real wage *relative to other workers*, whereas an increase in the general price level affects everyone more or less equally. The tendency of money wages to be sticky in the downwards direction, and the willingness of the unemployed to work at a lower real wage brought about by a rise in the price level, gives rise to a supply of labour function which is perfectly elastic with respect to the current money wage up to full employment. The Keynesian specification of the supply of labour in terms of algebra is:

Supply of labour

$l^s = l_f$ if $l^D < l_f$ (involuntary unemployment)

$l^s = f\left(\dfrac{W}{P}\right)$ if $l^D \geqslant l_f$ (neo-classical labour supply function)

labour supply rises when real wage rises
l_f = full employment
l^s = labour supply

The Keynesian labour supply function is depicted in the top graph of figure 2.7. This shows the demand and supply of labour with respect to the money wage rate, which is measured along the vertical axis. The current money wage rate is W_1. $0l_f$ labour is supplied to the economy at the current money wage rate. Once full employment, l_f, is reached more labour is only supplied if the money wage rate rises. As the price level is held constant along each supply curve, a rise in the money wage along any one supply curve means a rise in the real wage. Thus the rising portion of the labour supply curve is the same as a neo-classical labour supply function. (The supply of labour is treated more fully in chapter 3.) In this Keynesian labour market the demand for labour depends on the real wage rate. In the top graph of figure 2.7, the demand for labour curve is drawn with respect to the money wage. To know what real wage corresponds to each money wage rate we need to know the price level. So let us suppose that the price level is fixed at P_1. The demand for labour curve with respect to the money wage when the price level is P_1 is given by $D_1 D_1$ in figure 2.7. With the price level fixed at P_1, the lower is the money wage, the smaller is the real wage, and hence the greater is the demand for labour. At the real wage of W_1/P_1 the demand for labour is l_1, while the supply of labour is l_f. Involuntary unemployment is therefore $l_1 l_f$.

The second graph in figure 2.7 shows the short-run production function for a given quantity of capital and a given state of technology. From this we can see that if employment is l_1 the amount of real national output produced will be y_1. We have now got enough information to start tracing out an aggregate supply function. This is done in the bottom of graph of figure 2.7, which has the price level along its vertical axis and real national output along the horizontal axis. We know that if the price level is P_1, then the amount of real national output firms wish to supply is y_1. Thus point 1 is one position on the aggregate supply function.

To get another point on the aggregate supply function we need to find out what amount of output firms are willing to supply at a different price level, everything else remaining unchanged. So let the price level rise to P_2. This reduces the real wage implied by each value of the money wage measured along the vertical axis in the top graph of figure 2.7. Therefore the demand for labour at each money

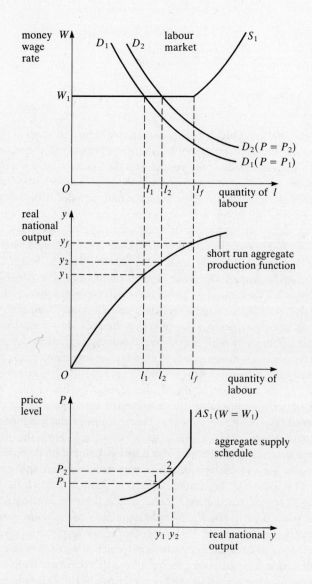

Figure 2.7. Deriving an upward-sloping aggregate supply schedule

wage rate is now greater: the entire demand for labour schedule has shifted up to the right from $D_1 D_1$ to $D_2 D_2$, as shown in figure 2.7. The demand for labour schedule is $D_2 D_2$ when the price level is fixed at P_2. But because workers are willing to accept a cut in real wages that comes from a rise in the price level, the supply of labour schedule $W_1 S$ *does not shift* when the price level rises. This is a crucial assumption. So, given the unchanged current money wage of W_1, a rise in the price level to P_2 increases the demand for labour to l_2. From the short-run production function we can see that firms now wish to supply y_2 real national output. Turning to the bottom graph, we record at point 2 that when the price level is P_2 firms wish to supply y_2 real national output. We now have one more point on the aggregate supply curve. By changing the price level we can get many more such points which trace out an aggregate supply schedule. Once full employment, l_f, is reached, a higher price level will not increase the supply of output. This is because labour in excess of l_f will only be supplied if the real wage rises. But a rise in the price level reduces the real wage. So once full employment is reached it is not possible to increase real output beyond y_f by raising aggregate demand and the price level. Thus the AS schedule becomes vertical at y_f, as it is assumed that once full employment is reached any rise in the money wage will be matched by an equivalent rise in the price level.

3.4. *Shifts in the aggregate supply function*

As already stated, two sets of variables are assumed constant for the purpose of deriving an aggregate supply function. One is the money wage rate and the other set encompasses those factors which determine the productive capacity of the economy – namely the quantity of capital, the size of the labour force and the state of technology. A change in any of these variables will shift the AS schedule, as indicated in figure 2.8.

If the money wage increases, then the supply of labour schedule depicted in figure 2.7 will shift upwards. At every price level the real wage is now higher, so firms demand less labour and wish to produce less output. Hence the AS schedule shifts up to the left in figure 2.8. If the productive capacity of the economy increases, due to growth in the capital stock or technological improvements, then the short-run production function shifts upwards. For any given level of employment and hence real wage – real output is greater. Then the AS curve shifts down to the right. An increase in the labour force can occur for a number of reasons: a rising working age population and increased labour force participation by married women have been the main factors in the post-war period. This is analysed in figure 2.7 as a shift to the right in the supply of labour schedule. In a Keynesian model this results in an extension of the upward-sloping part of the AS schedule and a rightwards shift in the vertical part. It would be a good idea to redraw figure 2.7 for yourself

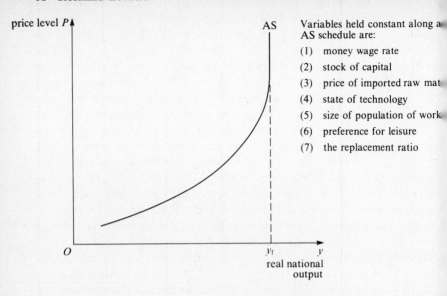

Figure 2.8.   Determinants of the position of the AS function

and derive new AS schedules due to changes in the money wage rate and in productive capacity.

3.5.   *The orthodox Keynesian AD/AS model*

A downward-sloping AD function together with an upward-sloping AS function constitutes the orthodox Keynesian model (in contradistinction to the radical one). It is a direct descendent of the model Keynes presented to the world in the *General Theory*. Its characteristic features are the assumption of a fixed money wage rate together with an upward-sloping AS schedule until full employment output is reached, whereupon it becomes vertical. The complete model is depicted in figure 2.9. The model is in equilibrium when the aggregate demand for real national output equals the aggregate amount firms are willing to supply. All three markets – goods, money and labour, are in simultaneous equilibrium. Then the equilibrium values of real national income and the price level are determined at the intersection of the AD and AS curves. When the AD schedule is AD_1, real output is y_1, and the price level is P_1.

   If the government increases its spending, reduces taxation or expands the money supply, then the AD schedule will shift up to the right, as shown in figure 2.9 from AD_1 to AD_2. The increase in aggregate demand enables firms to raise their

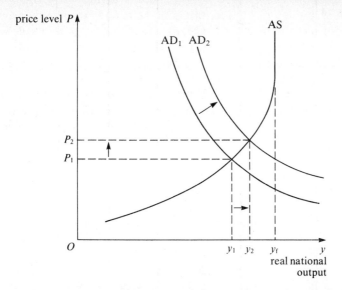

Figure 2.9. The Keynesian AD/AS model: the effect of an increase in aggregate demand

prices. The price level increases and, since the money wage remains unchanged, the real wage declines. Firms therefore demand more labour and, given the Keynesian supply of labour function, this extra labour is forthcoming even though the real wage has fallen. Thus firms are willing to supply more output to meet the extra demand and so real national output rises. This model displays a conflict between the objectives of reducing unemployment and keeping prices stable: real output and employment can only be increased via expanding aggregate demand if the price level is allowed to rise. In this view of how the economy works, demand management involves making a political choice as to how much of a rise in the price level to tolerate in relation to the level of unemployment thereby achieved, given that policy-makers know what the permanent trade-off relationship between the two variables is.

In an attempt to avoid the unpalatable choice between inflation and unemployment, policy-makers turned to incomes policy as a third internal policy instrument, which could be assigned to controlling inflation, thus permitting lower unemployment to be associated with balance of payments equilibrium. From the early 1960s to the late 1970s there were intermittent periods of incomes policy under both Conservative and Labour administrations.

4.   Monetarism

By the mid-1970s it was evident that economic performance had generally worsened, in the UK and in other better-performing western economies. With the benefit of hindsight, it can now be seen that from the mid-1960s both unemployment and inflation began rising, (see chapter 6, p. 162). The 1974–5 recession was the first post-war one in which real output fell absolutely rather than just growing more slowly. Since the mid-1960s each peak and trough of the business cycle has been associated with a higher level of unemployment than the equivalent stage of the previous cycle. In 1975 inflation rose to the unprecedented peacetime rate in the UK of 25 per cent. A stable Phillips trade-off between inflation and unemployment had vanished; higher and higher rates of inflation appeared to be required to keep unemployment at a given level.

4.1.   *The rise of monetarism*

The practice of Keynesian economic policy eventually succumbed to the attack mounted on it by monetarist economists. This change in UK official policy-making occurred in 1976 under the Callaghan Labour Government. Faced with a rapid depreciation of sterling, the Government – despite Left-wing opposition in the Party and in Cabinet – negotiated an IMF loan conditional on the adoption of mildly monetarist policies. These were a tighter monetary policy based on preannounced targets for the money supply and cuts in public expenditure. The more explicit and doctrinaire monetarism of the incoming Thatcher Government in 1979, marked the final eclipse of Keynesianism at the Treasury (at least up to 1986 – and very likely until 1988).

Academic monetarism started as a few dissidents in Chicago in the late 1940s, staunchly refusing to be moved by the Keynesian revolution. Gradually their ideas were taken up and developed by an increasing number of economists on both sides of the Atlantic. At first monetarists focused on excessive monetary growth as the prime cause of inflation; a theory which became more influential in the 1970s, following the experience of rapid monetary expansion and ensuing inflation under the Heath Government of 1970–4. At this stage of the debate between Keynesians and monetarists – in the 1960s – the argument was about the role of money as a determinant of aggregate demand. Monetarists maintain that changes in the money supply are the predominant cause of changes in nominal aggregate demand. They asserted the primary importance of monetary policy in contrast to the Keynesians' belief in its ineffectiveness. Thus a monetarist AD/AS model would have a much more price-elastic aggregate demand function than a Keynesian one. Some monetarists went as far as to claim that fiscal policy is totally ineffective. By the late 1970s this stage of the monetarist-Keynesian debate had reached a rough consensus. Orthodox Keynesians accept that monetary variables have a greater impact on aggregate demand than had been earlier acknowledged, while many monetarists agree that fiscal policy can affect real aggregate demand to some extent. (This debate was largely resolved in a series of conference papers – see Stein, 1976.)

Another and related aspect of monetarism is its critique of Keynesian demand management for being fundamentally misconceived. According to monetarists, expanding aggregate demand reduces unemployment for only a short while. After a couple of years the only effect is a higher rate of inflation, while unemployment is back to its original level. Some monetarists maintain that the long-run effect on unemployment is to increase it because the uncertainty brought about by inflation makes firms more cautious about capital investment and hiring and training labour. Economic growth is thus retarded.

4.2.   *The monetarist version of the AD/AS model*

The monetarist critique of Keynesian economic policy can be elucidated using the AD/AS model and so deriving a monetarist or neo-classical variant of it. (A neo-classical macromodel differs from a Keynesian one mainly with respect to its specification of the labour market.) In a neo-classical model the labour market equilibrates, or clears, like other markets, so that there is no involuntary unemployment. Thus I am classifying a monetarist macro-model as one with an upward-sloping AS curve. The crucial difference between a neo-classical and Keynesian AD/AS model can be demonstrated by assuming that the government expands aggregate demand in order to reduce unemployment. This policy has already been analysed with the help of figure 2.9. The AD curve shifts up an unchanged AS schedule because the money wage is assumed constant. The price level rises from P_1 to P_2 and so the real wage falls. Firms demand more labour and so employment rises, as does output from y_1 to y_2.

The crucial assumption of the Keynesian AD/AS model is that the money wage rate stays unchanged when the price level rises. But what if workers are unwilling to accept a cut in the real wage rate? If this is the case, the Keynesian supply of labour function does not hold: unemployment is not involuntary. Instead the neo-classical supply of labour function holds: the supply of labour is positively related to the real wage rate. If the price level rises, then in order to preserve the original *real* wage rate the money wage rate will rise. A rise in the money wage shifts the AS function up to the left. Monetarists argue that in this situation the money wage rate will adjust in response to a rising price level until the real wage is restored to its original level. Once the real wage is back to the value it had before the government increased aggregate demand, then the demand for labour will also be back at its original level and so will employment and real output.

Figure 2.10 illustrates the monetarist argument that an increase in aggregate demand can lead at best to at temporary increase in real output, but aggregate supply will not increase in the long run – that is, permanently – because money wages rise in response to higher prices. Initially the AD schedule is AD_1 and the AS schedule is AS_1. The initial equilibrium values for real output and the price level are y_1

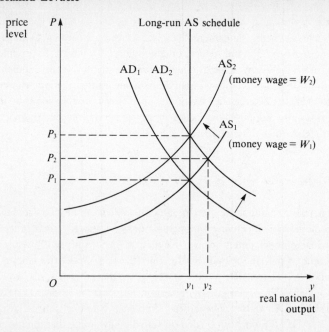

Figure 2.10. The monetarist or neo-classical version of the AD/AS model

and P_1. The government then tries to increase real output by expanding aggregate demand. The AD schedule shifts up to AD_2. At first the money wage rate is unchanged, so the economy moves up the AS_1 schedule. The price level rises and, with a constant money wage, the real wage falls. Consequently firms demand more labour and real output rises to y_2. But then money wages start rising in response to the higher price level because workers are unwilling to accept a cut in the *real* wage rate. As the money wage rises, the AS schedule shifts up to the left. To restore the original real wage the money wage will rise until the new AS schedule, AS_2, intersects the new AD_2 schedule at the original level of real output, y_1. You can see from Figure 2.10 that the real wage rate is unchanged. The vertical distance between AS_1 and AS_2 is the rise in the money wage rate. This equals the final increase in the price level, which is the distance between P_3 and P_1. An equiproportionate change in the money wage rate and the price level leaves the real wage rate unaltered.

If this is the way the supply side of the economy responds to an increase in aggregate demand, then expansionary fiscal and monetary policies can have only a temporary impact on real national output. Only while the price level has risen by more than money wages will the increase in real output persist. In the long run – in the sense of the period over which money wages adjust fully to the rise in the price level – there will be no expansion in real output in response to higher aggregate demand. The final result is just a higher price level. That monetarism had finally penetrated official thinking in the UK was clearly signalled by Prime Minister James Callaghan at the 1976 Labour Party Conference.

> We used to think you could spend your way out of a recession and increase employment by cutting taxes and boosting government spending. I tell you in all candour that that option no longer exists. It only worked, on each occasion since the war, by injecting a bigger dose of inflation into the economy, followed by a higher level of unemployment at the next step. That's the history of the last 20 years.

In the long run monetarists consider that the aggregate supply schedule is vertical: ultimately a rise in the price level does not result in any change in the amount of real output firms wish to supply. The long-run AS schedule is shown in figure 2.10 as a vertical line drawn from y_1. Thus monetarists distinguish between a series of short-run aggregate supply schedules which slope upwards with respect to the price level, and the vertical long-run aggregate supply schedule. The latter is the long-run equilibrium or 'natural' level of national output which would be attained when money wage and price changes have adjusted fully so that the market-clearing real wage rate is established.

The assumptions underlying the vertical aggregate supply schedule are depicted in figure 2.11. The top graph depicts the neo-classical labour market. Both the demand for and supply of labour depend on the real wage rate. At real wage w_e the labour market clears, l_e labour is employed, and y_e real output is produced. If the price level rises then over time the money wage adjusts upwards in the same proportion to preserve the real wage at w_e. Hence long-run employment and real output stay at l_e and y_e respectively; and the associated long-run equilibrium level of unemployment is called the 'natural rate of unemployment'. The natural rate of unemployment can imply quite a high percentage rate: anything between around 5 per cent and 13 per cent in the UK currently, depending on who makes the assessment. The natural level of real output grows over time as the capital stock expands, the employed labour force rises or technology improves. Thus the long-run AS schedule shifts to the right over time, though it may move backwards on occasions. The natural rate of unemployment is affected by those variables which shift the demand and supply of labour functions. So an enlarged quantity of capital for labour to work with, or an improvement in the skills of the labour force, will increase the demand for labour. Increased labour mobility or flexibility, which shifts down the supply of labour curve, will also reduce the natural rate of unemployment, given a static labour force.

In monetarist analysis the actual amount of real output, employment and unemployment in the economy fluctuate around their respective natural levels over the business cycle. If the price level temporarily rises more rapidly than the money

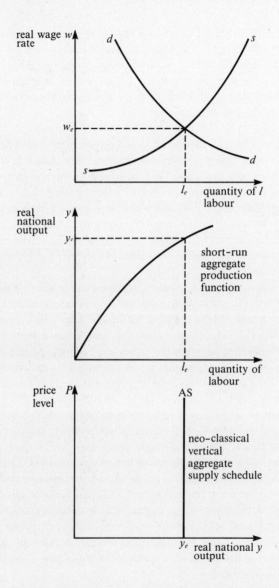

Figure 2.11.   Deriving a neo-classical long-run vertical AS schedule. *Note:* The money wage rises in proportion to the price level to keep the real wage at its market-clearing value w_e. Hence increases in the price level cannot increase the demand for labour.

wage rate, so that the real wage falls, there will be an increase in the quantity of labour demanded and employed. This effect is shown in a diagram such as figure 2.11 by a temporary shift of the labour supply curve down to the right. It is these temporary shifts in the labour supply function that give rise to short-run upward-sloping aggregate supply schedules. You may have noticed in figure 2.10 that the monetarist short-run upward-sloping AS curves are drawn without the vertical section at full employment that characterizes the Keynesian AS schedule. This is because monetarist models do not contain a physical capacity limitation on output, which determine a level of output, employment and unemployment denoted as 'full employment'. In monetarist models the productive capacity of the economy is limited by the amount of output and labour firms and workers are willing to supply, and this depends on what relative prices are perceived to be. The higher are the incentives to supply, the more intensively will existing physical and human resources be used. Thus output and employment can temporarily rise above their natural levels. Hence y_1 in figure 2.10 is the natural or long-run equilibrium level of real output, not its full-employment level. Full employment is a Keynesian concept and, like the natural rate, one that is not easy to quantify for a specific economy at a specific time.

4.3. *Monetarism in practice*

The Conservative Party, led by Margaret Thatcher, won the 1979 election with a policy package which included the explicit intention to implement monetarist policies. I wish to now consider briefly what are monetarist policies, how do they relate to other aspects of economic management as conceived by the Thatcher Government; and how have these policies fared?

Macroeconomists define monetarism relatively narrowly to mean a coherent set of economic theories and policy implications which attribute inflation to the excessive growth of the money supply, and deny that unemployment can be permanently lowered by increasing aggregate demand. These ideas have been explained in this chapter using the AD/AS model. Non-economists tend to interpret monetarism far more widely, to include policies aimed at reducing the economic role of government – by privatization and by cutting public expenditure programmes and taxation; and by enhancing the operation of free market forces. However, monetarism as understood by macroeconomists has no particular implication for the size of the public sector or of the role of market forces (see Laidler, 1982). Its main policy thrust is the need to combat inflation by means of monetary control. This, in turn, requires the government to refrain from financing its budget deficit by increasing the money supply.

There is, though, a distinct tendency for monetarists to advocate reduced budget deficits, if not a balanced budget, on the grounds that government borrowing raises interest rates and crowds out private sector investment. This financial 'crowding-out' hypothesis was discussed in chapter 1. In terms of the AD/AS model, complete financial crowding out would mean that an increase in government spending did not in fact raise aggregate demand because there is an equivalent reduction in private sector investment and consumption. Complete crowding out would mean the total ineffectiveness of fiscal policy. The empirical evidence to support complete crowding out is rather weak; partial financial crowding out, though, does occur, though its extent is a matter of conjecture. Partial financial crowding out means that the impact of increased government spending on aggregate demand is diminished.

The Thatcher Government began to implement a monetarist policy. Reducing inflation was accorded top priority: the means was monetary control. Incomes policy has been firmly rejected. In March 1980 it stated that:

> The Government intend to reduce public expenditure progressively in volume terms over the next four years. This change of direction is central to the achievement of [its] objectives. These are: to bring down the rate of inflation and interest rates by curtailing the growth of the money supply and controlling Government borrowing; to restore incentives; and to plan for spending which is compatible both with the objectives for taxation and borrowing and with a realistic assessment of the prospects for growth. (HMSO, 1980.)

In the 1980 Financial Statement and Budget Report the Government set out its Medium Term Financial Strategy (MTFS): an explicit commitment over the next 4 years to steadily declining targets for the rate of growth of £M3 and the PSBR as a proportion of GDP. (These are discussed more fully in chapter 7.)

Though £M3 failed to stay within the target range, there was nevertheless a considerable tightening of monetary policy, reflected in higher real interest rates and a 17 per cent appreciation of the exchange rate between 1979 and 1981. This, in fact, is entirely explicable by the monetary approach to the balance of payments. Monetary restriction meant an excess demand for money balances, which could only be satisfied by drawing in money from abroad and hence causing a balance of payments surplus accompanied by a rising exchange rate. Unemployment also rose rapidly during 1980 and 1981 and has continued to rise at a more moderate pace up to the time of writing (1986). Real GDP fell by 6.7 per cent between May 1979 and May 1981 - the trough of the latest recession. Since then real national output has recovered and by mid-1985 was 5 per cent above its peak 1979 value. Inflation - the one undoubted success associated with the policy - has been brought down and held steady at around 5 per cent since 1983.

In terms of the AD/AS diagram, the MTFS can be interpreted as a downwards shift in the AD function implemented in order to reduce the price level. This is shown in figure 2.12 as a shift from AD_0 to AD_1. Initially, this occurs along the original short-run aggregate supply function AS_0. Real output falls from y_0 to y_1

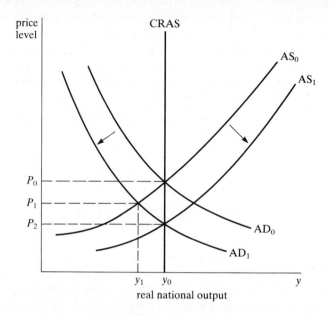

Figure 2.12. A restrictionary monetary policy

and the price level from P_0 to P_1. In a more realistic dynamic version of the AD/AS model it is inflation (the rate of increase of the price level) that falls, not the absolute level of prices. (This analysis is undertaken using the Phillips relation in chapter 6.)

In a monetarist AD/AS model the lower price level will, after some time, induce a downwards adjustment in the money wage and so the short-run AS function shifts to AS_1; real output returns to its previous level and prices fall to P_2. In the dynamic version of the model the rate of growth of money wages will adjust downwards in line with inflation. However, while the rate of increase of money wages has fallen since 1980 it has remained 2–3 per cent above the rate of inflation. Thus real wages have continued to rise despite mounting unemployment. There is little the government can do about this, given they consider incomes policies ineffective and inefficient, except enact new laws to reduce union power, dismantle minimum wage legislation, curb public sector wages and exhort the private sector to practise restraint. The Treasury's stated position is that if money wages rose more slowly real output, and especially employment, could grow faster within the framework set by the MTFS. In the context of the AD/AS model this means that the MTFS sets the AD function at AD_1 in figure 2.12. The further to the right the AS function goes, the higher the level of real output.

Though government rhetoric has insisted on adherence to the MTFS, it has in fact been far more flexibly interpreted than seemed the government's intention in 1980. As discussed much more fully in chapter 7, a more rapid growth in £M3 has occurred. The Chancellor, in his 1985 Mansion House Speech, stated that the £M3 target had, with hindsight, been set too low. Problems with controlling £M3 have, since 1982, caused the government to restate the MTFS in broader – and vaguer – terms in relation to other monetary aggregates, to interest rates, to the exchange rate and to the rate of growth of nominal GDP. Other important departures from the 1980 MTFS are that government expenditure in real terms has risen by an average of 1.8 percent a year rather than falling by 1.2 per cent per annum as originally planned (Levačić, 1986). Consistent with this is that the PSBR as a proportion of GDP has fallen less than originally intended. It fell from 5.4 per cent in 1978/9 to 3.3 per cent in 1981/2, since when it has declined very little. This compares to the original target of 1.5 per cent by 1983–4. And if receipts from public sector asset sales are added to the official figures for the PSBR it became 4.1 per cent of GDP (Congdon, 1985).

For purist monetarists, and for those who want a decisive contraction in the size of the state sector, the Thatcher Government has failed to live up to its rhetoric. However, its economic management policies have been distinctly different from the fine-tuning approach of the 1950s to 1970s, and from the more Keynesian policies advocated, with differing degrees of Keynesianism, by the opposition parties. Deliberate contracyclical demand management, with its associated budget deficit financing have been abandoned, to be replaced by an overriding concern with containing inflation by monetary means and keeping a tight rein on the size of the budget deficit. In the earlier post-war decades economic management, especially as practised by the Treasury, focused almost exclusively on policies designed to manipulate aggregate demand, supplemented at times by incomes policy or devaluation. Since 1980 much more attention has been paid to operating on the supply side of the economy. Both orthodox and radical Keynesians have also embraced this concern, though in different ways. These different notions of how to operate on the supply side of the economy are discussed in chapters 3, 4 and 9. In terms of the AD/AS framework these are all attempts to shift the aggregate supply function – especially the long-run AS function – to the right.

5.   Conclusion

This chapter has set out a largely geometric exposition of the AD/AS model with its different variants. These capture the essential features of the different varieties of Keynesian and monetarist perspectives on macroeconomic policy. The different forms of the AD and AS schedules specified are summarized in figure 2.13. The

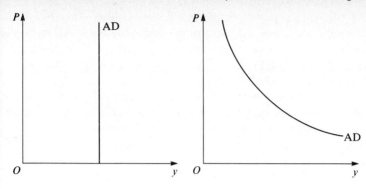

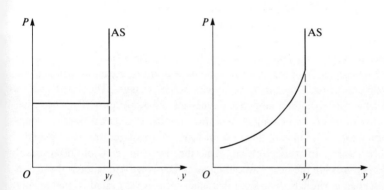

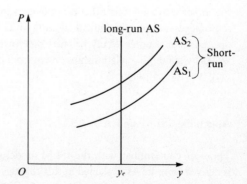

Figure 2.13. The variants of the AD/AS model

vertical AD function represents early post-war Keynesian views. These have now been superseded by a general acceptance of the downward-sloping AD function, though differences persist as to its slope: monetarists expect it to be less steep than do Keynesians. The main controversy in macroeconomics has now refocused on the aggregate supply function.

Radical Keynesians still adhere to an inverted L-shaped AS schedule. This is justified by the theory that inflation is due to structural forces within the economy pushing up wages and prices independently of the state of demand. The interaction of trade unions and oligopolistic firms practising mark-up price is regarded as the main source of inflationary pressure (see chapter 6, pp. 173–7). Thus the horizontal section of the AS function is depicted as shifting upwards over time. If the AD schedule intersects the AS function at less than full employment, then the traditional Keynesian remedy is still appropriate. An increase in aggregate demand will raise real output and lower unemployment without inducing any rise in prices. However, the uncompetitive state of British industry does require that a policy of demand expansion be accompanied by import controls designed to prevent a balance of payments crisis.

Moderate Keynesians consider the upward-sloping AS schedule to be a more realistic representation of the economy, and have absorbed the monetarist analysis of shifting short-run AS curves as money wages change. There has been a considerable convergence of moderate Keynesians and monetarists. The main issue which divides them is how long it takes the economy to adjust towards its long-run natural rate position and the scope for economic management in keeping the economy nearer to this position. On the extreme end of neo-classical macroeconomics are the new classical school, much more strongly represented in the USA than in the UK, who hold that adjustment is very rapid. Consequently the economy is never very far off the long-run AS schedule, and Keynesian demand management can only destabilize the economy by causing inflation.

These different approaches will be considered more fully in subsequent chapters. It is important to appreciate that the different variants of the AD/AS model represent sets of ideas, not people. Individual economists cannot be neatly pigeon-holed into one model or another. Many will base their own conclusions on how the economy works by combining relationships drawn from more than one stylized model. You may well do the same.

Appendix: ISLM and AD/AS

Those of you familiar with the ISLM model should note that the AD schedule is derived from it. As explained in this chapter, the goods and money markets are in equilibrium all along the AD schedule. Thus the AD schedule is the locus of points of intersection of the IS and LM curves. How the AD schedule is derived

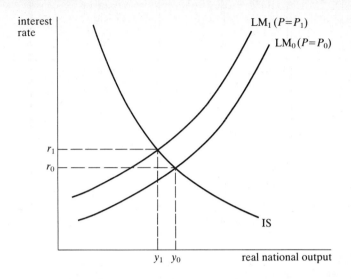

Figure 2.14.   Deriving the AD schedule from the ISLM model

from the ISLM model is explained with the help of figure 2.14. Changes in the price level shift the LM curve because the quantity of real money balances is affected. At a price level of P_0, the LM curve is LM_0. Real output is y_0. Now the price level rises; the quantity of real money balances is thereby reduced and the LM curve shifts up to the left to LM_1. As a consequence of the reduced value of real money balances and a higher interest rate, aggregate demand falls to y_1. Thus coordinates P_0, y_0 and P_1, y_1, are two points on an AD schedule. Without an assumption about aggregate supply the ISLM model is only a model of aggregate demand determination. It becomes a model of real output determination by assuming an inverted L-shaped AS schedule, though many textbook expositions do not make this explicit.

References

Backhouse, R. (1983) *Macroeconomics and the British Economy*. Martin Robertson, Oxford.
Congdon, T. (1985) *Whither Monetarism?* Centre for Policy Studies, London.
Dow, J. C. R. (1964) *The Management of the British Economy 1945-60*. Cambridge University Press, Cambridge.
Godley, W. and Cripps, F. (1983) *Macroeconomics*. Oxford University Press, Oxford.
HMSO (1944) *Employment Policy*. Cmnd 6527. HMSO, London.
HMSO (1980) *The Government's Expenditure Plans, 1980-1 to 1983-4*. Cmnd 7841. HMSO, London.

Keynes, J. (1963) *The General Theory of Employment, Interest and Money*. Macmillan, London.

Laidler, D. (1982) *Monetarist Perspectives*. Philip Allan, Oxford.

Levačić, R. (1986) 'State spending out of control?' *Economic Affairs*, 6(2), 4–8.

Radcliffe Committee (1959) *Report of the Committee on the Working of the Monetary System*. HMSO, London.

Stein, J. (ed.) (1976) *Monetarism*. North Holland, Amsterdam.

3

The Determinants of the
Natural Rate of Unemployment

ROSALIND LEVAČIĆ

Unemployment is now widely seen as the most pressing economic problem of our time. In the years 1983-5 the number of unemployed in the UK reached a post-war peak at around 3 million, or about 13 per cent of the labour force. Since 1979 unemployment has more than doubled. After the Second World War unemployment was at historically low levels, and the general view prevailed that the age of full employment, achieved by the application of Keynesian economic principles, had come to stay. But from the mid-1960s unemployment began to creep upwards while still fluctuating over the course of the cycle in economic activity. This is shown in figure 3.1, where the shaded bands indicate the cyclical downwards from peak (*P*) to trough (*T*). Since 1967 each recession has been associated with a higher level of unemployment than its predecessor. What is different about the latest cycle is that the recovery in real national output, which by mid-1985 was 7 per cent above its previous cyclical peak in 1979, was not as yet accompanied by any fall in unemployment. This pattern of secularly (long-term) rising unemployment since the mid-1960s is not unique to the UK but has been generally experienced by the developed economics, though there is now quite a wide dispersion in unemployment rates, as indicated in table 3.1.

Table 3.1. Average annual percentage rate of unemployment in selected OECD countries, 1960-85

	UK	USA	Japan	W. Germany	Italy	Sweden	Belgium	Spain
1960-4	1.8	5.72	1.4[a]	0.9	4.7	1.6	3.6	—
1964-9	2.0	3.8	1.2	1.2	5.6	1.8	3.4	—
1970-4	3.0	5.4	1.3	1.3	5.8	2.2	3.4	2.7
1975-9	5.2	7.0	2.0	4.4	6.9	1.9	9.3	5.8
1980-5	11.2	8.2	2.4	6.5	9.2	2.9	12.3	16.7

[a] 1962-4.
Source: OECD *Main Economic Indicators, Historical Statistics, 1960-79.* OECD Economic Outlook.

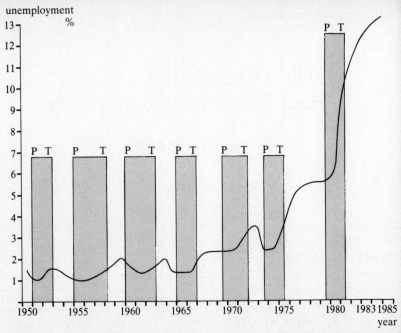

Figure 3.1. UK unemployment (%) 1950-85. *Source:* CSO. *Economic Trends.* Annual Supplement, 1984. Peaks and troughs for 1958-81 dated by CSO: for 1951-5. Dow, 1964.

When studying unemployment at the aggregate, or economy-wide level, there are two distinct aspects of it which require explanation: its secular rise over the last 20 years and its cyclical fluctuation. This chapter is concerned with the long-term behaviour of unemployment; in particular it considers the extent to which the secular rise in unemployment can be attributed to an increase in the 'natural rate of unemployment' – that is the level of unemployment consistent with the underlying general equilibrium of the economy and which cannot be permanently altered by government manipulation of aggregate demand. The concept of the 'natural rate of unemployment' was first introduced in chapter 2 and will be developed further in the course of this chapter. Chapter 6 discusses short-run fluctuation of the actual level of unemployment around its natural level and how this behaviour relates to variations in the rate of inflation.

1. Analysis of the Labour Market

Baldly put, unemployment is the difference between the amount of labour demanded by firms and public sector organizations, and the amount supplied by those seeking paid work. The quantity of labour demanded includes those already employed plus vacancies, while the supply of labour is made up of those in employment plus the unemployed. If the demand for labour fails to grow in line with an expansion of the labour force unemployment will inevitably result. The UK labour force has been rising since the late 1940s. In 1950 it was 23.5 million compared to 27 million in 1984. Much of this growth has been due to the rising proportion of women who work. Over the post-war period the female workforce has risen by over 50 per cent. Since the mid-1970s the number of young people of working age has also increased by almost a quarter. Overall the labour force has increased from 26.3 million in 1978 to 27.1 million in 1984. But the number of people employed fell from its post-war peak in 1979 of 25.4 million to 23.6 million in 1983. Since then employment has started to rise again: there was a net increase of 500,000 jobs up to mid-1985 but this was not sufficient to offset the rising labour force and reduce the unemployment rate. Furthermore, the Department of Employment expects the labour force to rise by over 750,000 between 1984 and 1991 and then stabilize. Two-thirds of this projected increase consists of women workers.

The specification of a demand for and a supply of labour function constitutes a labour market model which can then be used to analyse the possible determinants of unemployment. When modelling labour markets it must be borne in mind that labour is a highly heterogeneous commodity, with numerous dimensions. It embodies different kinds of skills, employed in a great variety of occupations and industries: it is differentiated by sex, age, race, unionization and geographic location – to list the main dimensions. Thus the economy consists of many interrelated labour markets whose boundaries are defined according to the problem being analysed. Since this chapter concentrates on a macroeconomic approach to unemployment I will use for formal analysis a model of a single aggregate labour market for the whole economy, which suppresses these differences. The purpose of the concept of an aggregate labour market is to simplify the analysis of whole economies. The significance of the differentiated characteristics of labour are captured either by introducing specific variables, such as the extent of unionization, into a formal macro-labour market model, or, in less formal terms, by a more intuitive consideration of their likely impact.

The analysis of the natural rate of unemployment undertaken in this chapter is conducted firmly within the framework of the AD/AS model of the economy, and focuses specifically on the position of the long-run aggregate supply function and how this has shifted over time. But this is just one key relationship, since it concerns the behaviour of the long-run equilibrium or 'natural' level of real output. The next link in the chain is the relationship between natural level of real output and the natural level of employment associated with it. The final link is the difference between employment and the labour supply, which is unemployment. A significant feature of the 1980s recovery is the sharp reduction in the UK in the amount of labour required to produce a given level of real output. If this occurs when the labour force is growing, real output needs to expand that much faster in order to prevent unemployment rising.

By focusing on the aggregate supply function, one is looking to labour market behaviour for explanations of unemployment, while at the same time undertaking aggregate level analysis. This requires specifying demand and supply functions for labour which are derived from assumptions about the behaviour of individual economic agents. The micro-level labour demand and supply functions are then transposed to the aggregate level with, admittedly, some sleight of hand. In chapter 2 I outlined the derivation of the aggregate supply schedule from labour demand and supply functions and the aggregate production function. Here I will recapitulate that material only to the extent that it bears directly on the determinants of the natural rate of unemployment. I will go more fully into the determinants of the labour supply, as this was barely touched upon in chapter 2. (For a more thorough exposition of labour market analysis readers should consult a microeconomics or labour economics textbook.)

1.1.   *The demand for labour*

Labour, capital, land and raw materials are the primary factors of production. Since national output is defined as value added, its quantity varies with the amount of labour, capital and imported raw materials used. The amount of output produced from a *given* quantity of inputs depends on the state of technology. Thus the general form of an aggregate production function is

$$y = f(l, k, rm, t)$$

where $y =$ real national output
  $l =$ labour employed
  $k =$ capital stock
  $rm =$ imported raw materials
  $t =$ state of technology.

In a very short-run analysis of the demand for labour the quantity of all the other inputs is held constant. If product and labour markets are perfectly competitive then profit-maximizing firms will equate the marginal physical product of labour with the real wage rate. The real wage which matters for firms is the money wage relative to the price of their product. At an aggregate level this is the price index of gross domestic output, known as the GDP price deflator or index of total home costs. The money wage deflated by this index is called the *real product wage*, to distinguish it from the real wage of relevance to workers, which is what their money wage will buy in terms of retailed goods and services, including imports.

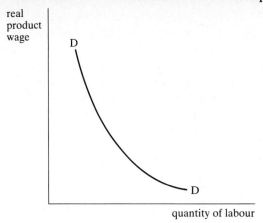

real
product
wage

D

D

quantity of labour

Figure 3.2. The demand for labour curve

If the marginal product of labour declines as more labour is put to work with fixed quantities of capital and raw materials and a given state of technology, then firms will only wish to employ more labour and supply more real output if the real product wage falls. Thus a firm's demand for labour is deduced to depend inversely on the real product wage. On this basis the aggregate demand for labour curve slopes downwards with respect to the real wage as depicted in figure 3.2.

The demand for labour curve will shift and/or alter its slope if there is a change in any of the variables assumed constant for very short-run analysis. An increase in the capital stock raises the capital/labour ratio and thus the marginal productivity of labour, enlarging the demand for labour. Similarly, technical progress can increase the marginal product of labour and, in a competitive economy, raise the demand for labour. (Though, in other circumstances, if the demand for output stays constant, technical progress could diminish the quantity of labour required. This is discussed much more fully in chapter 5.) A change in the price of raw materials or capital will affect the demand for labour, though the direction of this effect is not deducible from theory alone. This is because an increase in the price of any factor of production reduces the amount of output firms wish to supply. This is the income effect of a change in factor prices, and it works to reduce also the demand for those factors whose price has not risen. Against this, the substitution effect operates to raise the demand for labour to the extent that labour can be substituted for raw materials or capital which have become relatively more expensive. The longer the period of adjustment allowed for, the more scope there is for firms to find it worthwhile to substitute one factor for another in response to changes in relative factor prices.

Thus a rise in the real product wage can be expected to have both a short-run and a long-run impact on the demand for labour. In the short run there will be a movement up the short-run demand for labour curve; in the long run as raw materials and/or capital are substituted for labour, the short-run demand for labour schedule will shift or pivot down to the left. Thus the elasticity of the demand for labour with respect to the real wage will be greater in the long run than in the short run.

So far I have assumed perfectly competitive product and factor markets. The assumption of a perfectly competitive product market, which clears in equilibrium, means that the demand for labour is not affected by the level of aggregate demand. This is because each firm can sell all the output it wishes to in order to maximize profits. All that matters is the price of output relative to the money wage. If this rises then it becomes profitable to sell more output. However if the product market is imperfectly competitive then a firm's demand for labour depends on the elasticity of demand for output as well as the real wage. The aggregate demand for labour thus derived depends on the real wage rate and the level of aggregate demand for national output. The assumption of an imperfectly competitive labour market modifies, but does not alter, the basic analysis of the long-term natural rate of unemployment (e.g. Layard and Nickell, 1985). The level of employment and the amount of unemployment associated with it depends on the interaction of the demand for and supply of labour.

1.2. *Aggregate supply in a small open economy*

The assumption of competitive product markets is more realistic for a small open economy, whose firms face competition from foreign suppliers in tradeable goods, than it is for a closed economy. If we take the extreme case of a small open economy producing only tradeable goods (i.e. those traded internationally) and assume that international competition will ensure the price of any single good in a common currency is the same in all economies, after allowing for taxes and transport costs, then the aggregate demand curve facing such a country is horizontal as depicted in figure 3.3. In this case domestic firms are never constrained by deficient demand: they can sell as much as they want to at the price level P_1. Given this, how much they wish to produce is determined by the upward-sloping aggregate supply function. The only way the price level can be raised and, in effect, aggregate demand increased, is by a depreciation of the exchange rate. This raises the sterling price of internationally traded goods while leaving their foreign exchange price the same. Imports are dearer and exports more competitive, so domestic firms are willing to produce more output.

I have touched on the case of the small open economy producing traded goods only, to indicate the limitations of the notion that firms are constrained by inadequate demand. This is a feasible case for non-traded goods markets which are imperfectly competitive, but less so for firms producing exports or import substitutes. For them their international competitiveness – or the extent to which their costs remain below

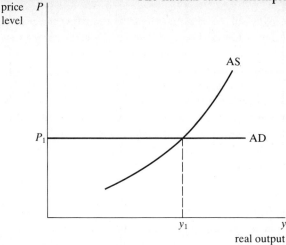

Figure 3.3.   Output determination in a small open economy producing traded goods only

the world price for their product – is a vital consideration. This depends both on the exchange rate (which determines the world price in terms of sterling) and on unit production costs. The latter are highly dependent on the conditions upon which labour is supplied to firms.

1.3.   *The supply of labour*

The supply of labour consists of all those in paid employment or who are self-employed – the employed labour force – plus the unemployed – those without jobs, but who are capable of working and are actively seeking work. This is a theoretical definition: the statistical measures of the employed labour force and the numbers unemployed are only approximate quantifications of their conceptual counterparts. The official statistics on the employed labour force are derived from population censuses and labour force surveys, and will be underestimates to the extent that those working in the black economy escape enumeration. In the UK the official unemployment statistics are obtained from a count on a given day each month of the number claiming unemployment and supplementary benefits or national insurance credits at Unemployment Benefit offices. All these claimants are not necessarily capable of work and actively seeking it: some are disabled, or are not actively seeking work, or may be employed in the black economy. Others who are without paid jobs and actively seeking work, but not claiming benefit, are not counted as unemployed. This applies to many unemployed married women who are not entitled to state benefits. Unemployment statistics produced by the OECD for member countries are based on labour force surveys which ask people for their employment status and record them as unemployed if they are available for work, without a job and actively seeking one. The definition of what is meant by actively looking for work is thus crucial in determining what is meant by unemployment, and hence how many people are in this category. The OECD thus adjusts the UK unemployed statistics to be consistent – as far as is possible – with their definition of unemployment, which is the one adopted by the International Labour Office in 1954. The way unemployment is measured statistically is an important consideration for empirical studies which seek explanations for unemployment. They use statistical measures of unemployment and so are explaining these rather than an ideal conceptual definition of unemployment.

The size of the labour force depends on the size of the population of working age – i.e. above school-leaving age and below retirement. Not all the population of working age participate in the labour force, or wish to. Some are full-time students, some work within the home caring for dependants – the major category being women with young children – some retire early and some choose not to work for other reasons. As already mentioned, the steadily rising participation rate of women in the labour force has been a major element in its post-war growth. This participation rate is affected by social mores concerning attitudes to working mothers, by changing technology which enables women to replace domestic labour by bought-in domestic appliances and convenience goods, and the technological and economic factors encouraging employers to provide increasing numbers of part-time jobs.

The participation rates, together with the sizes of the male and female population of working age, determine the size of the labour force. In addition, some above retirement age also work, and so are included in the labour force. But as well as deciding to participate, workers also make choices about how many hours to work. Although most employers usually stipulate basic working hours, workers still have some discretion over their hours. Some jobs involve more hours than others – part-time jobs can be chosen, overtime worked or moonlighting undertaken.

One variable to which economists have given great attention, both as a determinant of the participation rate and of the number of hours worked, is the real wage rate received by workers. The neo-classical AD/AS model, as outlined in chapter 2, is typified by an aggregate labour supply curve which slopes upwards with respect to the real wage rate. The hypothesis that the supply of labour depends on the real wage rate is arrived at by analysing the choices made by members of households when deciding whether to participate in the labour force and, if so, how many hours to work. These choices depend on a comparison of the benefits of working relative to those of not working. The main benefit from working is the income thereby earned, and this depends on the real wage rate earned per hour and on the number of hours worked. The benefit of not working consists of any income then received, such as income from financial assets and unemployment benefit, and the value of time spent on domestic activities or as leisure. So, for example, a married woman's decision about participation is deduced to depend on her husband's income, the value of her time spent on domestic work and on the non-pecuniary benefits of working, as well as the real wage per hour she can earn. Having decided to participate, then the decision for a part-time or full-time job will be influenced by the same set of variables.

Whether or not the supply of labour is positively related to the real wage or not, is ultimately an empirical matter. This is because a rise in the real wage enables a worker to gain her previous income by working fewer hours. This is the income effect of a rise in the real wage and it may induce workers to supply less labour. But a rise in the real wage increases the opportunity cost of 'leisure' – one more hour spent on leisure or domestic work costs more in forgone income. This is the substitution effect, and it always works to increase the individual's supply of labour. Provided a negative income effect does not dominate the positive substitution effect, a rise in the real wage will increase an individual's supply of labour.

Empirical research indicates a distinct difference between the short-run and long-run response of the supply of labour to real wages. Over the long run, as real wages have risen in line with living standards, the average number of hours worked per week by full-time workers has declined. In the 1950s adult male manual workers put in about 48 hours per week on average; this had fallen to around 44 hours by the late 1970s. In the short run one would expect the level of real wages to be more important in inducing marginal workers to participate in the labour force and existing workers to supply overtime. There is evidence that in the short run workers' supply of labour does respond positively to changes in their own real wage, though this is much stronger for women's labour supply than that for men's (see Greenhalgh and Mayhew, 1981; Heckman et al., 1981).

1.4. Frictional and structural unemployment

In a labour market characterized by a demand for labour curve which slopes downwards with respect to the real wage rate and a supply of labour schedule which slopes upwards with respect to the real wage, the market clearing or equilibrium real wage is that which equates the demand and supply of labour. Market clearing in labour markets, unlike many other markets, is still associated with the coexistence of some unsatisfied buyers and sellers: there are firms with vacancies and unemployed workers searching for jobs. So even in the 'full employment' years of the 1950s (as you can confirm from figure 3.1) unemployment in the UK did not fall below 1 per cent, and averaged 1.7 per cent between 1948 and 1966.

These features of labour markets are explained by the particular characteristics of exchange involving labour services. Unlike primary commodity markets and financial markets (often called auction markets), the buyers and sellers of labour are not able quickly to exchange information about prices and quantities, and so speedily establish an equilibrium price. Both firms and workers need to search for information about the quantities and quality of labour being demanded and supplied at various rates. A worker looking for a job needs to find suitable vacancies, make applications, attend interviews and then decide – if offered a specific job – whether or not to accept it. The decision depends on balancing the pros and cons of acceptance. On the plus side is the immediate income from the job, but on the minus side is forgoing the opportunity of searching longer, and possibly getting a better job offer. In the course of applying for jobs the searcher learns more about the job conditions and wage offers he is likely to get, and this accretion of information will be used to decide on the acceptability of each job offer. Employers also need to search, especially when hiring from the external labour market, and will gain information about the supply of labour from the number of job applicants and job acceptances received in response to specific wage offers. So, because information about labour market is imperfect and costly to acquire, both vacancies and unemployment coexist all of the time.

The unemployment attributable to the search activities of firms and workers is known as *frictional unemployment*. While it is not possible to estimate with any great accuracy the amount of frictional unemployment in the economy, a number of variables are thought to influence its level. One is the amount of income maintenance (in the form of unemployment and supplementary benefit) the unemployed receive relative to their income when working. This variable is often called the *replacement ratio*. The higher the replacement ratio the lower is the opportunity cost of remaining unemployed by rejecting job offers and continuing to search for something better. If the average duration of unemployment increases, even if the number of people becoming unemployed in a year stays the same, the average number unemployed at any one time will be higher. In addition, the higher the replacement ratio the more attractive is the option of quitting a job to search for a better one.

So even if every individual labour market in the economy were cleared, there would still be some frictional or search unemployment. But individual labour markets will not be in continuous equilibrium: they have to adjust to a stream of changes in the conditions of demand and supply. On the supply side there arise new technological developments and ways of organizing production, new sources of supply and changes in the relative prices of raw material inputs. On the demand side, consumer tastes can change. For a particular domestic industry, demand often falls because of new competition from substitute products developed by other industries or from foreign manufacturers who can supply cheaper or better-quality products. Changes in these product market variables will be reflected in the demand for labour. Inter-sectoral shifts in the demand for labour would not cause longer-term disequilibrium in the labour market if the supply of the various kinds of labour could adjust quickly enough in response to relative wage changes. The mismatch of skills in demand with those supplied can persist for long periods, as it takes time to acquire new skills; nor is everybody equally capable of acquiring any given skill.

A further problem is the geographic immobility of labour, which is exacerbated by the expense and difficulty of moving house. So in some labour markets vacancies will exceed unemployment, while in others an excess supply of labour prevails. The unemployment associated with disequilibrium in individual product and labour markets brought about by continuous changes in the conditions of demand and supply within those markets is termed *structural unemployment*.

If wages fell in industries and regions with high unemployment relative to wages in markets with relatively low unemployment, this would induce labour to move to regions and industries with higher net demand for labour. Such a relative wage movement would also assist adjustment by increasing the quality of labour demanded in regions and industries with excess labour supply. Structural unemployment persists because relative wages fail to adjust so as to bring into equilibrium the demand and supply of labour in regional and sectoral labour markets.

1.5.   *The natural rate of unemployment*

The aggregate labour market is in equilibrium if there is no tendency for the average real wage rate in the economy to change in response to either an overall excess demand or excess supply of labour in the economy. In a neo-classical model such an equilibrium is also associated with market clearing; i.e. the overall demand and supply of labour are equal. But this overall balance in the demand and supply of labour coexists with vacancies and frictional and structural unemployment. The notional aggregate labour market clears when the number and distribution of vacancies and unemployment in the various micro-level markets is such that there is neither an upward nor downward pressure on the average real wage. The amount of unemployment consistent with the aggregate labour market being cleared, so that the market clearing aggregate real wage rate is established, is termed the *natural rate of unemployment*. Thus the natural rate of unemployment includes frictional and structural unemployment. But if the actual rate of unemployment exceeds the natural rate then only some of the frictional and structural unemployment is included in the natural rate.

The natural rate of unemployment is depicted diagrammatically in figure 3.4. The supply of labour schedule is TLF. As the real wage rate rises more people participate in the workforce. Curve ELF indicates the amount of labour willing to accept jobs at each real wage rate. The demand for labour, excluding vacancies, is given by curve *dd*. The market clearing real wage, w_e, is the wage at which the number of workers willing to accept job offers equals the demand for labour, excluding vacancies. At this real wage rate the number of vacancies is such that employers neither wish to raise nor lower the real wage to alter the flow of job acceptances.

The distance between curve TLF and curve ELF is the difference between the supply of labour, l_s, and the amount of employment offered and accepted. Thus

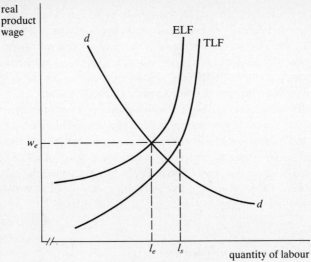

Figure 3.4.   Determining the natural rate of unemployment

$l_e l_s$ is the amount of natural employment caused by structural changes in the economy and induced by the process of search on the part of workers and firms. The distance between the ELF and TLF curves increases as the real wage falls because I am assuming that unemployed workers search longer for work as the opportunity cost of doing so falls. Though the distance between the ELF and TLF supply curves when the labour market is in equilibrium gives the natural rate of unemployment, the statistically measured rate of unemployment may well be different. For example, the quantity of labour willing to work at the market-clearing real wage, w_e, is l_s. But there are additional people willing to work at a real wage above w_e but not below it. However they may well appear in the unemployment statistics, either because they are collecting welfare benefits or because they indicate in labour force surveys that they are available for and seeking work. Such surveys do not yield information on whether the unemployed are seeking work at above the market-clearing real wage. Hence the measured rate of unemployment may well be above the theoretical natural rate. It is the measured rate of unemployment that empirical studies attempt to explain. Hence we need to distinguish between the theoretical rate of natural unemployment and its measured rate. It is also possible that measured unemployment could be below the theoretical natural rate.

2.   Determinants of the Natural Rate of Unemployment

Having set up a labour market model which focuses on the determination of the natural rate of unemployment, we can now examine those variables which are thought to influence both the theoretical and measured natural rate of unemployment. This is done in order to consider the extent to which these variables explain the observed rise in unemployment and suggest policy measures to combat unemployment. I shall categorize the determinants of the natural rate of unemployment according to whether they operate on the demand side or the supply side of the labour market, starting with the former.

2.1. Non-wage labour costs

The cost to a firm of employing labour consists not just of wages. It also includes statutory and private welfare benefits in cash and kind – such as maternity and sick pay, holidays and recreational facilities – training and employers' taxes – which take the form of national insurance contributions in the UK. These non-wage labour costs have generally increased in industrial countries since the mid-1960s. In Britain they rose from around 10 per cent of total labour costs in 1968 to 18 per cent by 1981. In particular, the real level of employers' NI contributions doubled between 1967 and 1982 (Robinson and Dicks, 1983), though they have been progressively cut recently, especially for the low-paid.

The effect of increases in the non-wage labour costs is to shift the demand for labour with respect to the real product wage down to the left, as shown in figure 3.5. The market-clearing real wage falls to w'_e and employment falls to l'_e. How does this increase unemployment? Well in the first place frictional unemployment rises if jobless workers take longer to search for and accept job offers now that the real wage has fallen. Second, there will be an increase in statistically measured

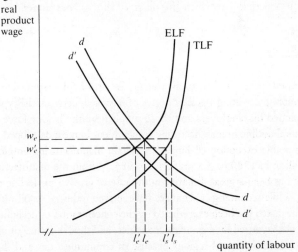

Figure 3.5.   The effect on unemployment of a fall in the demand for labour

unemployment if those who have lost jobs, but are unwilling to work at the lower real wage, are recorded as unemployed.

2.2. *Employment protection legislation*

Another factor, which it is argued increases firms' labour costs and so reduces the demand for labour, is the employment protection legislation introduced in the 1960s and 1970s. This has made it more difficult and expensive for firms to declare redundancies or dismiss workers. Though this kind of legislation initially reduces unemployment, it is likely to increase it over the long run as firms become more reluctant to hire labour because it is difficult and costly to dismiss workers.

2.3. *Slow-down in labour-productivity growth*

The demand for labour curve will also shift down to the left if there is a reduction in the marginal productivity of labour. The large jump in oil prices in 1973/4 and 1979, which occurred as a result of OPEC's co-ordinated pricing and output policies, had this effect. As explained in section 1, a rise in the price of imported raw materials reduces firms' profits and thus the amount of output they are willing to supply. It is generally thought that this income effect had a stronger depressing impact on the demand for labour than the substitution effect which induces firms to substitute labour for energy. Some economists have attributed part of the rising unemployment in industrial economies to a general slow-down in the rate of growth of labour productivity to which the oil price shocks contributed.

2.4. *Structural change*

The increased pace of structural change is also held responsible for rising unemployment by creating a greater degree of mismatch between the types of labour skills demanded by employers and those supplied by the labour force. There has been a general decline in manufacturing employment in most developed economies, with the notable exception of Japan. In Britain manufacturing employment fell from 7 million in 1980 to 5.5 million by 1985. Within the manufacturing sector itself there has been a great disparity in the rate of growth or decline of different industries, while technological changes have altered industry's skill requirements. The skill mismatch has been exacerbated by the concentration of declining industries in regions not favoured by expanding industries, and the reluctance of unemployed workers to leave depressed regions because of community ties and the difficulty of obtaining rented accommodation if they relocated. The widening gulf between registered vacancies and unemployment, which started to appear in the late 1960s, is interpreted as indicative of structural change.

2.5. Inflation

It is also argued that high rates of inflation increase unemployment. This is because rapid inflation is linked to greater variability in actual and expected rates of inflation, and hence greater uncertainty about relative prices. It is argued by monetarists that such uncertainty inhibits firms from investing and hiring labour, and that markets cannot perform their allocative function properly because relative price signals get confused with general price rises. Stable prices – or at least mild inflation – are therefore seen as a precondition for economic growth. A comparison of the growth performance and inflation experience of different countries does little to substantiate or negate this argument, as growth depends on so many factors other than the behaviour of the price level, though some econometric studies have claimed that the variability (i.e. variance) of inflation is linked to unemployment (e.g. Froyen and Wand, 1984).

Turning now to the supply side of the labour market, several variables are singled out in the literature as influencing the natural rate of unemployment.

2.6. Taxes and import prices

Direct and indirect taxes place a wedge between the wage a firm pays and its value to workers in terms of the consumption goods it will buy. If the labour supply is positively related to workers' real consumption wage, then an increase in income and indirect taxes reduces the real consumption wage for a given level of pre-tax wages. Consequently, the supply of labour curve, TLF, and the supply of job acceptances curve, ELF, in figure 3.6 shift up to the left. This results in a higher market clearing real wage and a fall in employment. Measured unemployment increases if those who are now without jobs, but were previously working, are recorded as unemployed. A rise in import prices has a similar effect as it reduces the real consumption wage associated with a given real product wage. So the rise in imported oil prices in the mid-1970s not only decreased the demand for labour but also placed upward pressure on wage rates.

2.7. The replacement ratio

In making an economically rational decision about whether to participate in the labour force and, if so, how long to spend searching before accepting a job offer,

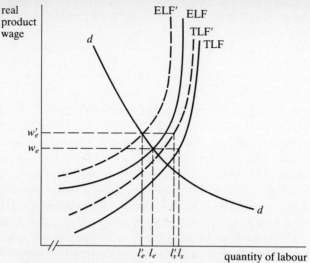

Figure 3.6.   The effect of a reduction in the labour supply

an individual will weigh the advantages of not working against those of working. The benefits from being without a job are the time available for leisure and domestic activities and any unemployment or supplementary benefits to which the individual is entitled. The opportunity costs of not working are the loss of income and of any personal and social standing attached to being in employment. The replacement ratio is the size of the individual's or household's income when not in work relative to after-tax income from working. The larger the replacement ratio the less incentive there is to participate in the labour force in the first place, and so the level of measured unemployment will be higher. A higher replacement ratio also induces people to spend longer searching for a job, and so increases the amount of frictional unemployment. On the basis of the calculations rational workers would make, it is hypothesized that the natural rate of unemployment is positively related to the replacement ratio. This hypothesis is highly controversial: its opponents fear that the implied policy solution is to reduce the incomes of the unemployed and so increase poverty and the unequal distribution of income. One problem with testing the hypothesis is the difficulty of calculating appropriate replacement ratios. This is because households' benefits vary with their personal circumstances, such as the time spent unemployed, number of children and housing costs, and the extent to which they claim the benefits to which they are entitled. Some calculations are of the hypothetical benefits a specific type of unemployed household would be entitled to; others are survey data on actual benefit received. It is fairly well agreed that replacement ratios rose between 1968 and 1978 (Atkinson, 1981; Dilnot and Morris, 1983) and have been falling since then, because the government abolished earnings-related unemployment benefit and made unemployment benefit taxable. These measures have reduced the replacement ratio for short-term unemployment.

2.8. *Union power*

Finally there is what many consider a crucial factor in explaining the high level of the natural rate of unemployment – the power of trade unions. Once unions enter the picture the assumption of a perfectly competitive labour market has, of course, to be dropped. Various ways of modelling a labour market characterized by collective wage bargaining are used. A popular one is to depict unions as bargaining over the wage level and leaving firms to decide on how much employment they will offer at the agreed wage rate. This can be depicted diagrammatically as in figure 3.7, which represents an economy with a fully unionized, homogeneous labour force. The effect of unionization is to set a floor to the real wage rate, w_1, which is above w_e – its market-clearing level in a competitive economy. Consequently, a smaller-quantity of labour is demanded and employment is lower – at l'_e – with unionization. However the total labour force now supplied is l'_s, giving a natural unemployment level of $l'_e l'_s$, which is larger than the unemployment level of $l_e l_s$ brought about by a competitive labour market in equilibrium.

However, even in Britain the labour force is not fully unionized. The proportion of the labour force unionized peaked at 55.4 per cent in 1979, having climbed quite markedly from 44 per cent in the 1960s. In 1978, 80 per cent of manual workers were covered by union agreements, while a further 7 per cent had minimum wages set by statutory Wages Councils. By 1984 the unionization rate had declined to 45 per cent (Oswald and Turnbull, 1985).

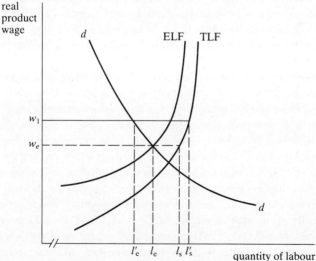

Figure 3.7. The effect of union power

If the labour market is segmented into a unionized and a non-unionized sector, then the workers who cannot find work in the unionized sector when the real wage is raised above its market-clearing level will seek work in the non-unionized, competitive sector. This will lower the real wage there until the demand and supply of labour are equalized. Hence one would not expect partial unionization to increase unemployment in the economy as a whole; only to reduce employment in the unionized sector. But if the real wage in the non-unionized sector is prevented from falling to its market-clearing level then the kind of model depicted in figure 3.7 applies, and the natural rate of unemployment is higher than it would be if the market-clearing real wage prevailed. It has been argued (for example by Minford, 1983a) that such a floor is set to the real wage in the non-unionized sector by minimum wage legislation and social security benefits. When the social security and tax systems impose high marginal effective tax rates on low income earners, there is little economic incentive for them to seek work. Workers whose marginal product is low will be unable to find jobs which pay them more than social security, and firms will not offer such low-paying jobs, knowing that there will be few, if any, takers.

2.9. 'Too high' real wages

This chapter's analysis of labour market behaviour has been conducted in terms of labour demand and supply functions which interact to determine an equilibrium real wage and level of employment. If the actual real wage is above its market-clearing level then unemployment can be attributed to the real wage being 'too high'. However, of itself, this statement says little about the causes of a high natural rate of unemployment. The reasons for the real wage being above its market-clearing level have to be sought from those factors which determine the position and slope of the labour demand and supply curve, i.e. the variables that have been discussed in the last few pages.

The analysis so far undertaken has been couched in terms of changes in these exogenous variables shifting the labour demand or supply curves to produce a new equilibrium with higher unemployment, especially higher measured unemployment. There is an additional dimension of analysis which focuses on reasons why labour markets adjust back slowly to equilibrium when subject to exogenous shocks, such as oil price rises, exchange rate fluctuations or demographic changes. So if the demand for labour falls because of a sudden drop in labour productivity, as occurs when raw material prices rise significantly, then the real wage remains above its market-clearing level for some time. Similarly youth unemployment, which has increased more rapidly than adult unemployment, is explained in a Department of Employment study (Wells, 1983) as arising from the failure of youth wage rates to adjust downwards relative to adults' wages in response to the increased supply of young people on the labour market.

3. Empirical Evidence

To disentangle the empirical evidence on the determinants of the natural rate of unemployment and the extent to which it can account for observed levels of unemployment is no easy matter. I shall consider some of the empirical evidence under three headings – time series data on real wages; econometric estimation of labour market equations and simulations with econometric models. To observe a rise in the real product wage over time is consistent with the hypothesis that factors such as union power have pushed the labour supply curve upwards over time, and so caused a reduction in employment relative to what it would have been otherwise. However, rising real wages are also consistent with a rising demand for labour due to technical progress increasing the marginal product of labour. While the latter process operates in all growing economies over the long run, the existence of supply-side forces in the UK economy pushing up wages is widely reflected in the accumulated empirical evidence and in policy debates. Linking wage pushfulness with unemployment is less widely accepted, though it appears strongly in the work of moderate Keynesians such as Nickell and Layard (see references). Also the two-way relationship between price and quantity – or wages and unemployment in this case – complicates the interpretation of data. An upward shift in the labour supply curve raises real wages and increases unemployment, but the resulting excess supply of labour puts some downward pressure on the wage rate. If the labour market adjusts, then high and rising unemployment will reduce the rate of increase of wages.

3.1. *Data on the real wage rate*

The behaviour of the real product wage in the UK over the post-war period is indicated in figure 3.8. It rose almost continuously until 1976, dipped sharply in 1977 as a result of the Labour government's incomes policy, and returned to its previous peak around which it has hovered. The real product wage rose rapidly between 1967 and 1976, when unemployment was on a rising trend. However, since the appearance of even higher levels of unemployment in the 1980s it has held steady. To sustain the argument that high real wages since 1980 explain yet higher unemployment one needs to show that the gap between the actual real wage rate, and that required for a given level of unemployment, has widened in recent years. One important factor that can explain such a widening gap is increased international competition in traded goods in both domestic and export markets, especially from newly industrialized countries. Furthermore, other developed countries are containing their unit wage costs more successfully than Britain. Some evidence of this is given in table 3.2. The first three columns show the percentage changes in hourly earnings in manufacturing. How these rises affect unit labour

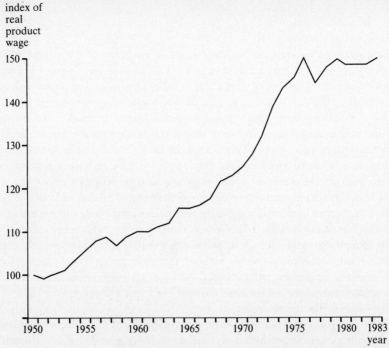

Figure 3.8. The real product wage in the UK, 1950-83. *Note:* The real product wage is calculated as the average basic weekly wage rate for manual occupations (male and female) in all industries and services, deflated by the index for total home costs (the GDP deflator at factor costs) and indexed at 1950 = 100. *Source: CSO Economic Trends*, Annual Supplement, 1984.

Table 3.2. International comparison of labour costs

	Hourly earnings in manufacturing: percentage changes (average)			Unit labour costs in manufacturing: percentage changes (average)		
	1963-73	1973-83	1984	1963-73	1973-83	1984
USA	5.2	8.0	3.9	2.4	7.0	−0.5
Japan	14.5	9.2	4.6	3.9	2.8	−4.4
W. Germany	8.6	6.3	2.4	4.0	4.4	−0.8
France	9.5	14.4	8.1	3.1	10.8	4.0
UK	9.0	15.1	8.1	4.8	14.3	4.1
Italy	11.0	21.1	10.9	5.3	16.4	7.8
Canada	7.1	10.7	5.2	2.4	9.9	−2.0

Source: OECD Economic Outlook, June 1985, p. 40.

costs will depend on how much labour productivity improves. The marked feature of the UK economy over the past 5 years is that firms have responded to high labour costs by shedding labour in order to increase labour productivity. This rose by 12 per cent between 1980 and 1984 – a high rate for the UK. The resulting rate of change in unit labour costs is given in the last three columns of table 3.2.

As can be seen, the UK has experienced a relatively high rate of increase in unit labour costs. A relatively large rate of increase in unit costs in terms of sterling can be offset by depreciating the exchange rate. The problem with this option is that it raises import prices and hence retail prices. This stimulates further upward movements in money wages so that the initial competitive advantage is nullified, unless there is continually accelerating inflation. For these reasons the current government is reluctant to allow the exchange rate to depreciate.

3.2.   *Estimating labour market equations*

There is now accumulating a body of empirical literature concerned with estimating labour market equations specified along the lines of the labour market model outlined in this chapter. The real wage rate appears to be a significant determinant of the demand for labour, and a consensus is emerging that the elasticity of demand for labour with respect to the real wage rate is in the order of -0.5 to -1.0 (Nickell, 1982; Nickell and Andrews, 1983; Layard and Nickell, 1985; Minford, 1983b; HM Treasury, 1985; Symons and Layard, 1984). By also estimating a labour supply function (or wage determination equation) in which independent variables appear – such as the replacement ratio, taxes, and union power – it is then possible to solve the estimated equations for the value of the natural rate of unemployment. The researchers present these results as likely orders of magnitude which need further confirmation. All the variables listed in section 3 as determinants of the natural rate of unemployment (except the variance of inflation) have been found significant in most of the studies surveyed here. Of the tax variables, employers' NI contributions appear to have the strongest impact on unemployment. The majority of studies found that the replacement ratio has some effect on unemployment (Rau, 1984) though the effect is generally modest and occurring in the 1970s. Nickell and Andrews' (1983) estimate of an unemployment elasticity of -1 with respect to the replacement ratio reflects the median result, in contrast with Minford's (1983) unusually large elasticity of -2.5. The 1970s slow-down in productivity growth, employment protection legislation (measured by unfair dismissal cases), and structural change (measured as the absolute percentage change in manufacturing employment) all have some explanatory power. Union power emerges as a strong explanatory factor, though there are problems in measuring it. The estimated union/non-union wage differential performs better than the unionization rate. The former has continued to rise throughout the period, from 4 per cent in 1963 to 12 per cent

Table 3.3.   Estimates of the causes of changes in the unemployment rate (male) 1956–83

	1956–66 to 1967–74	1967–74 to 1975–9	1975–9 to 1980–3
Employers' labour taxes	0.58	1.06	1.57
Replacement ratio	0.74	−0.14	−0.20
Union power	1.15	1.36	1.15
Real import prices	−0.50	1.60	−1.35
Structural change	0.19	0.29	0.88
Incomes policy	—	−0.49	0.86
Change in natural rate	2.16	3.68	2.91
Demand factors	−0.11	−0.54	3.68
Total 'explained' change	2.05	3.14	6.59
Actual change	1.82	3.01	7.00

Source: Layard and Nickell (1985).

in 1983 (Metcalf and Nickell, 1985). Nickell and Andrews (1983) estimate that 'the impact of unions on employment via their effect on real wages has been of the order of 400,000 since the War' (p. 202).

A summary of a set of estimates of the contribution of the various determinants of changes in unemployment is given in table 3.3. Four periods are distinguished, 1956–66, 1967–74, 1975–9 and 1980–3, and the estimated average contribution of the explanatory variables to the percentage rate of unemployment is compared over consecutive periods. The first six variables are determinants of the natural rate of unemployment. Incomes policy appears here because, if successful, it exerts a downward pressure on real wages and reduces unemployment, as in the years 1975–9 compared to 1967–74. (Its positive impact in 1980–3 as compared to 1975–9 is presumably due to its absence in these years – given that it could have been successfully implemented over 6 years or so.) The estimated increase in the natural rate of unemployment over the periods is shown in the seventh row, and the estimated contribution of aggregate demand variables is indicated in the eighth row.

In terms of the AD/AS model the estimates of the factors affecting the size of the natural rate of unemployment are to be interpreted as shifting the AS function. When a change in a variable, such as union power, shifts the AS function up to the left along a given AD curve, the quantity of aggregate demand is reduced. The impact of this on unemployment is included as part of the increase in the natural rate. The separate aggregate demand variables are those which *shift* the AD function.

According to these results changes in aggregate demand reduced unemployment in the first two compared periods, but contributed to unemployment in 1980–3 compared to 1975–9. These estimates are consistent with the rising trend in

Table 3.4. Estimates of the natural rate of unemployment (males)

	1955–66	1967–74	1975–9	1980–3
Natural unemployment rate	1.96	4.12	7.80	10.72
Actual unemployment rate	1.96	3.78	6.79	13.79

Note: Actual rate assumed equal to natural rate 1955–66.
Source: Layard and Nickell (1985).

inflation over the 1967–80 period, and the subsequent shift to a more deflationary macroeconomic policy in order to bring down inflation. Estimates of the natural rate of unemployment over the post-war period made in the same study are reproduced in table 3.4. These estimates are of interest because they indicate the relatively modest scope for reducing unemployment by expanding aggregate demand, perceived by economists who are critical of the Thatcher government's economic policies and support the Employment Institute and its Charter for Jobs. If the natural rate of unemployment were around 10.7 per cent, compared to an actual rate of 13.8 per cent for the labour force as a whole in 1985, then just over three-quarters of a million unemployed, out of a total of 3.4 million, is due to deficient aggregate demand.

3.3. *Simulations with econometric models*

Some simulations have been done with econometric models to see what would be the impact on output, employment, and unemployment of cutting the rate of growth of nominal wages and hence reducing the real wage rate below what it would otherwise be. The results of such simulations depend on the structure of the model being used, the values given to the relevant coefficients – such as the elasticity of employment with respect to the real wage – and what is assumed about fiscal and monetary policy over the period of the simulation. The significance of the policy assumption is explained using the AD/AS model in figure 3.9. A reduction in the real wage is modelled as shifting the AS function to the right. If the government maintains the nominal money stock constant the real money supply will expand and interest rates fall. This is an accommodating monetary policy; it results in an increase in aggregate demand as the AS schedule shifts down a fixed AD schedule. The natural level of real output expands to y_1 and so the natural rate of unemployment falls. This is as a consequence both of real wages falling and aggregate demand being allowed to increase because of the lower price level. The AD/AS model is static in order to remain simple, and assumes changes up or down in the price level. The econometric models are dynamic in that the analysis is undertaken in terms of changes in the rates of price and wage inflation, and in

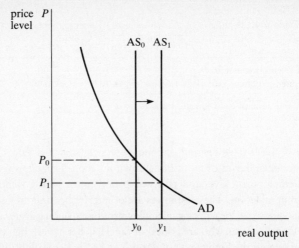

Figure 3.9.   An increase in aggregate supply induces an increase in the level of aggregate demand

the rate of growth of real wages. Monetary and fiscal policy are accommodating if the government does not reduce the rate of growth of the nominal money supply or of nominal government expenditure when inflation falls due to the cut in real wage growth. According to the Treasury's simulations on its own model (Treasury, 1985), a reduction in the rate of growth of nominal wages sufficient to ensure that real wages are 2 per cent lower than otherwise predicted would, after 3 years, increase employment by 1.4 per cent, if policy is accommodating, or by 1 per cent if tax and interest rates stay unchanged. It was this simulation that underlay the Chancellor's (Nigel Lawson) claim that a 1 per cent fall in the average level of real earnings relative to its current trend would mean, 150,000 to 200,000 more jobs. Similar simulations on the models have produced both less and more optimistic results, depending on how sympathetic the model builders are towards government policy. However, there is a considerable measure of agreement that a lower rate of growth of nominal and hence real wages would allow the government to relax its monetary and fiscal stance. The double stimulus of lower real wage growth plus the induced expansion in aggregate demand would be the most effective way to reduce unemployment. Although real wage reductions can be readily simulated in models, how they are to be achieved in practice remains an intractable problem.

4.   Policies to Reduce the Natural Rate of Unemployment

The upward pressure on real wages exerted by collective bargaining, and its impact on the natural rate of unemployment, can be tackled in two ways – incomes policies or legislative and political measures to reduce trade union power.

4.1. Prices and incomes policies

Various forms of prices and incomes policies have been either tried or proposed, both in the UK and elsewhere. The term covers a variety of schemes whereby the government directly intervenes to influence the price and money wage setting behaviour of firms and trade unions both in the public and private sectors. A prices and incomes policy aims to restrain money wage increases and associated price increases and ideally to keep money wages rising in line with the growth of labour productivity. Prices and incomes policies may be statutory limitations on price and incomes increases, with legal penalties for disregarding them. However the problems of enforcing such legislation and the unpopularity of doing so when statutory incomes policies have been resorted to, in the UK, has made governments wary of this approach. Another alternative is for the government to bargain with the trade unions, promising reflationary policies, tax cuts, social benefit increases or legislation to enhance trade union power, in return for wage moderation. The 1974-9 Labour government entered into such a 'social contract' with the TUC. This had some success in bringing down wage increases in 1976 and 1977, but broke down in the winter of 1978/9. The general conclusion that has emerged from econometric studies of incomes policies is that while they have some short-term impact on the rate of wage increases, over the longer run they have been ineffective in Britain. The Thatcher government has eschewed incomes policies except for holding down pay increases in the public sector. The Alliance Parties and their moderate Keynesian supporters are the main advocates of incomes policy. Failing a voluntary agreement, many favour a tax-based incomes policy whereby firms would be taxed on the extent to which their wage bill increased faster than the norm specified by government. Whether such a policy would exert sufficient pressure on firms to withstand union wage demands, and would be administratively feasible, is questionable.

4.2. Increasing competition in the labour market

The Thatcher government has instead favoured measures designed to increase competition in the labour market. It has introduced legislation aimed at reducing trade union power. The 1980 Employment Act withdrew unions' legal immunity from civil action against secondary picketing, and requires a vote of at least 80 per cent of a union's membership before a new closed shop can be created. The 1982 Employment Act extended similar periodic voting requirements to enable existing closed shops to continue. By more narrowly defining a trade dispute it further reduced unions' legal immunities and made selective dismissal of strikers possible. The 1984 Trade Union Act was intended to reduce the incidence of strikes by requiring secret ballots of members to secure a majority in favour of strike action. In addition, the government has abolished some Wages Councils which set minimum wage rates in many low-paid occupations. The remaining ones have had their remit narrowed to setting basic wage rates only for adult workers. It is also proposed to extend for all firms the length of employment before an employee can make a claim for unfair dismissal from 6 months to 2 years.

4.3. *Improved training and mobility*

Other supply-side measures aim at improving the quality and mobility of the labour force in order to give the labour supply the characteristics sought by employers. A major initiative in this field is the Youth Training Scheme started in April 1983. It caters for 16- and 17-year-olds, providing them with work experience with an employer who should provide training plus college-based education. The government aims to extend the scheme to all 16- and 17-year-olds while reducing this age group's entitlement to social security benefits. There are various other schemes such as the 1982 Enterprise Allowance Scheme which pays unemployed people who start their own business with at least £1000 of their own money, £40 a week for a year. Various educational initiatives are being attempted, such as the Technical Vocational Education Initiative in schools sponsored by the Manpower Services Commission in conjunction with local education authorities, or the Open College for adult training.

4.4. *The tax and social security systems*

The government has already reduced the replacement ratio by abolishing earnings-related unemployment benefit and making unemployment benefit liable to tax. It has been further diminished by raising the post-tax income of the low-paid by reducing their NI contributions. Employers' NI surcharge has been removed, and lower employer NI rates for the low-paid were introduced in the 1985 budget, while the upper earnings limit was abolished. This makes low-paid labour, whose unemployment rates are highest, relatively more attractive to employ.

This litany of supply-side measures is not exhaustive, but it should be sufficient to convey their general characteristics. They are detailed, micro-level measures, often directed at very specific parts of the labour market, in contrast to the broad aggregate-level policies of demand management. Many operate at too disaggregated a level for their impact to be traced out in any detail in a highly aggregated macroeconomic model. In terms of the AD/AS model these measures would, if effective, shift the AS function to the right and so reduce the natural rate of unemployment.

5. Conclusion

This chapter has used a particular theoretical framework for analysing the determination of the underlying long-run rate of unemployment, ignoring any cyclical fluctuations in aggregate demand which cause actual unemployment to deviate from its natural level. I think it is fair to say that mainstream macroeconomics has embraced the natural rate of unemployment concept in place of the earlier notion of a full-employment equilibrium. However, the acceptance of the natural rate concept still leaves considerable scope for disagreement over (a) the extent to which fluctuations in aggregate demand can cause temporary deviations in unemployment about its natural level; (b) how far actual unemployment in the 1980s is above its natural level and can be permanently reduced by increased government expenditure; and (c) the extent to which a cut in the rate of growth of real wages would reduce unemployment, and whether this could be best achieved by incomes policy or by increasing competition in the labour market. These issues will be pursued further in some of the following chapters. The next chapter analyses unemployment from a Keynesian perspective by considering the role of deficient aggregate demand. Chapter 6 takes up the first issue listed above. In the context of discussing the interconnection between unemployment and inflation, it examines how changes in nominal aggregate demand can cause unemployment to fluctuate around its natural level.

References

Atkinson, A. B. (1981) 'Unemployment benefits and incentives'. In Creedy, J. (ed.) *The Economics of Unemployment in Britain*. Butterworths, London.

Dilnot, A. W. and Morris, C. N. (1983) 'Private costs and benefits of unemployment: measuring replacement rates'. In Greenhalgh, C. A., Layard, P. R. G. and Oswald, A. J. (eds) *The Causes of Unemployment*. Oxford University Press, Oxford.

Dow, J. C. R. (1964) *The Management of the British Economy 1945-60*, Cambridge University Press, Cambridge.

Froyen, R. T. and Wand, R. (1984) 'The changing relationship between aggregate price and output: the British experience', *Economica*, 51 (201).

Greenhalgh, C. and Mayhew, K. (1981) 'Labour supply in Great Britain: theory and evidence'. In Hornstein, Z., Grice, J. and Webb, A. (eds) *The Economics of the Labour Market*. HMSO, London.

Heckman, J. J., Killingsworth, M. and McCurdy, T. (1981) 'Empirical evidence on static labour supply models: a survey of recent developments'. In Hornstein, Z., Grice, J. and Webb, A. (eds) *The Economics of the Labour Market*. HMSO, London.

H. M. Treasury (1985) *The Relationship between Employment and Wages: empirical evidence for the UK*. London.

Layard, R. and Nickell, S. (1985) 'The causes of British unemployment', *National Institute Economic Review*, no. 111 (February).

Layard, R. and Symons, J. (1984) 'Do higher real wages reduce unemployment?', *Economic Review*, (3).

Metcalf, D. and Nickell, S. J. (1985) 'Jobs and pay', *Midland Bank Review*, Spring.

Minford, P. (1983a) *Unemployment: cause and cure*. Martin Robertson, Oxford.

Minford, P. (1983b) *Labour market equilibrium in an open economy*. In Greenhalgh, C. A., Layard, R. R. G. and Oxwald, A. J. (eds) *The Causes of Unemployment*. Oxford University Press, Oxford.

Nickell, S. J. (1982) 'The determinants of equilibrium unemployment in Britain', *Economic Journal*, no. 92.

Nickell, S. J. and Andrews, M. (1983) 'Trade unions, real wages and employment in Britain 1951-79'. In Greenhalgh, C. A., Layard, P. R. G. and Oswald, A. J. (eds) *The Causes of Unemployment*. Oxford University Press, Oxford.

Oswald, A. J. and Turnbull, P. J. (1985) 'Pay and employment determination in Britain', *Oxford Review of Economic Policy*, 1(2).

Rau, N. (1984) 'Does unemployment benefit affect unemployment?', *Economic Review*, 1(4).

Robinson, B. and Dicks, G. (1983) 'Employment and business costs', *Economic Outlook*, 8(4).

Symons, J. and Layard, R. (1984) 'Neoclassical demand for labour functions in six major economies', *Economic Journal*, 94 (December).

Wells, W. (1983) 'The relative pay and employment of young people', *Research Paper 42*, Department of Employment, London.

4

Demand-deficient Unemployment

VIVIENNE BROWN

1. Introduction

Fifty years ago, in 1936, the rate of unemployment was 13 per cent. In that year John Maynard Keynes published *The General Theory of Employment, Interest and Money*. Although by that time Keynes was already well known, it was this book that secured his reputation as one of the most outstanding and controversial economic theorists of this century. Whilst writing the *General Theory* Keynes wrote to George Bernard Shaw:

> To understand *my* state of mind, however, you have to know that I believe myself to be writing a book on economic theory which will largely revolutionize – not, I suppose, at once but in the course of the next ten years – the way the world thinks about economic problems. When my new theory has been duly assimilated and mixed with politics and feelings and passions, I can't predict what the final upshot will be in its effect on action and affairs. But there will be a great change . . . (Keynes, 1973b, pp. 492-93.)

The *General Theory* lived up to Keynes's expectations. As a book on economic theory it did present a powerful challenge to the existing accounts of how the economy works; and when mixed with politics and passions, it became the basis of the post-war consensus that full employment was one of the major policy objectives for the government. (For a wider discussion of this see Thompson, 1984.)

One reason for the impact that Keynes's book made was that it was the first systematic attempt to examine how the level of aggregate demand for goods and services affects the level of output and employment. Keynes was not the first to think along these lines, nor did he rule out other influences, but he was the first to systematically put forward a theoretical framework for examining the importance of aggregate demand in determining output and employment. In Keynes's time it was orthodox to identify high real wages as the cause of unemployment. Keynes did not rule out the effects that real wages could have on unemployment, but he emphasized the crucial importance of aggregate demand. This was linked very closely in Keynes's work with the argument that the economic system is not self-adjusting within a reasonable period of time. Keynes argued that the economy could get locked into a situation of unemployment with no inherent mechanisms of self-adjustment to pull the economy out of the slump.

But like all revolutions, the so-called Keynesian revolution has been questioned, as both the Keynesian challenge and the Keynesian consensus have in their turn become the established orthodoxy. Keynesianism has been challenged by the monetarism of Professor Milton Friedman and by the school of new classical macroeconomics. At a policy level this 'monetarist revolution' in economic thinking has been reflected in the UK by the monetarist policies that Mrs Margaret Thatcher's government has been implementing since 1979. In this more critical environment, Keynesian economists have had to clarify and sharpen their argument as to how demand-deficient unemployment can occur in an economy. It has also reopened one of the issues that was in dispute in the 1930s when Keynes wrote the *General Theory*; viz. the relation between real wages and employment. This issue centres on two basic questions: first, do changes in aggregate demand have a systematic effect on output and employment? and second, if so is this achieved by affecting real wages? As you have seen from chapter 2, the monetarist answer to the first of these questions is no, because their answer to the second is yes: if workers make an adjustment for inflation when bargaining to secure a given real wage, then the aggregate supply curve is vertical and changes in aggregate demand cannot affect output and employment. The policy implication is that governments cannot affect output and employment by demand management policies.

In this chapter I shall examine some Keynesian approaches to these two basic questions for macro-theory and policy, and I shall use the AD/AS framework of analysis to do this, as it is the main arena within which these theoretical differences have been discussed. I shall argue that these approaches are united in answering the first question in the affirmative, but that different Keynesian approaches provide different answers to the second question. This then raises the issue of how we portray the supply side of the economy – the labour market and the conditions of production as represented (if inadequately) by the aggregate production function – and we shall see here that different emphases have been suggested within a broadly Keynesian approach.

In section 2 I shall concentrate on the goods market by examining aggregate demand as this has traditionally been regarded as the cornerstone of a Keynesian approach to demand-deficient unemployment. This section is largely empirical as I shall examine the recent movements in the main components of aggregate demand, but I shall also examine theoretically how these movements may be related to changes in output and employment by using the 45° diagram. In section 3 I shall extend this analysis by incorporating the price level and the supply side of the economy, and it is here that I shall build on the AD/AS model as set out in chapter 2. In section 4 I shall examine the implications of this for the labour market, by considering how demand-deficient unemployment may be represented in a model of the labour market.

2. The Effect of Aggregate Demand on Output

In this section I am going to examine the experience of the UK economy in the 1970s and early 1980s, concentrating on the post-1979 period. During this period unemployment rose sharply; between the cyclical peaks of 1973 and 1979 it rose from 0.6 million to 1.2 million, and from 1979 to 1984 it rose from 1.2 million to 3.0 million. It is notoriously difficult for economists to agree on measurements of the different causes of unemployment, but there seems to be strong evidence that inadequate aggregate demand has been a significant factor in causing unemployment, and that its importance has increased in the more recent period. It has been estimated that demand deficiency accounted for about 27 per cent of the increase in male unemployment between the periods 1967-74 and 1975-9, while it accounted for about 73 per cent of the increase between the periods 1975-9 and 1980-3 (Layard and Nickell, 1985; for other estimates see Nickell, 1982; and Artis et al., 1984).

If we are to understand the links between aggregate demand and employment, we must first be able to identify which components of aggregate demand were low or falling during this period. Once we can identify the source of weakness in aggregate demand we can then consider the immediate causes of unemployment during these years, and we are also in a position to review the policy implications.

To examine this we need to use the basic categories of aggregate demand, where aggregate demand (e) is composed of demand for consumption goods (c), demand for investment goods by the private sector (i), government demand for goods and services (g), and net exports or net foreign demand for the country's output ($x - b$). Thus, aggregate demand in real terms is:

$$e = c + i + g + (x - b)$$

In order to examine the reasons for changes in output we need to account for the components of aggregate demand which were inadequate. Figure 4.1 shows the main components of aggregate demand during the period from 1973 (the previous peak year prior to 1979) to date. In this graph we can see 1973 and 1979 as the peak years. Between 1979:3 (i.e. third quarter) and 1981:3 GDP fell by 5.8 per cent. When we look at the components of aggregate demand, however, we see a varied picture. Consumers' expenditure has very roughly followed the same pattern as GDP (as consumption is the major component of GDP that is hardly surprising) but it remained relatively robust over the 1979-81 period, falling by only 3.7 per cent

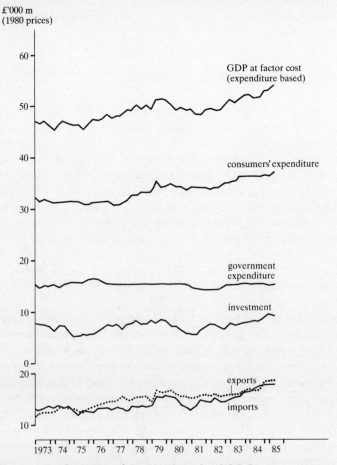

£'000 m
(1980 prices)

Figure 4.1. *Components of aggregate demand and G.D.P., 1973:1 to 1985:2*
Notes: 1. components of aggregate demand are at market prices
     2. prior to 1978 the aggregates may differ from the sum of the components
Source: Economic Trends Annual Supplement, 1986, pp. 17, 55.

between 1979:2 and its lowest level in 1980:4. This can be explained in terms of a rise in real wages which counteracted the high personal savings ratio. Exports too have largely followed a procyclical pattern, reflecting the increasing synchronization between the UK's economic cycle and that of its major trading partners, as well as the effect of cyclical factors on the competitiveness of UK exports. I shall return to this again when I come to consider the post-1979 years in more detail. Imports are strongly procyclical, reflecting the high marginal propensity to import. Investment (fixed investment plus stock changes) has been very strongly

Table 4.1. Cyclical and inflation adjusting the public sector financial balance, UK, 1973-84 (percentage of GDP)

	Public sector financial balance	Structural, i.e. cyclically adjusted, balance	Inflation-adjusted structural balance
1973	− 3.8	− 4.8	− 2.6
1974	− 5.7	− 5.7	− 2.6
1975	− 7.2	− 5.9	− 3.0
1976	− 6.7	− 5.2	− 2.1
1977	− 4.2	− 2.8	+ 0.3
1978	− 4.9	− 4.5	− 1.5
1979	− 4.4	− 4.4	− 1.2
1980	− 4.9	− 2.5	+ 1.1
1981	− 3.6	+ 1.0	+ 4.8
1982	− 2.8	+ 2.6	+ 6.1
1983	− 3.6	+ 1.7	+ 3.8
1984	− 4.3	+ 0.5	+ 3.8

Source: Miller 1985, table 2.
Note: A minus sign denotes a deficit, and a plus sign denotes a surplus.

procyclical throughout this period. From 1973:1 to 1975:1 it fell by 35.3 per cent and from 1979:3 to 1981:1 it fell by 35.5 per cent, and it did not reach its 1979:3 peak until 1984:4.

Looking at government expenditure the most striking impression is just how constant it has been for most of the period. It was relatively unchanged during the periods 1977:1 to 1980:4 and 1982:4 to 1985:2 at about £15.5 million on a quarterly basis, although in between these two periods it fell quite noticeably. These periods of stability, however, obscure a long-run decline in public sector fixed investment from the 1973-6 level and a corresponding increase in government consumption.

Assessing the macroeconomic effects of fiscal policy as a whole – whether it has been expansionary or contractionary overall – is a very complicated exercise, and must include not only the exhaustive expenditures of consumption and investment, but also transfer payments such as social security payments, pensions, and interest payments on the national debt. One approach to this has been to assess the overall state of fiscal stance by calculating summary measures of the total government deficit/surplus incorporating various adjustments for cyclical factors and changes in the rate of inflation. One such estimate is shown in table 4.1.

The first column shows the unadjusted figures for the public sector financial balance. This shows an increased deficit during the earlier recession 1974/5, and a tightening in 1981 and 1982. The second column shows the effect of adjusting for cyclical factors by taking into account the automatic stabilizers of the tax and benefit system (i.e. what would the government's budgetary policy have implied for an economy with a 'trend' level of activity and unemployment?) According to these figures 1975 was much less expansionary, and the period 1980 to 1982 was extremely contractionary, compared with the unadjusted figures. Between 1979 and 1982 the balance swung from a 4.4 per cent deficit to a 2.6 per cent surplus – a massive contraction amounting to 7 per cent of GDP over 3 years. The third column shows the effects of including an adjustment for inflation as well as for cyclical changes, as it takes into account the effects of inflation on the real value of the government's debt and on the interest payments on that debt. Here we see a roughly similar pattern, although showing higher surpluses and smaller deficits than in column 2, such that over the period as a whole there was a net surplus rather than a net deficit, as column 1 shows. During 1979-82 the balance again shows a contraction of around 7 per cent, suggesting that it is the cyclical adjustment rather than the inflation adjustment which points to the fiscal contraction of those years.

Given the complexity of these sorts of calculations there is considerable scope for different estimates to be put forward and, hence, for controversy as to their basic usefulness, although all these estimates show a massive tightening of UK fiscal policy during the period 1979-82 with a slight relaxation since then. As an example of the difficulties involved in calculating these estimates, consider the calculation of the cyclically adjusted or structural budget which entails taking a view as to what the underlying trend rate of growth is in the economy. This is clearly a contentious issue at the moment. (For a discussion of some of these points see Allsopp, 1985; for alternative estimates see Biswas *et al.*, 1985; Layard *et al.*, 1984; and Miller, 1985.)

So far I have simply looked at the change in the components of aggregate demand. Together they add up to the overall change in GDP (as they must do according to the national income accounting identities). But if we want to understand the causes of a recession or upturn in activity, we have to examine the factors which influence these components of aggregate demand. Only in this way can we hope to identify the immediate causes of the change in aggregate demand rather than simply describe the change.

What caused the recession of 1979-81? The first point to notice is that the recession of 1979-81 was superimposed on a longer-term recession associated with the OPEC oil price rise of 1973-4. Unemployment had been rising during the 1970s and even when recovery came, in 1975-9, this was at a lower growth rate than in previous years. During these years exports and investment were weak, the savings ratio was increasing and fiscal policy was becoming more deflationary, but real wages were rising, which helped to bolster consumers' expenditure, and stockbuilding had been high.

In 1979 there was the second oil price rise. During 1979-81 the previous counteracting influences of rising wages and high stockbuilding failed to operate at a time when Margaret Thatcher's first government took office with an electoral commitment to reduce inflation and reduce the extent of government economic activity. Thus, instead of counteracting the contractionary tendencies of those years with an expansionary fiscal policy, the UK government was espousing an overtly contractionary policy which reinforced the other adverse tendencies. Estimates of the change in fiscal stance for that year show a much more restrictive fiscal policy in the UK than in any other major country. Allsopp (1985) cites figures which show that the inflation-adjusted structural balance changed between 1978 and 1981 by +6.9 per cent of GDP for the UK, by +0.9 per cent for the USA, by +2.0 per cent for Japan, by −0.1 per cent for Germany, and by +1.4 per cent for the OECD. (Note: a plus shows an increased surplus/reduced deficit and a minus shows an increased deficit/reduced surplus.) Alternative estimates for the period 1979 – 81 show a similar pattern: a +5.0 per cent change for the UK and a +0.7 per cent for the EEC as a whole (Layard et al. 1984).

In addition to this increasingly restrictive fiscal stance, the government introduced its Medium Term Financial Strategy in 1980 with the purported aim of reducing the rate of inflation. From one point of view the rationale for the MTFS was to provide an argument for reorientating fiscal policy away from the macroeconomic objectives of stabilizing the economy and promoting full employment, and towards the control of inflation (Buiter and Miller, 1983). According to this view the main anti-inflationary impetus was actually coming from the restrictive fiscal policy. The official government explanations, however, emphasized the ineffectiveness of fiscal policy in determining the real variables of the economy whilst emphasizing the need for fiscal policy to be subordinated to monetary objectives.

Whatever the arguments for the MTFS, it was accompanied by high interest rates and a sharp rise in the exchange rate. The high interest rates led to massive destocking from the high levels of 1979 as they raised the cost of borrowing to finance such stocks, and they also reduced firms' plans for investment in fixed capital. In addition, these high rates of interest made sterling more attractive to hold at a time when oil revenues were strengthening the pound, and so the exchange rate of the pound against foreign currencies rose sharply such that international competitiveness worsened by about 30 per cent. Exports suffered as a result of this, with the manufacturing sector taking the brunt of the fall in export demand. By mid-1980 the first impact of the world recession hit the UK economy, and this too weakened exports. (For more detailed accounts of the recession see Buiter and Miller, 1981; Surrey, 1982; and Artis et al., 1984, in addition to works already referred to.)

As a large source of the reduction in aggregate demand is clearly investment, it is worth taking a longer look at this component of aggregate demand. We have

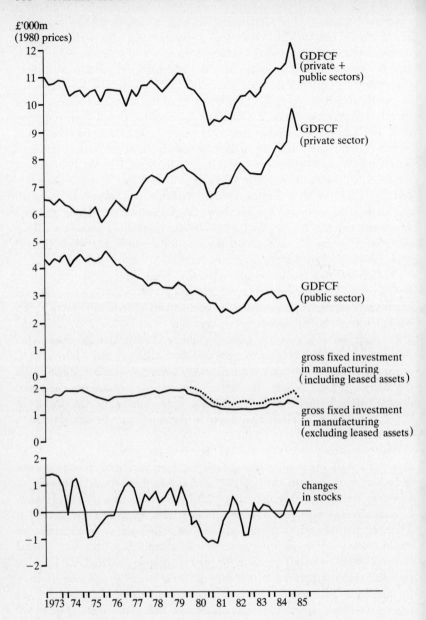

Figure 4.2. *Selected investment indicators, 1973:1 to 1985:2*

Note: GDFCF = Gross Domestic Fixed Capital Formation

Source: Economic Trends Annual Supplement, 1986, pp. 17, 55, 57, 58; and *Monthly Digest of Statistics*, Table 1.8, various editions

seen that investment is strongly procyclical, and that during 1979–81 it fell by an amount greater than the fall in output itself. Figure 4.2 shows various investment indicators, including public sector gross domestic fixed capital formation which was included in government expenditure in figure 4.1. Investment is generally subdivided into gross domestic fixed capital formation and the value of physical increase in stocks and work in progress. Between 1979:3 and 1981:2 both categories of investment fell: gross domestic fixed capital formation fell by 15.4 per cent and stocks/work in progress fell by £4656 million (at 1980 prices); that is stocks fell by an amount equal to 12.4 per cent of the 1981 level of fixed capital investment. The last year previous to this period when fixed capital investment had been lower than the 1981 level was 1967, whilst the 1979 level from which it fell had been the highest level recorded. If we examine the *private* sector gross domestic fixed capital formation, we find that it fell by 15.3 per cent between its peak 1979:4 and its trough 1981:1, whilst gross fixed investment in manufacturing industry fell by 37.8 per cent between 1979:1 and 1981:4, and has still not regained the 1979 level, even when leased assets are included, as the 1985 levels had still not reached the 1980 levels. (For a discussion of leased assets see *Bank of England Quarterly Bulletin* (1985) and chapter 9, below.) To find the last year when fixed investment in manufacturing industry was lower than the early 1980s we have to go as far back as the late 1950s and early 1960s. Public sector fixed capital formation fell by 31.1 per cent between 1979:3 and 1981:1, and this low level was repeated in 1985. These changes in investment are shown in figure 4.2 for the period 1973:1 to 1985:2 (chapter 9 also discusses changes in investment).

In summary we can see that the massive increase in unemployment during the short period 1979–81 was the result of a severe tightening of government fiscal and monetary policy which reduced real demand in the economy and helped to contribute to a loss of external competitiveness at a time when the second oil price rise was also putting upward pressure on the pound. These effects were compounded by the onset of the world recession in 1980, itself partly the result of the contractionary policies of other European governments (although these were less contractionary than the UK's). Since then, UK fiscal policy has become slightly less restrictive: the inflation-adjusted structural public sector financial surplus fell from 6.1 per cent of GDP in 1982 to 3.8 per cent in 1984, although there are indications that it is currently (1985/6) tightening again. In addition there has been some easing in interest rates and the exchange rate. These factors have helped to turn the economy round, so that since 1981 GDP has been growing at about 2.5 per cent a year, roughly the trend rate of growth just before the 1979–81 recession. But unemployment has failed to fall. Why is this?

In order to maintain a target level of unemployment two conditions must be met. First, the long-term growth of real spending must be sufficient to counteract both the long-run increases in labour productivity and the long-run increases in the labour force. Second, any cyclical reductions in real spending relative to trend which increase unemployment have to be compensated by increases in real spending relative to trend in order to put the cyclically unemployed (i.e. demand-deficient unemployed) back to work. Thus, even if the rate of growth of the UK economy were to continue at 2–3 per cent per annum, this is merely putting the economy back onto its trend growth rate, but without any reduction in the demand-deficient unemployment, i.e. the economy is growing at its trend rate but at lower level.

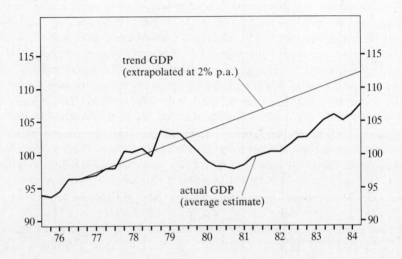

Figure 4.3. Actual and trend real GDP (index 1980 = 100). *Source:* Dornbusch (1985), p. 9.

This is illustrated in figure 4.3. Here we can see that a return to the trend growth rate during 1981–4 will not eradicate the gap between trend and actual GDP; for this we need some years of 'catching up' when the level of aggregate demand is above the trend level. This can also be depicted using a very simple static Keynesian 45° diagram, as shown in Figure 4.4. In this figure the expenditure function E^*F^* represents the trend expenditure function with a level of output O_y^*. The contractionary policies together with a high exchange rate push the expenditure function down to E^1F^1. Since then there has been some slight easing and the expenditure function has begun to increase up towards E^*F^*, but in order to reduce the demand-deficient unemployment expenditure must for a short time exceed E^*F^* and rise to some level such as E^2F^2. As this unemployment is reduced, fiscal policy would be adjusted to return the expenditure function back to its trend level E^*F^*.

What kinds of policies could the government pursue, and how expansionary should they be? The first point to notice is that during the years 1979–84 the net accumulated surplus on the adjusted public sector financial balance was equivalent to 18.4 per cent GDP (see column 3, table 4.1, above), and the ratio of government debt to GDP has fallen by about a third since 1970 (Miller, 1985, table 1), so there is considerable scope for a more relaxed approach to fiscal policy. It is generally emphasized, though, that this looser fiscal policy should be accompanied by a tight monetary policy to prevent the exchange rate falling. Investment incentive schemes could then be used to counteract the domestic effects of high interest rates on investment.

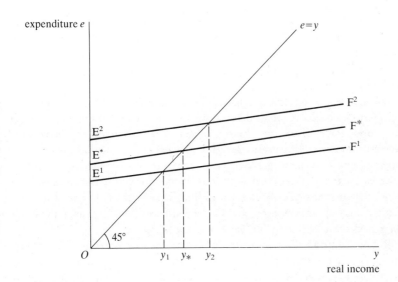

Figure 4.4

The second point, though, is that different fiscal programmes have very different employment effects, and the best mix of such policies is not clear-cut and will clearly depend on political priorities as well as on economic objectives. An indication of these differences is provided in table 4.2. This shows that tax cuts are the most expensive way of generating jobs (the increased consumer spending sucks in imports), whereas employment programmes are the cheapest. Most commentators agree that a phased mix of such measures would be the most beneficial in order to balance out the immediate employment effects of the employment programmes with the more long-term effects of measures that increase public and private investment

Table 4.2. Employment effects of £1 billion increase in PSBR (in numbers of workers affected)

Tax cuts	Public infrastructure investment	Public current expenditure	Employment programmes
17,000–21,000	38,000	65,000	488,000

Notes
(1) The figure for public infrastructure investment is an average across different categories.
(2) £1 billion represents about 0.33 per cent of GDP.
Source: Dornbusch (1985), p. 23.

programmes. In terms of a general order of magnitude for such a reflationary package, about £4–5 billion p.a. for 2 years with a gradual phasing out has been suggested (Dornbusch, 1985, p. 24). Alternative estimates have shown that these employment effects could be achieved even with a fixed money supply (Walker and Davies, 1985a).

It is also argued that expansionary policies such as these should be carried out on a European basis. As pointed out above, exports are very susceptible to changes in world trade. Thus the European countries are together sharing high unemployment levels that are not being reduced by the contractionary policies operated by all the countries individually, as these policies are affecting all countries via their exports. As generalized contraction is producing widespread unemployment, so a concerted, phased expansion would bring benefits to all. Layard *et al.* (1984) call for a European expansion, and Oudiz and Sachs (1984) examine the case of an expansion led by the USA, Japan and Germany.

But would such expansion reintroduce inflationary pressures into the economy such that any demand expansion would simply be at the price of higher inflation with little long-term effect on unemployment? This is a serious question, and to consider it properly we need to move on from the simple 45° diagram and take up the AD/AS model developed in chapter 2. This will be the subject of the next section.

3.   Putting a Keynesian AD/AS Model to Work

Once we include the price level within a general framework of aggregate demand and supply, the unity of the Keynesian approach, which we saw exemplified in the simple 45° diagram of the previous section, begins to evaporate. Now there are competing Keynesian accounts of the relation between changes in aggregate demand and changes in output, and their effects on prices. As a result there are differences of view on the inflationary consequences of demand expansion, and on the implications of this for achieving a significant reduction in unemployment without a fall in real wages.

One interpretation of the Keynesian approach emphasizes that the aggregate supply curve is an inverted L shape, such that increases in aggregate demand directly secure increases in output without any inflationary consequences. This case is illustrated in Figure 4.5. Here we can see that an increase in aggregate demand from AD_1 to AD_2 will increase output from Oy_2 to Oy_2 without any increase in the price level which remained constant at OP. As you will remember from chapter 2 this AS curve is based on constant average and marginal costs such that producers are prepared to increase output without any increase in prices.

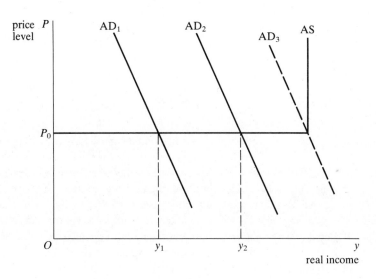

Figure 4.5

This would be the case, for example, in the presence of underutilized capacity. In this case real wages too would remain constant as the unemployed labour force could be put back to work at the going nominal wage rate, i.e. the labour supply curve is horizontal at the existing nominal wage rate. Referring back to our two basic questions on p. 106 this approach would answer yes to the first question and no to the second.

Another interpretation of the Keynesian approach argues that the AS curve is upward sloping, that producers will only increase output if the price level rises relative to a nominal wage rate. This case is illustrated in figure 4.6. In this case the AS curve is based on a diminishing marginal product of labour. As output

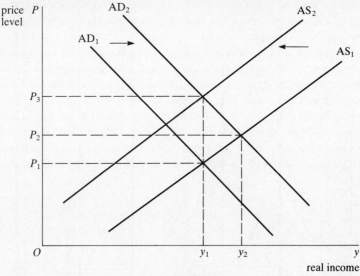

Figure 4.6

increases, the marginal product of labour falls and marginal costs rise. The profit-maximizing producer will increase output only if there is a fall in the real wage paid to labour. This is illustrated in figure 4.6 where there is an increase in aggregate demand from AD_1 to AD_2. The price level rises and the real wage falls given the existing nominal wage rate, and output increases from Oy_1 to Oy_2. The crucial question for this approach is – will the workers continue to accept the reduced real wage? If they do then an increased output is the result of the increase in aggregate demand. If they do not, then the increase in nominal wages to restore the real wage rate is illustrated by a leftward shift in the AS curve. If workers fully compensate for the rise in the price level, the AS curve shifts to AS_2. All that has been achieved is an increase in the price level from OP_1 to OP_3 without any permanent increase in output. Referring back to the two basic questions on p. 106 this approach answers yes to both questions. Increases in aggregate demand can permanently increase output, but only if workers accept a reduction in their real wages; alternatively, temporary increases in output can be secured for as long as workers accept reduced real wages.

The model represented by figure 4.5, which I shall call the radical Keynesian model, claims that prices are determined exogenously and so do not respond to changes in the level of aggregate demand. Aggregate demand can be increased right up to the full employment level AD_3 without any repercussions on the level of prices. In this model the price level is determined by exogenous factors such as the level of money wages and the price of imported goods. Although this approach rightly underlines the importance of excess capacity in providing the conditions for expansion, it overlooks the difficulties connected with this, such as bottlenecks in the supply of certain component parts, shortages of certain types of skilled labour, and the effect of the dismantling of spare capacity during the recession. It thus overlooks the extent to which the productive capacity of the economy has itself been eroded by the period of recession and spare capacity, an erosion which is also reflected in the fall in investment during the recession period, as we saw in the previous section. Thus, by claiming that supply can expand at constant prices, and that the existing spare capacity and unemployed labour has only to be put back to work, this approach argues against there being any inflationary repercussions of expansionary policies, the problem that many believe is the root of the weakness of Keynesian reflationary policies.

The model represented in figure 4.6, which I shall call the orthodox Keynesian model, accepts the short-run neo-classical production function as a basis for analysing the cyclical movements of the economy. This means that output can expand if and only if there is a reduction in real wages; any movement along the aggregate production function entails a fall in the marginal product of labour. Whereas the radical Keynesian model accepts the notion of spare capacity, i.e. the unemployment of capital, in an unproblematic way, the orthodox Keynesian model eliminates it altogether by assuming that output can increase only if the existing capital stock is used more intensively by a larger labour force which requires that workers must accept a reduced real wage. This notion of spare capacity cannot accommodate the idea of *idle* capacity – that some capital is just not being used at all, that some factories are closed down and some lorries are not put on the road. As there is no idle capacity that can be put back to work to generate more jobs, but only a more intensive use of existing capacity, the only way that output can expand is by a movement along the marginal productivity curve – and this entails lower real wages for the profit-maximizing firm. Whereas the radical Keynesian model postulates a horizontal AS curve, the orthodox Keynesian model postulates a vertical AS at the going real wage. By accepting the short-run neo-classical aggregate production function, the orthodox Keynesian result is identical to the monetarist result except to the extent that workers are subject to money illusion or can be persuaded to accept lower real wages via an incomes policy.

For each of these two examples of Keynesianism there are difficulties with the way that the unemployment of physical resources has been understood and incorporated into the model. The radical Keynesian approach assumes that excess capacity can simply be put back to work again without cost when the upturn in activity comes, but this overlooks the significance of capital scrapping and company liquidations, as well as the deterioration of mothballed equipment. The orthodox Keynesian approach effectively assumes away the problem by basing its analysis on an unchanged capital stock.

If we are to go beyond these accounts of Keynesianism and its alleged failures in policy-making, I think we have to take seriously the issue of what it is that we mean by the unemployment of capital as well as of labour, and that means taking seriously the supply-side consequences of changes in aggregate demand. It means that we must examine more closely the notion of excess capacity – as the radical Keynesian model has tried to do – and we must be able to relate this to the issue of price determination such that the supply side of the economy does have an impact on the level of prices – as the orthodox Keynesian model has tried to do. This means considering a third version of the Keynesian AD/AS model. (This is discussed at greater length in Brown, 1986.)

Throughout most of the *General Theory* Keynes assumed that the capital stock was fixed – hence his reliance on a short-run aggregate production function where the level of output is inversely related to the real wage. But the level of capital stock *in use* in the economy cannot remain fixed if there is scrapping of capital ahead of schedule, or if there is excess capacity such that the actual utilization rate is less than the planned utilization rate. But it is unrealistic to assume that all output adjustments are achieved by working a given capital stock more or less intensively as the number of workers is increased or reduced. Some, if not the major part, of the adjustment must be borne by a reduction in the amount of capital actively in use; equipment is lying idle, lorries are not put on the road and entire factories are closed down. Hence, the Marshallian assumption of a fixed short-run stock of capital *in use*, which Keynes adopted and which macroeconomics has continued to employ ever since, is not strictly tenable. This means that changes in aggregate demand which bring about changes in the amount of capital in use must have immediate supply-side implications.

In addition, if the level of fixed investment changes, then the planned capital available in the economy cannot remain fixed. If investment should fall, this means that (ceteris paribus) the planned level of capital in existence will also fall. The extent to which this level of capital is actually put to work will, of course, depend on the actual degree of capital utilization, although generally we would expect that (actual) utilization and investment are positively correlated.

This reduction in the level of capital in use in the economy is represented by a downward shift in the production function from $q = q(l, \bar{k})$ to $q = q(l, \hat{k})$ as shown in figure 4.7. Here we see that the level of capital in use in the economy falls from $\bar{k}$ to $\hat{k}$ and it is this that underlies the downwards shift of the production function.

The reductions in fixed investment during the recessionary periods of 1973–5 and 1979–81 were clearly shown in figure 4.2, above. Private sector fixed capital formation fell 1973/4 and 1979/81 but has been on a rising trend during the decade 1973/83. Public sector fixed capital formation, however, fell not only during the recession years but also in every other year in the period 1974–82; the 1983 and 1984 levels picked up only to the 1980 level. Gross fixed investment in

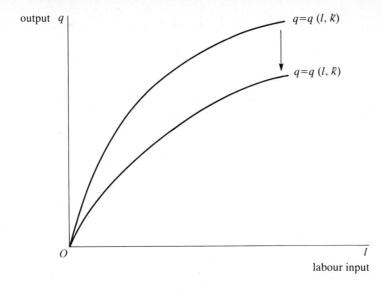

Figure 4.7

manufacturing had still not regained the 1979 level by 1984, even when leased assets are included.

It is much harder to calculate the effects of these fluctuations and declining trends in investment on the level of the capital stock *in use* in the economy, estimates of which are notoriously unreliable. Firstly an estimate has to be made of the capital stock available, and then the degree of capacity utilization has to be assessed. In calculating the capital stock available, the estimate of the gross capital stock depends on the length of life assumed, and this is a considerable source of error. The average life of capital goods in manufacturing in 1980 was assumed by the CSO to be over 30 years, but this is probably an overestimate. Certainly assumptions about asset lives are likely to be less reliable during periods of technological and structural change, or during long periods of excess capacity when capital equipment may be scrapped ahead of schedule. To arrive at the net capital stock an allowance has to be made for depreciation on the grounds that the flow of capital services declines with the age of the capital stock.

Estimates of capacity utilization have been based on the answers to a question in the CBI *Industrial Trends Survey*, which asks firms whether they are working below capacity. Figure 4.8 shows the percentage of firms answering 'no' (i.e. those firms working at or above capacity) for the period 1962-82. Here the cyclical pattern of capacity utilization is clearly visible: capacity utilization is at its greatest during the four peaks of economic activity, 1964-5, 1969, 1973 and 1979.

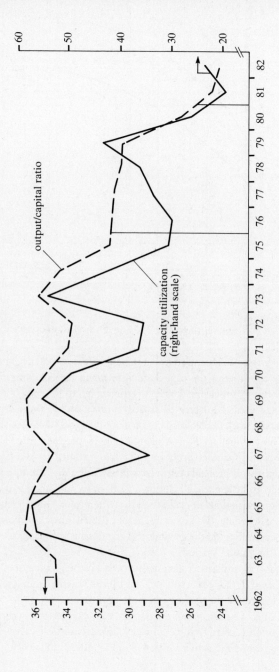

Figure 4.8. Ratio of manufacturers' output to gross capital stock (including leased assets) and CBI measure of capacity utilization. *Source: National Institute Economic Review* (1983), p. 24.

Figure 4.8 also shows the ratio of manufacturing output to the gross capital stock. This ratio also fluctuated cyclically for the past three cycles of economic activity, but since 1973 it has fallen each year. Assuming that the productivity of the capital stock in use has not fallen, this suggests that idle capacity has been increasing steadily since 1973. This in turn suggests that the level of capital used in the calculation of the output/capital ratio is an overestimate. It has been calculated (*National Institute Economic Review*, 1983, pp. 23–5) that these two data series on capacity utilization and the output/capital ratio would be reconciled if the gross capital stock had been growing between 1974 and 1979 by about 3 per cent a year less than the CSO estimate as a result of accelerated scrapping following the low levels of capacity utilization. In this case the true rate of scrapping would be nearly three times greater than allowed for in the official estimates. If this is so it reveals the extremely damaging effects that the recession had on the economy's capital stock, and it underlines the importance of investment in any reflationary programme. But does it mean that output is already constrained by an inadequate capital stock, and that reflationary measures would therefore fail because of supply limitations, as Robinson (1985) has argued? Evidence that this is not the case can be found in the answers to another question on the CBI survey, which asks manufacturers what are the factors limiting their output over the next 4 months. In answer to this, 79 per cent reported 'shortages of orders or sales' as a constraint on output, whereas only 17 per cent mentioned plant capacity.

This reduction in the capital in use in the economy is represented on the AD/AS diagram by a *shift* to the left of the AS curve (and not by a movement along it). This is shown in figure 4.9. The fall in aggregate demand is shown by the leftwards shift of the AD curve from AD_1 to AD_2. This is followed by a leftwards shift of the AS curve from AS_1 to AS_2. Clearly output falls from Oy_1 to Oy_2, but what happens to the price level? This is indeterminate as it depends on the relative shifts of the AS and AD curves. As I have drawn the diagram the price level remains constant, and this may be taken as an alternative rationale for a horizontal AS curve of the radical Keynesian type. Indeed, the neo-classical model of the perfectly competitive industry shows that in the long run expansion can take place at a constant level of costs if all firms face the same cost structure. But this is clearly unrealistic when considering the macroeconomy. The extent of the shift of the AS curve in relation to the AD curve depends on the prevalence of spare capacity, the actual reduction in investment, the types of industries affected and the effect on expectations. Thus, nothing *a priori* can be said about the direction of the change in the price level.

But what happens when the expansion in activity eventually comes about and the diagram is reversed when AD increases from AD_1 to AD_2? What can be said about the supply-side response here? In this case we would expect the AS curve to shift to the right from its low position of AS_2, but how far will it shift? Again, this cannot be settled on *a priori* grounds. It depends on how much of the excess

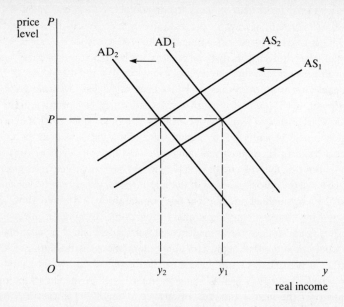

Figure 4.9

capacity has been scrapped and how much that is still available can be put back to work without considerable start-up costs. This will depend partly on the length and depth of the recession, the pattern of company liquidations, and on how fast technology is changing. It also depends on how responsive investment demand is to the upturn in economic activity, and how available the necessary skilled workforce is. These are factors that will clearly vary from one recession to another and from one country to another. As remarked above, one of the worrying features of the current recession is that there is some evidence of a reduction in the capital stock resulting not only from the reduced levels of investment, but also from the scrapping of excess capacity.

By modelling the supply-side implications of changes in demand and economic activity we have seen how aggregate demand and supply are not independent of each other. The greater the supply-side response, the greater is the possibility that expansionary demand management policies can be carried out without inflationary repercussions. Hence, important factors determining how much reflation (or less contraction) is possible without generating higher inflation, are how much spare capacity there is existing in the economy and the extent to which firms can expand output without driving up costs. Another important factor relates to the precise mix of fiscal policy that is used to reflate demand. In the previous section it was noted that different fiscal programmes have different implications for employment generation, but they also have different implications for investment, both private and public. Thus a reflationary fiscal package would need to achieve a balance between those programmes that are rich in new employment but not in investment and those, such as public infrastructure programmes or investment incentives, that generate less new employment in the short term but are competitively viable in the longer term.

This underlines the importance of seeing the more general interconnections between the demand and supply sides of the economy. We have seen that any reflationary programme will generate new investment as well as putting idle capacity back to work. An increase in government expenditure can include public investment projects as well as current expenditure, and would enable the government to reverse the steady decline in government investment that has been evident since the early 1970s. Tax changes can have demand and supply effects: a reduction in personal income tax may have supply-side effects if people are thereby encouraged to work harder, as well as the traditional demand effect of increasing consumers' expenditure. The above discussion of capacity problems in UK industry suggests, though, that a policy that was too reliant on such tax cuts would meet balance of payments problems as a result of increased imports. Reductions in the employers' National Insurance contributions reduce the cost of labour to firms, and so provides an incentive for firms to employ more labour. In addition, fiscal changes which operate solely on the demand side can affect supply via their effect on firms' expectations. If firms believe that the government will provide the macroeconomic conditions required for sustained growth, they are far more likely to undertake the long-term investment programmes that are themselves a major prerequisite for such sustained growth (cf. Matthews, 1968).

Thus, Keynesian policies for fiscal reflation are no longer based on the view that, if aggregate demand is kept high enough, the supply side will automatically take care of itself. Rather, they are based on the view that the structural changes required in the economy are more likely to be forthcoming in an expansionary environment, and that the appropriate mix of reflationary fiscal measures needs to take into account the supply side as well as the demand side effects. This emphasis on the supply side also raises a much wider question about the need for a more sustained approach to industrial policy, a question which is taken up in chapter 9.

The issue of the interdependence of demand and supply also brings us to the thorny question of the 'natural rate of unemployment'. Some commentators think that the notion of the natural rate of unemployment has done more harm to Keynesian notions of demand management than any other single notion put forward by the monetarists. Even studies which show that about three-quarters of the rise in unemployment between the late 1970s and the early 1980s was caused by a deficiency of aggregate demand (i.e. fiscal contraction and world recession), also show how the natural rate of unemployment has been increasing steadily over this period and stood at 10.72 per cent by 1980–3 (Layard and Nickell, 1985). But many economists are coming to feel that the constant upward revisions to the NRU suggest that there is something faulty about the concept itself, and that the NRU does not actually denote the long-term equilibrium rate of unemployment but rather is very closely linked to the actual rate of unemployment itself (see e.g. Metcalfe, 1984; Morris and Sinclair, 1985).

If, as this chapter has emphasized, aggregate demand and supply are not independent of each other, then it makes no sense to specify the NRU in terms of supply-side factors alone as these are partly determined by the state of demand. Thus, the orthodox Keynesian/monetarist distinction between short-run deviations of unemployment from the NRU caused by inappropriate levels of aggregate demand, and the long-run determination of the NRU by supply-side factors, turns out not to be a viable one, as both the NRU and the actual rate of unemployment are affected by demand-side factors. If in the present situation both AD and AS have shifted to the left, as in figure 4.9, this would be interpreted as a rise in the natural rate of unemployment but, as we have seen, a reversal of this decline would not necessarily result in any increase in inflation.

The NRU is based on the analysis of the augmented Phillips curve and denotes that level of unemployment when expectations of inflation are fulfilled. If unemployment falls below this level then inflation increases, whilst if unemployment rises above this level inflation falls. But in the UK inflation has more or less stabilized at around 5 per cent or so since 1982, but unemployment has not fallen. And this is at a time when the government has put into effect measures to 'free' the labour market, such as changes in trade union legislation, the removal of some wage protection from the low-paid, the reduction of the replacement ratio and a reduction in the levels of employers' national insurance benefits.

The NRU is expressed as a relation between the changes in inflation and the level of unemployment. But in fact, a high level of unemployment seems to be stabilizing with a constant rather than a falling rate of inflation. Thus, economies are getting locked into a situation where inflation is levelling off at a high level of unemployment, and where the NRU has simply followed the rising unemployment rate on its upwards path. Indeed the NRU is generally calculated as 'the actual rate adjusted upwards for the increase in inflation and for the excess rate of real wage growth' (Layard *et al.*, 1984, technical appendix, p. 4) – the Phillips curve has been shifting out even though the rate of inflation has been falling. But this does not imply that a reduction in unemployment must cause a rise in inflation – that will depend on how the fall in unemployment is actually achieved, and we have seen in this chapter that various policy mixes are possible. Indeed, in this sense there is nothing very natural about the NRU.

Some economists are more optimistic that a reflationary policy could be non-inflationary, and point out that, apart from the dangers of an appreciating exchange rate which could be counteracted by a tight monetary policy, an export-led recovery would pose the same problem with respect to wage inflation but that no-one uses this to argue against an export-led expansion. To the extent, however, that nominal wages might increase substantially during a reflation, various schemes have been proposed to reduce such wage increases. One type of scheme could be an incomes policy which would try to restrain nominal pay increases, perhaps within a broader agreement including fiscal reforms and a prices policy.

Basically, such incomes policies try to overcome the 'prisoners' dilemma' characteristic of individual pay settlements. The problem here is that what is rational behaviour for the individual bargaining group is not rational behaviour for all taken together. The solution therefore is to alter the institutional environment of pay bargaining such that this distinction is removed and all groups reach agreement jointly. Another type of scheme relies on providing a system of incentives and penalties to induce pay bargaining within certain prescribed limits, e.g. an inflation tax where wage increases above a norm are liable to tax (see Morris and Sinclair, 1985).

We are now in a position to provide answers to the two basic questions raised on p. 106. The answer to the first question is yes, the government can increase output by increasing demand; and the answer to the second is no, this increase in demand is not predicated on workers receiving a reduced real wage. This is because the increase in output follows from *increasing* the productive potential of the economy, represented by an upwards shift of the production function as more capital is put to work (a reversal of the movement shown in figure 4.7) and not by a movement along an existing production function which implies a lower marginal productivity. This will be shown in more detail in section 4.

So far I have considered the relation between changes in aggregate demand and output, and have emphasized the need to focus on the interdependence between aggregate demand and aggregate supply in modelling the unemployment of labour and resources. But how does this link up with the labour market and changes in the level of employment and of real wages? I will now consider this question.

4.   Aggregate Demand and the Labour Market

We have seen in section 3 that increased output need not be based on a declining real wage rate, although increases in nominal wages may have inflationary consequences. But how does this measure up with the Keynesian (and neo-classical) accounts of the labour market which suggest that increases in output can be secured only if real wages fall? According to this view the low level of aggregate demand causes a fall in the price level which, given existing nominal wages, makes real wages higher than the market clearing rate. In this approach the reduced aggregate demand influences the demand for labour via its effect on real wages; as real wages rise, employers move upwards along their demand curve for labour and unemployment results. This unemployment may then be seen as the result of sticky nominal wages or of the difficulties involved in trying to reduce the real wage by downward

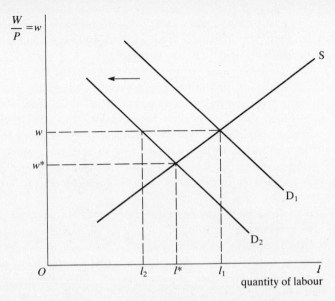

Figure 4.10

adjustments in the nominal wage. Either way, the real wage does not fall and so unemployment emerges.

Whereas this type of Keyensian account sees the demand for labour responding only to the real wage and not to the actual fall in aggregate demand, the analysis presented in section 3 suggests another route by which the demand for labour is affected by a fall in aggregate demand.

The impact of a fall in aggregate demand on unemployment may be easily understood at a common-sense level. If a fall in aggregate demand for goods and services causes a fall in firms' output, it leads firms to reduce their demand for labour, so that redundancies occur and unemployment rises. But how does this square with the theoretical model of the labour market used in chapters 2 and 3 above, where firms' demand for labour was determined by the real wage rather than aggregate demand or the level of output. These firms employed labour up to the point where the marginal product of labour matched the real wage, and no mention was made of aggregate demand or sales. How does a fall in aggregate demand, through reducing output, affect employment and unemployment? (For a useful survey of theories of unemployment see Lindbeck and Snower, 1985).

We have seen in section 3 that one key to providing an answer to this question is the interdependence of aggregate demand and aggregate supply. When aggregate demand falls, so too does the level of the capital stock in use in the economy. We have seen that this causes the (two-dimensional) production function to shift downwards from $q = q(l, \bar{k})$ to $q = q(l, \hat{k})$ where $\hat{k} < \bar{k}$. It also directly affects the demand for labour; as the capital in use falls, so does the marginal product of labour at existing (real) wage rates. This means that the demand curve for labour shifts downward and to the left. This is shown in figure 4.10 where the demand for labour falls from D_1 to D_2.

The demand curve for labour shows what is demanded on the assumption that firms use labour up to the level where its marginal productivity equals the real wage. If the marginal productivity for any level of labour were lower than previously, that level would only be employed if the real wage were lower too. Alternatively, at the existing real wage rate, the quantity of labour demanded would fall from Ol_1 to Ol_2. The effect of the fall in aggregate demand, then, is the fall in employment from Ol_1 to Ol_2 at the existing wage rates. This reduction in employment is what I term demand-deficient unemployment, and is shown by $l_2 l_1$.

It is important to notice that demand-deficient unemployment is caused by factors exogenous to the labour market, i.e. by the effect of changes in aggregate demand on the amount of capital in use in the economy. Given existing wage rates, unemployment of $l_2 l_1$ results, but this unemployment is not caused by an excessive wage rate, nor will it be eradicated by a fall in the wage rate. But you may be asking, surely a reduction in the wage to Ow^* will eliminate unemployment by establishing a market-clearing level of real wages? There are two major difficulties with this. First, arguments about a movement *along* the demand curve for labour in response to a reduction in the real wage presuppose that the demand curve itself does not shift. But this amounts to assuming that the level of aggregate demand is unaffected by changes in the wage rate. This is an instance where we must consider the general equilibrium, as well as the partial equilibrium, effects of a wage reduction, as we must consider whether such a general wage reduction would have any effect in the goods market. Keynes considers this question in the *General Theory* (chapter 19) when he takes on board the question of the self-adjusting character of the labour market as the core element in the classical argument that the economic system as a whole is self-adjusting. Keynes's argument here is that it cannot simply be assumed that aggregate demand will remain unchanged when wages fall; to do so would be to make the mistake that the *ceteris paribus* assumption appropriate for partial equilibrium analysis is also appropriate for general equilibrium analysis.

The question for us now, in the inflationary 1980s, is to consider the case of a fall in real wages brought about by an increase in money wages less than the rate of inflation. How would such a fall in real wages affect aggregate demand? In order to answer this question it is necessary to consider the net effect of the change in wages on all the components of aggregate demand. The short answer to such a complex question is that there is no simple answer. There would initially be a redistribution of income from wage-earners to profit-receivers, so the question is – who has the higher propensity to consume and what are the employment-generating effects of this expenditure. In so far as people on a lower income have a higher marginal propensity to consume, we would expect a reduced expenditure, unless firms felt optimistic enough to spend their increased income on new investment projects. Overall, the effect is a most uncertain one. The problem is that if the fall in wages were to reduce aggregate demand, the demand for labour curve would shift even further to the left. If a market-clearing level of employment existed, it would actually be below Ol^*.

A second difficulty involved in relying on wage cuts to restore employment is that even if the demand for labour curve remained unchanged, the wage cuts would not restore employment to the former level Ol_1, which is what is required if the demand-deficient unemployment is to be eliminated. At best wage cuts could restore only an employment level of Ol^* – the new natural rate of employment. This shows how the natural rate is itself partly dependent on demand factors and points to the difficulty of simply accepting a market-clearing level of employment as a full employment level. In this case the reduction in employment would be equivalent to l^*l_1, but it would be reclassified as voluntary unemployment and so would be made invisible. This is further exacerbated by the 'discouraged worker effect', where some workers give up searching for work and effectively resign from the active labour force. This is the case for many married women, for example, who redefine

Table 4.3. Unemployment and real wage effects of various policy changes in the Treasury model (after 4 years)

	Percentage change in		
	Employment	Real wages	Inflation
Nominal wages down 2 per cent, No policy-induced real demand change	+0.34	−0.60	down
Policy-induced real demand increase No change in wage pressure	+0.89	+0.73	up
Nominal wages down 2 per cent Policy-induced real demand increase	+1.16	−1.27	? probably down

Notes
(1) Row 1 is derived from table C, p. 49 and row 3 from table B, p. 48 of the Treasury (1985). We assume that the numbers can be adjusted *pro-rata*.
(2) Row 2 is taken from table 3 in Andrews *et al.* (1985) and corresponds to a 3.25 per cent rise in government spending on goods and services.
(3) The real demand increase is generated by maintaining cash limits in nominal terms and by cutting taxes to keep the PSBR/GDP ratio constant.
Source: Nickell (1985), table 2, p. 107. Similar results can also be found in Andrews (1985) and Walker and Davies (1985b).

themselves as housewives when they lose their job without any prospect of another one, and so drop out of the labour force altogether. In terms of our diagram of the labour market, this would be represented by a leftward shift of the supply curve. In this case, too, the resulting market-clearing level of employment is less than it would have been if the demand for labour had not fallen, and in this case too the unemployment becomes invisible (see the discussion in Metcalfe, 1984, p. 61).

In spite of these theoretical difficulties, estimates have been made of the effect on total employment of a change in real wages. Such results are shown in table 4.3. The first row shows that a 2 per cent reduction in nominal wages would result in an increase in employment of about 0.34 per cent after 4 years. Real wages would fall by about 0.6 per cent, lower than the nominal fall because the rate of inflation also falls. Thus a small increase in employment is feasible under these conditions. If, however, the 2 per cent fall in nominal wages were accompanied by a policy-induced real demand increase by cutting taxes to keep the PSBR/GDP ratio constant, then the employment effect is increased by about 3½ times.

In these circumstances it would be technically possible to keep the post-tax consumption wage constant in spite of the fall in the real value of gross pay, by making the appropriate tax adjustments. The main problem, though, with this kind of simulation using the Treasury model is that no indication is given as to how nominal wages might actually be reduced. One commentator has remarked that it corresponds to 'if-only' analysis, but concludes that wishful thinking is scarcely analysis (Andrews *et al.*, 1985, p. 52).

Another question that arises is why don't some workers accept a reduced real wage in order to secure employment? This is the question that has bedevilled much analysis: are workers subject to money illusion, or are they concerned with relativities rather than absolute wage levels, or is it the periodic rather than continuous nature of wage agreements that underlies the apparent stickiness of wages in the presence of unemployment? Part of the answer to this must be that the price of labour is just not like the price of any other good. It embodies social norms of justice and fairness, so that it is not regarded as socially acceptable for unemployed workers to be paid less than the going rate in order to secure employment (Solow, 1980). And if wage rates were to fluctuate to achieve market-clearing there would have to be a considerable degree of fluctuation in wages.

The emphasis of this chapter, however, suggests another approach to the question of why unemployed workers do not accept lower wages in the face of demand-deficient unemployment. On what basis can workers rationally accept that their labour has become less productive, that their marginal product has fallen, and that the economy can afford only a lower wage to a smaller workforce? This runs counter to commonly held notions of productive advances in industry and increases in workers' productivity. In this case outlined here, the solution to unemployment is not to reduce wages but to increase aggregate demand and the amount of capital in use and so increase the demand for labour back to D_1.

Rather than a policy of wage-cutting (in an age of inflation – of nominal wages increasing less than the rate of inflation), this chapter has emphasized a policy of demand expansion with a particular regard to the importance of stimulating investment, both public and private, and the need to formulate a long-term industrial policy. This chapter's emphasis on the amount of capital in use does not provide support, therefore, for a policy of demand expansion based on tax cuts which would simply fuel a consumer boom outrunning industry's capacity to supply. In the present circumstances of relatively free trade and a high marginal propensity to import (itself the outcome of industry's supply difficulties) this would simply result in excessive pressure on the balance of payments.

5. Conclusion

This chapter has reviewed several approaches within Keynesianism to the general question of how demand-deficient unemployment can occur. It has argued that the Keynesian acceptance of the Marshallian conception of the short run as the appropriate time-period of analysis has obscured the significance of changes in the capital actually in use in the economy. The chapter argued that this adoption of the Marshallian short-run period of analysis is an incoherent one when the level of capital in use in the economy is changing, and that the integration of these capital adjustments strengthens Keynesianism's traditional argument that there is an absence of self-adjustment mechanisms to eradicate demand-deficient unemployment. The chapter also showed how the adoption of an approach in which the supply-side implications of changes in demand are recognized, can provide an effective argument for non-inflationary policies to increase output and employment.

References

Allsopp, C. A. (1985) 'Monetary and fiscal policy in the 1980s', *Oxford Review of Economic Policy*, 1(1), 1–19.

Andrews, M. J., Bell, D. F., Fisher, P. G., Wallis, K. F. and Whitley, J. D. (1985) 'Models of the UK economy and the real wage-employment debate', *National Institute Economic Review*, 112, 41–52.

Artis, M. J., Bladen-Hovell, R., Karakitsos, E. and Wolatzky, B. D. (1984) 'The effects of economic policy', *National Institute Economic Review*, 108, 54–67.

Bank of England (1985) 'Developments in leasing', *Bank of England Quarterly Bulletin*, 25, 582–5.

Biswas, R., Johns, C. and Savage, D. (1985) 'The measurement of fiscal stance', *National Institute Economic Review*, 113, 50–64.

Brown, V. (1986) *Capital, Demand-deficient Unemployment and the Labour Market*, The Open University, Faculty of Social Sciences Working Paper no. 1 (New Series).

Buiter, W. H. and Miller, M. (1981) 'The Thatcher experiment: the first two years', *Brookings Papers on Economic Activity*, 2, 315-79.

Buiter, W. H. and Miller, M. (1983) 'Changing the rules: economic consequences of the Thatcher Regime', *Brookings Papers on Economic Activity*, 2, 305-79.

Dornbusch, R. (1985) *Sound Currency and Full Employment*. Employment Institute, London.

Keynes, J. M. (1973a) *The General Theory of Employment, Interest and Money*. Macmillan, London.

Keynes, J. M. (1973b) *Collected Works*, vol. xiii. Macmillan, London.

Layard, R. and Nickell, S. (1985) 'The causes of British unemployment', *National Institute Economic Review*, 111, 62-85.

Layard, R., Basevi, G., Blanchard, O., Buiter, W. and Dornbusch, R. (1984) *Europe: the case for unsustainable growth*, Centre for European Policy Studies, Paper 8/9.

Lindbeck, A. and Snower, D. J. (1985) 'Explanations of unemployment', *Oxford Review of Economic Policy*, 1(2), 34-59.

Matthews, R. C. O. (1968) 'Why has Britain had full employment since the War?', *Economic Journal*, 78, 555-69.

Metcalfe, D. (1984) 'On the measurement of employment and unemployment', *National Institute Economic Review*, 109, 59-67.

Miller, M. (1985) 'Measuring the stance of fiscal policy', *Oxford Review of Economic Policy*, 1(1), 44-57.

Morris, D. and Sinclair, P. (1985) 'The unemployment problem in the 1980s', *Oxford Review of Economic Policy*, 1(2), 1-19.

National Institute Economic Review (1983) 'The capital stock', Appendix B to Ch. 1, 'The home economy', Section 11, 'The medium term', 106, pp. 23-5.

Nickell, S. (1982) 'The determinants of equilibrium unemployment in Britain', *Economic Journal*, 92, 555-75.

Nickell, S. (1985) 'The government's policy for jobs: an analysis', *Oxford Review of Economic Policy*, 1(2), 98-115.

Oudiz, G. and Sachs, J. (1984) 'Macroeconomic policy coordination among the industrial countries', *Brookings Papers on Economic Activity*, Part 1, pp. 1-64.

Robinson, P. W. (1985) 'Capacity constraints, real wages and the role of the public sector in creating jobs'. In Kay, J. (ed.) *The Economy and the 1985 Budget*, Basil Blackwell, Oxford, pp. 40-50.

Solow, R. M. (1980) 'On theories of unemployment', *American Economic Review*, 70, 1-11.

Surrey, M. J. C. (1982) 'Was the recession forecast?', *National Institute Economic Review*, 100, 24-8.

Thompson, G. (1984) 'Economic intervention in the post-war economy', In McLennan, G. *et al.* (eds) *State and Society in Contemporary Britain*. Polity Press, Cambridge.

Treasury (1985) *The Relationship Between Employment and Wages*, H.M. Treasury, London.

Walker, J. and Davies, G. (1985a) 'The UK economy: analysis and prospects' *Oxford Review of Economic Policy*, 1(1), 21-34.

Walker, J. and Davies, G. (1985b) 'The UK economy: analysis and prospects', *Oxford Review of Economic Policy*, 1(2), 20-33.

5

Unemployment and Technology

GRAHAME THOMPSON

1. Introduction

The Roman emperor Vespasian (AD 69–79) is said to have opposed the use of water power because he felt it might create unemployment (Derry and Williams, 1970, p. 252). Thus the concern with 'technological development' and its effect upon employment is by no means a new phenomenon. However, it is probably since the advent of large-scale automation in the 1960s that the ability of economic and technological growth to create *additional* employment opportunities has become a major issue. This uncertainty has been multiplied by the widespread deployment of microelectronic technology in industry and commerce during the late 1970s and early 1980s.

This chapter is concerned with whether a purely technological cause of unemployment can be isolated. By this is meant unemployment which arises as a consequence of product and process innovations, in distinction to it being either the result of impediments in the labour market which act to keep the price of labour above its equilibrium level *or* the result of a lack of aggregate demand.

As we shall see, the problem is to give a precise definition to 'technologically induced unemployment'. This involves three aspects:

(a) a consideration of the way technology appears in theoretical discussions of technical and economic change;
(b) an empirical problem of isolating that part of overall unemployment attributable solely to technological developments, as opposed to a range of other causes of unemployment; and
(c) a problem of distinguishing technological unemployment from that due to the slow adjustment of market-clearing wages after technological change has occurred.

These three features are of course interlinked.

It was pointed out in chapter 2 that the state of technology and methods of organizing labour are two arguments of the short-run production function, which appear as components in determining the aggregate supply schedule. But while both

134

of these positively affect the marginal product of labour, their impact on the demand for labour is ambiguous. It is this ambiguity that is at the heart of this chapters analysis – technological change and any accompanying changes in the way labour is organized in the process of production may or may not increase the demand for labour and hence increase or decrease employment. We shall therefore be dealing with the short-run production function in this chapter but I shall also be opening up some remarks about what might be termed the long-run production function as well. In both cases this chapter focuses on the supply side of the economy, and upon what underlies the shape and position of the aggregate supply curve.

2. Technology and Technical Change

For the purposes of this chapter we can define technology as 'the application of science to the plant, machines, tools and processes available for the execution of production tasks at a given time, and the rationale underlying their utilization'.

This is a wide definition, capturing the embodiment of technology in capital goods and techniques. This parallels the distinction already mentioned in the introduction between product technologies and process technologies. Technological change not only affects production goods (the means of production) it affects the processes or techniques of production as well, involving the organization of the production line, the relationships between different aspects of firms or 'enterprises' overall production effort and so on. Of course, it also affects consumption goods, particularly consumer durables.

The point here is that technology is always 'embodied' in something else. It does not exist independently of that in which it is embodied. Ultimately technology is a relationship between science and its application to the art or manner of producing things – a relationship which is only made manifest through its effects. One of these 'effects' could be unemployment, so we always have a problem of attribution of effect to cause involved here, which is where empirical work arises. This is further discussed in section 6.

In simple neo-classical economic theory technical change is what enables an economy to produce more with given amounts of labour and capital inputs. In the context of the effects of technical change on employment (rather than on capital use) this is measured by an increase in labour productivity. An increase in labour productivity implies a reduction in the amount of labour required to produce a given volume of goods. Thus the problem of unemployment follows as a consequence of conceiving production in terms of this relationship between inputs and outputs. But there is an additional element here which concerns the rise in real incomes occasioned by an increase in productivity. Technological change creates a problem of unemployment in that it widens the gap between potential and actual output. This gap is akin to the Keynesian problem of demand deficiency and in

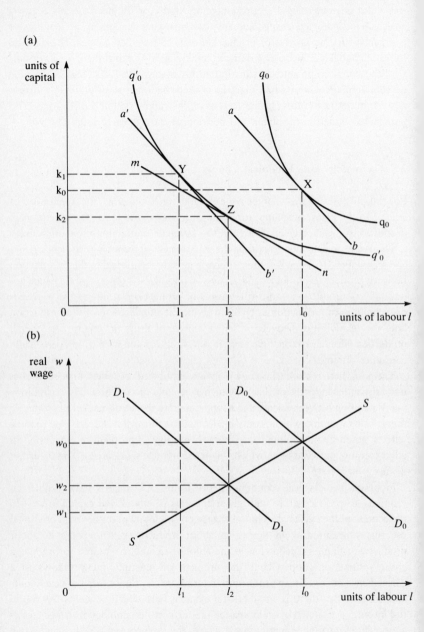

Figure 5.1. Technical change and the demand for labour

this sense the neo-classical and Keynesian analyses are quite compatible. However, within Keynesian theory the increase in per capita income has an expansionary effect on aggregate demand which could increase employment. Thus it is possible for technological change to more than offset the contractionary effects that it has on employment through an increase in labour productivity (Hussain, 1983, p. 15).

Figure 5.1 translates some of these preliminary remarks into a more analytical framework. This can illustrate the general conditions for neo-classical technological unemployment to exist, and from it can be generated the policy implications that arise in the context of the analysis. This analysis relies upon the technique of isoquants, which show the combinations of labour and capital inputs necessary to produce any given level of output. These embody a particular technology and method of organizing production, and here it is assumed that the possibility of continuous substitution between capital and labour input holds to produce the output.

In figure 5.1(a) we assume that the initial situation is typified by equilibrium output as represented by isoquant q_0 at point X where l_0 units of labour and k_0 units of capital are employed. The position in the labour market consistent with these production characteristics and this level of output is shown in figure 5.1(b). The demand and supply curves of labour, $D_0 D_0$ and SS respectively, are assumed to be in equilibrium with employment levels at l_0 and the real wage rate at w_0. The real wage rate w_0 in figure 5.1(b) is translated into the relative price of capital and labour in figure 5.1(a) by the price line with slope ab, tangent to isoquant q_0 at point X. Let us suppose that a technological change now occurs which is capital-intensive in character. This means that the marginal productivity of capital (MP_k) increases relative to the marginal productivity of labour (MP_l) or $(\Delta MP_k / \Delta MP_l) > 1$.

Such a shift in relationship between capital and labour is shown in figure 5.1(a) by isoquant q_0'. This isoquant is skewed round towards the capital axis, since the technological change is more capital-intensive: it shifts the proportionate relationship between the inputs of labour and capital needed to produce the same output. It is also pushed in towards the origin showing that fewer inputs are actually needed. With the same relative price relationship between capital and labour $(a'b')$, the same level of output as before can now be produced at point Y on isoquant q_0'. Under the circumstances shown, this implies an increase in the units of capital required (to k_1) but a reduction in the units of labour required (to l_1) to produce the output.

Perhaps this is the result that might be expected with a technological change: it increases the capital used but decreases the labour used. However, this is not the end of the matter. If we look to the bottom half of the figure it can be seen that there is a short-run technologically induced unemployment of l_0-l_1. The demand curve for labour has shifted in to the left as a result of the technological change, i.e. to $D_1 D_1$. But at the real wage rate w_0 the labour market is no longer in equilibrium. There is a tendency for labour to offer itself at a lower wage rate. For instance, some labour would be willing to offer itself at a lower real wage rate w_1 under these circumstances. Eventually the labour market will restore itself to equilibrium at lower wage rate w_2 by moving down the new demand curve D_1D_1 and along the supply curve SS. Some of the potentially unemployed labour will be re-employed as the relative price of capital and labour changes and as the new lower wage rate w_2 becomes established.

This change in relative prices brought about by technological change can be seen in figure 5.1(a). As the price of labour falls relative to the price of capital, there is a substitution of labour for capital and a movement around the isoquant to point Z. This is the point of tangency between the new relative price line mn and isoquant q'_0 which is consistent with the restored equilibrium in the labour market. Under the circumstances shown this eventually leads to fewer units of capital, k_2, employed than before the technological change, and fewer labour units, l_2, although proportionately there is a greater reduction in labour than in capital (hence capital-intensivity). We might think of the introduction of microelectronic-based technologies as an instance of this, since it could result in both a reduction in labour use and a reduction in the units of capital employed. Technologically induced unemployment is now l_0-l_2 (rather than l_0-l_1), and there is nothing that labour can immediately do to increase employment prospects. If real wages had been 'sticky' downwards, unemployment could have been higher and capital use greater than before the change.

It should be clear from the above analysis that a capital-intensive innovation could lead either to a decrease in the amount of capital units employed, as in the case discussed above, or to an increase in the amount needed to produce the same level of output. This would depend upon the precise shape and position of the isoquants (which in turn are dependent upon the pre- and post-technical change marginal productivities of the two inputs concerned) relative to the price lines.

The technological innovation represented in figure 5.1 is *labour-saving*. The same level of output as before can now be produced by employing fewer units of labour. Formally speaking, a labour-saving innovation is one where the following condition holds, given a fixed level of output:

$$l_t - l_{t+1} > 0$$

where l_t = the technologically determined labour input required to produce a unit of output prior to the technological change, and l_{t+1} = the labour input required to produce a unit of output after the technological change.

If this difference is greater than zero, the technological change has enabled the given output to be produced with less labour input.

An analogous case to the labour-saving one just analysed would be a *capital-saving* innovation. As with the labour-saving examples we can formally state the condition for a capital-saving innovation. This is the case when the following condition holds, given a fixed level of output:

$$k_t - k_{t+1} > 0$$

where k_t = the technologically determined capital input required to produce a unit of output prior to the technological change and k_{t+1} = the capital input required to produce a unit of output after the technological change.

We have now defined a labour-saving and a capital-saving innovation. But in the spirit of the remarks made above about per capita income effects, such innovations might actually lead to more or less labour use or to more or less capital use via output changes. Thus in addition to these labour or capital *savings* or *using* examples, we need to further distinguish a labour or capital *displacing* or *employing* case. Given the emphasis on the employment consequences of technological innovations in this chapter we concentrate on the labour-displacing and labour-employing cases.

In these latter cases we are allowing for a possible change in the level of output, with output being either cut back or stimulated as a result of the technological change, rather than held constant as in the earlier examples. Let us first take the case where a technological innovation leads to an output change such that labour is displaced. That is what happens if the technological change leads to a decrease in the actual level of employment independently of its effect upon $l_t - l_{t+1}$. Similarly a labour-employing case will be what happens if a change in technology leads to a change in output that leads to an increase in employment, again regardless of its impact upon $l_t - l_{t+1}$.

For instance, looking back at figure 5.1, if output grew after the technological change it would end up somewhere on an isoquant to the right of q'_0. If it finally came to rest on an isoquant to the right of Z, yet to the left of labour use l_0, the innovation would have been *labour-displacing*. This is because the level of labour units used is still not as high as before the innovation. However, if it expanded on to an isoquant where labour use was *more* than at l_0 the innovative would be *labour-employing*. It would have stimulated a greater use of labour than before. Similar reasoning can be brought to bear on the *capital-displacing* and *capital-employing* cases.

Clearly any innovation or wave of innovations may be *both* labour-saving and capital-saving. Alternatively it may be *just* capital-saving or labour-saving. These possibilities could have different labour use consequences. In addition innovations could be either labour-employing or labour-displacing, again with different overall employment implications. Thus, in determining the aggregate labour-saving and capital-saving effects and aggregate labour-employing or labour-displacing effects of innovations, the aggregate supply of innovations and their diffusion must be considered. Overall employment changes will depend upon a weighted summation of sectoral labour-saving innovations (or labour-using ones) – i.e. on productivity effects, and on the ouput consequences of this – i.e. on real income effects. This will in turn depend upon which sectors introduce innovations and how labour-saving (or labour-using) these innovations are and on any income effects (Jones, 1983). We return to this issue in section 6 below, in the context of attempts that have been made to calculate empirically the possible aggregate employment consequences of the current round of technological innovations.

The relationship of this analysis to Keynesian demand-deficient unemployment can work in two ways. On the one hand real income effects of increases in productivity (labour or capital) could expand aggregate demand. On the other hand an explicit policy option in the context of the situation depicted in figure 5.1 would be to deliberately expand aggregate demand. This could stimulate output and shift the demand curve for labour out again to the $D_0 D_0$ position, thereby restoring long-run equilibrium in the labour market.

An alternative policy option to try and restore labour market equilibrium could be product price subsidies. Such subsidies could increase the demand for the products in question (other things remaining equal) and since the demand for labour is a derived demand, the demand curve for labour would also shift. A sufficiently large product price subsidy could thus encourage an expansion of output, i.e. a movement on to a higher isoquant, and once again restore labour use to the original l_0 position.

3. Supply-side Adjustments and Skills

There is an alternative policy response on the above context which does not tackle the demand side but looks to the supply side to offer a possible adjustment mechanism. In the analysis conducted around figure 5.1 the labour employed was treated as homogeneous. It was implicitly assumed to be either skill-specific to the particular configuration of output under consideration, or unskilled labour. Thus when its use was altered by the change in technique due to technological development, it remained unemployed in the absence of any further adjustments or policy response. But there are two different was of linking production to technologies. One involves the question of the kinds of operations involved in industries, while the other involved the kinds of skill or occupational categories involved. Let us now look into this second aspect as up to now we have concentrated on the first.

Consider the position represented in figure 5.2 (which relies upon Cooper and Clark, 1982). The two axes of this figure measure unskilled labour (l_u) and skilled labour (l_s) respectively. These can be combined together to produce given levels of output as indicated by the isoquants. We ignore capital in this diagram.

The assumption underlying this analysis is that the combination of skilled and unskilled labour used to produce output q is dependent upon relative wage rates.

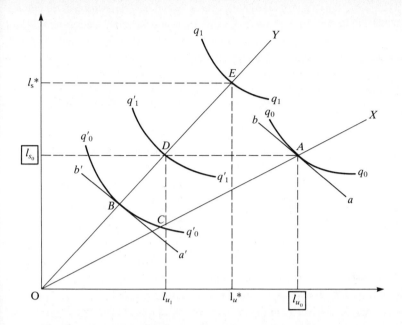

Figure 5.2. Technologically induced unemployment with different skills

We begin the analysis at 'full employment' point A. Here output q_0 can be produced. This point is determined by three factors: (i) the full employment levels of skilled and unskilled labour, l_{s_0} and l_{u_0} (the total labour force is thus equal to $l_{u_0} + l_{s_0}$) combined with: (ii) the isoquant representing the q_0 production level, which is tangential at this point to: (iii) the relative wage rate of skilled to unskilled labour as denoted by the slope of the line ba in this case.

Technological change now makes the production of the same level of output possible at q'_0. This technological change is not neutral with respect to the skill combination of labour required, however. In fact it is assumed to be biased so that at the fixed relative wage rates denoted by the slope ba ($=$ slope $b'a'$) a larger proportion of skilled to unskilled labour is required to produce a given unit of output. It is more 'skill-intensive'.

Given this new situation the expansion path for output is through point B, and employers will continue to employ workers until some constraint an output is reached. Assuming there is no immediate constraint on the demand for the product, the new output employment position is reached at point D on the q'_1 isoquant, when all the available skilled labour is employed. This leaves a 'technologically induced' unemployment of unskilled labour equal to $l_{u_0} - l_{u_1}$.

If relative wages had been fully flexible it would have been possible to employ skilled and unskilled workers in the proportions in which they were available. This would require a fall in the wages of unskilled labour compared to skilled labour. Notionally this would imply a movement around the isoquant q_0' to point C - i.e. a change in the relative price of skilled to unskilled labour such that the slope of this ratio became tangential to the isoquant at C. The movement would then be along the expansion path OX on to a new isoquant through point A but parallel to q_0'.

Given an inflexibility in wages, however, D becomes the output position on isoquant q_1' and because of unemployment some potential output is lost. Clearly, a policy response here could be for unemployed skilled labour to retrain to become skilled. Under these circumstances an expansion of output could ensue, encouraging a movement along the expansion path OY to point E on isoquant q_1. At this point all potentially employable labour with its new mix of skills has found employment $(l_u^* + l_s^* = l_{u_0} + l_{s_0})$.

But supposing that to either encourage this retraining, or as a consequence of it happening, the relative price of skilled to unskilled labour has changed permanently, then different expansion paths to the ones shown in figure 5.2 would have resulted. Clearly, any change in skill pattern is very likely to put pressures on relative wage changes in the direction of skilled labour. This is going to change the slope of the wage ratio line in figure 5.2, and as a result lead to a different tangential position with the relevant isoquant.

4. The 'New Technology' and Unemployment

Up to now the chapter has laid out a particular analytical framework for considering some of the possible consequences of technical change on employment. Before we go on to evaluate this and introduce some other approaches it will be useful to review exactly what the issue of technical change amounts to under contemporary conditions. This is the aim of this section.

The major contemporary concern with technology and unemployment relates to the present round of computer-based information systems and electronic robotic manufacturing systems that are gradually being introduced into the production, service and distribution sectors of the economy. It is important to recognize that the impact of the new technology purely in the manufacturing sector is likely to be quite variable. This is because this sector itself is a very heterogeneous one. It comprises a number of sub-sectors, operations and processes not all of which will be affected to the same extent by this new technology, or necessarily in the same way. There are significant differences in the potential for its application as between footwear manufacture and iron and steel production, for instance. Operations such as design, assembly, packaging, transport, textual information processing, and so on, are all likely to be differently affected; indeed, some of them are unlikely to be affected much at all. In addition, the technologies within different sub-sectors of manufacturing (e.g. plastics, mechanical engineering, food processing) are themselves quite heterogeneous, and may also be going through their own technological revolutions, such as the introduction of biotechnology and genetic engineering into various areas, the development of ceramic, acoustic and optical technologies, etc. This makes the employment impact of the progressive introduction of microelectronic and robotic technologies into a range of areas itself variable and difficult to predict with any accuracy.

In addition, whilst a basic division within economics and followed in this chapter is between the manufacturing and the service sector industries, it should be remembered that some 25 per cent of labour in manufacturing is itself of a 'service' character, involving managerial, supervisory and clerical skills and occupational categories. Significant in*tra*-sectoral shifts in employment patterns may emerge, therefore, which do not register as in*ter*-sectoral shifts. It is with inter-sectoral shifts that much of the analysis of the impact of microtechnology on employment is concerned; the presumption being that labour displaced from the manufacturing sector will find employment in the service sector. Thus there can be two sets of conventional economic classification operating here. Whether an occupation counts as 'service' or 'manufacturing' (one convention) is different from whether the industry or sector in which workers are employed counts as being in the service or manufacturing sector (another convention). But shifts may occur in either of these as a result of technological change.

As mentioned above, one way of linking 'industries' to 'technologies' is through the specification of the operations that they involve; another is through the skill or occupational composition of those employed in such operations. It is these two aspects of the new technology that are highlighted here.

4.1. *What is the new technology?*

In 1978 the UK Advisory Council for Applied Research and Development published a report entitled *The Application of Semi-conductor Technology*. In this (p. 4) it provided a useful list of the attributes of the new micro-chip technology, stating that:

> [it] is the most influential technology of the twentieth century because: (i) it both extends and displaces a wide range of intellectual and intuitive skills; (ii) it is all pervasive; (iii) it is still advancing rapidly; (iv) it is very cheap and getting cheaper; (v) it will become abundantly available from international sources; (vi) it has exceptional reliability.

With respect to these characteristics a range of commentators have pointed out how its application could increase productivity dramatically such that economic growth might now produce a new reduction of jobs in the economy rather than enhancing job prospects. Barron and Curnow (1981), in a study carried out between 1976 and 1977, predicted a 16 per cent job loss in the UK because of microelectronic technology over the following 15 years. Jenkins and Sherman (1979) suggested a loss of 1 million jobs by 1983, 3.8 million by 1993, and over 5 million by 2003. In addition, trade unions such as ASTMS have suggested losses of 2.6 million office jobs by 1985; APEX predicted a more modest figure of about 250,000 by 1983 (all reported in Whitley and Wilson, 1982).

What there commentaries are referring to are two somewhat distinct realms of application of semiconductor technologies – one with respect to the 'factory', broadly speaking, and the other with respect to the 'office'. In both cases job losses are predicted. But the actual technologically based processes involved in each of these two areas are not the same.

4.1.1. *In the factory*

The type of considerations that have prompted predictions of the kind mentioned above in the context of the factory are summed up in Jenkins and Sherman's description of development in Japanese television set manufacture:

> In 1972 Hitachi employed 9,000 on colour TV production; in 1976 this was down to 4,300; the story is similar with other large manufacturers. National Panasonic's workforce fell from 9,875 to 3,900 and Sony from 4,498 to 2,278. In all, the big seven Japanese colour TV producers almost halved their labour force from nearly 48,000 to 25,000. In the same period the number of TV sets manufactured rose by 25% from 8.4 million in 1972 to 10.5 million in 1976. It has been achieved by an immense investment in product and process design (Jenkins and Sherman, 1979, p. 91).

They go on to point out how robots were increasingly being programmed to perform quite sophisticated tasks–such as the assembly of a Ford motor governor with 13 components in one-third of the time taken by an expert assembler. The Japanese company Hitachi, having developed a robot with seven micro television cameras and linked to a mini lightweight computer which can process both visual and tactile information, harnessed this to the assembly of spherical vacuum cleaners. The assembly operation took just 2.5 minutes. IBM computers were being used to assemble the eight sub-sections of a typewriter in 45 second. Other more sophisticated consumer durable production will follow a similar pattern of development, it is suggested.

These points emphasize the assembly operations that were being performed by robots of various kinds. Whilst increasingly these are being programmed with the aid of micro-chip-based computer technology, the majority of robots are still 'numerically' controlled by simple 'loop-tape' or card systems.

In addition most robots are still used for relatively simple tasks such as welding, spraying, loading and assembly functions. Some are used to remove metal and non-metal pieces from lathes and milling machines. While Sweden had the highest per capita robot population in the early 1980s, and Japan the highest overall number, the rate of installation and use was accelerating in the USA and other European countries, particularly in the UK. A parallel development to this quantitative increase in the use made of robots involves a qualitative change in the manner of their use. Robots have in some cases been linked to machine tools and their associated manufacturing techniques and organizational procedures to form what are known as flexible manufacturing systems (FMS). These FMS were originated in the late 1960s in the USA. They involve a linked system of manufacture which itself can be re-set and re-programmed to produce different variations of the product. Various processes of fabrication, assembly and transportation within the factory are thereby linked together, either around simple numerically controlled machine tool operation (SNC-MT) or increasingly around computer numerically controlled machine tool operation (CNC-MT). These are then combined into assembly and movement sub-systems and further into entire manufacturing processes to develop an integrated and flexible overall production process on a continuous line basis.

One important point with respect to the FMS is that their introduction has been rather slow in developing. In 1982 there were 30–40 FMS installed in Japan, 22 in the USA, and 17 in West Germany (compared with 8–10 in the UK). However, further FMS were in the planning stage (Rempp, 1982, p. 69). Such FMS are what Diebold (1952) and others seemed to have partly in mind as the 'fully automated manufacturing control systems' of the 1950s, and it has taken 30 years for only 22 of these to be introduced in the USA. Admittedly, though, their introduction seems to be accelerating during the late 1970s and early 1980s with the added power and precision that microelectronic technologies can give. The number of separate parts or 'work pieces' in each of these FMS also varies between the countries referred to above, with Germany having the largest numbers (eight separate FMS with between 100 and 200 'work pieces' integrated together). Germany is followed by Japan and the USA (and presumably by the UK) in the extent of its average number of 'work pieces'.

In fact it is these separate 'work pieces', or numerically controlled machine tools that have escalated in number since the 1960s (particularly their computerized variant), something referred to by Jenkins and Sherman above when describing the number of robots working in Japanese industry. But these are not necessarily integrated into flexible and combined systems of production. The main reason why more FMS were not introduced in industry during the first 20 years of their existence, according to the study by Rempp from which most of this information is drawn, concerned the cost of these large integrated systems. They require huge capital investment and, without very careful planning and organization, can prove to be economically inefficient. They rely upon volume production and the fact that the system can be re-tooled and re-organized to produce updated models or products with the same or similar characteristics. Production savings arise from the fact that materials have a known location on the shop floor and can be easily entered into the production process. In addition, reliability of output is increased. This means that savings are mainly in terms of the time taken to complete tasks (some 40 per cent savings) and in time spent checking, rejecting and reworking produced output. In general terms the survey conducted by Rempp (1982) showed that (a) technical efficiency was lower for the FMS than feasibility studies had suggested, and (b) economic efficiency in terms of overall cost reductions compared with the nearest best alternative (rather than with the older replaced technique) were also much less than anticipated (in fact in some cases they were more costly). This confirms the need to be sceptical about manufacturers' and consultants' claims about the advantages of FMS, and not simply to extrapolate job consequences from manufacturers' proposals.

The main advantage of FMS would seem to be the labour productivity changes induced by their introduction. Table 5.1 shows the actual productivity differentials calculated for various combinations and forms of machine tool operation as a result of the substitution of FMS for conventional machine tool and simple numerically controlled machine tool operations.

The first column of figures shows the labour productivity increases (this is clearly not the same as the total factor productivity changes, which would have to include the effects of capital productivity as well). The final column gives the percentage manpower savings induced by the introduction of the various processes. These vary from an average of 50 per cent to as much as 85 per cent.

In summing up the analysis of the effects of manpower demand as a result of these developments in West Germany, Rempp calculated a loss of some 42,000 machine operators' jobs between 1975 and 1980. But this was offset by the creation of about 20,000 new numerically controlled jobs – all to produce the same level of output. Thus there was an important *intra*-sectoral accommodation even before any *inter*-sectoral shifts began to occur. He predicted a maximum overall reduction

Table 5.1.   Manpower savings through SNC–MT and FMS (operators only)

Transition from/to	Labour productivity increase factor	Manpower savings for operators (%)
Conventional MT/SNC-MT	2.0–3.0	50–70
SNC–MT/FMS	1.3–2.2	25–50
Conventional MT/FMS	2.2–5.5	60–85

Note: MT = machine tool; SNC-MT = simple numerically controlled machine tool; FMS = flexible manufacturing system.
Source: Rempp, 1982, table 6, p. 81.

in skilled machinist manpower as a result of FMS developments to 1990 of only 10,000 (Rempp, 1982, p. 85). Thus here we have a case of both a reduction in the numbers employed in the sector and a rearrangement of the remaining employees' skill profile. But clearly the net impact on employment in the economy overall, as a result of these technological changes, cannot be judged by looking at one sector or branch in isolation. This is returned to in section 6 below.

In addition there is another level at which the intra-sectoral or intra-industry rearrangement of skills and occupations can be viewed. One element not mentioned so far concerns the likely impact of the new technology on the need for supervisory, managerial and other 'service' back-up in connection with automated plants of the FMS variety. Perhaps ironically, such new technology can lead to the need for more managers and supervisors to control the dislocated labour processes so established. These systems were conceived, to a large extent, in terms of an ultimate in control technology, virtually eliminating the need for human management as well as direct labour. But by and large this has not proved to be the case. Thus the new technology may be no more revolutionary in its control possibilities than previous generations of technical change. It is severely limited in this respect particularly by software developments. An FMS, for instance, involves the following three 'dimensions' to its operations:

(1) computer-controlled machine tools capable of being programmed to change tools or heads, and capable of stand-alone operations;
(2) a materials handling system which automatically moves parts randomly between stations, controlled by a computer or programmable controller;
(3) an executive or 'host' computer with the functions of (a) storing programmes for down-loading to machines, (b) handling the scheduling of parts to machines, and (c) collecting management information.

Anyone familiar with the study of operations research (the discipline involved with modelling integrated systems of this character) will realize that this represents a formidable overall programming problem, and even theoretical models developed to solve it can be very complex and problematical (see Canuto *et al.*, 1983, for instance). As a result, inefficiencies in the actual running of systems have to be overcome with *ad hoc* procedures involving supervisory personnel and the application of manual activities.

4.1.2. *In the office*

These warnings about the inefficiencies of the strict application of new technology are particularly important within non-manufacturing sectors. So far the discussion has concentrated on the role of microelectronic technology with respect to the plant and shopfloor organization of production. But 'production' for economists has a wider significance than this. It is in the service sectors, and particularly the office, where microelectronic technology in the form of information technology and 'telematics' (the integration of communications and information systems with visual displays) has been most rapidly advancing. This has led to the idea of an 'electronic office' in which previously labour-intensive clerical and secretarial skills are drastically reduced to a few routine tasks connected through an elaborate and integrated computer-guided information gathering, recording and processing system. But again such a 'production process' is fraught with difficulties of implementation. The tasks of secretaries, typists, clerks and the like are not simply reducible to an abstract set of electronically guided procedures, but involve liaison, 'manning' the office, discussion and judgement, etc, which require the necessary supervisory and managerial skills and functions. Additional tasks may also be generated, which open up new job prospects in these areas.

Office mechanization started in the second half of the nineteenth century. In 1850 the quill pen had not yet been fully replaced by the steel nib pen, but taking pen to paper was still the main form of office work. During the 1880s and 1890s the typewriter began to replace this activity. It introduced a precision technology for writing and recording which was as revolutionary as the present introduction of micro-chip technology into the office. With the typewriter came an increase in the size of offices and in their number, in the number of people employed in them and in the variety of jobs – thus employment increased as a result. It also had a profound effect on the social composition of the office and its organization. Office work had remained a male occupation well after the introduction of women workers into factories, but this was rapidly transformed at the turn of the century with the demise of writing as the main office activity.

During the first half of the twentieth century, further refinements of existing office technologies were undertaken and new ones introduced. Amongst these were the teletypewriter, automatic telephone switching, ticker tape, the electric typewriter, duplicating machines and copiers, adding machines and calculators, even small off-set printing presses and data-processing equipment operated by punch paper cards. All these *product* innovations were based upon mechanical operations first and foremost. But they also had implications for the *processes* of office 'production'. The 'pre-industrial office' existed, and indeed still exists, as one involving little systematic organization between its parts. Each person does his, or more often her, job more or less independently and each can maintain a different style of work – moving about between parts of the office as necessary. The 'industrial office' by contrast is more akin to the production line of a factory. Tasks are fragmented and standardized. Successive groups of clerks and typists carry out only incremental steps in the processing of documents or in the answering of specific inquiries.

These two office 'designs' are still the predominant ones in the 1980s. They have typified the period of the rapid growth of office work throughout this century. What we are witnessing now, however, is a series of product innovations no longer based upon mechanical operations but upon electronic ones, and this is again having a significant effect on the design or organization of the office. The 'information-age office' can use this new technology to some extent to preserve or even reintroduce the values of the 'pre-industrial' office, while at the same time handling large volumes of complex information. It can also 'disperse' the office into a number of different locations as microelectronic equipment becomes smaller, lighter, portable and cheaper, and as integrated systems of information and easy access data banks develop. The full consequences of these developments are not altogether clear in terms of the number and forms of jobs, but it is now becoming cheaper to communicate electronically than on paper, so paper as the main 'raw material' in the office may soon disappear or be severely diminished. At least an intra-sectoral shift of employment opportunities is happening within the office. Telephone operators, stenographers and key punch operators declined in numbers between 1972 and 1980 in the USA, numbers of typists were more or less constant, but secretaries and particularly computer and peripheral equipment operators significantly increased in number (the latter by 170 per cent – Guiliano, 1982, p. 129).

The general issue posed by this somewhat rapid survey of the prospects for the microelectronic technologies in various production environments, and the practical experience of their use, is whether they will have the effect of reducing employment either within a particular sector or with respect to the economy overall. We have already seen in sections 2 and 3 the complexity of analysing the potential interdependencies set up in an economy by technological change. This raises once again the appropriate framework for conducting such an analysis, and understanding the empirical tendencies just outlined in the previous section.

5. Some more Dynamic Problems

5.1. A question of time

In the formal analysis of sections 2 and 3 both 'static' and 'dynamic' elements were involved. The main body of the analysis was couched in a comparative static framework, involving tendencies towards equilibrium, while the discussion of possible adjustments to the emerging situation (retraining, changes in relative prices) slipped into a more dynamic framework. As was pointed out in the context of that analysis 'wage ridgidity' was one of the elements that might lead to a higher 'technological unemployment', and for a longer period of time, than under a fully price flexible system. A flexible economy could thus compensate for the immediate detrimental employment effects of innovations, at least after some period of time. Hence, one of the reasons for a continuation of technological unemployment may be the non-instantaneous adjustment of prices, and particularly the rigidity of wages. This produces disequilibrium in the labour market, though as we shall see below this need not be the only cause of a disequilibrium under conditions of rapid technological change. Thus we may be able to isolate something called 'technological unemployment', but this is only pertinent over a certain period of time. As far as the analysis conducted around the simple neo-classical assumptions of figure 5.1 was concerned the definition of technological unemployment arising there could be 'that unemployment resulting from a fall in demand for labour due to a shift in the production function brought about by the introduction of some new technology'. But this leaves out of account the two main possible adjustment mechanisms discussed subsequently, i.e. that demand may be stimulated in some way, or supply-side retraining adjustments initiated. These raise the time scale over which the analysis is to be conducted.

To put this into a slightly more formal framework we can set up a (linear) labour market clearing model as follows:

$$1 \qquad Q^D = \alpha_1 D - \alpha_2 w$$
$$2 \qquad Q^S = \beta_1 S - \beta_2 w$$
$$3 \qquad Q^D \rightleftharpoons Q^S$$

where Q is the quantity of labour in the occupation or sector, w the relative wage rate, D and S are vectors denoting shifts in demand and supply curves, and α, β are the respective demand and supply parameters. Equation 1 is the demand for labour, equation 2 the supply of labour, and equation 3 the condition integrating supply and demand.

Given this formulation, structural change enters the system via sustained shift in either the demand or supply schedules. When this happens the usual assumption is to view adjustments taking place via changes in relative wages which thereby clear the market. This is equivalent to equation 3 holding as an equality, and a fourth and often less openly acknowledged equation being added to express the mechanism of 'supply and demand adjustment'.

$$4 \qquad \frac{d_w}{dt} b(Q^D - Q^S); \ b' < 0, \ b(0) = 0$$

Equations 1 to 4 with an equality in 3 comprise the conventional market model. However, if the market does not clear through relative wage adjustment in the period over which the variables are measured, the model should be altered to reflect disequilibrium phenomena. A limiting if perhaps unrealist case of disequilibrium would be where relative wages are absolutely rigid. This would mean making equation 3 an inequality and putting $b' = 0$ in 4, and dropping the condition $b(0) = 0$. In this strong disequilibrium case, labour market adjustment would take the form of quantity adjustments as reflected in relative excess demand or supply $(Q^D - Q^S)$. Thus while in the conventional price adjustment case, structural change leads to changing relative wages in order to re-allocate employment, in the disequilibrium case, relative quantity adjustments will take place and be reflected in changing shortages and surpluses of labour (Withers and Freebain, 1983, p. 114).

5.2. Long waves

In the case just analysed disequilibrium holds, but the system is not truly dynamic. It is in the context of the *extent* and *depth* of economic disruption caused by a wave of technological innovations that a more dynamic *and* disequilibrium approach has been developed. Could the disruption be so extensive as to produce a lengthy period of structural disequilibrium in an economy and thereby undermine the significance of other forms of unemployment? This is the kind of claim those supporting the idea of technologically induced 'long waves' have made. These long waves theories give a central importance to technological change either in inducing an investment-led recovery from the bottom of the depression or in stimulating a recession by introducing process innovations which displace labour and upset established demand patterns.

It will be useful to chart the course of such long waves to see exactly how technological change is thought to fit into the overall pattern and to allow us to explore some of its implications.

Let us begin with an upswing. During this period conditions are conducive to preliminary scientific and technical work; R and D expenditures are likely to be high given the buoyant nature of demand, fundamental research will be well funded during expansionary phases, and so on. The major new technologies generated will stimulate both new investment and new employment on a large scale in anticipation of cost savings and higher profit. Thus substantial new branches of economic activity are formed. As a result of this rapid technological change and increasing competition, relative prices of new goods fall and their cost advantage increases. The main employment effect during this upswing is thus likely to be a steep increase in employment. There will also probably be shortages of specific types of labour which will create an upward pressure on wages and ultimately induce labour-saving innovations.

But, it is suggested, after perhaps two or three decades when the new branches of industry have been firmly established, their role as generators of additional new employment diminishes and may eventually disappear. This could be because of a slow down in new investment as the limits on the expansion of demand appear. Such a loss of impetus for the growth of employment in the new industries is reinforced by the acceleration of labour-displacing technological changes, and economies of scale which arise from the success of the new technology itself. Thus during the downswing so induced, competitive pressures within the industry may become stronger, capital intensity grows and investment continues, but labour-saving and material-saving technological changes become increasingly important.

The question that has exercised long-wave theorists a good deal, and which has caused the greatest dispute amongst them, focuses on the way the depression 'bottoms out' and how the upswing is begun. Probably the most influential approach is that first advanced by Schumpeter and later extended by Mensch. Schumpeter considered the irregular clustering of innovations to be crucial for development. He suggested that these innovations 'bunch' in cycles. This leads to a competitive struggle to gain advantage through the early adoption of a new innovation in terms of products and processes. Thus the most important firms for him were those that served as the vehicles for action, and the real engines of the system were the innovating entrepreneurs that organized these firms.

Crucial to this process is the way innovations are thought to 'swarm' or 'bunch' intensively during particular, relatively short periods. Such an *innovation* cycle may well happen some time after the main and fundamental research has been completed and *inventions* established. It is the putting of these inventions into a relationship with each other by establishing product and process innovations associated with them, and the further insertion of these into a competitive economic structure where spillovers and interdependencies abound, that is crucial to launching the upward cycle referred to above.

Mensch subsequently stressed the role of *basic innovations* which created the new leading sectors. These only occur under pressure of demand saturation of the existing leading sectors when entrepreneurs are looking for new and profitable investment opportunities. Once entrepreneurs invest in these new risky sectors, turbulent technological development begins in the same direction which results in *improvement innovations* of products and production processes. It is pointed out that microelectronics is one of these *innovation-packed* sectors that has been growing during the depression of the late 1970s and early 1980s and which has wide dispersal possibilities through other sectors (e.g. Freeman *et al.*, 1982 and Freeman, 1983).

5.3. *Structural disequilibrium*

What this approach stresses is the *structural re-organization* of the economy during the successive cycles, as new leading sectors come into existence and then subsequently decline in importance. The (competitive) environment within which firms operate is one of struggle and motion. It is a dynamic environment, rather than an equilibrating one. The essential forces of growth are innovation and selection with the augmentation of capital stocks more or less tied to these processes. While firms (and entrepreneurs) may seek profit and may innovate or imitate to achieve higher profits, there is no emphasis on careful calculation over well-defined choices (i.e. maximization subject to constraints to produce an optimum). This has led a number of commentators to see the kind of process discussed above as falling well outside the strict theoretical purview of either Keynesianism or neoclassical analysis (Nelson and Winter, 1974).

To try and make these issues clearer let us return to figure 5.2. The analysis began there at a 'full-employment' equilibrium (point A) and eventually reached another full-employment equilibrium position (point E).

Only if there were a continual series of technical improvements (or other shifts in economic variables) that continually 'upset' these adjustment mechanisms would the tendency towards equilibrium be of necessity continually disrupted. It is this latter kind of process that could be characterized as describing a sectoral or structural *disequilibrium*. In the case discussed in section 5.2, this is largely the effect of technological innovations which disrupt labour markets in particular, as well as engendering rather wider obstacles to any equilibrating tendencies. If pursued, this kind of argument could be used to suggest that far from simply reproducing a tendency towards a *shifting equilibrium*, this process makes those very tendencies themselves conceptually problematical and the notion of an equilibrium itself suspect. (There seems to be no particular reason why the term 'equilibrium' should be given any privileged theoretical status.)

These arguments have been stressed by those supporting the idea of structural or technological unemployment. An economic system in which innovation and competition co-exist will have sectoral disequilibrium built into its very structure, it is argued. At times of innovation it is technological change above all else which is responsible for unemployment in some declining sectors and the lack of employment opportunities in others (though other compensating economic factors may be working themselves out as stressed above in section 5.2).

Now, it is not necessary to support *all* of the arguments associated with long cycles (their supposed 50-year length for instance) and the central role attributed to 'technological developments' in generating the cycle, to see the pertinence of some of the disequilibrium ideas that have been drawn from the theory. Clearly capitalist economies are subject to fluctuation, though not necessarily on a rigid fifty-year basis which is itself dependent upon the clustering of technological innovations. But the latest round of technological developments could be of some importance in the context of unemployment, and arguably is having an impact on restructuring the sectoral composition of employment during the present recession. The general point here, however, is to stress the possible importance of an approach which highlights the structural disequilibrium in the economy under present conditions. If this is accepted, then strictly speaking an analysis conducted in the context of the 'partial equilibrium' approach of figures 5.1 and 5.2 may miss important elements of the actual processes involved. A more overtly 'dynamic' theory is called for.

The implication of these remarks is to see 'technical unemployment', in the terms analysed above, as a sub-category of a rather larger set of determinants of unemployment which can be termed 'structural' (Standing, 1983). Such structural unemployment has been generally defined as resulting from a *qualitative* mismatch between the demand for labour and the supply of suitable workers. This emphasizes the *non-quantitative* aspects of any mismatch: the available labour is deemed unsuitable. Within this broad definition a number of forms of structural unemployment have been identified: that which is skill-dependent; that resulting from immobility of labour between different regions; that dependent upon various demographic characteristics of the labour force, e.g. gender, age or racial categories which serve to structure particular types of people into particular types of jobs; and even that which is sectorally specific and 'wage rigid' to particular industries or parts of the economic structure. In this context 'technological unemployment' could be added as another such structural division associated with the introduction of technological innovations into particular productive sectors, altering the demand for labour in those sectors.

A crucial feature of the existence of these structural divisions within the economy (but not the only one) is the relative rigidity of the wage rates that operate in relation to them. Wages are not seen to be perfectly flexible between sectors – indeed for the purpose of the analyses it is these inflexibilities of wages that serve to demarcate the boundaries of the 'structure' itself. The structure of the economy is partly determined by the fact of rigid wages existing between different sectors. Movement of labour between sectors of the economy is then fairly inflexible, and not dictated by relative wage rate changes caused by the interaction of the demand and supply of labour. Adjustments are 'quantity' adjustments in the first instance which, because of wage rigidities, are not flexibly determined by the wage movements that typify the differences between sectors, as more conventional theory would have it. In fact this relative wage rigidity in the economy itself presents 'obstacles' to the movement of labour between sectors or occupations and this leads to a slow adjustment of labour to new requirements. This is the very mechanism which thereby establishes just that 'structural unemployment' (this was found to be the case by Withers and Freebain (1983) with Australian data for instance). Structural unemployment could thus simply be defined as 'that which is concentrated in particular sectors of the economy', and could in principle be the result of a wide variety of causes. It could include those mentioned above and additionally things like shifts in consumer demand, or the introduction of competitive imports and so on. (Note that the use of the term 'structural unemployment' in this chapter is somewhat different from its use in chapter 2 where structural unemployment comprises part of the 'natural rate of unemployment'. Such a 'natural rate' conception is not involved in this chapter analysis.)

6.   Technological Unemployment at an Aggregate Level

One important remaining problem is to consider the empirical evidence with respect to the employment consequences associated with structural shifts between sectors in the economy. Of major concern here is whether the growth of service sector jobs, broadly conceived, can compensate for the decline in manufacturing jobs as a result of the introduction of widespread microelectronic mechanization and other labour-displacing technologies. This concerns interdependencies both within sectors (intra-sectoral shifts in employment) and between sectors (inter-sectoral shifts in employment), as well as income and output effects. In this context we have an opportunity to explore the possible net impact of labour-saving, labour-using, labour-employing and labour-displacing innovations affecting the contemporary economy.

A further issue is the capacity of the service sectors to absorb displaced labour in the traditional manner, given it too is increasingly being affected by the new microtechnology. But like the manufacturing sector the service sector is not homogeneous. While word processors in the office can, it is claimed, increase productivity by 100 per cent over the conventional typewriter (CPRS, 1978, p. 768), it is questionable whether new technology will have more than a marginal impact on the productivity of health or social service manual workers, for instance. Generally it seems that office, printing, financial and insurance services are likely to feel the impact of new information-based technology more forcefully than the health, social service and educational occupations.

What is needed, then, is some way of netting out these possible impacts on different sectors. An intermediate form of this 'economy-wide impact' approach is illustrated by the use of input–output models. These models first simulate the structure of any economy in terms of a matrix of physical inputs and outputs linking the various sectors and industries in an economy. Technical change appears in this model when the same range of consumption goods are produced with different arrays of inputs, some of which will be new inputs embodying the new technology. Apart from the greater differentiation of physical inputs, the other advantage of this approach over simple neo-classical models is the explicit focus on employment multipliers. This means that, at each stage of production, employment before and after the technical change is calculated but any labour 'displaced' by innovations is offset against the labour 'used' to produce those innovations, and so on down the line of the interdetermined production process. In general a decrease in the employment multipliers leads to an increase in unemployment.

Problems abound in the calculation of these multipliers, particularly when new products are being introduced into the output arrays, but a large-scale study using this technique was undertaken in the early 1980s for the Austrian economy (Leontief, 1982). This constructed an inter-industry model for the economy using 1976 production and price data. It included service industries as well as manufacturing industries in order to cover comprehensively the interdependencies within the economy. Such an input – output model was then used to predict the *net* impact on jobs of the introduction of the 'new technology' into all the sectors of the economy. The results of this exercise are shown in table 5.3 under a number of different assumptions for the year 1990. Three different states of technology

Table 5.3. Effects of technological developments on the Austrian economy

	1976 (actual)	Unchanged work week		Shorter work week		
		No mech.	Full mech.	No mech.	Partial mech.	Full mech.
Average working week (hours)	42.1	39.6	39.6	35.3	35.3	35.3
Unemployment (1000 persons)	55	220	386	29	165	76
Employment (1000 persons)	3,222	3,221	3,056	3,413	3,277	3,366
Percentage unemployment	1.7	6.8	12.6	0.1	5.0	2.2

Source: Adapted from Leontief, 1982, p. 164.

change are assumed (termed 'mechanization' in the table columns): no mechanization, partial mechanization, and full mechanization. In addition some assumptions about the average length of the working week were made, as shown in the top row of the table. The bottom row shows the percentage unemployment estimated to result in 1990 as compared to the actual 1976 level. The importance of the change in the hours of the working week is clear. At an unchanged working week - with full mechanization, unemployment is forecast to be 12.6 per cent as compared to 1.7 per cent in 1976. With a shorter working week (35.3 hours) and full mechanization, this percentage unemployment drops to 2.2, per cent very close to the 1976 level. Thus the introduction of 'new technology', on the basis of this analysis, need have little impact on overall unemployment if there are compensating reductions in the hours worked. The reason why 'partial mechanization' leads to worse results than 'full mechanization' is that it relies heavily on imported equipment, which does not create as many domestic jobs.

A similar comprehensive analysis to this, which shares some of its features but which relies upon a different modelling technique, was employed by Whitley and Wilson (1982) to look at the UK economy. The input–output technique used by Leontief in the Austrian example compares the total requirements of primary and intermediate inputs for the generation of a given output, first with one set of technologies and then another. A criticism of this is that the technique does not generally take into account the demand impact of the new technology itself. Whitley and Wilson augmented the input - output approach to include this. They employed a large multisectoral macroeconomic model of the UK economy ('The Cambridge growth model') which has equations explaining consumption, employment, exports, imports, prices, investment and wages as well as an input–output sector which determines intermediate demand. There are 49 employing activities in this model and each element of demand is considered to be a function of prices, incomes, tastes and technological changes. Labour supply is assumed to be exogenous, but labour demand is determined by output and technology. In the presence of any disequilibrium in the labour market, the wage rate change, which has feedback effects on prices. But the labour market is not infinitely and immediately flexible in the model, so unemployment can exist (Stoneham, 1983, p. 192). Whitley and Wilson used this model to simulate what the effect might be of an accelerated change in technological innovation after 1985, on UK employment prospects to 1990. The benchmark for these simulations was the assumption that within such a change the UK would continue to become less competitive relative to its competitors (in both price and non-price terms) at the same rate as experienced during the 1960s and 1970s. As a result the simulations carried out did *not* represent forecasts of the likely developments in the UK economy as a result of the advent of microelectronic technology; rather they provided a vehicle for considering some neglected, but nevertheless important, *compensatory effects* on employment that might offset the initial displacement effects.

Table 5.4.   Accelerated pace of technological change in the UK: impact compared to the benchmark simulation

	Initial direct displacement effect[b] (1)	Price and cost compensation effects (2)	Domestic demand compensation effects[c] (3)	Non-price effects on trade (4)	Overall effect (5)
Employment (thousands)					
Mechanical engineering	− 34	19	15	19	19
Instrument engineering	− 6	3	1	1	− 1
Electrical engineering	− 31	13	6	10	− 2
Textile fibres	− 1	—	—	1	—
Textile nes[a]	− 23	7	1	8	− 7
Leather, clothing etc	− 13	7	2	3	− 1
Paper and board	− 2	1	—	1	—
Printing and publishing	− 23	12	4	3	− 4
Rubber	− 4	2	—	1	− 1
Manufactures nes[a]	− 10	4	1	4	− 1
Communication	− 37	14	10	6	− 7
Distribution	− 94	50	26	8	− 10
Insurance etc	− 46	11	7	6	− 22
Professional services	− 16	3	2	1	− 12
All industries nes[a]	—	29	67	34	130
Whole economy	− 342	175	142	106	81

[a] nes = not elsewhere specified.
[b] The effect of decreasing the required labour input per unit of output ratio with all else constant.
[c] Primarily increases in investment.
Source: Whitley and Wilson, 1982, adapted from table 2, p. 491.

Table 5.4 shows the results of these simulations for 1990 compared to the benchmark view, as outlined above. The initial labour displacement occasioned by the faster take-up of the new technology is offset by increases in demand resulting from cost and price reductions and beneficial labour productivity changes. There is then a second round of compensations due to changes in investment, changes in intermediate demand and improved trade performance from improved non-price competitiveness. These amount to the 'real income' effects' discussed in section 2.

The first column shows the level of the direct displacement effects for a number of industries implied by productivity increases resulting from the introduction for the 'new technology'. The second column shows the compensating effects arising from reduced prices and costs for product lines already being produced – it is assumed there is some increase in demand as costs fall because of the more efficient new technology, these effects being based upon various behavioural relationships estimated on historical data embodied in the macro-model. The domestic demand compensation effects in column 3 are mainly due to the higher level of investment demand required to embody the new technology. In addition it includes *new product demand* and the changing structure of intermediate demand. Finally the effect of improve non-price competitiveness on foreign trade is given in column 4. The overall impact is specified in column 5.

While the initial direct displacement effect was in the order of 340,000 lost jobs over the period, it can be seen that the overall effect on employment is some 80,000 jobs higher in 1990. Thus the compensating effects more than offset the direct displacement effect of the technological changes.

The above results were calculated on the basis of a fixed exchange rate but the authors argued that even if the exchange rates were allowed to be flexible, and responded to some of the current account implications of the overall results (a worsening by over £4.5bn), there would be no appreciable change in their results (Whitley and Wilson, 1982, pp. 492–3).

7. Conclusions

The chapter has been less concerned with accounting for the rise in unemployment in the late 1970s to early 1980s period than were chapters 3 and 4. Rather it has concentrated on whether a specific form of unemployment can be isolated that appears a consequence solely of technological change. It has attempted both to provide a definition of 'technological unemployment' and to assess some of its empirical manifestations. In so doing we have seen how different ideas about the relationship between technical change and unemployment depend, at least in part, on the conception of production that underlies economic analysis, and on the dynamic trajectories thought to characterize capitalist economies.

Technological unemployment is perhaps best analysed as a variant of the more general form of unemployment termed 'structural unemployment'. This involves a qualitative mismatch between the demand for labour and the supply of suitable workers with the attributes or features required of that demand. If we characterize the long run as a situation involving a continual dynamic process of readjustment or structural disequilibrium in which unemployment appears as a necessary feature of the technological advance and innovations so introduced within this process, simple quantitative adjustments organized via changes in the relative price of labour need not provide suitable adjustment mechanisms even in the short run to eliminate 'technological unemployment'.

References

Barron, I. and Curnow, R. (1981) *The Future with Micro-electronics: forecasting the effects of information technology*. Frances Pinter, London.

Canuto, E., Menga, G. and Bruno, G. (1983) 'Analysis of flexible manufacturing systems'. In Wilson, B. *et al.* (eds) *Efficiency of Manufacturing Systems*. Plenum Press, New York.

Central Policy Review Staff (1978) *Social and Employment Implications of Micro-electronics*. Cabinet Office, London.

Cooper, C. M. and Clark, J. A. (1982) *Employment, Economics and Technology*. Wheatsheaf Books, Sussex.

Derry, T. K. and Williams, T. I. (1970) *A Short History of Technology from the Earliest Times to AD 1900*. Oxford University Press, London.

Diebold, J. (1952) *Automation: the advent of the automatic factory*, Van Nostrand, New York.

Freeman, C. (ed.) (1983) *Longwaves*. Frances Pinter, London.

Freeman, C., Clark, J. and Soete, L. (1982) *Unemployment and Technical Innovation*, Frances Pinter, London.

Guiliano, V. E. (1982) 'The mechanization of office work', *Scientific American*, 247(3), 125-34.

Hussain, A. (1983) 'Theoretial approaches to the effects of technical change on unemployment'. In Bosworth, D. L. (ed.) *The Employment Consequences of Technological Change*. Macmillan, London.

Jenkins, C. and Sherman, B. (1979) *The Collapse of Work*. Eyre Methuen, London.

Jones, D. (1983) 'Technological change, demand and employment'. In Bosworth, D. L. (ed.) *The Employment Consequences of Technological Change*. Macmillan, London.

Leontief, W. W. (1982) 'The distribution of work and income', *Scientific American*, 247(3), 152-64.

Nelson, D. D. and Winter, S. G. (1974) 'Neoclassical *v.* evolutionary theories of growth', *Economic Journal*, 84, 886-905.

Rempp, H. (1982) 'The economic and social effects on the introduction of CNC machine tools and flexible manufacturing systems'. In Bekemans, L. (ed.) *European Employment and Technological Change*. European Centre for Work and Society, Masstricht.

Standing, G. (1983) 'The notion of structural unemployment', *International Labour Review*, 122(2), 137-53.

Stoneham, P. (1983) *The Economic Impact of Technological Change*. Oxford University Press, London.

Whitley, J. D. and Wilson, R. A. (1982) 'Quantifying the employment effects of micro-electronics'. *Futures*, December, pp. 486-95.

Withers, G. and Freebain, L. (1983) 'Structural change and labour market adjustment'. In Weisbrod, B. and Hughes, H. (eds) *Human Resources, Employment and Development*, vol. 3. Macmillan, London, for the International Economics Association.

6

Inflation and unemployment

ROSALIND LEVAČIĆ

1. Introduction

Inflation and unemployment have become twin problems for macroeconomic policy as, in the course of the 1970s, increasing difficulty was experienced in western economies in combining a relatively stable general price level with a reasonably low level of unemployment. In each post-war decade the average rate of inflation rose, until the 1980s when governments made greater efforts to bring down the rate of inflation. As noted in chapter 3 (see table 3.1) unemployment has also been on a rising trend, and has remained high in a number of major economies, excluding the USA and Japan, despite the recovery in real national output since the 1980/1 recession. The behaviour of inflation and unemployment in the UK since the early 1950s is shown in figure 6.1 and related to the stages of the trade cycle dated by peaks (P) and troughs (T).

The experience of rising and high inflation during the 1970s, together with the failure of traditional demand management techniques to produce a sustained reduction in unemployment, led to a reorientation of macroeconomic policy in Britain and elsewhere. Chapter 2 discussed the shift from Keynesian demand management policies to monetarist and supply-side policies. The purpose of this chapter is to re-examine the theoretical foundations of the contrasting macroeconomic policy scenarios currently advocated by the major political parties. The different perspectives on how the economy works, and the related policy conclusions, are explained using the variants of the AD/AS model set out in chapter 2. In addition, a dynamic extension of the AD/AS model – the Phillips relation – is developed in order to investigate the extent to which there is a trade-off between inflation and unemployment. This question is of great importance for policy, because reducing inflation and unemployment are both regarded as policy objectives. As discussed in chapter 1, knowledge of the nature of the trade-off between inflation and unemployment is crucial in formulating macroeconomic policy. If inflation and unemployment are inversely related so that there is a permanent trade-off between them, then it is possible to have lower unemployment but at the cost of higher inflation. This used to be the consensus view in the 1950s

161

per cent

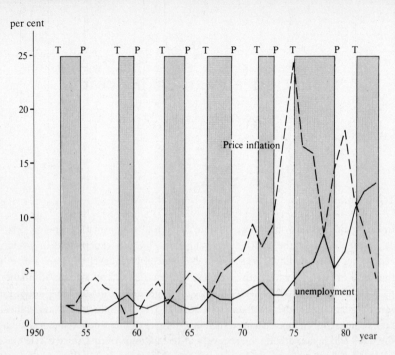

Figure 6.1. Cycles in inflation and unemployment, UK, 1953–85. *Source:* data from *Economic Trends* and Dow, 1964.

and 1960s. But in the 1960s monetarists began to argue that the trade-off between inflation and unemployment is only temporary: in the long run it does not exist. So, if the government tries to reduce unemployment by raising aggregate demand, the long-run effect will be higher inflation but no decrease in unemployment. These ideas came to be very influential in policy-making in the late 1970s and early 1980s. Yet another argument, put by radical Keynesian critics of monetarism, is that inflation and unemployment are totally unrelated, even in the short run. Consequently the government can reduce unemployment permanently by raising aggregate demand.

The issue of whether or not there is any trade-off between inflation and unemployment is part-and-parcel of the great puzzle of macroeconomics, which has preoccupied economists for generations. The puzzle is this: 'What determines how much of a change in *nominal* output is due to a change in *real* output and how much due to a change in *prices*?' Given that a change in the nominal money supply changes nominal output, does all the effect come through on the price level only, or does some of the effect appear as a stimulus to real output? If real output is so affected, how long do these real effects persist? Or is it the case, as argued by the Cambridge Keynesians, that the relationship is the other way round? Is the dominant causal link that from changes in economic activity and in the price level to changes in the money supply?

Using the AD/AS model to analyse changes in real output and the price level, helps in understanding ideas about the relationship between inflation and unemployment because unemployment is presumed to vary inversely with real output, while inflation is a continuously rising price level. The AD/AS model identifies three possible permutations of price level and real income changes which make up the increase in nominal income brought about by an increase in aggregate demand. These three cases are shown in figure 6.2.

(a) Vertical aggregate supply function: all the nominal output increase is due to an increase in the price level.
(b) Upward-sloping aggregate supply schedule: nominal output increase is made up of both an increase in the price level and in real output.
(c) Inverted L-shape aggregate supply function: all of the nominal output increase is due to an increase in real output.

Because the AD/AS model, as developed here using graphs, is static, it analyses changes in the price level rather than in the rate of inflation. However its dynamic implications are readily drawn: a continually upward shifting AD schedule will give rise to inflation in cases (a) and (b), whereas an upward-shifting horizontal portion to the AS schedule will produce inflation in case (c). Cases (a) and (c) depict contrasting theories of inflation. The former illustrates the monetarist theory that inflation is due to excessive growth in the money supply pushing up AD: the latter illustrates the radical Keynesian theory that inflation is due to social forces pushing up nominal wages independently of the state of demand. In the intermediate case (b) inflation due to increased nominal aggregate demand gives rise to some increase in real output and hence some reduction in unemployment. This view of how the economy works underlies the proposition that there is a trade-off between inflation and unemployment.

The taxonomy set out in figure 6.2 forms the structure for this chapter. Section 2 outlines monetarist and radical Keynesian theories of inflation: section 3 examines the nature of the trade-off between inflation and unemployment. Is the trade-off permanent, as mainstream Keynesians still believe to some extent, or is it only temporary, as monetarists have argued? Or does it not exist at all? This is argued by both new classical macroeconomists and radical Keynesians, but for different reasons.

2.   Theories of Inflation

I will start with the oldest approach to inflation derived from the quantity theory of money: it underlies cases (a) in figure 6.2

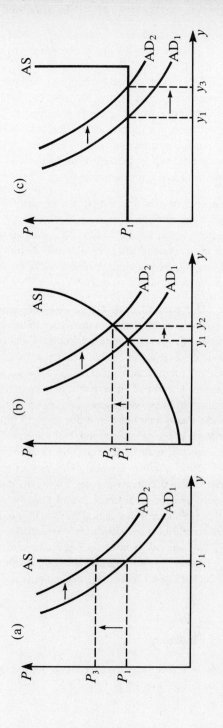

Figure 6.2. The effect on the price level and real output of an increase in aggregate demand

2.1. *The quantity theory of money*

The simplest way to introduce the link between money and the price level is to consider an economy in which real national output cannot be increased in the short run as no more capital and labour are forthcoming. Since nominal output (Y) is real output (y) times the price level (P) then, given the assumption of a fixed real output, nominal output can only change if the price level changes. The quantity of money circulating in the economy in relation to the value of nominal output is called the velocity of circulation of money, V. The velocity of circulation is the nominal value of output, Y, divided by the stock of money, M^S. Hence, by definition, we have the identity

$$1 \qquad\qquad V \equiv \frac{y \cdot P}{M^S} \equiv \frac{Y}{M^S}$$

Equation 1 states that the lower the quantity of money in circulation relative to the value of nominal output, the higher is the velocity. Velocity can be thought of as the number of times the stock of money in the economy turns over in a given period, such as a year. If nominal output rises in value but the stock of money stays the same, then money must be changing hands (or bank accounts) more quickly than before, i.e. the stock of money is turning over more often: hence velocity has risen.

If we multiply the elements of equation 1 by M^S we get

$$2 \qquad\qquad V \cdot M^S \equiv y \cdot P \equiv Y$$

This is the famous quantity theory equation, and states that nominal national output is identical to velocity times the stock of money.

As it stands, equation 2 is an identity because it is derived from the definition of velocity. It can only become a *theory* of price level determination if further assumptions are made about the behaviour of some of the variables involved. One assumption is that real output is fixed. The second is that velocity is constant. Given these assumptions, then it follows from equation 2 that any change in the money supply (whether an increase or a decrease) must lead to a proportionate change in the price level in the same direction. A doubling of the money supply leads to a doubling of the price level.

But so far, the explanation of the link between changes in the money supply and changes in the price level does not say how this change in the price level comes about. All one knows is that it must occur in order to preserve the identity expressed in equation 2. What we need to specify is a *transmission mechanism* whereby an increase (or decrease) in the stock of money brings about a new equilibrium price level. In order to specify such a transmission mechanism we need to bring in the concept of the *demand for money* introduced in chapter 2. For the moment let us assume that money is held only as a medium of exchange for financing transactions and that this demand depends positively on the nominal value of national output. The higher nominal national output is, the more nominal money balances people wish to hold. So the demand for money function can be written as

3 $$M^D = z(y \cdot P)$$

The coefficient z has a positive value of less than one, and indicates that the demand for money is some constant fraction, z, of nominal output. The money market will be in equilibrium if the total stock of money in the economy is willingly held, i.e. if the demand for money equals the supply of money, as expressed in equation 4.

4 $$M^D = M^S$$

If we now replace M^S in equation 2 – the quantity theory equation – by M^D, we get

5 $$M^D \cdot V = y \cdot P = Y$$

Dividing through by V gives

6 $$M^D = \frac{1}{V} \cdot y \cdot P \frac{Y}{V}$$

Comparing equation 6 with equation 3 we see that the coefficient z in the demand for money function is the same as the reciprocal of velocity ($1/V$), when the money market is in equilibrium. You can think of this relationship between the demand for money and velocity intuitively. The higher is z, the more money people want to hold in relation to the nominal value of national output. But if people are holding on to money for longer, then it is turning over more slowly, i.e. velocity is lower. Therefore a high z means a low V and vice-versa. Thus the demand for money is the inverse of the velocity of circulation of money.

The demand for money is the key to the transmission mechanism underlying the quantity theory's relationship between changes in the stock of money and resulting changes in the price level. Let's suppose we start off in a situation of monetary equilibrium. We know from equation 6 that

7 $$M_o^S = M_o^D = \frac{1}{V} \cdot y \cdot P_o$$

(The subscript o indicates the original equilibrium values.)

Now there is an exogenous increase in the money supply to, say, M_1^S. But the demand for money is initially still M_0^D so there is an excess supply of money in the economy. For monetary equilibrium to be restored, the demand for money must increase until it equals M_1^S. Given the assumptions that real output and velocity are constant, then this required increase in the demand for money can only come about if the price level increases. The reason that the price level increases is that people try to get rid of their excess money balances by spending them on goods and services. (In the AD/AS model, excess money balances are also spent on other financial assets, such as bonds and this lowers interest rates.) Thus an excess supply of money results in an increase in aggregate demand. If real national output cannot be increased then there is an excess demand for national output. This results in an increase in prices as firms find their customers willing to pay more. As the price level, and with it nominal output, rises, the demand for nominal balances (see equations 3 and 6) increases proportionately. The price level will stop rising when the demand for nominal money balances is once more equal to the supply of money. When the demand for and supply of money are once more in equilibrium, the source of excess demand in the goods market has also been removed, so the price level stops rising.

The quantity theory view of price level determination is illustrated in figure 6.2(a) in terms of the aggregate demand and supply model. The inclusion of a money market enables us to derive a downward-sloping aggregate demand schedule. Each schedule is drawn for a fixed *nominal* stock of money. But as the price level falls along a given AD schedule the value of *real* money balances, M/P, rises. Consequently aggregate demand increases. An increase in the nominal money supply shifts the AD schedule up to the right from AD_1 to AD_2. The price level rises from P_1 to P_2.

Since the price level depends on the stock of money, then inflation, which is a continuously rising price level, is explained in the quantity theory by the rate of growth of the money supply. What rate of growth of the money supply will cause inflation depends on what is happening to real output. If real output is growing over time, at say 3 per cent a year, then (given a constant z) the demand for nominal money balances is also growing at 3 per cent. Only if the money supply grows at more than 3 per cent a year will the price level be rising too. So in this theory, inflation is due to an 'excessive' rate of growth of the money supply, i.e. a rate of growth which is faster than the demand for money would be growing if there were no inflation.

2.2. *Keynesian critique of the quantity theory*

The version of the quantity theory I have just explained pre-dates Keynes and is known as the 'old' or 'classical' version of the quantity theory. It predicts a direct and proportionate relationship between the money supply and the price level, whereby prior changes in the money stock cause changes in the price level.

Keynesians have criticized this quantity theory prediction and have done so by questioning its assumptions: first, the fixity of real output. If real output is variable because firms have spare capacity then an increase in aggregate demand caused by an expansion in the money supply will result in more real output being produced. If the aggregate supply function is horizontal then *all* of the increased demand will be met by higher real output and there is no change in the price level. If the aggregate supply function is upward-sloping then the increased demand will be met partly by an increase in real output and partly by an increase in the price level. But in the latter case the price level will rise by *less* than the increase in the stock of money.

The second line of attack by Keynesians has been on the constancy of velocity assumption. Look again at equation 6. If velocity falls when the money supply increases (i.e. if z in equation 3 rises) then the demand for money will increase. In the most extreme Keynesian case, velocity would fall so much, because people are willing to hold on to all the extra money balances rather than spend them, that no excess aggregate demand would be created by expanding the money supply. No increase in nominal output would therefore occur. So the more velocity falls (i.e. the more z rises) following an expansion in the money supply, the smaller the consequent increase in nominal output (which, remember, in Keynesian analysis would, at less than full employment, be made up of some increase in real output).

It is an empirical fact that observed velocity, that is Y/M^s, is not constant. Over the past 15 years the velocity of £M3 has been quite variable. It fell from 3 in 1970 to 2.4 in 1974 and then peaked at 3.5 in 1980. Since then it has fallen back to 2.5. A change in velocity is the same as a change in the demand for money. (This was expanding in section 2.1 by showing that $z = 1/V$). An important factor causing z to change is the rate of interest. If the rate of interest falls, interest-bearing financial assets become less attractive to hold relative to money, so the demand for money rises. The inclusion of the interest rate as a determinant of the demand for money is equivalent in equation 3 to making z vary with the interest rate. Anything that causes z to rise means that more money is held relative to the value of nominal national income. So a fall in the interest rate causes z to rise and velocity to fall.

Rapid changes in the range of financial assets available and in the services offered by different kinds of financial institution are cited as the principal reason for the recent decline in £M3 velocity and its increased variability. If velocity is not constant, but falls when the money supply is increased because the rate of interest is thereby reduced, then there is not a fixed proportional relationship between changes in the money supply and changes in the price level. Early Keynesians rejected the quantity theory on the grounds that the dependency of the demand for money on interest rates made velocity unstable.

2.3. Modern quantity theorists

The basic message of the classical quantity theory, that price level changes are due to money supply changes, has in the post-war period been taken up by monetarist economists, of whom Milton Friedman is probably the best known. One of the central propositions of monetarism is that 'inflation over any substantial period is always and everywhere a monetary phenomenon, arising from a more rapid growth in the quantity of money than in output' (Friedman, 1980). Monetarists have responded to the Keynesian attack on the old quantity theory by accepting the empirical facts that velocity is not constant and real national output is not continuously at its long-run equilibrium value, and have restated the quantity theory in a modern form so as to take account of these facts. In his restatement of the quantity theory in 1956, Friedman argued that the causal link between exogenous changes in the money supply and subsequent changes in the price level does not require constant velocity: velocity can be varied as long as it behaves predictably, because it is a stable function of its determining variables. A central proposition of monetarism is that there is a *stable* demand for money function: the demand for money varies predictably with changes in its determinants, in particular income and interest rates.

The other aspect of the modern version of the quantity theory is that changes in the money supply are recognized to affect real output in the short run, though not in the long run. In the long run, according to monetarists, an 'excessive' rate of growth of the money supply will only be reflected in a higher price level. If changes in the money supply affect real national output in the short run but not in the long run, then increased aggregate demand can reduce unemployment in the short run but can have no effect on unemployment in the long run (i.e. there is a short-run trade-off between inflation and unemployment but no long-run trade-off). These ideas will be examined more closely in section 3. Thus the modern restatement of the quantity theory rescues the old quantity theory by adopting its propositions for the long run but not for the short run.

The proposition that increases in the stock of money can have *real* effects (i.e. on real national output) as well as monetary effects (on the price level) can be demonstrated with the AD/AS model, as in figure 6.3. Here the aggregate demand schedule slopes downwards and the aggregate supply schedule upwards. An increase in the nominal money stock shifts the aggregate demand schedule up from AD_1 to AD_2. Firms are only willing to supply additional real output in response to increased demand if prices rise. At the new equilibrium real output has increased from y_1 to y_2 while the price level has risen from P_1 to P_2. So the increase in nominal national income can be split up into a rise in prices and a rise in output.

When the aggregate demand schedule shifts up along an unchanged aggregate supply schedule, the price level rises but money wages are assumed to stay the same.

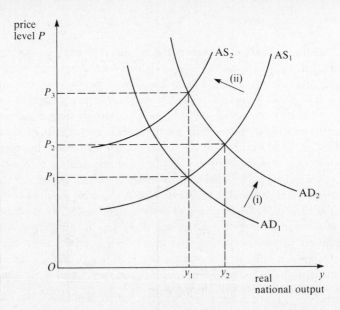

Figure 6.3. Inflation generated by money wages adjusting in response to increases in aggregate demand

Real wages therefore fall. Given the assumption underlying the upward-sloping aggregate supply schedule, which is that in the short run the marginal product of labour declines as output expands, the fall in real wages is needed in order to induce firms to respond to increased aggregate demand by increasing employment and real output as depicted in figure 6.3. But if workers react to the decline in real wages by demanding and getting higher money wages, then the aggregate supply schedule shifts up to the left as shown in figure 6.3. (Remember that the money wage rate is constant along any given aggregate supply schedule.) Given that money wages rise in response to the increase in the price level, so as to restore the original real wage level, then the new aggregate supply schedule AS_2 will intersect the new aggregate demand schedule AD_2 at the original level of output. Consequently, real national output declines to its initial level of y_1 and employment falls also.

If the government then responds to the rise in unemployment by expanding aggregate demand once more, the whole sequence is repeated. For this process to continue, thus generating inflation, monetary policy needs to be accommodating, so that the nominal quantity of money grows in line with the increased demand for nominal money balances generated by the rising price level. You should note that in this analysis the price level rises both when the real output expands from y_1 to y_2 and when it contracts from y_2 to y_1. In this story, money wages and hence the aggregate supply schedule rise in response to increases in nominal aggregate demand which are due to the government's monetary and fiscal policy.

2.4. Keynesian views on the role of nominal aggregate demand in causing inflation

Many economists would accept that changes in the money supply can and do cause inflation. What is disputed is the universality of the monetarist theory of inflation, expressed in the quotation from Friedman at the beginning of section 2.3. It is widely accepted that once real output has reached its upper limit, then increases in the supply of money must lead to rising prices. Keynesians, though, see not only money, but any factor which leads to an excess level of aggregate demand, as causing inflation. Hence increased government expenditure or reduced taxation would also shift the aggregate demand schedule up to the right and could generate inflation.

While the monetarists' emphasize on money as the prime cause of inflation is disputed, a necessary role for money in the inflationary process is now widely accepted. A consensus has emerged that increases in the price level brought about by non-monetary factors still have to be accommodated by a growing money supply. If nominal output rises because prices are increasing, then the demand for nominal money balances also grows, given that velocity is not infinitely flexible in the upwards direction. If this demand for money is not satisfied by commensurate increases in the money supply, then aggregate demand will be cut back as people build up their stock of real money balances. While monetarists see this process as restraining price increases, Keynesians consider that most of the impact will be on real output, which will decline. Hence they recommend an accommodating monetary policy which prevents real output from declining in response to shifts in aggregate demand or supply. Monetarists, however, disapprove of such accommodating monetary policy because it encourages inflation.

2.5. Summary on inflation due to increased aggregate demand

An increase in aggregate demand can be due to an increase in any of its components, but monetarists see growth in the money stock as the prime motivating force behind inflation. The monetarist theory of inflation is based upon two assumptions:

(1) A stable demand for money functions.
(2) Changes in the money supply are exogenous. To quote Friedman and Schwartz (1963): 'Monetary changes have often had an independent origin; they have not been simply a reflection of changes in economic activity.'

The monetarist transmission mechanism is that an exogenous increase in the money supply produces an excess supply of money. These excess money balances generate an increased demand for goods and services. Economic activity is stimulated for a while and the price level rises permanently. Continuously excessive growth in the money supply results in continuous inflation. However, monetarists do point out that money supply changes can only be exogenously determined in a closed economy or in an open economy within a flexible exchange rate system: the domestic money supply is endogenous for an open economy with a fixed exchange rate. If a country is on a fixed exchange rate, then a balance of payments surplus, resulting for example from a decline in aggregate demand, leads to an inflow of foreign exchange and hence to an expansion of the domestic money supply; conversely a balance of payments deficit brings about a contraction in the domestic money supply. So in the post-war period the UK could only have had an exogenous money supply since 1972 when sterling was floated. And even since then there has been some central bank intervention in the foreign exchange market. All this is explained more fully in chapter 8.

Overall, then, most economists accept that money does have a role to play in the inflation process: a growing money supply is necessary to enable inflation to continue, even if it is not the dominant causal factor.

2.6. *Inflation due to supply-side factors*

Up to now I have been outlining explanations of inflation which stress increases in nominal aggregate demand as the prime cause. The supply side of the economy may well be affected and the aggregate supply schedule may shift, but the adjustments occur in response to changes initiated on the demand side. Now I am going to consider supply-side changes which occur independently of changes in aggregate demand.

2.6.1. *Increased energy costs*

One example of a supply-side shock is sudden and large increases in the prices of primary commodities, as occurred with oil in 1973/4 and 1979/80. In chapter 3 these factors were analysed as causing a downward shift in the demand for labour schedule. A decrease in the quantity of raw materials used in production diminishes the marginal product of labour and so reduces the demand for labour. In terms of the AD/AS model, such a decline in labour productivity causes an upward shift (to the left) in the aggregate supply schedule. Because of the increased cost of energy, firms are only prepared to supply output at a higher price than before. Real output falls, and with it falls employment, while the price level rises.

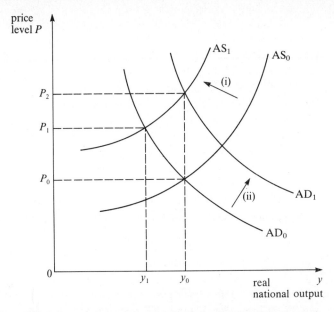

Figure 6.4. Inflation generated by a decrease in aggregate supply

2.6.2. *Trade unions and inflation*

Another important way in which the aggregate supply schedule could be shifted up to the left is by organized labour securing an increase in money wages which occurs *independently of the state of demand*. The independence between increased money wages and aggregate demand is an important condition. If money wages rise only in response to a prior increase in prices then this would be part of the inflation process set in motion by excess aggregate demand. For trade union action to be a cause of inflation, the effect of trade union power on money wage rates must, at least partly, be independent of the state of demand so that money wages rise more than they would under competitive market forces. The effect on the price level and real output of such an increase in money wages is also shown by figure 6.4. The aggregate supply schedule shifts up from AS_0 to AS_1, because the underlying supply of labour schedule has shifted in the same direction. Real wages rise and so real output falls from y_0 to y_1. The price level rises, but not by enough to offset the rise in the money wage, so that the real wage increases.

However, the upward shift in the aggregate supply schedule shown in figure 6.4 accounts for a once-and-for-all increase in the price-level. As in the earlier analysis of demand-side initiated inflation, a sequence of AS and AD shifts is required to generate inflation. For inflation to be set in motion by supply-side changes, there must be an aggregate demand response. Let's assume that the government reacts to the decline in real output caused by the upward shift in the aggregate supply schedule, by some combination of reflationary monetary and fiscal policy aimed at restoring output to its old equilibrium level of y_0. The aggregate demand schedule shifts up to AD_1, real output rises to y_0, and the price level to P_2. If trade unions then respond to the fall in real wages brought about by the rise in the price level, the AS schedule again shifts up to the left and the whole sequence is repeated. Thus a continually rising price level is observed.

For this inflationary process to continue, it is necessary for the money supply to expand in order to accommodate the higher nominal value of transactions. Given that velocity does not rise indefinitely, there would be an excess demand for money if the money supply were not increased. In order to build up their money balances people would spend less and this would ultimately stop the rise in prices. So, as I have already mentioned, many economists who reject the view that money supply growth is the main cause of inflation, still accept that growth in the money supply is required if inflation is to persist.

The view that inflation is generated primarily on the supply side of the economy is popular amongst British Keynesian and radical economists, particularly those at Cambridge. They consider that wages are set by collective bargaining and so determined by sociological and political factors, not by the forces of demand and supply (Cripps, 1977). In addition, Cambridge Keynesians argue that firms in modern capitalist economies operate in oligopolistic markets and therefore do not set prices in relation to the demand for their products. Rather prices are set as a fixed mark-up over average costs and so are known as 'administered' prices. If money wages rise, firms mark up product prices accordingly. Since firms are able to mark up prices in this way they do not put up much resistance to unions' wage claims.

The radical Keynesians consider that workers aspire to a certain target real wage which is determined by their previous experience of real wage growth. So if wages had been growing in the past at 3 per cent a year, in line with the underlying growth in labour productivity, and then productivity declined to 1 per cent a year, workers would continue to press for an annual 3 per cent rise in real wages. Another idea is that workers in one country wish to emulate living standards abroad. So workers in a country with a relatively poor economic performance will press for a real wage growth which is higher than the economy can deliver. The result is inflation.

In this view of the inflation process, trade unions bargain for a money wage which is expected to secure the aspiration real wage. The money wage target will therefore be set so as to compensate for any factors which have reduced, or threaten to reduce, real wages. Increased taxation will cause unions to demand higher money wages in order to protect the level of real take-home pay. Similarly, compensation will be sought for increased retail prices due to higher import prices. The higher the expected rate of inflation, the greater will be the increase in money wages needed to attain a given real wage target. The view that money wage increases depend on expected future inflation and that money wage levels will adjust upwards following a devaluation is also held by monetarists. The difference between monetarists and Keynesians here is that the latter stress the role of political and sociological factors in determining the aspiration real wage and that some Keynesians deny the state of aggregate demand has any influence on the aspiration real wage.

In the Cambridge Keynesian account of the inflationary process, money plays a purely passive role. As the price level rises, so does the demand for nominal money balances. The financial system always responds by supplying the amount of money which is needed as a medium of exchange to finance transactions and as a liquid store of wealth. So in this view the money supply is endogenous – it responds to prior movements in nominal national income – in contrast to the monetarist approach in which money supply changes are exogenous. If the money supply is endogenous, then the aggregate demand schedule shifts up automatically, without government action, in response to wage and price rises.

2.6.3. *Conflict theories of inflation*

Some radical economists have amended the sociological-cum-political view of wage inflation to depict it as the outcome of the conflict between workers and capitalists over the shares of wages and profit in national income. At the aggregate level this conflict is analysed in terms of the proportion of national expenditure which benefits workers.

Workers as a whole receive as gross wages the national income minus the share going to capitalists in the form of gross profits. (These include rent and interest payments.) Out of their gross wages workers have to pay the state direct and indirect taxes, but get from the state transfer payments, goods and services. The difference between workers' tax payments and the government expenditure received by them may be positive or negative. A further adjustment for the resources at workers' command in an open economy must be made for exports and imports of goods and services. Exports are unavailable for workers' consumption, but these are offset by imported consumer goods. Thus a deficit in the balance of trade enables workers to consume more than if the balance of trade were in surplus. Changes in the government budget position or in the balance of payments position worsen or ameliorate the basic conflict between capitalists and workers as to how national income should be apportioned between gross wages and gross profits. But the focus of the struggle remains that over wages and profits.

An example of a conflict model of inflation is Rowthorn's (1977), in which class conflict is the engine that drives the inflationary process, rather than the more diverse and complex patter of interest group conflict that pluralists emphasize. Rowthorn's theory of wage inflation is similar to that of the Cambridge Keynesians in that workers are assumed to have a target real wage. The difference between the real wage workers receive and that they desire is termed the aspiration gap. However, Rowthorn argues that the level of aggregate demand does influence the rate of wage and price inflation. The higher the level of demand, and the lower is unemployment, the greater the bargaining power of unions. As unemployment rises, so the power of firms to resist wage demands increases. Thus wage inflation depends negatively on unemployment via its effect on unions' bargaining power.

2.7.   *Theoretical approaches to inflation: an overview*

To summarize then, theories of inflation fall into two distinct categories – those emphasize the role of nominal aggregate demand, in particular excess monetary growth, and those stressing structural factors operating on the supply side of the economy. But these explanations of inflation are not necessarily mutually exclusive. Exogenous changes in the money supply can operate at the same time as supply-side pressures. In any country over a particular period one factor can be dominant, while elsewhere, or at different times, other causes predominate.

There is also a certain conjunction of views. Many Keynesians who regard supply-side factors, especially unions and oligopolistic firms, as the prime engine behind inflation also accept that these structural forces could not generate inflation without accommodating monetary and fiscal policies. Many British economists who are sympathetic to monetarist ideas, nevertheless see union power as a crucial factor pushing up wages in the UK institutional context. North American monetarists have paid much less attention to unions as the level of unionization there is considerably lower. However, unlike Keynesians – and in particular the radical variety – UK monetarists see union power as causing a higher natural rate of unemployment rather than inflation. Union wage pushfulness only causes inflation if the government responds by allowing the money supply, and hence nominal aggregate demand, to expand. This is the scenario depicted in figure 6.4. The moderate Keynesian wing also subscribes to this view and treats union power as a determinant of the natural rate of unemployment. (See the empirical work referred to in chapter 3.)

The radical Keynesian view that wage push causes inflation but not unemployment is based on specific assumptions about how the supply side of the economy works. The radical Keynesian assumptions are represented by the inverted L-shaped AS function. Structural forces within the economy, such as union power or worker aspirations and militancy, push the horizontal portion of the AS function upwards over time, as depicted in figure 6.5. If the AD schedule is vertical, because the real quantity of money has no impact on aggregate demand, then real output remains unaffected by wage pushfulness. However, if the AD curve slopes downwards, because aggregate demand falls as a rising price level reduces the real value of the money supply, then wage push reduces real national output. This is because the higher price level causes deficient aggregate demand, not because the real wage has been pushed over its market clearing level. Given this, it is recommended that

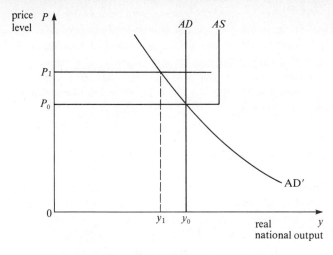

Figure 6.5.   The radical Keynesian view of inflation

the government accommodate wage push by expanding the money supply, since it is held that unemployment has no impact on the rate of growth of money wages. If the money supply is completely endogenous then it will expand in response to rising prices, and so the AD function will shift up to the right without any action on the part of the government.

Thus the characterization of modern Keynesians as emphasizing the role of supply-side factors in generating inflation in no way contradicts their emphasis on aggregate demand in determining the level of economic activity, employment and real output. Although Keynesian and monetarist theories of *inflation* can be distinguished in terms of an emphasis on supply-side factors by Keynesians and on demand-side factors, particularly the money supply, by monetarists, both sets of explanations encompass shifts in the aggregate demand *and* supply schedules.

Section 2 has concentrated on monetarist and Keynesian theories of inflation and used the AD/AS model to show how different assumptions about how the economy works lead to different theories regarding the causes of inflation. Section 3 extends the analysis by examining the interrelationship between inflation and unemployment in the context of the question of whether or not there is a trade-off between these two variables.

3.   Unemployment and inflation: is there a trade-off?

When investigating the nature of the trade-off between unemployment and inflation I shall be using a dynamic counterpart to the static aggregate supply function of the AD/AS model. In an AD/AS model with an upward-sloping AS schedule, as depicted in figure 6.2(b), a rise in the price level induces firms to supply more real output when the AD schedule shifts up an unchanged AS schedule. The dynamic counterpart to this is that higher inflation results in higher output and employment and lower unemployment. The nature of this trade-off, known as the Phillips relation, is considered in this section, while the related policy implications are discussed in section 4.

3.1. *A permanent trade-off between inflation and unemployment*

In the 1960s the general view prevailed that there is a permanent trade-off between unemployment and inflation. The policy implications of this are important. They are that the government can permanently lower unemployment, but at the cost of a permanently higher but stable rate of inflation. These ideas developed out of a seminal article by Phillips (1958) on the relation between unemployment and the rate of change of money wage rates in the United Kingdom 1861–1957. He hypothesized that money wages would rise faster the lower the level of unemployment, basing this hypothesis on standard demand and supply analysis.

> When the demand for a commodity or service is high relative to the supply of it we expect the price to rise, the rate of rise being greater the greater the excess demand. Conversely when the demand is low relative to the supply we expect the price to fall, the rate of fall being greater the greater the deficiency of demand (Phillips, 1958).

Phillips's hypothesis that the rate of change of money wages, $\Delta W/W$, depends on the level of unemployment, u, is expressed algebraically as:

$$8 \qquad\qquad \frac{\Delta W}{W} = f(u)$$

where f is specified as an inverse functional relationship. Phillips also hypothesized that the relationship is non-linear, i.e. it is not a straight line. Money wages rise more rapidly when the labour market has excess demand than they fall when there is excess supply of labour.

In order to test this hypothesis statistically, using some of the techniques of econometrics, Phillips assembled data on the annual rate of change of hourly money wage rates and the percentage rate of unemployment from 1861 to 1957. These measures of money wages and unemployment were averages for different trades over the whole economy. The earlier statistics were gathered from trade union returns, which in the nineteenth century were much patchier in their coverage than

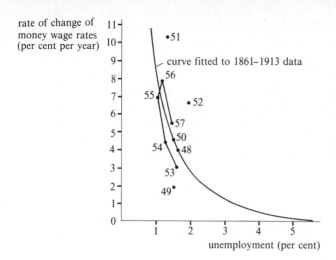

Figure 6.6.   The Phillips curve and observations for 1948-57. *Source:* Phillips, 1958, figure 10).

the government figures collected in the post-war period. Most statistical studies of the relationship between unemployment and inflation have, like Phillips, used aggregated data, though some later studies have disaggregated by region or broad occupational groups. Phillips found his hypothesis supported by the evidence, and his name has been given to the inverse non-linear relationship between the rate of change of money wages and unemployment. The Phillips curve or relation is shown in figure 6.6. The main curve was fitted to data from 1861 to 1913, and it seemed significant that most of the observation for 1948-57 lay near this curve. A few years lie well away from the curve. Phillips argued that these were mainly due to money wages adjusting to increased import prices in specific years, and that this seemed 'to occur very rarely except as a result of war'.

3.1.1.   *The relationship between wage inflation and price inflation*

Phillips argued that from the wage inflation–unemployment relationship can be derived an equivalent relationship between price inflation and unemployment. In other words one can move interchangeably between the rate of change of money wages and the rate of change of prices by making a suitable adjustment for changes in labour productivity.

To understand how this is done, consider the three basic components which, by definition, must make up the ex-works price of final input: (i) raw materials; (ii) labour costs; (iii) gross profits, which includes the cost of using capital plus an element of net profit (or loss!). If we are concerned only with value added, as we are when valuing the national output - then the elements which make up the average price level are the price of imported raw material inputs, unit labour costs and the gross profit margin. If we assume a constant gross profit margin and constant import prices then we can concentrate on the factors which make up unit labour costs. The unit labour cost, or labour cost of a unit of output, is identical to the number of labour hours which are needed to make the product times the hourly money wage rate. The number of labour hours required to make a unit of output measures the physical productivity of labour: if the productivity of labour increases, this means that the number of labour hours required per unit of output decreases. So if the money wage rate stays constant and labour productivity increases, unit labour costs fall. With a constant gross profit margin this would result in a price cut. However, if money wages are rising at say 2 per cent a year and labour productivity is also rising at 2 per cent a year, unit labour costs remain constant since the one effect exactly offsets the other. With a constant gross profit margin, prices remain unchanged. However if money wages are rising at 5 per cent a year while labour productivity increases at 2 per cent, unit labour costs will rise - at 3 per cent a year. So, given a constant profit margin and constant import prices, we have the general relationship:

9 $\quad\begin{matrix}\text{rate of change}\\\text{of prices}\end{matrix} = \begin{matrix}\text{rate of change of}\\\text{of money wages}\end{matrix} - \begin{matrix}\text{rate of change of}\\\text{labour productivity}\end{matrix}$

$$\frac{\Delta P}{P} = \frac{\Delta W}{W} - \frac{\Delta L}{L}$$

If we then substitute $\Delta W/W$ in equation **9** by $f(u)$ from equation **8**, we get

10 $$\frac{\Delta P}{P} = f(u) - \frac{\Delta L}{L}$$

This state that inflation varies inversely with the level of unemployment and the rate of growth of labour productivity.

Equation **10** is the alternative version of the Phillips relation in terms of price inflation rather than wage inflation. Inflation and unemployment are inversely related and so there is a trade-off between the two variables. The price inflation version of the Phillips relation has become more widely used than the wage inflation version.

3.1.2. *The policy implications of the Phillips relation*

By deducting from the rate of change of money wages the long-run annual average rate of increase of labour productivity, which was about 2 per cent over the years 1861–1957, Phillips estimates a relationship between price inflation and unemployment. He estimated that zero inflation would require about 2.5 per cent unemployment.

Phillips' study was highly influential, and spawned a large number of empirical studies of the determinants of inflation, particularly in the UK and the USA. A good number of these studies done in the 1960s supported Phillips' findings that inflation is inversely related to the level of unemployment. It was widely accepted in the 1960s that the price of full employment was a steady rate of inflation of somewhere between 2 and 4 per cent in the UK and about 5.5 per cent in the USA (Samuelson and Solow, 1960). There appeared to be a trade-off between the two policy objectives, low unemployment and stable prices. The Phillips curve was seen as offering a menu of policy choices. Various combinations of unemployment and inflation, given along the Phillips curve, were attainable, and it was up to governments to select the preferred combination.

3.2. Expectations and the Phillips relation

In the late 1960s the Phillips relation began to show signs of instability. From 1968 onwards in the UK both inflation and unemployment began to rise. Figure 6.7 shows the steady drift rightwards in the observations of inflation and

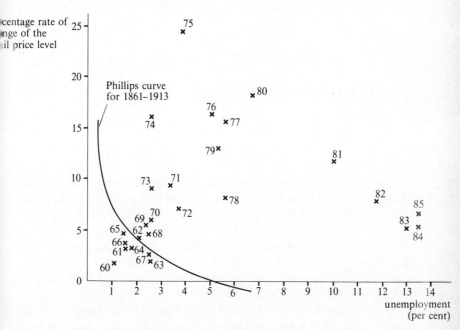

Figure 6.7. The breakdown of the Phillips relation, 1960-85

unemployment during the 1970s and early 1980s. This experience was replicated, though not usually to the same degree, in other Western economies.

3.2.1. Friedman's critique of Phillips

At around the same time, Milton Friedman – in his Presidential address to the American Economic Association in 1968 – declared that the permanent trade-off between inflation and unemployment embodied in the notion of a stable Phillips curve lacked a credible theoretical rationalization. He pointed out (Friedman, 1968, 1975) that there is nothing in standard microeconomic theory that would lead one to expect that inflation could cause a permanent reduction in the level of unemployment. Thus Phillips was mistaken in relating changes in the *money* wage to the state of excess or deficient demand in the labour market. If there is excess demand for labour then price theory predicts that *real* wages will rise in order to clear the market. If there is excess supply of labour real wages will fall towards their market clearing level.

In making changes in real wages the centrepiece of his analysis, Friedman offers an explanation of both the original observation by Phillips of an apparently stable trade-off between inflation and unemployment and the later drift to the right in the observations of the two variables. The crux of Friedman's argument is that there can be a temporary trade-off between inflation and unemployment, but that it cannot be sustained. In the long run no trade-off between inflation and unemployment exists: lower unemployment cannot, in the end, be bought at the cost of a higher steady rate of inflation.

3.2.2. No permanent trade-off between inflation and unemployment

Having stated the basic outline of Friedman's – and the monetarist – position, that there is no permanent trade-off between inflation and unemployment, I would now like to go into it more fully to see how this conclusion is arrived at.

The AD/AS model has already given us some insight into how the explanation is developed. Have another look at figure 6.3. Expansionary monetary and fiscal policies initially shift the aggregate demand schedule up an existing aggregate supply schedule, determined by the current money wage level. Prices start rising from P_1 to P_2. Money wages are temporarily fixed so real wages fall. As a result the demand for labour rises, and so does output. So initially there is a rise in real output as well as in the price level. But as prices rise, workers seek to adjust their money wages in line with prices. As this happens the aggregate supply schedule shifts up to the left until real wages return to their original level. As this adjustment occurs the demand for labour and real output fall back to their original level. The increase in real output is just temporary, but there is a permanent rise in the price level.

The difference between this story and Keynes's version in *General Theory* is that Keynes believed money wages to be 'sticky'. This stickiness was associated with involuntary unemployment, which meant that unemployed workers were willing to work at lower real wages than those currently in existence. Hence, in a depression, the supply of labour does not depend on the real wage rate. A rise in the price level would not cause an upward and compensating adjustment in the money wage rate. On the other hand, neo-classical economists believe that all economic agents – including workers – are rational, and that this rationality implies that the supply of labour depends on real wages. If there is an excess supply of labour the real wage rate will be bid down to its market-clearing level. If the price level rises, money wages will adjust upwards to restore the real wage level. If a rising price level causes money wages to rise, then the AS function is shifting up to the left. (See chapter 2, pp. 57–69 for an explanation of the differences between Keynesian and neo-classical labour market analysis.)

But neo-classical economists need to explain why the AS function does not shift straight away up to AS_2, because if it did they would have no explanation for short-run variations in real output and employment. The key question is then 'why do workers work more hours when aggregate demand increases even though real wages have not risen?' The Keynesians' answer to this question is that this happens because there is involuntary unemployment due to the failure of markets to adjust properly, so that prices, and especially wages, are sticky. For the neo-classically inclined, this answer will not do, because sticky prices imply economic agents are irrational: price and wage adjustment would benefit both employers and workers, and yet it does not occur. The neo-classical answer to why the AS schedule does not shift instantaneously in response to increased demand is that economic agents base their plans to buy and sell on mistaken expectations about future prices.

To see the key role played by expectations of inflation, let us begin with an economy which is in equilibrium at a stable price level and at its 'natural' level of output – say y_1 in figure 6.3. (To keep the analysis simple no growth is assumed. If growth is allowed for then the natural level of output is increasing over time.) This natural level of output is associated with a natural level of employment and of unemployment. (This concept of equilibrium was introduced in chapter 2, p. 69, and the natural level of unemployment forms the central focus of chapter 3.) Monetarists argue that the natural level of unemployment cannot be affected by changing the level of aggregate demand. Increasing aggregate demand can bring unemployment below its natural level only temporarily. I will now spell out this reasoning in more detail.

We start with an economy which has zero inflation and is at its natural level of unemployment (u_N). It is at point A in figure 6.8. However, the government believes that there is a stable Phillips relation: unemployment can be brought down – at the cost of some permanent but relatively low inflation. The government

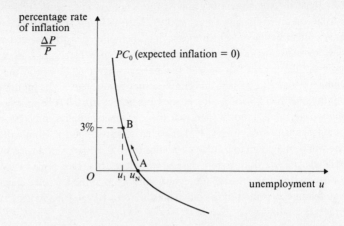

Figure 6.8. Moving up a short-run Phillips curve

introduces expansionary fiscal and monetary policies which raise aggregate demand and the price level, and so move the economy up the Phillips curve to point B. Inflation rises to 3 per cent and unemployment falls to u_1. The reason unemployment has fallen is that inflation reduces the real wage rate paid by employers, since at first prices rise more rapidly than money wages. The increased level of demand causes goods prices to rise, or at least firms can anticipate such an upward movement. Firms also bid up money wages in order to attract more labour. Workers, however, having experienced a stable price level in the past, do not at first anticipate any inflation. They therefore mistakenly perceive the rise in money wages as indicating a rise in real wages and so supply more labour. Consequently unemployment falls below the natural rate and real output rises. The economy has thus moved from point A in figure 6.8 to point B, along a Phillips curve which corresponds to zero expected inflation.

But after some time of actually experiencing 3 per cent inflation, workers begin to realize that assuming zero inflation is mistaken. Their expectations about inflation are gradually raised upwards and, as this happens, the money wage rate is adjusted upwards in order to restore the previous real wage. As the actual real wage rises the demand for labour falls. The supply of labour also falls, since workers no longer mistakenly anticipate an increase in real wages. The level of output returns to its original level, and unemployment rises back to its natural rate. But though the economy is back at the natural rate of unemployment, inflation is now at 3 per cent, sustained by a growing money supply, so the economy is not at point A in figure 6.8. The Phillips curve has moved out – as shown in figure 6.9 – to PC_1 which corresponds to a 3 per cent expected inflation.

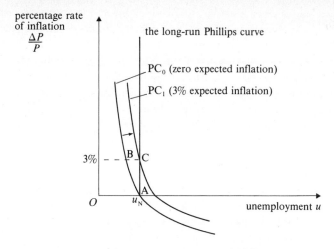

Figure 6.9. The expectations-augmented Phillips curve

3.2.3. The expectations-augmented Phillips relation

Thus the Phillips curve is not stable: it shifts as expectations about inflation change. The position of each downward-sloping Phillips curve depends on what rate of inflation is on average expected to occur in the near future. For instance in figure 6.9, Phillips curve PC_0 corresponds to zero expected inflation, while PC_1 corresponds to 3 per cent expected inflation. Each of these Phillips curves is a short-run curve since its position will change as expectations about inflation change.

This modified Phillips curve is known as the *expectations-augmented Phillips curve*. According to the expectations-augmented Phillips relation, inflation does not only depend on unemployment, it also depends on the expected rate of future inflation. Assuming no growth in labour productivity, the algebraic expression for the expectations-augmented Phillips curve is:

$$\textbf{11} \qquad \frac{\Delta P}{P} = f(u) + \alpha \cdot E\left(\frac{\Delta P}{P}\right)$$

where $E(\Delta P/P)$ stands for expected inflation and α is a coefficient which has a value between zero and 1. Thus α is an expression of the extent to which prices and wages adjust in line with expected inflation.

If money prices and wages are adjusted upwards to fully reflect expectations about inflation, then $\alpha = 1$. On the other hand, if money wages rise less than inflation, then real wages fall as a result of inflation, and α is less than 1. So if inflation gets higher, real output will rise permanently. But if people do not allow for the full effect of anticipated inflation on the real value of money wages, then they can be said to be suffering from 'money illusion' and are in that sense behaving irrationally. As monetarists consider that economic agents do behave rationally, they take α to equal 1.

Let us continue the argument in this section by assuming that money wages adjust upwards fully in response to expected inflation, and that the inflation rate people expect adjusts to become equal to the actual rate of inflation. Hence the α coefficient in the expectations-augmented Phillips relation is equal to 1.

With expected inflation now at 3 per cent and equal to the actual rate of inflation, and money wages fully adjusted for inflation so that real wages have risen back to their original level, the demand and supply of labour are once again consistent with the natural rate of unemployment. The economy is now at point C in figure 6.9 with unemployment at its natural rate but with inflation running at three per cent. The return of the economy to a point such as C, where the level of unemployment is back to its natural rate, means that there is no permanent trade-off between unemployment and inflation. In other words, the long-run Phillips curve is vertical, passing through points like A and C, each on a short-run expectations-augmented Phillips curve.

Another way of seeing that the long-run Phillips curve is vertical is to subtract $\alpha \cdot E(\Delta P/P)$ from both sides of equation 11 and put $f(u)$ on the left-hand side. Then we have

$$12 \qquad f(u) = \frac{\Delta P}{P} - \alpha \cdot E\left(\frac{\Delta P}{P}\right)$$

And if $\alpha = 1$, then

$$13 \qquad f(u) = \frac{\Delta P}{P} - E\left(\frac{\Delta P}{P}\right)$$

Now, in the long run, actual and expected inflation must be equal because if actual inflation were not the same as expected inflation then people's expectations would be continuously falsified by experience. People would then realize that their expectations were mistaken and so would alter them. Changed expectations mean changed behaviour and so the economy could not be in a long-run or steady-state equilibrium. So in the long run (i.e. in steady-state equilibrium) actual and expected inflation must be equal. So substituting $E(\Delta P/P)$ for $(\Delta P)/P$ in equation 13 gives

$$14 \qquad f(u) = \frac{\Delta P}{P} - \frac{\Delta P}{P} = 0$$

If $f(u) = 0$, the labour market is in equilibrium and unemployment is at its natural rate. Its value can be found by solving equation 14: i.e. it is that value of u which makes $f(u)$ equal to zero. Thus in the long run, when expected and actual inflation are equal, inflation has no effect on the level of unemployment. Hence the natural rate of unemployment is consistent with any level of inflation. A point such as C in figure 6.9 is a position of steady-state equilibrium. When actual and expected inflation are equal, so that people's expectations are being confirmed by experience, they have no incentive to change their behaviour. Steady-state equilibrium is used as a reference point towards which the economy adjusts, rather than as a state which an actual economy can attain, buffeted as it is by continual changes. The natural rate of unemployment is that level which would exist were the actual and expected rate of inflation the same. The natural rate of unemployment is thus consistent with any rate of inflation provided the inflation rate is correctly anticipated. This is why the natural rate of unemployment is often referred to as the *non-accelerating inflation rate of unemployment* which, mercifully, is abbreviated to NAIRU. The NAIRU is consistent with any rate of inflation, provided that rate is fully anticipated by economic agents.

In analysing and investigating the determinants of unemployment it is important to distinguish between short-run cyclical changes in unemployment and long-run changes in the underlying trend of unemployment. The latter is the 'natural' rate or the NAIRU. In the monetarist approach, short-run cyclical variations in unemployment are due to deviations in the actual rate of unemployment about the NAIRU. These cyclical variations in unemployment are the result of mistaken expectations about inflation, whereas long-term changes in the natural rate of unemployment are due to real factors – those detailed in chapter 3.

The expectations-augmented Phillips curve and its associated concept of a NAIRU tie in closely with the monetarist reformulation of the quantity theory. Changes in the rate of growth of the money supply can generate short-term changes in real output and employment as well as long-term price level changes. The quantity theory alone can only explain price level changes, so it is nowadays seen by monetarists as a theory of long-run price level determination. The short-term adjustments are modelled using AD/AS and Phillips curve analysis. The initial response of the economy to an increased rate of growth of the money supply is for real output and employment to rise. But as expectations about inflation catch up with the actual rate of inflation, real output and employment return to their 'natural' levels while inflation remains permanently higher. So higher inflation is related to high rates of monetary growth and is consistent with a wide range of values for the natural level of unemployment which is determined by real, micro-level variables. Fluctuations in unemployment and real output around their natural levels are induced by unstable monetary policy. Hence the monetarist recommendation is that the money supply should grow at a constant and known rate. This would eliminate government-induced monetary disturbances and so stabilize the economy. In this view Keynesian demand management policies are mistaken because they lead to instability and inflation.

4.   Policy Implications of Different Inflation – Unemployment Trade-offs

The variant of the AD/AS model, characterized by a downward-sloping AD curve and an upward-sloping AS schedule which, when made dynamic, give rise to an expectations-augmented Phillips relation, represents the broad middle ground currently occupied by monetarists and moderate Keynesians. Within this shared analytical framework there remains considerable disagreement over the extent to which actual unemployment is currently above the NAIRU, and on the scope for demand management and incomes policies in helping the economy to adjust back to its 'natural' equilibrium. Moderate Keynesians favour a greater role for demand management and incomes policy, whereas neo-classical supply-siders place much greater emphasis on micro-level measures to improve the workings of market forces – as discussed in chapters 3 and 9. In the remainder of this chapter I want to focus on a specific and important macroeconomic policy issue. This is the implication for demand management policy of the various possible forms of the inflation–unemployment trade-off. The whole gamut of positions from radical Keynesian to new classical can be categorized according to the kind of unemployment–inflation trade-off postulated. These are that there is a permanent trade-off, a temporary trade-off, or no trade-off at all.

4.1.   *A permanent trade-off*

If there is a permanent trade-off, then there is a definite and long-term choice to be made between inflation and unemployment. In the 1950s and 1960s the cost of full employment was thought to be around 3–4 per cent inflation a year, and this was generally regarded as an acceptable price to pay. As a result of the policy experiences of the 1970s and the work of monetarists, moderate Keynesians accept that the Phillips curve has shifted outwards and that the slope of the long-run Phillips curve is steeper than that of the short-run curve. In other words, the long-run trade-off is agreed to be much less favourable than the short-run one. Some moderate Keynesians go along with a vertical long-run Phillips curve, while others maintain that there is still some permanent trade-off. They argue that running the economy with a high level of unemployment increases the natural rate of unemployment: enforced idleness permanently reduces the productivity of those workers who become unemployed and causes firms to scrap capital equipment, so diminishing the country's stock of capital below what it would otherwise be. (These ideas were discussed in chapter 4.) Radical economists using the conflict approach argue that the unemployment costs of reducing inflation are very high. If organized labour and big capital are both powerful it will require a severe recession to bring down wage and price inflation. If real wages remain high then capitalists respond by scrapping uneconomic plant in order to improve labour productivity and restore profitability. This creates 'a permanent reserve of unemployed labour, sufficiently large to cow workers into submission' (Rowthorne, 1977, p. 237).

4.2.   A temporary trade-off

For those who subscribe to the expectations-augmented Phillips relation, the cost of reducing inflation is, at worst, a temporary rise in unemployment. Higher unemployment in the near future will bring lower inflation and the same or even lower unemployment in the more distant future. A policy of reducing inflation results in a temporary increase in unemployment: it is the reverse of the process whereby increasing inflation temporarily reduces unemployment. In terms of the Phillips curve, the economy initially moves down an expectations-augmented Phillips curve when inflation is reduced.

Figure 6.10 illustrates what happens when a policy of bringing down inflation is implemented. Let us suppose we start off in a steady-state equilibrium with expected and actual inflation both equal to 15 per cent. Unemployment is therefore at its natural rate so the economy is at point D on that diagram. The government succeeds in reducing inflation to, say, 10 per cent. But if expected inflation lags behind actual inflation, then for a while expected inflation exceeds the actual rate of 10 per cent. Workers, however, bargain for money wage increases on the basis of their expectations about inflation. Money wages rise more rapidly than prices,

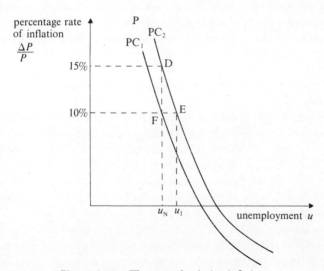

Figure 6.10.   The cost of reducing inflation

so real wages rise. More labour is consequently supplied, but less is demanded by firms and unemployment rises. If expected inflation remains at 15 per cent then the economy moves down the expectations-augmented Phillips curve PC_2 in figure 6.10 from point D to point E. If you turn back to figure 6.7 and look at the observations for 1980-5, you will see that they are consistent with this explanation. But as expectations of inflation adjust towards the new lower inflation rate, so the short-run Phillips curve moves down towards the left. PC_1 in figure 6.10 corresponds to a 10 per cent expected inflation rate. At point F the expected and actual rate of inflation are once more equal at 10 per cent, and unemployment has fallen back to its natural rate.

The crucial factor determining the unemployment costs of a lower rate of inflation in this adjustment mechanism is expectations. The longer it takes expectations of inflation to adjust, the greater the excess of expected over actual inflation, and the longer this gap persists. Consequently the real wage rate remains above its market-clearing level for longer, resulting in higher unemployment for a longer time. So how expectations are formed is important in determining these adjustment costs. When the expectations-augmented Phillips relation was first developed, it was assumed that expectations of future inflation depended on past values of inflation. So the longer it took for expectations of inflation to catch up with experience, the higher would be the adjustment costs. This way of forming expectations is called *adaptive expectations* because the expected future value of a variable adapts to past experience of that variable.

However, the adaptive expectations hypothesis is unsatisfactory, especially to economists who think that economic agents behave rationally. To see why, consider an economic agent who thinks that the rate of inflation depends on current and past rates of growth of the money supply. To predict future inflation on the basis of past inflation, and to ignore the information about future inflation given by the money supply figures, would then be irrational; it would be rational to base expectations of inflation on past and current values of the money supply. Expectations are deemed rational when they are based on all the available relevant information.

The use of *rational expectations* for all sorts of variables, not just inflation, was an important development in macroeconomics in the 1970s. In the context of the Phillips curve, rational expectations imply more rapid adjustment than do adaptive expectations, for as soon as economic agents observe that the government has cut the rate of growth of the money supply in order to reduce inflation, expected inflation falls. The faster expectations adjust, the less the real wage rate is held above its market-clearing level by mistaken expectations about inflation.

So even amongst those who accept the expectations-augmented Phillips relation, there is considerable disagreement about the size of the unemployment costs of reducing inflation. At one end of the spectrum are moderate Keynesians who consider that the labour market is characterized by institutions and practices which result in slow adjustment. They therefore consider that adjustment costs will be high and so question whether it is worth embarking on a costly anti-inflation programme via monetary contraction. At the other end of the spectrum are economists who adopt the rational expectations view. They argue that if the government adopts a clear, pre-announced programme for reducing the rate of growth of the money supply, and convinces economic agents that the policy will not be changed, then expected inflation will fall rapidly, making the adjustment costs low.

4.3. *No trade-off: a vertical aggregate supply schedule*

If expectations are rational so that when the rate of growth of the money supply is cut, expectations of inflation fall at the same rate as actual inflation, then the real wage rate remains unchanged. In figure 6.10 this would be depicted as an instantaneous shift in the short-run Phillips curve from PC_2 to PC_1. So, in effect, the short-run Phillips curve is also vertical. The economy moves instantaneously from D to F and so the unemployment costs of reducing inflation are zero.

One implication of this argument is that the government cannot reduce unemployment by deliberate fiscal or monetary policy actions. This is because economic agents, having rational expectations, will correctly anticipate the future inflation arising from these policies and will immediately adjust all money prices upwards. In terms of the AD/AS model this means that the short-run upward-sloping aggregate supply schedule will immediately shift up to the left when the government increases nominal aggregate demand (see figure 6.3). In effect, the short-run aggregate supply schedule is vertical. These arguments are associated with the new classical school of macroeconomists who came to prominence in the USA in the mid to late 1970s.

4.4. *No trade-off: a horizontal aggregate supply schedule*

As shown in section 3, Cambridge Keynesians also maintain that there is no trade-off between unemployment and inflation, but for them this is because the aggregate supply schedule is horizontal up to full employment. This specification of aggregate supply is directly tied to their view that inflation is due to social forces which determine real wage aspirations independently of the state of demand. To them monetarist policies to control inflation are utterly wrong-headed: reducing nominal aggregate demand by means of monetary restriction will increase unemployment but it will not reduce inflation. In fact, it has been argued that inflation might even get higher because slower economic growth increases the gap between actual and target real wages. So the way expectations are formed, and how expectations affect economic behaviour, are of crucial importance in determining the nature of the relationship between unemployment and inflation, as explained more fully in Levačić (1984).

4.5. The current policy debate

The incoming Conservative government of 1979 made a more explicit and complete abandonment of Keynesian policies than its Labour predecessors, giving priority to reducing inflation by controlling the growth of the money supply. In their view, getting back to low inflation is a prerequisite to improving Britain's long-term growth rate. The government stated its attitude to economic management as follows:

> The Government has deliberately not set its targets in terms of the ultimate objectives of price stability and high output and employment because these are not within its direct control. It has instead set a target for the growth of the money supply, which is more directly under its influence and has stated that it will frame its policies for taxation and public expenditure to secure a deceleration of money supply growth without excessive reliance on interest rates. (Memorandum on Monetary Policy, House of Commons Treasure and Civil Service Select Committee 1979–80, vol 2, HMSO, 1980, p. 9.)

The implementation of this policy was accompanied by a large and rapid increase in unemployment – as you can see from figure 6.7. From 1980 to 1983–5, inflation fell from 18 per cent to 5 per cent but unemployment rose from 6.8 per cent to 13 per cent. The results lend comfort neither to those who argue on the basis of rational expectations that the adjustment costs would be low, or to those who maintain that inflation is entirely sociologically determined and bears no relation to the level of aggregate demand. While this experience has narrowed the range within which most unemployment cost estimates lie, there still remains considerable disagreement over the extent to which the rise in unemployment was due to long-term structural factors affecting the natural rate of unemployment or to inadequate aggregate demand arising from world recession and inappropriate government policy. (See chapters 3 and 4.)

In fact, the Conservative government did not adopt as restrictionary a fiscal stance as first announced in 1980. Over the years government expenditure has crept upwards and has, in fact, increased in real terms at 1.8 per cent a year (Levačić, 1986). The ratio of PSBR to GDP has declined, but by not so much as first intended, and £M3 has grown more rapidly than originally envisaged. By 1985 targeting the rate of growth of £M3 was virtually (and quietly) abandoned in favour of keeping interest rates high in order to maintain the exchange rate within an unofficial target range. These monetary aspects of policy are taken up more fully in the next chapter.

But although the Thatcher government's macroeconomic policy was not as restrictionary as first intended, it was still criticized as too tight from a broad spectrum of opinion ranging from moderate Keynesian to the extreme left. There are also repeated calls from the moderate centre for an incomes policy to bring down the NAIRU. In terms of the AD/AS model an incomes policy would help to lower unemployment by dampening the rise in money wages which would otherwise occur in response to the higher prices and lower unemployment brought about initially by expansionary government policy. That the price- and wage-setting behaviour in the UK seems particularly prone to offset the employment-generating effects of expansionary government policy is borne out in a number of empirical studies (e.g. Grubb *et al.*, 1982; Sachs, 1979; OECD, 1985).

The nature of these results is graphically conveyed in figure 6.11, which relates a measure of short-run real wage rigidity to the percentage rise in unemployment for a number of OECD countries. The OECD measure of short-run real wage rigidity is the percentage rise in money wages in response to a rise in consumer prices, divided by the (absolute) response of money wages to a rise in unemployment.

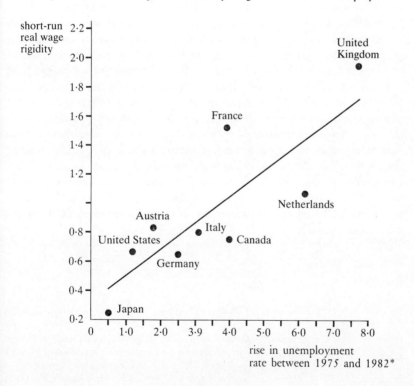

Figure 6.11. Short-run real wage rigidity and unemployment (*percentage points of unemployment)

A rapid response of money wages to prices means that the AS function shifts up rapidly in response to an upward shift in the AD schedule. If money wages rise rapidly in response to inflation, while being little affected by rising unemployment, then a country has high real wage rigidity, as does Britain. In these circumstances an incomes policy is, on the face of it, an appealing remedy, as it should reduce real wage rigidity. But even disregarding any loss in allocative efficiency because an incomes policy impedes relative price adjustments, devising and implementing an effective, long-lasting prices and incomes policy in the UK remains, so far, in the realms of wishful thinking.

5. Conclusion

This chapter complements chapter 3 by considering the short-run cyclical determinants of unemployment and the role of inflation and inflationary expectations in causing unemployment to deviate from its natural rate. This analysis provides the theoretical foundation for the Conservative government's economic policies. It is also the theoretical framework for moderate Keynesians' criticisms of that policy for being too deflationary, relying excessively on monetary policy and neglecting the possibilities of incomes policy. From the other end of the spectrum, the Thatcher government has been criticized by 'free-market/monetarist' economists for being too interventionist and for maintaining too high a level of government spending. In contrast to these positions the radical Keynesian perspective rejects the concept of a natural rate of unemployment. It perceives deficient aggregate demand and lack of direct government control of the economy at the micro-level as the main causes of unemployment. From a radical perspective, inflation in a capitalist economy characterized by class conflict can only be held down, if at all, by high unemployment. Thus the contrasting views as to how the British economy should be managed are based on different theories about the way the economy operates and, in particular, on how the supply side of the economy responds to changes in aggregate demand.

References

Cripps, F. (1977) 'The money supply, wages and inflation', *Cambridge Journal of Economics*, 1, 101–12.
Dow (1964) *The Management of the British Economy*. Cambridge University Press, Cambridge.
Friedman, M. (1956) 'The quantity theory of money: a restatement', in Friedman, M. (ed.) *Studies in the Quantity Theory of Money*. University of Chicago Press, Chicago.
Friedman, M. (1968) 'The role of monetary policy', *American Economic Review*, 58, 1–17.
Friedman, M. (1975) *Unemployment v. Inflation? An evaluation of the Phillips curve*. Institute of Economic Affairs, London.

Friedman, M. (1980) 'Memoranda on monetary policy'. House of Commons, Treasury and Civil Service Committee (July).

Friedman, M. and Schwartz, A. (1963) *A Monetary History of the United States 1867-1960*. National Bureau of Economic Research Studies in Business Cycles No. 12, Princeton University Press, Princeton, NJ.

Grubb, D., Jackman, R. and Layard, R. (1982) 'Causes of the current stagflation', *Review of Economic Studies*, XLIX(5), 707-30.

Levačić, R. (1984) 'The expectations controversy', *The Business Economist*, 16(1), 20-9.

Levačić, R. (1986) 'State spending out of control?', *Economic Affairs*, 6(2), 4-8.

Levačić, R. and Rebmann, A. (1982) *Macroeconomics*, 2nd edn. Macmillan, Basingstoke.

OECD (1985) 'Employment and unemployment', *OECD Economic Outlook*, no. 37 (June).

Phillips, A. W. (1958) 'The relation between unemployment and the rate of change of money wages in the United Kingdom, 1861-1957', *Economica*, 25, 283-99.

Rowthorne, R. (1977) 'Conflict, inflation and money', *Cambridge Journal of Economics*, 1, 215-39.

Sachs, J. (1979) 'Wages, profits and macroeconomic adjustment: a comparative study', *Brookings Paper in Economic Activity*, no. 2, pp. 269-332.

Samuelson, P. and Solow, R. (1960) 'The problems of achieving and maintaining a stable price level – analytical aspects of anti-inflation policy', *American Economic Review*, 50, 77-94.

7

Controlling the money supply

DAVID COBHAM

1. Introduction

This chapter concentrates on one particular instrument of macroeconomic policy, the money supply. This is an instrument which has become much more important since the mid-1970s and indeed in the early 1980s it appeared to be almost the only, and certainly the most important, macro-instrument. At the simplest level it is widely (but not universally) argued that the money supply exerts a strong influence on the growth of nominal income. And if the analysis of the expectations-augmented Phillips curve (chapter 6) is accepted then over the long run the money supply may be seen as the primary means of reducing and/or preventing inflation. However, as will become obvious, the money supply is an instrument which has been difficult to control precisely, and whose control has been the focus of sharp controversy.

Section 2 starts by looking at the history of monetary control in the UK since the 1960s: this will provide an introduction to the techniques which have been used in monetary policy and to the problems associated with them which have led to a number of different techniques being used at different times; it should also whet the appetite for the more rigorous and more general discussion which follows. Section 2 then considers the various definitions of the money supply which are used in the UK.

Section 3 considers the specific problems experienced by the monetary authorities in trying to control monetary growth in a more analytical way than was possible in section 2, taking each of the 'counterparts' to monetary growth in turn.

Since it will be clear that these problems have been considerable, the question naturally arises whether there is not some alternative method of monetary control which would be more satisfactory. Section 4 examines in some detail the principal candidate for this role, namely 'monetary base control'.

The principal aims of the chapter, then, are to explain how the monetary authorities try to control the money supply, to examine the problems which have arisen in the course of their efforts and to consider the main alternative method of monetary control which has been suggested. The key question to be borne in mind throughout the chapter, to which the concluding section directly addresses itself, is, 'Can the money supply be controlled?'.

2. Two Decades of Monetary Control in the UK

This section starts by surveying the experience of monetary control in the UK; to do this it is necessary to say something about what is meant by the money supply. A number of 'monetary aggregates' (i.e. various definitions of the money supply) are discussed later, in section 2.3, but for the moment it is useful to assert without explanation two points which provide a background to the review of monetary control. First the definition of the money supply on which monetary policy has concentrated, and on which this review focuses, is a broad definition which includes bank deposits in deposit accounts as well as current accounts: M3 or (excluding foreign currency deposits) sterling M3 (£M3). Second the change in this broad definition of the money supply can be related to a small number of *credit counterparts* (again this is discussed in more detail later), as follows:

1   Δ broad money supply
         = public sector budget deficit
         $- \Delta$ private sector lending to public sector
         $+ \Delta$ bank lending to private sector
         + external flows,

where Δ stands for 'the change in'. It is, however, most important to remember that equation 1 is an *identity* (that is, it is true by definition); in particular there may well be all sorts of linkages between the terms on the right-hand side, so that it should not be assumed that an exogenous increase in any one of those elements will necessarily be fully reflected in the growth of the money supply (this point is examined more carefully in section 3.5, below).

2.1. *The pre-1979 experience of monetary control*

From the late 1950s to the early 1970s the UK monetary authorities (by which is meant primarily the Bank of England, but also the Treasury) paid very little attention to any measure of the money supply. Their emphasis was more on a somewhat amorphous concept of 'liquidity' (roughly, money plus financial assets that are close to money) which they tried to control mainly through direct limits ('ceilings') on bank lending to the private sector; interest rates were also considering important but they were set primarily with reference to the UK's balance of payments position, being raised when it was weak and lowered when it was strong.

However this system of monetary control attracted heavy criticism during the 1960s, on the grounds that it inhibited competition between banks (since each bank's ceiling was set by reference to the current size of its balance sheet there was little scope for extra dynamism on the part of individual banks), because it created an incentive for the evasion of the controls (e.g. by the setting up of secondary or tertiary banks outside the scope of the controls), and because it became increasing 'leaky'. The system was therefore replaced in 1971 by a new system of monetary control, 'competition and credit control' (CCC), under which both direct controls on bank lending and the interest rate cartel which the banks had been operating at the same time were scrapped, and monetary control was supposed to be exercised via the effect of interest rates on the demand for bank credit. However the CCC system was less efficient than had been hoped, mainly because the demand for bank credit turned out to be much less interest-elastic than had been expected, and it is generally thought to have contributed to the very high rates of monetary growth during the reflationary period of the 1971–3 Heath–Barber 'dash for growth'.

Thus by late 1973/early 1974, after 2 years of exceptionally rapid monetary growth, with expansion halted by capacity constraints and labour shortages and with inflation beginning to accelerate rapidly, the authorities not only changed their macro-policy towards gradual deflation but also significantly modified the system of monetary control. Where under CCC they had attempted to exercise control by operating via interest rates on bank lending to the private sector, the third item on the right-hand side of equation 1, they now introduced a new instrument, the supplement special deposits scheme or 'corset' (an indirect limit on bank lending imposed via a limit on bank deposits), and began to try to exercise control by manipulating the first and second items on the right-hand side of equation 1 as well, namely the public sector deficit, or to be more precise the public sector borrowing requirement (PSBR) and private sector lending to the public sector, also referred to as 'net sales of public sector debt to the private sector'. In principle the PSBR was under the authorities' direct control though in practice the control was often very imprecise (see section 3.1 below); public sector debt sales the authorities tried to control mainly via interest rates, offering higher rates to encourage larger sales (larger private sector lending).

At the same time official thinking on monetary policy, which in the 1960s had emphasized interest rates, moved strongly towards an emphasis on the monetary aggregates. From late 1973 the authorities set themselves definite (but unpublished) targets for M3 and they thought about the achievement of these targets specifically in terms of the counterparts to money supply growth as set out in equation 1. The main reason for this shift of emphasis away from interest rates and towards monetary aggregates was that with higher and more variable inflation it was more difficult to use the interest rate as the instrument of monetary policy. It is usually argued that *nominal* interest rates rise more or less automatically with inflation, for they consist of an 'expected inflation' component and a 'real interest rate' component, the latter being the component that indicates the thrust of policy. But when inflation is high and variable it is hard to separate these two components of the nominal interest rate since expectations of inflation may be high but cannot be directly measured, no that the use of the interest rate as an instrument becomes more complicated and less precise.

In 1974 and 1975 monetary control seems to have been reasonably successful, but in 1976 there was a prolonged sterling crisis with repeated falls in the sterling exchange rate which threatened to bring about a reacceleration of inflation. The authorities found the crisis extremely difficult to deal with, but one of the measures they took in their efforts to restore confidence to the financial markets was the Chancellor of the Exchequer's announcement in July that the growth of M3 over the financial year 1976/7 'should amount to about 12 per cent'.

This statement, reaffirmed towards the end of 1976, was the first official published target for money supply growth in the UK. It was introduced in the specific context of a prolonged and acute sterling crisis, in the hope of convincing the financial markets of the seriousness of the government's resolve to stabilize the economy. However, monetary targets of this sort were introduced in a number of countries during the mid-1970s – Germany and Italy in 1974, Canada, the USA and Switzerland in 1975, France as well as the UK in 1976 – for a number of reasons. First, the announcement of a monetary target should make it easier for the private sector to make its own economic forecasts and should therefore help to stabilize the economy. Second, the announcement of a target might have an independent impact on expectations of inflation, pushing them down, for example, more quickly than they would otherwise have fallen and therefore reducing the unemployment cost of lowering inflation (in terms of the expectations-augmented Phillips curve analysis of chapter 6 a monetary target might help the short-run Phillips curve to shift inwards more rapidly). And third, the announcement of a monetary target means that the authorities are setting out in advance a standard by which their own behaviour can be judged, so that there is much more political pressure on them to keep to that standard; their willingness to accept that political pressure should increase the credibility of their policy. The main disadvantage of a target is that the flexibility with which policy can respond to unforeseen events is reduced; but with 1-year targets this disadvantage is limited, since most unforeseen events will have relatively little impact on the economy within 1 year, and the target for the next year can be set to take account of them. It should be noted that this case for monetary targets does not rest exclusively on monetarist rather than Keynesian assumptions about the workings of the macro-economy and the causes of inflation, although it fits much more readily with the former. It should also be noted that to a considerable extent monetary targets are a substitute for a fixed exchange rate – a point which is explained in the next chapter.

The experience of monetary targeting in this period was mixed, as can be seen from table 7.1, with an undershoot of the target in 1976/7 but several overshoots

Table 7.1.　Monetary targets, 1976-9

Period	Target (%)	Outturn (%)
1976/7*	12	9.7
April 1976 to April 1977	9-13	7.5
April 1977 to April 1978	9-13	15.6
April 1978 to April 1979	8-12	11.3
October 1978 to October 1979	9-12	13.6
June 1979 to April 1980	7-11	10.9
June 1979 to October 1980	7-11	17.7

*The target for 1976/7 was in terms of M3, but all other targets were in terms of £M3. All figures refer to growth at annual rates.
Sources: Bank of England Quarterly Bulletin, Economic Trends, various issues.

in the following years. One response to these overshoots was the introduction of overlapping or 'rolling' targets in October 1978; these were designed to reduce the acute pressures often generated towards the end of target periods.

2.2.　*Monetary targets 1980-4: the medium term financial strategy*

The new government which came to power in May 1979 had a rather different view of the appropriate objectives and instruments of macro-policy from that of its predecessor: on the former it attached much more weight to the objective of reducing inflation and much less to that of reducing unemployment, and on the latter it attached overriding importance to a single policy instrument, that of monetary policy. Compared to the 'pragmatic' or 'practical' monetarism of its predecessor the new government's monetarism was both more 'hard-line' and more a matter of faith; in more theoretical terms the new government had strong sympathies for the rational expectations or new classical version of monetarism, as opposed to the more orthodox (adaptive expectations) monetarism of the previous government. In terms of the AD/AS framework developed in chapter 2 the government was inclined to believe that the AS curve was vertical in the short as well as the long run, so that there was no serious unemployment cost to be paid for the reduction of inflation.

Initially the new government simply 'rolled' the target for £M3 forward 1 year. Later the initial target was extended up to October 1980. However in the 1980 Budget the government introduced the first version of its medium term financial strategy (MTFS), which set out targets for £M3 growth and for the PSBR for each of the next 4 years. The underlying idea was that announcing targets for this longer time period would give more certainly to the private sector, have a greater impact on inflation expectations and constitute a stronger earnest of the government's

Table 7.2.   The medium term financial strategy

	1980/1*	1981/2	1982/3	1983/4	1984/5	1985/6
MTFS targets for £M3 growth (%) as per:						
1980 FSBR†	7–11	6–10	5–9	4–8		
1981 FSBR		6–10	5–9	4–8		
1982 FSBR			8–12	7–11	6–10	
1983 FSBR				7–11	6–10	5–9
Actual £M3 growth	18.5	13.0	11.4	10.2	11.9	
MTFS targets for PSBR as percentage of GDP at current market prices, as per:						
1980 FSBR	3¾	3	2¼	1½		
1981 FSBR		4¼	3¼	2		
1982 FSBR			3½	2¾	2	
1983 FSBR				2¾	2½	2
Actual PSBR percentage of GDP	5.7	3.4	3.2	3.2	3.2	

* The period for the monetary targets is the 14 months from the February of the first year to the April of the second, rather than the financial year as such.
† Financial Statement and Budget Report.
Sources: Financial Statement and Budget Report, Bank of England Quarterly Bulletin, Economic Trends, various issues.

commitment to the reduction of inflation. In other words all three reasons for monetary targets given in section 2.1 would apply more strongly; while at the same time monetary growth would be gradually reduced. For the long term the government was probably aiming to reduce monetary growth further until it could eventually be fixed at the rate of underlying productivity growth: this was the policy proposed by Friedman (1959) and often referred to as his 'money supply rule'. Such a 'monetary rule' requires the government to eschew all 'discretion', that is fresh decision-making in the light of current circumstances, in monetary policy and nearly all discretion in fiscal policy too, and therefore represents a much more *laissez-faire* kind of macro-policy than the active stabilization policy promoted by Keynesians and practised in the 1950s and 1960s.

On the other hand announcing targets for a longer time period also increases the disadvantage of monetary targets, in that it limits to a substantial degree the flexibility of policy in response to unforeseen events and exogenous factors. In the event such factors had a major impact on the MTFS, particularly in its first 2 years. As table 7.2 shows, the target for 1980/1 was substantially overshot, that for 1981/2 was also exceeded, though by a smaller margin, and only in 1982/3 did £M3 growth finally come within the target range. Furthermore the second version of the MTFS, presented in the 1981 Budget, retained the original *rates* of growth for £M3 on a 'base' which was now much higher than had previously been expected because of the 1980/1 overshoot. The 1982 version not only incorporated a second instalment of this 'base drift' but also substantially increased the target range for 1982/3, from the 5–9 per cent first thought of to 8–12 per cent. Thus the more accurate attainment of the targets in the later years of the MTFS reflects to an important extent the adjustment of the targets, rather than greater technical facility in meeting them.

What was responsible for these problems in the MTFS? Two points need to be made here. First, part of the overshoot of 1980/1 reflected a process of 'reintermediation' after the abolition of the 'corset' in June 1980, and therefore exaggerated the underlying growth of £M3 (conversely it implied that the observed growth in 1979/80 had been an underestimate of the true underlying rate). 'Reintermediation' means the process by which financial transactions that had been pushed outside the banking system under the distorting impact of the corset now came back into the system, thereby artificially inflating the growth of bank deposits and therefore also of the money supply; however this phenomenon is discussed in more detail in section 3.3 below. Second, during the first 2 years of the MTFS considerable controversy arose over whether £M3 was the appropriate measure of monetary policy, since a number of other indicators, ranging from the narrower monetary aggregates such as M0 and M1 (see section 2.3 below) through interest rates and exchange rates to output and employment, suggested that monetary policy was extremely tight at a time when £M3 growth appeared from the figures to be rather lax.

Such a phenomenon could be explained, and was so explained by the Treasury, as the result of a shift in the demand for £M3 relative to the demand for other monetary and liquidity aggregates. There were three possible but controversial reasons for this shift, if indeed it had occurred:

(1) structural changes in the banking system, in particular the banks' entry into the mortgage market for which purpose they began to bid more strongly for deposits;

(2) an increase in the ratio of savings to personal income, possibly in response to the 1980 rise in inflation (the ratio appears to rise and fall regularly with inflation), with a proportion of the additional savings being held in the form of bank deposit accounts; and

(3) an increase in desired liquidity more generally, perhaps as a result of the increased uncertainty about employment prospects and wider economic developments.

Thus this phenomenon, and official recognition of it, appears to have led to an official policy decision not to tighten monetary policy further so as to attain the targets. It also brought about two further shifts in the 1982 version of the MTFS. First the authorities specified the target range as applying to two other monetary aggregates, M1 and PSL2, as well as £M3 (in the event all three grew at very similar rates in 1982/3). Second, although the 1981 version of the MTFS had registered some willingness on the part of the authorities to consider other indicators of monetary tightness as well as £M3, the 1982 version went much further in this direction, with the Financial Statement and Budget Report stating that 'Interpretation of monetary conditions will continue to take account of all the available evidence, including the behaviour of the exchange rate'; it also stated that the target ranges for 1983/4 and 1984/5 would be reconsidered nearer the time, taking account of structural and institutional changes. With 1982/3 monetary growth within the target range the 1983 version retained the ranges (referred to more emphatically that before as 'illustrative ranges') and the general reasonings of the 1982 version. The 1984 and 1985 versions gave target growth rates for 1984/5 for £M3 and for M0, a much narrower measure of the money supply than M1, together with illustrative ranges for these aggregates for the following 4 years; thus the period of the MTFS was extended again but the later years' ranges were definitely not to be understood as targets. Continued overshooting of £M3, and continued doubts about the relevance of this aggregate, led the Chancellor of the Exchequer, in a speech of October 1985, to announce the effective suspension of the £M3 targets; however the Bank of England has been keen to emphasize that the growth of broad monetary aggregates such as £M3 is still being monitored and taken seriously by the authorities in their analysis of monetary developments, and as of late 1985 it was difficult to foresee the implications of the Chancellor's statement and decision.

Finally do these problems experienced in operating the MTFS mean either that the MTFS had no effect on the economy since its targets were not in fact attained, or that the 'monetarist' government was not in fact pursuing 'monetarist' policies? In both cases the answer seems to be 'no'. It is clear that although £M3 growth was well above target the growth of nominal GDP, which is after all a large part of what monetary growth is aimed at, was much closer to its implied targets (Budd, 1982); while the government's primary objective, inflation, which had initially risen higher than the government had anticipated, probably fell more rapidly than expected from its peak in the second quarter of 1980. More importantly, however, it can be argued that the essential purpose of the MTFS *was* fulfilled, in so far as it was widely believed that the government would adhere to a strategy of sustained deflation, even if the relevant numbers changed over time: this is the basic case argued by Fforde (1983), who was an adviser to the Governor of the Bank of England throughout this period. Thus despite all the problems which the MTFS encountered it can be argued that as it operated over this period it *did* involve a restrictive monetary policy and that this restriction *did* exert a deflationary influence on the economy. However the nature of that influence is not entirely clear: some economists would argue that the major immediate cause of deflation was the fiscal contraction due to public expenditure cuts and tax increases, rather than the monetary contraction due to tight monetary growth, while Buiter and Miller (1983, p. 364) have argued that 'the MTFS has progressively become a strategy for fiscal contraction as the PSBR targets, initially said to be secondary to the monetary targets, have come to dominate the design of macroeconomic policy'. Thus there is still widespread disagreement over the contribution to macroeconomic policy and performance made by the MTFS, and it is left here as an open question.

2.3. *The money supply*

The definition of money is a subject of considerable controversy. The simplest definition is 'notes and coin in circulation plus bank deposits', but the problem is which bank deposit to include and indeed how, for this purpose, to define a 'bank' – for example, should building society deposits be regarded as money? These questions are not easily answered; instead a variety of the definitions actually used in the UK will be considered here.

Table 7.3 shows which of a number of financial assets are regarded as components of which of a number of monetary aggregates. The two most commonly used aggregates in the UK have been M1 and £M3 (sterling M3). M1 consists essentially of notes and coin in circulation plus sterling sight deposits, while £M3 consists of M1 plus sterling time deposits; in both cases only those deposits held by the non-bank private sector. M3, which was widely used before the introduction of £M3 in December 1976, consists of £M3 plus the foreign currency deposits of the private sector. PSL1 and PSL2 ('private sector liquidity') are broader aggregates introduced only in 1979; they exclude the longer-term bank time deposits included in £M3 and M3 but include a range of liquid financial assets, notably, in the case of PSL2, building society deposits. Table 7.3 also shows M2, an even more recently introduced aggregate often referred to as 'transactions balances', that is money held only for the purpose of making transactions; and what the Bank of England calls the 'wider monetary base', more often referred to as M0, a rather different aggregate which consists of the commercial banks' holdings of notes and coin plus their balances at the Bank of England, together with notes and coin in circulation.

The amounts outstanding for each component and each aggregate at mid-February 1984, and the changes in the aggregates since February 1983, are also shown in the table: M1 is roughly 300 per cent larger than M0; M2, £M3, M3 and PSL1 are all about 250 per cent larger than M1; and PSL2 is another 50 per cent larger still. There is nothing particularly surprising here but two additional figures help to put table 7.3 in perspective: non-residents' holdings of sterling bank deposits (in UK banks) totalled £22,481m at the end of 1982, and their holdings of foreign

Table 7.3. Monetary aggregates for the UK

Item	Amount outstanding 15 Feb. 1984 (£m)	M1	M2	£M3	M3	PSL1	PSL2	M0[7]
Notes and coin in circulation	11,531	×	×	×	×	×	×	×
Private sector sterling sight bank deposits:								
non-interest-bearing	19,018	×	×[1]	×	×	×	×	
interest-bearing	11,951	×	(×)[1]	×	×	×	×	
Private sector sterling time bank deposits	56,106		(×)[1]	×	×	(×)[2]	(×)[2]	
Private sector foreign currency deposits	16,754				×			
Private sector holdings of other money market instruments[3]	2,668					×	×	
Private sector holdings of savings institution deposits and securities[4]	65,699		(×)[1]				×	
Certificates of tax deposits[5]	1,798					×	×	
Notes and coin held by banks	1,170							×
Balances of commercial banks at Bank of England[6]	778							×
Total outstanding at 15 Feb. 1984 (£m)		42,500	120,682	98,806	115,360	102,688	168,414	12,888
Change since 18 Feb. 1983 (£m)		4,339	12,284	861	12,399	8,537	18,043	744

[1] M2 includes only the 'retail' element of these categories of bank and savings institution deposits.
[2] PSL1 and PSL2 include only those private sector sterling time bank deposits with less than 2 years to maturity.
[3] Deposits with local authorities, bank bills and Treasury bills.
[4] Mainly shares and deposits with building societies and National Savings deposits and securities (net of savings institutions' holdings of bank deposits).
[5] Gross in the case of PSL1, net of building societies' holdings for PSL2. The figure given is gross.
[6] Only those balances which are defined as 'operational deposits' (as opposed to 'cash ratio deposits') are included in M0.
[7] The monthly data for M0 are calculated as averages of weekly levels – as averages of the levels on all the Wednesdays of the month.
n.a. Not available.

Sources: data, seasonally adjusted where possible, from *Bank of England Quarterly Bulletin* and *Financial Statistics*, various issues; for full discussion of aggregates and components see 'Changes to monetary aggregates and analysis of bank lending', in *Bank of England Quarterly Bulletin*, March 1984.

currency bank deposits in UK banks totalled £304,451m; the latter figure indicates the size of the international money market that exists in the City of London.

Monetary policy in the UK has generally attached most importance to M3, and since 1977 to £M3. There are three reasons for this. First, early studies seemed to show that M3 was more closely related to other economic variables than M1 (e.g. Goodhart and Crockett, 1970). Second, there is a strong argument that narrower measures of money such as M1 are in practice demand-determined, since depositors can switch between sight and time deposits at will. Third, the growth of M3 and £M3 can conveniently be related to changes in a small number of 'counterpart' items, the assets which correspond to the liabilities of the money supply, in a way which is not possible for M1.

For the banks as a whole assets must equal liabilities; in very simple terms deposits must equal lending. Thus for a very simple monetary economy where there are no foreign currency bank deposits, no non-resident holdings of bank deposits and no bank loans in foreign currency or to non-residents,

$$2 \qquad\qquad M^S = C + D$$

and

$$3 \qquad\qquad D = Lg + Lp$$

where M^S is a broad definition of the money supply, C is notes and coin in circulation, D is bank deposits (both sight and time), Lg is bank lending to the public sector and Lp is bank lending to the non-bank private sector. Substituting from equation 3 into equation 2 and rewriting the equation in terms of *changes* (that is, the difference between one period and the next), gives

$$4 \qquad\qquad \Delta M^S = \Delta C + \Delta Lg = \Delta Lp$$

(where Δ means 'the change in'). Next consider what is called the 'public sector financing identity', which states that the public sector's deficit must be exactly covered by the sum of the various sources of finance to the public sector:

$$5 \qquad\qquad PSD = \Delta C + \Delta Lg + \Delta Gp$$

where PSD is the public sector's deficit, and ΔGp, is the non-bank private sector's lending to the public sector, that is the public sector's borrowing from the non-bank private sector. Equation 5 can be rearranged to obtain

$$6 \qquad\qquad PSD - \Delta Gp = \Delta C + \Delta Lg$$

which is then substituted in equation 4 to obtain

$$7 \qquad\qquad \Delta M^S = PSD - \Delta Gp + \Delta Lp.$$

Now equation **7** is valid for a closed economy, but for an open economy it is necessary to include external flows, that is flows of money into or out of the economy from or to the rest of the world. This will not be demonstrated because it gets rather complicated, but the result obtained is

8
$$\Delta M^S = \text{PSD} - \Delta Gp + \Delta Lp + \text{EF}$$

where EF is 'net external flows'. Equation **8** is, of course, the same as equation **1** above. Thus the change in the broadly defined money supply can be related in a convenient and straightforward way to the counterpart items of the right hand side of equation **8**, especially the deficit of the public sector, whereas this is not possible for a narrow definition of the money supply which includes sight deposits but not time deposits, since there is no corresponding distinction between types of bank assets.

For the UK, however, these relationships are somewhat more complicated, as can be seen from table 7.4. This is primarily because UK banks both lend to, and take deposits from, non-residents as well as residents, and in foreign currency as well as in sterling; the UK public sector also borrows directly from overseas via sales of certain types of security, especially guilt-edged securities (government bonds) and Treasury bills, and these transactions are included in 'net external flows'.

Finally the introduction of a number of new definitions in the UK in recent years has occurred mainly in response to innovation and structural change in the monetary system which have made the existing measures less satisfactory. On the one hand the growth of interest-bearing sight deposits has made the M1 definition (which includes them but excludes other interest-bearing deposits) anomalous, and it is now increasingly recognized that M1 has ceased to be a useful measure of money. The M2 definition has been introduced as an alternative measure of narrow money, and M0 (the bulk of which is notes and coin in circulation) is also used partly in this context. On the other hand PSL2 has been introduced as a broader

Table 7.4. Monetary growth and its counterparts, 1984/5 (£million)

Public sector borrowing requirement	10,274
minus net sales of public sector debt to private sector	− 12,486
plus change in sterling lending to private sector[1]	18,607
equals sum of domestic counterparts	16,395
plus net external flows	− 1,894
minus minor adjustments[2]	− 2,558
equals change in £M3	11,943

[1] Sterling lending by banks plus purchases of commercial bills by the Issue Department of the Bank of England.
[2] Increase in banks' net non-deposit liabilities.
Source: Bank of England Quarterly Bulletin, September 1985.

aggregate which is less susceptible to some of the distortions that have affected £M3 in recent years (see section 2.2).

3. The Problems of Monetary Control

This section examines the problems of monetary control touched on in section 2 in a more analytical and less chronological way. It discusses the problems experienced by the monetary authorities in trying to control monetary growth by controlling each of the counterparts to monetary growth.

3.1. *Controlling the PSBR*

On a pure Keynesian view of macro-policy the primary instrument of policy is fiscal policy, that is variations in the levels of expenditure and the rates of taxes and benefits. The PSBR, the budget deficit that results from the levels and rates chosen, is of no intrinsic significance: it can be large or small, positive or negative, whatever is implied when expenditures and taxes are set at the levels required to attain macro-policy objectives such as full employment. However, on a monetarist view the PSBR can be seen as one of the counterparts of monetary growth, as set out in section 2.3 above, and in this case its size becomes important for reasons other than the effects on the economy of the levels of public expenditure or rates of tax involved, since other things being equal (which they are often not) a higher PSBR will increase the rate of monetary growth.

In the 1960s and early 1970s the UK authorities may be said to have taken a broadly Keynesian view of the workings of the economy; in any case fiscal policy (levels of expenditure and rates of tax) were set by the Treasury and the resulting PSBR was treated by the monetary authorities as something given to them from outside. However from 1974 as the authorities became more concerned with monetary growth, which they considered specifically in terms of the counterparts as set out in section 2.3 above, they inevitably turned their attention to the possibility of 'controlling' the PSBR so as to meet more easily their (explicit or implicit) monetary targets. This connection was taken even further in 1980 in the MTFS, which set out targets for the PSBR as a percentage of GDP as well as for the growth of £M3 (see table 7.2, above).

There are two separate ideas involved in 'control' of the PSBR which are often conflated: one is accuracy, that is whether the government can hit its PSBR target; the other is reduction, that is whether the government can reduce the PSBR below some allegedly 'excessive' level. As regards accuracy there are three major problems for the government. First, the size of the PSBR depends partly on the levels of economic activity and employment: the higher these levels the larger the tax revenues (particularly income taxes but also expenditure taxes) the government will be receiving and the lower the amount of unemployment and other benefits it will be paying out. However, the government may be unable to forecast them accurately, since they depend on many factors outside its direct control. From a Keynesian point of view income-related taxes and expenditure of this sort are 'automatic stabilizers' in the sense that they cause the budget deficit to automatically increase when the level of activity declines in a recession, thereby partially offsetting the decline, and to automatically decrease in a boom, thereby partially reducing the boom. Another way of putting this is to say that part of the effect of exogenous influences on income is displaced from income onto the budget deficit. For a government which wants to reduce the budget deficit and/or public expenditure for some other reason (such as to contribute to a reduction in monetary growth) there is a special problem here, for expenditure cuts can be expected to reduce income, so that the reduction in the budget deficit or PSBR from an expenditure cut is likely to be smaller than the original cut (though it can easily be demonstrated that under normal conditions the PSBR *will* fall).

A second problem is that the size of the PSBR will also be affected by inflation, which again the government may not be able to forecast accurately. On the receipts side the effects of higher than forecast inflation are

(a) to raise in real and nominal terms the receipts from income tax in so far as the tax thresholds and allowances are not adjusted in line with inflation;
(b) to raise in nominal but not real terms the receipts from taxes such as VAT which are levied on an *ad valorem* basis (i.e. as a fixed percentage of the price); and
(c) to reduce in real but not nominal terms the receipts from indirect taxes such as those on alcohol, petroleum products and tobacco which are levied on a specific basis (i.e. as so many pence per pint/gallon/ounce, etc.).

On the expenditure side the effect of inflation will depend on the way in which expenditure is planned and controlled. Essentially there are two ways of doing this in the short term of the budgetary period: one to plan and control in real or volume terms (so many teachers, so many hospital beds, etc.), the other to plan and control in cash terms (that is, by allocating fixed amounts of money to each area of expenditure). With volume planning higher than forecast, inflation will increase nominal but not real expenditure; while with cash control higher than forecast, inflation will reduce real but not nominal expenditure. The net effect of inflation on the PSBR as a whole will depend on the expenditure control system in use, and the share of the various kinds of taxes in total revenue; in principle it could go either way. A further complication is the 'relative price effect' which measures the extent to which the prices which the public sector pays for labour and other goods and services rise at a different rate from the overall rate of inflation; this can vary sharply from year to year, and has in the past been particularly affected by the comming and going of incomes policies.

A third problem is the broader question of the accuracy or efficiency of the control mechanism for government expenditure. Without going into detail it can simply be stated that the coordination of the whole range of public expenditure is a vast bureaucratic undertaking, and it may be impossible to control the total precisely particularly in the short run without unacceptable disruption in particular areas of expenditure.

These three problems also impinge on the question of controlling the PSBR in the sense of 'reduction' rather than accuracy. But here there is also an obvious political problem. Investigations of the politics of public expenditure such as Heclo and Wildavsky (1981) have emphasized the extent of the political infighting between ministries and departments in Whitehall, as well as between political factions in the Cabinet. Public expenditure cuts as a method of reducing the PSBR will necessarily offend, and therefore face obstruction from some vested interests within, as well as outside, the administrative system.

In fact there have been major differences between the forecasts made for the PSBR in the annual budgets and the actual or 'outturn' figures. In particular there were very large overshoots in 1974/5 and 1975/6, which were largely responsible for the changeover from the system of volume control used since the 1960s to the use of cash limits on most items of expenditure as from 1976/7. However this changeover was followed immediately by 2 years of substantial undershoot and then by a continuing pattern of large though somewhat smaller errors in both directions, so it is clear that cash limits do not get rid of the problems of public expenditure control, though they may well change the nature of the problems.

It is clear then that controlling the PSBR is far from straightforward in principle, and that large errors have occurred in both directions at different times in the past. PSBR control is therefore an inefficient and inflexible instrument for controlling monetary growth, although that assessment does not mean that control is unnecessary or irrelevant.

3.2. *Public sector borrowing from the private sector*

The acquisition of public sector debt by the non-bank private sector, that is public sector borrowing from the private sector, is a negative item in equation 1 or table 7.4 above. *Ceteris paribus* the larger this item in absolute terms the smaller is the amount the public sector has to borrow from the banking system and/or from overseas, and the lower is monetary growth. Moreover, an increase in the PSBR accompanied by increased borrowing from the private sector does *not* cause an increase in monetary growth. Thus, although the public sector can always borrow what it wants from the banks, the extent to which it borrows from the non-bank private sector, instead of from the banks, has a crucial impact on the rate of monetary growth.

The most important means by which the public sector borrows from the private sector is through the sale of 'gilt-edged' securities (or simply 'gilts'); these are government bonds, which carry a fixed interest payment and will be redeemed at some specified date in the future. The public sector also borrows significant amounts by issuing Treasury bills, various forms of National Savings debt (National Savings certificates, Premium Bonds, etc.), 'tax instruments' such as Certificates of Tax Deposits which enable firms to set money aside now for the payment of future taxes, and various kinds of local authority bills, bonds and deposits. While local authority debt sales are generally flexible and sensitive to interest rates they cannot be used by the monetary authorities as an instrument of monetary control because of the (relative) independence of the local authorities. Sales of National Savings debt and tax instruments, on the other hand, tend to be difficult to vary in the short run because of the administrative costs of changing interest rates; while sales of Treasury bills are only a short-term (usually 3 months) means of raising finance, they are bought mainly by the discount houses and the banks, and they are generally more important for the authorities' influence on interest rates than for their contribution to funding the PSBR. Furthermore gilts are quantitatively much more important, typically amounting to about 75 per cent of total central government debt outstanding, while National Savings account for some 15 per cent and Treasury bills for only 1 per cent. (Local authority debt is typically twice as large as National Savings debt, but less than half as large as outstanding gilts.) Thus for controlling monetary growth attention is concentrated on gilt-edged securities.

In the 1950s and 1960s the authorities believed that gilts sales could not be readily varied for monetary control purposes. They attached great importance to maintaining relatively stable prices for gilts, in order to maximize the long-term demand. However many academic economists argued that the authorities could and should be more positive in varying the terms on which they sold gilts (and hence the return on them to investors) in order to control the quality of sales. There was a long and sometimes very technical controversy on this question, but the criticisms were gradually diffused during the 1970s as the authorities became more aggressive in their sales tactics. This change in the authorities' behaviour occurred partly under the pressure of much larger PSBRs on the one hand and of their own greater concern for monetary growth on the other hand; but in the context of the higher levels and greater volatility of both inflation and interest rates it had in any case become impossible to stabilize gilts prices. Thus the authorities began from the mid-1970s to vary interest rates and gilts prices more frequently and more strongly in order to control the sales of gilts. There were also two other changes in their policies in this area. First, from the late 1970s they began to sell gilts on an instalment basis, with part of the price payable immediately and the rest over the next few months, in order to smooth out the pattern of uneven sales which had developed and which caused considerable pressures at times in the financial markets. Secondly, by the early 1980s they were regularly selling index-linked gilts, which carry a low nominal interest rate but whose redemption price is linked to the retail price index; the demand for these is generally more stable and consistent since investors are protected by the indexation against losses in the real values of their investments.

Over the past few years then, as a result of these policy changes, the authorities have been reasonably successful in selling the amount of gilts they wished. Indeed they have frequently sold more than their initial forecast as other factors (e.g. PSBR overshoots) obliged them to increase debt sales in order to adhere to their monetary targets. Moreover they frequently 'overfunded' in the first half of the 1980s, that is they sold more debt than was necessary to cover the PSBR, in order to exert a negative effect on overall monetary growth. However the regular use of overfunding led to other problems (it created a number of distortions to the structure of financial flows in the economy), and the Chancellor of the Exchequer announced in October 1985 that it had been abandoned.

3.3. *Bank lending to the private sector*

Section 2 mentioned the use of direct limits on bank lending to the non-bank private sector during the 1960s, and the attempted use of interest rates to control such lending in the CCC period. Both techniques were regarded as unsuccessful; the first mainly because of the distortion and evasion it induced and the second mainly because of the low interest-elasticity of the demand for bank credit.

It should also be mentioned here that up to 1981 the banks were required to maintain various kinds of reserve ratio. Under CCC all the banks were required to maintain a 12½ per cent ratio between a certain set of 'reserve assets' and their 'eligible liabilities' (roughly equivalent to sterling deposits other than those of other banks). Furthermore in the technique of 'Special Deposits' the authorities had a means of increasing the required ratios, by obliging the banks to deposit in the Bank of England extra funds not counted as liquid or reserve assets in proportion to their deposits. At first sight this might appear to give the authorities a means of controlling bank lending. However the ratios were never used in this way: the authorities never set out to restrict the supply to the banks of liquid or reserve assets (or cash) with the idea that, given their fixed minimum reserve ratios, the banks would be obliged to adjust their lending and deposits accordingly. In any case the authorities were unable to control that supply themselves since some of the relevant assets were assets issued by the private sector or within the banking system itself, rather than by the central bank or government. Instead the ratios were used to strengthen the authorities' control over the general level and structure of interest rates, in accordance with their concern with 'liquidity'.

Given the rejection of direct limits on lending, and of control through the reserve ratios, together with the recognition that the response of the demand for bank credit to interest rates is both small and very slow, the control of bank lending poses a considerable problem for the authorities. The only other specific technique which has been tried is the Supplementary Special Deposits Scheme, according to which banks were obliged to deposit extra funds with the Bank of England on a sharply rising scale in so far as the growth of their 'interest-bearing, eligible liabilities' (IBELs) exceeded specified norms. The scheme was used intermittently between 1973 and 1980, but by the latter date it was clear that the corset was increasingly subject to evasion, partly but not only as a result of the abolition of exchange controls in 1979, which enabled banking transactions to be diverted outside the UK and the control of the UK authorities without difficulty; it was therefore scrapped in 1980, and is unlikely ever to be reintroduced.

The problem of controlling bank lending has also been made more difficult by the banks' shift over the 1970s from 'asset management' to 'liability management': the former, as practised by the banks in the 1950s and 1960s, meant that they reacted to pressure by acting on their assets, essentially by rationing their lending to the private sector in the short term while reducing their lending to the public sector and increasing that to the private sector over the long term. During the 1970s, however, the banks went over to liability management, in which they react to pressure by acting on their liabilities, especially by bidding in the wholesale markets to attract deposits and by rearranging their various types of liability.

All the authorities are left with, then, is the possibility of a small and slow influence on the demand for bank credit via interest rates. Under the present arrangements bank lending to the private sector *cannot* be controlled in the short run. The authorities can only try to forecast it and then manipulate the other counterparts of monetary growth, especially debt sales, to offset the forecast change in bank lending. Thus during 1981 and 1982, for example, when bank lending was unexpectedly high the authorities pursued a policy of overfunding. However as noted in the previous section overfunding was abandoned in 1985. This leaves the authorities without an effective weapon for short-term control of broad money, but as noted in section 2.2 above the Chancellor downgraded the targeting of broad money at the same time.

3.4. *External flows*

The 'net external flows' shown in table 7.4 consists of the overall balance of payments surplus (a positive item) or deficit (negative) and a number of other flows, including (as a negative item) overseas lending to the public sector in the form of purchases of gilt-edged securities, Treasury bills, local authority debt, etc., and (as a positive item) the banks' transactions (lending net of deposits) with non-residents and in foreign currency with residents.

The precise determinants of the various flows involved are quite complex, but a simple generalization which will suffice for present purposes is that the total of net external flows can be expected to be positive when the balance of payments is in surplus and/or the exchange rate is appreciating, and negative when the balance of payments is in deficit and/or the exchange rate is depreciating. The government can of course try to influence the total, most obviously by intervening in the foreign exchange market as a buyer or seller of foreign currency. Without such intervention a non-zero overall balance of payments surplus or deficit cannot occur; but when the exchange rate is fixed the amount of intervention is endogenously determined as the obverse of the overall surplus or deficit. However there are good reasons why increasing or decreasing external flows is rarely used as a technique of monetary control.

First if the exchange rate is fixed the government cannot decide independently how much to intervene in the foreign exchange market. Secondly the effect on the balance of payments and/or exchange rate of such interventions will generally run counter to the government's overall policy objectives: for example, if the authorities wish to reduce monetary growth in order to reduce inflation, they would have to sell foreign currency in exchange for sterling in order to make 'net external flows' negative; but that would depreciate the exchange rate and depreciation tends to stimulate inflation (these relationships are discussed in more detail in chapter 8). There have been occasional exceptions such as the abolition of exchange controls in 1979, which may have been intended partly to reduce the total of net external flows by stimulating an outflow of investment in order to reduce monetary growth (though a more important objective was probably to restrain the appreciation of sterling). But on the whole it seems clear both that this item is thoroughly unsuitable for use as a technique of monetary control and that there have been few attempts to use it in this way. On the contrary external flows have sometimes created considerable difficulties for monetary control. For example the capital inflows of 1977 threatened to jeopardize the government's monetary target until it abandoned its implicit exchange rate target (thereby reducing the inflows). In 1979–81 the government avoided this problem by allowing the exchange rate to appreciate sharply, but that created problems in turn by causing a drastic deterioration of the competitiveness of UK industry.

3.5. *Interactions*

So far in this section the counterparts to monetary growth have been considered in turn, one by one. But it is of course possible that there are important interactions between some of these counterparts.

Consider first the relationship between the PSBR and public sector borrowing from the private sector: a reasonable empirical generalization about the behaviour of the UK monetary authorities since the war is that they have been concerned to avoid what they have seen as excessive monetary financing of public sector deficits; in other words they have in general tried to vary their sales of public sector debt in line with the size of the deficit. Now they have not always succeeded in this, and the relationship is far from precise, but the existence of such a relationship even in a fairly rough-and-ready form means that there is an important interaction between these two counterparts to monetary growth.

Secondly consider the relationship between the PSBR and bank lending to the private sector. In the 1960s macroeconomic policy often took the form of 'package' which combined elements of fiscal and monetary policy; in other words both would be expansionary at one time and both contractionary at another. This means that during this period the PSBR (fiscal policy) and bank lending to the private sector (monetary policy) had some tendency to move together. However such a relationship has been much more difficult to detect in recent years.

Thirdly consider public sector borrowing from the private sector and bank lending to the private sector. The more gilts the public sector sells to the private sector the less funds are available (*ceteris paribus*) for lending to companies in the form of purchases of equity or bonds. This is the basic story of the process called 'financial crowding out', and there is at least some *prima facie* evidence of such a process over some recent periods. The effect may be that companies borrow more heavily instead from the banks, so that these two counterparts (one of which enters monetary growth with a negative sign) tend to move together. Alternatively they may move together because the authorities are deliberately overfunding in order to counteract variations in bank lending, as discussed in section 3.3 above.

Finally take the relationship between the sum of the three domestic counterparts of monetary growth, that is $PSBR - \Delta Gp + \Delta Lp$, and net external flows. In chapter 8 it will become clear that there are reasons for thinking that particularly under fixed exchange rates when the sum of the domestic counterparts is relatively high net external flows will be negative, but when the former is relatively low the latter will be positive.

Thus many sorts of interaction between the counterparts of monetary growth are possible, and many sorts of interaction have occurred in different periods. It is for this reason that investigations of the relationships between monetary growth and the individual counterparts, notably the PSBR, have not discovered any relationships which are significant and stable over time: it is not the case that monetary growth in the UK has been consistently dominated by the PSBR, or indeed by any other counterpart.

3.6. *Conclusions*

This section has looked at the various problems faced by the monetary authorities in controlling each of the counterparts to monetary growth, and at the interactions between the counterparts. The most important conclusions to emerge are that monetary control by the methods which the UK authorities have used is far from straightforward; and that they have had most success in influencing public sector borrowing from the private sector by variations in interest rates.

4.   An Alternative Approach to Monetary Control

It is hardly surprising that the problems experimented by the authorities should have led to proposals for other methods of monetary control. Kaldor (1982), for example, has argued for stricter forms of direct credit controls, while the Liverpool model economists (Minford *et al.*, 1984) regard the PSBR as the key determinant of monetary growth so that PSBR control is the principal means of monetary control. However the proposal which has attracted most attention, and which is the focus of this section, is the proposal for the money supply to be controlled by means of control of the 'monetary base' – the method commonly referred to as 'monetary base control'. The discussion considers in turn how monetary base control is supposed to work, the main controversies surrounding it, and the debate which occurred on this subject in the UK between (roughly) 1978 and 1982.

4.1. *Monetary Base Control: the Proposal*

The basic idea underlying this proposal is that banks tend to keep a fixed ratio between their deposits and their reserves, either because they choose to do so on the basis of considerations of banking 'prudence' or because they are legally obliged to do so. According to this proposal the monetary authorities – instead of trying to limit the PSBR, sell more gilt-edged securities or restrict bank lending in other ways – would control the monetary base (also referred to as 'high-powered money'), which is usually defined as banks' reserves plus notes and coin in circulation; the total money supply is thought to be stably related via a 'monetary base multiplier' or 'high-powered money multiplier', to the stock of high-powered money, so that control of the latter implies and enables control of the former. In algebraic symbols,

9
$$M^S = C + D$$

where M^S is the money supply, C is notes and coin in circulation and D is bank deposits (the distinctions between sight and time deposits, etc., are ignored in this simple exposition). Secondly,

10
$$H = R + C$$

where H is the stock of high-powered money and R is banks' reserves (their holdings of notes and coin and their balances at the central bank). Now dividing equation 9 by equation 10 produces

11
$$\frac{M^S}{H} = \frac{C + D}{R + C}$$

and dividing the top and bottom of the term on the right-hand side of equation 11 by D (dividing *both* top *and* bottom by the same number leaves the value of the whole term unchanged), gives

12
$$\frac{M^S}{H} = \frac{C/D + 1}{R/D + C/D}$$

which can be rewritten as

13
$$M^S = H \cdot \frac{C/D + 1}{R/D + C/D}$$

The right-hand side of equation 12 is called the high-powered money multipler, and equation 13 shows that the money supply is equal to the stock of high-powered money times this multiplier. Notice that the value of the multiplier here depends on R/D and also on C/D: the latter is relevant in so far as the more cash the private sector wishes to hold the less will be available to be held by the banks as (part of) their reserves.

As it stands equation 13 is purely the result of manipulating identities and says nothing of interest. But suppose (i) that the stock of high-powered money is fixed exogenously by the monetary authorities, (ii) that the ratio C/D of cash to deposits is constant, reflecting a decision by the public always to hold certain proportions of their money balances in cash and deposits respectively, and (iii) that the ratio R/D of reserves to deposits is constant, reflecting either the prudential behaviour of banks in maintaining a certain proportion of reserves against the withdrawal of deposits or a reserve ratio imposed on the banks by the monetary authorities. On the basis of these assumptions the high-powered money multiplier becomes constant and H is exogenous, so that equation 13 becomes a behavioural equation saying how the money supply is determined. If these assumptions hold, then control of the stock of high-powered money will enable the authorities to control the money supply itself.

In fact it is not necessary for the two ratios C/D and R/D to be constant: if they are *stable* and *predictable*, that is they vary only within a limited range and in ways that can be predicted, then the high-powered money multiplier will itself be stable and predictable, and the monetary authorities can allow for likely changes in the multiplier when they are deciding by how much to vary H in order to obtain a given change in M^S. Thus most advocates of monetary base control will readily agree that the ratios are not constant: C/D is likely to fall in response to a rise in the interest rate on time deposits, as people and companies switch their holdings of money from cash to interest-bearing time deposits, while R/D is also likely to fall in response to a rise in the interest rate on bank loans, as banks try to increase their lending to take advantage of the rise (subject of course to any legally imposed minimum reserve ratio). But small and predictable variations of this sort in these ratios, and hence in the high-powered money multiplier, are not regarded as problems for monetary base control.

What then would the authorities have to do under monetary base control if, say, they wanted to reduce the money supply by 5 per cent? First they would work out how much H needed to be reduced, given any likely change in the multiplier. Then they would bring about the required decrease in H. This they would do by means of 'open market operations', the name given to the process by which the authorities sell (and buy) government securities on the open financial market. The point of doing this is that such sales (*ceteris paribus*) reduce the banks' reserves, for the buyers of the securities write cheques on their bank accounts payable to the government, and the way in which such payments are made involves a transfer from the banks' own accounts at the Bank of England to that of the government. Thus the banks' balances at the Bank, and hence their reserves, will be reduces; they will therefore be obliged to reduce their deposits (for example, by reducing their outstanding lending) in order to maintain their R/D ratios at the desired (or legally imposed) minimum level. Hence the money supply will be reduced by the required amount.

Finally it should be noted that within the general category of monetary base control there are a number of different schemes possible. These schemes differ first in their definitions of the monetary base. It is widely agreed that for monetary base control to be effective the authorities must be able to control precisely the amount of the monetary base available to the banks. Thus although standard definitions include notes and coin held by the public as well as banks' reserves it might be preferable to exclude the former, since the public's demand for cash (the ratio C/D) may fluctuate significantly in the short run – indeed Duck and Sheppard (1978), in their contribution to this debate, argued for the creation of a new financial asset, 'reserve deposits' at the Bank of England, which could only be held by banks, precisely in order to eliminate the variability introduced into the multiplier by including notes and coin in circulation. Second the various schemes differ over whether they envisage a mandatory (legally imposed) reserve ratio or rely on banks' prudential behaviour to establish a stable ratio. And third the control involved may range from tight day-to-day control to a much looser arrangement known as the 'indicator system' version of monetary base control, in which movements in the monetary base merely trigger interest rate adjustments by the authorities.

4.2. Monetary base control: the controversial issues

There are four principal issues involved in the long-standing controversies over monetary base control. First, would the C/D and R/D ratios, and therefore the multiplier itself, be sufficiently stable and predictable to serve as the basis for monetary control? and if not, can they be made stable and predictable enough without this imposing costs which would outweigh the benefits of monetary base control? Opponents of monetary base control argue that if the banks have some freedom of choice over the reserve ratio (e.g. if there is no mandatory ratio at all, or only a prescribed *minimum* ratio) the actual R/D ratio would be unstable; but if the banks were required to maintain a specific ratio (e.g. if there is a legally imposed minimum together with penalties to discourage substantial holdings of 'excess reserves' above the required minimum) then the pressures on the banks would lead to 'disintermediation', that is a re-routing of financial flows away from the banks, of a similar kind to that which occurred under direct credit controls in the 1960s and under the corset in the 1970s. Moreover, opponents argue, the C/D ratio is not stable either, being liable to sharp changes in response to structural changes in the banking system such as the extension of credit cards or an increase in the number of people whose incomes are paid directly into their bank accounts. Thus the multiplier must itself be unstable and unpredictable. On the other hand the advocates of monetary base control, who mostly favour non-mandatory reserve ratios, assert that the multiplier would be sufficiently stable, and that the resulting system of control, though possibly imperfect, would be less so than any of the alternatives: in particular it has the advantage of being relatively simple to operate, whereas the present system of monetary control, for example, is complicated and difficult to operate and, according to the advocates of monetary base control, produces a monetary growth rate which is highly volatile and often excessive.

The second issue concerns the exogeneity of the stock of high-powered money. Opponents of monetary base control tend to argue that the measures needed to make H entirely subject to the authorities' control would affect the operation of policy elsewhere in an unacceptable way. For example, since banks' reserves are affected by central bank intervention in the foreign exchange market (purchases and sales of foreign currency for domestic currency from or to the banks' customers result in increases and decreases of the banks' balances at the central bank) this intervention would have to be ended; that is exchange rates would have to be allowed to be perfectly flexible. Similarly there would at least be some pressure to balance the government's budget since a government deficit *ceteris paribus* increases bank reserves. Lastly the central bank would have to greatly reduce, if not eliminate altogether, its role as lender of last resort to the banking system, since that may require it to inject reserves in order to preserve the financial viability of an individual bank which is in difficulty. Most of the advocates of monetary base control, on the other hand, favour flexible exchange rates anyway, and would be glad to see budget deficits greatly reduces. They argue that under monetary base control the central bank would still be able to act as lender of last resort when it was really needed, though not on a day-to-day basis.

The third issue is the degree of instability of interest rates which is entailed by this method of monetary control. Opponents argue that, particularly with strict forms of monetary base control, interest rates would become highly unstable, and more so than under (for example) the present system of control, while advocates emphasize the degree of instability in the present system and argue that the more stable monetary growth which would occur under monetary base control would make financial markets more confident and thereby lead to *less* instability of interest rates.

Finally the opponents of monetary base control have argued that strict monetary base control would impose such tight constraints on the banks that they would be obliged to curtail the facilities they offer to their customers, particularly in the case of overdraft loans, a form of finance which is highly flexible and therefore of great value to the banks' customers but which exposes the banks to unforeseen increases in their lending and deposits. The curtailment of such facilities would, it is argued, in turn impose certain costs on the non-bank private sector. Advocates of monetary base control, on the other hand, have tended to play down the importance of the structural changes which it might impose on the banking system and the costs that would be involved.

What these various issues add up to is the question of whether monetary base control will 'work' and/or whether it can be made to work at an acceptable cost. In short the advocates argue that it could be made to work at a cost which will be far outweighed by the benefits of more stable and more precisely controlled monetary growth, while the opponents argue that even if these alleged benefits were attained they would be outweighed by the various costs involved: distortions to financial markets (disintermediation and interest rate volatility), constraints on macro-policy more generally (e.g. the need for flexibility of exchange rates), and structural changes in the banking system which reduces its ability to service the rest of economy.

4.3.   *Monetary base control: the recent debate in the UK*

The proposal for monetary base control became the subject of considerable public debate in the UK in the late 1970s, in the course of which all the arguments discussed in section 4.2, and more, were well aired. Various schemes for monetary base control were put forward, notably by Duck and Sheppard (1978), and by economists in or close to the City of London. The main opposition to the proposal came from the Bank of England, in a paper by three of its monetary experts (Foot *et al.*, 1979) and in the joint Bank of England–Treasury Green Paper on Monetary Control (1980).

In the end monetary base control was not implemented. There seem to be two main reasons for this. First, by late 1980 interest and attention had shifted away from the question of the appropriate *techniques* of monetary *control* to the question of what sort of *objectives* monetary policy should be pursuing: as discussed in section 2.2 the medium term financial strategy ran into considerable difficulties (to which monetary base control was simply irrelevant) and was modified in various ways. Thus some of the impetus behind the idea was lost. Secondly, although it is impossible to be sure of this, it seems likely that the strong defence of the existing system put up by the Bank of England, together with a few minor reforms, succeeded in changing, or at least unsettling the minds of some of the original supporters of monetary base control.

The minor reforms introduced in 1980 and 1981 concerned first the Bank of England's operations in the money market and secondly the reserve ratios of the banks; they were initially put forward by the Bank as changes which were desirable in themselves but might also form part of an evolution towards monetary base control. The first of these sets of changes is highly technical, but their effect is that the authorities now operate more flexibility in lending to the discount houses, market forces have a larger and more immediate influence on short-term interest rates, and the political attention previously focused on changes in minimum lending rate (the Bank's previous minimum rate for lending to the discount houses) has been diffused. More broadly these changes involve a withdrawal by the Bank from day-to-day lender of last resort operations. As regards the banks' reserve ratios, these were scrapped altogether in 1981 so that the banks are no longer required to keep reserves equivalent to any particular proportion of their reserves. In effect the Bank is now encouraging individual banks to find and adopt definite non-mandatory reserve ratios appropriate to their individual circumstances.

As of late 1985 it looks unlikely that monetary base control will be introduced in the foreseeable future. M0 is now being regularly targeted though not, it seems, with any idea of causation running from M0 to £M3 or other monetary aggregates. The present Chancellor of the Exchequer, Mr Nigel Lawson, is known to have been sympathetic to the proposal in 1979, but he has stated that he does not intend to reopen the debate. The Bank of England remains (so far as is known) as opposed to the idea as it has always been. And the evidence since the changes of 1980–1 is of considerable variability in the high-powered money multiplier.

5. Conclusions

In section 1 of this chapter its principal aims were given as 'to explain how the monetary authorities try to control the money supply, to examine the problems which have arisen in the course of their efforts and to consider the main alternative method of monetary control which has been suggested'.

Sections 2 and 3 discussed at some length how the authorities try to control the money supply: although in the 1960s monetary policy was neither directed towards control of monetary growth nor considered as of more than secondary importance, it is clear that since the mid-1970s the monetary authorities in the UK have been making considerable efforts to control it using a variety of techniques which all operate primarily on the counterparts of monetary growth. Over the medium term control of the PSBR is seen as important, but in the short term the manipulation of public sector borrowing from the private sector by means of variations in the terms on which gilt-edged securities are sold has been the primary weapon of monetary policy. As regards bank lending to the private sector, a considerable range of techniques has been tried, but hopes of short-term control have effectively been abandoned. Finally the external flows counterpart cannot be satisfactorily used for purposes of monetary control.

In the course of the chapter a variety of problems experienced by the authorities in trying to control the money supply have been mentioned. These range from the technical problems of controlling public expenditure through the problems of unforeseen capital flows to the rather different problems of the strong sterling appreciation associated with the first year of the medium term financial strategy. However there is also some room for doubt about the main alternative method of monetary control, monetary base control.

The key question of the chapter is: 'can the money supply be controlled?' The answer appears to be 'probably yes, but not precisely and not in the short run and not without costs of various kinds'; and the more general point that emerges from the discussion is that monetary control in a financially sophisticated economy such as the UK's is a complex business, not amenable to simple solutions. This point is underlined by the Chancellor of the Exchequer's speech of October, 1985, in which the targeting of £M3 was downgraded and the practice of overfunding officially abandoned, but no very clear alternatives were put in their place.

References

Bank of England–Treasury (1980) *Monetary Control*, Cmnd. 7858. HMSO, London.
Budd, A. (1982) 'The economy after the 1982 Budget'. In Kay, J. (ed) *The 1982 Budget*. Basil Blackwell, Oxford.

Buiter, W. H. and Miller, M. H. (1983) 'Changing the rules: the economic consequences of the Thatcher regime', *Brookings Papers on Economic Activity*, 2, 305-65.

Duck, N. W. and Sheppard, D. K. (1978) 'A proposal for the control of the UK money supply', *Economic Journal*, 88, 1-17.

Fforde, J. S. (1983) 'Setting monetary objectives', *Bank of England Quarterly Bulletin*, 23, 200-8.

Foot, M. D. K. W., Goodhart, C. A. E. and Hotson, A. C. (1979) 'Monetary base control', *Bank of England Quarterly Bulletin*, 19, 149-59.

Friedman, M. (1959) *A Program for Monetary Stability*. Fordham University Press, New York.

Goodhart, C. A. E. and Crockett, A. D. (1970) 'The importance of money', *Bank of England Quarterly Bulletin*, 10, 159-98.

Heclo, H. and Wildavsky, A. (1981) *The Private Government of Public Money*, 2nd edn. Macmillan, London.

Kaldor, N. (1982) *The Source of Monetarism*. Oxford University Press, Oxford.

Laidler, D. (1982) *Monetarist Perspectives*. Philip Allan, Oxford.

Minford, A. P. L., Marwaha, S., Matthews, K. and Sprague, A. (1984) The Liverpool macroeconomic model of the United Kingdom', *Economic Modelling*, January, pp. 24-62.

8

Managing the open economy

DAVID COBHAM

1. Introduction

The aim of this chapter is to analyse how the problems of macroeconomic policy and the way in which it operates are affected by an economy's being 'open', that is being integrated into and interdependent with the economies of other countries.

Section 2 focuses on how this openness impinges on policies of domestic reflation under fixed exchange rates. Section 3 discusses whether the possibility of changing the exchange rate provides an extra 'degree of freedom' for macroeconomic policy by eliminating or weakening the 'constraint' imposed by openness with a fixed exchange rate. Section 4 considers the choice between fixed and flexible exchange rates more generally, looking at experience since the breakdown of the Bretton Woods system, and at the theoretical arguments on each side. The final section reviews the main conclusions reached in terms of the implications of openness for macroeconomic policy.

2. Demand Management in a Fixed Exchange Rate Open Economy

This section examines the implications of openness for policies of domestic reflation under fixed exchange rates, starting with the Keynesian analysis in section 2.1, and proceedings to the 'monetary approach' analysis in section 2.2; section 2.3 considers whether import controls could provide a solution to the conflict which can occur in the Keynesian analysis between internal and external balance.

2.1. *The Keynesian analysis*

Traditional Keynesian analysis of open economies concentrates primarily on the current account or balance of trade, that is exports *minus* imports, rather than the overall balance of payments which includes capital flows, and within that framework it focuses separately on the determinants of exports and imports (chapter 1).

The crucial assumption is that a country's imports vary positively with its national income via the 'marginal propensity to import', which refers to the proportion of an increase to income which is spent on additional imports. There may also be some part of a country's imports which is exogenously fixed, and of course imports are assumed to depend on their relative price – relative that is to domestically produced goods and services; however in a fixed exchange rate situation the relative price effect can be regarded as secondary.

Since one country's imports are other countries' exports, an individual country's exports will depend in a similar way primarily on the incomes of other countries. For a small open economy it is assumed that changes in its level of income will have negligible effects on the income of other countries so that from the point of view of domestic demand management its exports can be taken as given. If, however, such effects (even for larger economies) are integrated into the analysis the qualitative nature of the results below is unchanged, although the quantitative results will differ.

Now what happens in a simple Keynesian model of the economy if the government increases its own expenditure or reduces taxes in order to stimulate the economy? The answer is that income will increase, and therefore imports will increase too. Exports, on the other hand, depend on foreign incomes, which are unchanged, and therefore remain at their original level so that the balance of trade deteriorates.

More formally in the simple Keynesian model of income determination, given the following behavioural functions:

$$C = a + bYd$$
$$Yd = Y - tY$$
$$I = \bar{I}$$
$$G = \bar{G}$$
$$X = \bar{X}$$
$$H = q + jY$$

where C = consumption, Y = income, Yd = disposable income, t = tax rate, I = investment, G = government expenditure, X = exports and H = imports; and the following equilibrium condition:

1    $$Y = C + I + G + X - H$$

the equilibrium level of income is

2    $$Y = \frac{(a + \bar{I} + \bar{G} + \bar{X} - q)}{1 - b + bt + j}$$

This result can now be used to work out the balance of trade, B, which is equal by definition to the difference between exports and imports:

$$B = X - H = \bar{X} - q - jY,$$

3
$$= (\bar{X} - q) \quad \frac{j(a + \bar{I} + \bar{G} + \bar{X} - q)}{1 - b + bt + j}$$

Multiplying and dividing $(\bar{X} - q)$ by the denominator of the second term on the right-hand side (which leaves its value unchanged) gives

$$B = \frac{(\bar{X} - q)(1 - b + bt + j)}{1 - b + bt + j} - \frac{j(a + \bar{I} + \bar{G} + \bar{X} - q)}{1 - b + bt + j}$$

which can be simplified by cancelling out the X and q terms where possible to

4
$$B = \frac{(\bar{X} - q)(1 - b + bt) - j(a + \bar{I} + \bar{G})}{1 - b + bt + j}$$

From equation 4 it can be seen that as Y rises B falls; and from equation 4 it can be seen that demand management policy to raise Y by means of an increase in G leads to a fall in B. It is also clear from equation 2 that j, the marginal propensity to import, enters positively into the denominator of the multiplier: this means that the larger j is, the smaller is the multiplier (because the leakages from the circular flow of income are larger). Now the size of j is one aspect of the 'openness' of an economy (there are other aspects such as the lack of restrictions on international trade or, indeed, on international capital flows), so what equation 2 implies is that the more open the economy the smaller is the multiplier.

What emerges from this analysis, then, is that when domestic income rises in an open economy imports rise but exports remain unchanged; the balance of trade therefore deteriorates, and this deterioration means that income rises by less than it would otherwise have done since the balance of trade enters positively into the determination of the national income. For demand management policy the implication is that attempts to stimulate the domestic economy, raise national income and lower unemployment will be partly dissipated in increased imports rather than increased domestic production. In terms of the aggregate demand/aggregate supply analysis developed in chapter 2, the larger a country's marginal propensity to import, and therefore the more open it is, the smaller will be the shift in the aggregate demand schedule which results from a given change in fiscal or monetary policy.

Furthermore these conclusions are reinforced by any relaxation of the rather simple assumptions of this analysis. For example if absolute and relative prices are allowed to vary, domestic reflation is likely to raise the domestic price level via an increase in demand and/or an improvement in the bargaining position of trade unions, and the consequent loss of competitiveness in international markets will lead to a reduction in exports and an increase in imports, exacerbating the deterioration of the balance of trade. Secondly it is widely regarded as plausible that imports are determined partly by the rate of change of national income as well as its level: the idea is that the more quickly demand increases the more difficulty domestic producers have in increasing supply at the same speed, and so the more imports are 'sucked' in. If that is so it provides a further reason why domestic reflation, which increases the rate of change as well as the level of income, should worsen the balance of trade. And thirdly consider the incorporation of capital flows in the balance of payments: in Keynesian analysis these are assumed to be determined mainly by relative interest rates, in which case expansionary domestic policies which usually involve lower interest rates will lead to increased net capital outflows (or reduced net inflows) so that the deterioration in the balance of payments will exceed that in the balance of trade.

The clear conclusion, then, is that domestic reflation will in general worsen the balance of payments. This does not mean that there will necessarily be a conflict between the objective of 'internal balance' – full employment (plus price stability) – and that of 'external balance' – zero balance of payments deficit – but it does mean that such a conflict is possible, for in this analysis there is no reason why the level of income at which full employment occurs should also be the level at which imports are such that the balance of payments deficit is zero. The conventional Keynesian response to this possible dilemma has been to argue that demand management policy on its own cannot attain the two objectives of internal and external balance. For this reason attention has been directed to a search for other policy instruments such as the exchange rate, which is considered in section 3 below, and import controls which are discussed in section 2.3.

2.2. *The monetary approach to the balance of payments*

The monetary approach to the balance of payments (MAB) involves a rather different method of analysis which focuses on the overall balance of payments rather than the balance of trade, and views it in terms of the supply and demand for money. Its modern form, as developed by both IMF economists and academic monetarists, represents a development out of, and in some respects against, the Keynesian approach. However, it also claims to have its roots in the eighteenth- and nineteenth-century classical theory which originated with David Hume's 'price-specie-flow' mechanism.

Chapter 7 explained the identity between the growth of the money supply (ΔM^S) and that of its credit counterparts:

5
$$\Delta M^S = \text{PSD} - \Delta Gp + \Delta Lp + \text{EF},$$

where PSD is the public sector budget deficit, ΔGp is public sector borrowing from the private sector, ΔLp is bank lending to the private sector, and EF is net external flows, the main component of the latter being the balance of payments surplus. If the first three items on the right-hand side are lumped together as the growth of the *domestic* counterparts or 'domestic credit expansion' (DCE), equation 5 can be written as

$$6 \qquad \Delta M^S = DCE + EF$$

Alternatively such a relationship for a simple monetary economy (it is more complicated for the UK) can be derived from the equality between the two sides of the balance sheet of the whole banking system (commercial banks *plus* central bank): the liabilities of the system are notes and coin in circulation and deposits, i.e. the (broadly defined) money supply, while the assets are lending to private and public sectors, i.e. domestic credit (DC), and the central bank's holdings of gold and foreign exchange reserves (FA):

$$7 \qquad M^S = DC + FA$$

Taking first differences (that is the change in each item between one period and the previous period) gives

$$8 \qquad \Delta M^S = DCE + \Delta FA$$

where DCE is the change in the domestic assets of the banking system and ΔFA is the change in its foreign assets (gold and foreign exchange reserves). This relationship is the starting point for the MAB; essentially the MAB involves an analysis of the effect of variations in DCE on ΔFA (the balance of payments surplus) *for a given* ΔM^S.

It is convenient to start by discussing the MAB formally with the help of some 'extreme' assumptions appropriate for a very small, very open economy on a fixed exchange rate which allow precise but simple analysis; those assumptions can then be relaxed in a way more appropriate for a medium-sized open economy and in a less formal analytical framework. It may be helpful to think of the underlying relationships in the following way: DCE is the potential increase in the supply of money from domestic sources; if this potential increase is more than the increase that the economy 'requires', then when the exchange rate is fixed the economy gets rid of the excess through a balance of payments deficit; while if the potential increase is less than the economy requires it obtains more money via a balance of payments surplus. The actual mechanisms by which excessive (inadequate) DCE results in a balance of payments deficit (surplus) are various: they involve people and firms altering their spending on goods and services and/or on assets when they find their actual money holdings differ from what they desire, and in principle the mechanisms will include changes in both current and capital account flows. However the focus of attention and analysis here is with the balance of payments as a whole.

The MAB starts by assuming that in equation **8** ΔFA is the dependent variable and ΔM^S and DCE are independent variables, the latter determined by the policy decision of the monetary authorities (though as was shown in chapter 7 it may not be easy for them to control monetary growth) and the former determined by the change in the demand for money, ΔM^D (it is assumed that the money market always clears, i.e. $M^S = M^D$ and $\Delta M^S = \Delta M^D$). Equation **8** can therefore be rearranged to give

$$9 \qquad\qquad \Delta FA = \Delta M^D - DCE$$

which says that the change in foreign exchange reserves, in other words the balance of payments surplus, is equal to (and determined by) the change in the demand for money minus the increase in domestic credit. The demand for money is assumed to depend on three things – real income, prices and interest rates. In that case the change in the demand for money, ΔM^D depends on the change in those three things. There are three very particular, 'extreme' assumptions about those three things, assumptions which are argued to be appropriate for a very small, very open economy, and which are convenient here:

(a) The domestic price level is equal to (and determined by) the world price level expressed in domestic currency: this assumption, often referred to as the 'Law of One Price', can be at least partially justified on the grounds that national markets, at least for raw materials and many manufacturers and some services, are integrated into single world markets, so that the normal processes of supply and demand prevent the price level in one country diverging from the world level in the same way as they prevent the prices of most goods and services in Edinburgh diverging from those in Glasgow.

(b) There is permanent 'full employment' and a constant rate of growth of potential output so that the rate of growth of real income is constant: this assumption can only be (inadequately) justified by appealing to neo-classical views of the self-equilibrating capacity of a capitalist market economy; however the real world range of variation in the growth rate of real income may be small in comparison to the variation in DCE, so that the assumption is a convenient, and not too misleading, simplification.

(c) The domestic interest rate is equal to (determined by) the world interest rate: this can be justified on the grounds of the substantial degree of integration of national capital markets in the real world (particularly as a result of the functioning of the Eurocurrency markets).

Now the effect of these assumptions is to pin down the change in the demand for money, ΔM^D: it depends on the change in real income which is now, by assumption, exogenous and constant; on the change in the domestic price level, that is the domestic rate of inflation, which is now, by assumption, tied to the world price level/rate of inflation; and on the change in the domestic interest rate which is similarly tied to the world interest rate. ΔM^D is therefore determined entirely by factors which are independent of and exogenous to domestic monetary policy, DCE, so that all fluctuations in DCE are reflected wholly in fluctuations (in the opposite direction) in ΔFA. *Ceteris paribus* any increase in DCE will worsen the balance of payments while any reduction in DCE will improve it. Moreover in this model there can be no conflict between internal and external balance such as occurs in the Keynesian analysis, since by assumption there is continuous full employment. There is only one effective policy instrument – DCE – but there is only one relevant policy objective – the balance of payments – which can be adequately controlled by DCE. On the other hand the MAB analysis agrees with the Keynesian analysis in implying unequivocally that expansionary domestic policies (though in this model there is no reason why there should ever be undertaken) would worsen the balance of payments.

For a medium-sized, not quite so open, economy such as that of the UK, however, the extreme assumptions may be applicable in the long run (3-4 years) but are not realistic for the short run. They should be modified to allow for (a) the possibility that the domestic price level can rise (fall) above (below) the world price level but to a limited extent only, particularly in response to an increase (decrease) in DCE; (b) the possibility that real income growth and the level of employment can fluctuate, rising (falling) particularly in response to an increase (decrease) in DCE; and (c) the possibility that domestic interest rates may fall (rise) below (above) world rates to a limited extent, particularly in response to an increase (decrease) in DCE. One way of viewing these modifications is as referring to an expectations-augmented Phillips curve type of analysis in which unemployment can fluctuate in the short run either side of the natural rate with inflation varying in the opposite direction, but with expected inflation dominated by the world rate of inflation (chapter 6). The implication is that a part of the effect of fluctuations in DCE will be reflected in fluctuations in the growth of the demand for (and therefore supply of) money, but it can be argued that the major impact of DCE fluctuations will still fall on the balance of payments when the exchange rate is fixed.

On these more moderate assumptions then internal balance is not guaranteed in the short run but there are forces which work to restore unemployment to the natural rate if it diverges from it. In the long run at least there is no conflict between internal and external balance since a rate of DCE which maintains external balance (ΔFA = 0) will in the long run keep unemployment at the natural rate, with domestic inflation exactly equal to the world rate. There are now two relevant policy objectives (full employment and the balance of payments) but two policy instruments – demand management policy here is dominated by monetary policy (DCE) but there is some role for fiscal policy. Finally the analysis still implies that expansionary policies will worsen the balance of payments, although in the short run, in contrast to what happens in the extreme assumptions model above, expansionary policies will increase the level of domestic activity as well (in the long run, however, demand management policies will have no effect on the level of unemployment which will return to the natural rate).

2.3. Import controls as an extra policy instrument

One of the reactions of Keynesian economists (and of important political forces) to the perceived conflict between external and internal balance has been a search for additional policy instruments, including that of import controls. The basic idea here is that, if imports were controlled to prevent the deterioration of the balance of trade which is predicted by the Keynesian analysis of section 2.1 to accompany policies of domestic reflation, then there would be no problem in using such policies to attain internal balance.

In terms of the algebra of the Keynesian analysis import controls are commonly thought of as setting the value of imports at a fixed level independent of the level of national income, that is as setting $H = q^*$, say, with $j = 0$. Equations 2 and 3 of the model will now be modified to the following:

2a
$$Y = \frac{(a + \bar{I} + \bar{G} + \bar{X} - q^*)}{(1 - b + bt)}$$

3a
$$B = X - H = \bar{X} - q^*$$

In this case clearly reflation has no implications (adverse or otherwise) for the balance of trade and with external balance achieved by the appropriate use of import controls the instruments of demand management policy (G and t) can be set at whatever levels are necessary for internal balance.

However the above analysis is far from satisfactory: what it in fact does, in setting $H = q^*$ and $j = 0$, is to model the *desired effects* of import controls rather than modelling the policy instrument that the government is to manipulate (which is the normal practice in analysing fiscal policy, for example). The obvious candidates as policy instruments here are tariffs and quotas. The former are essentially taxes on imports which raise their prices in domestic markets and therefore lead to a decline in the demand for them. There are two points (at least) which need to be considered:

(1) that the effect on the total value of imports would depend on the relevant elasticities of demand and of the supply of import substitutes, but might also

depend on demand pressure, as measured by the level and/or rate of change of national income; and

(2) that the widespread introduction of tariffs would raise the general price level, which might have various other effects also.

Quotas, on the other hand, are physical limits on the volume of imports. In principle they can be designed so as to achieve the precise effect desired on the volume of imports, and to produce a significant income for the government corresponding to that from tariff revenues in the forms of the proceeds of import licences sold by the government to importers. However their effects on the prices of imported goods are less predictable, and will indeed depend on the various factors, elasticities and demand pressure, which determine the volume effect of tariffs. It should be clear then that import controls cannot be properly evaluated within this simple Keynesian model, but that they are at least rather more problematical than appears at first sight, once the nature of the controls and the manner of their operation is taken into account.

Finally what are the predictions of MAB with respect to tariffs and quotas? In principle the automatic tendencies towards internal balance mean that there is no conflict between that and external balance, and therefore no need for import controls. However it is still possible to ask the question within the MAB framework: how would import controls affect the balance of payments? The answer is that they would affect the overall balance of payments (as opposed to a part or the whole of the current account) only if they affect DCE or M^D: in equation 9 that an increase in ΔM^D or a reduction in DCE will increase ΔFA, as the supply of money adjusts via the balance of payments to the demand. Import controls can only affect DCE by increasing the income of the government and so reducing its budget deficit (without there being any offsetting change in any of the other counterparts of monetary growth). On the other hand they may have the effect of raising M^D by increasing prices or (if the domestic output of import substitutes is increased, though this is strictly incompatible with the internal balance assumptions) income; however any such effect is likely to be a once-for-all effect on the level, rather than a permanent effect on the *growth* rate, of prices or income, in which case M^D will be raised once and for all but the underlying ΔM^D will remain the same. Thus in the MAB analysis import controls can bring about only a temporary improvement in the balance of payments.

3. Exchange Rate Manipulation as a Solution

Section 2 established that in the Keynesian analysis the openness of an economy on a fixed exchange rate constitutes an obstacle to, or a constraint upon, domestic policies of reflation in so far as such policies will normally cause a deterioration of the balance of trade; policy-makers are therefore confronted with the dilemma that the use of the instrument of demand management policy to attain one objective, that of internal balance, frequently worsens the economy's position with respect to another objective, that of external balance. A number of problems involved in the use of import controls to solve the dilemma were also identified. This section focuses on another instrument, that of the exchange rate. First section 3.1 surveys the evolution of thinking within the Keynesian tradition about the ability of exchange rate changes to correct balance of trade disequilibria, and about whether the use of the exchange rate as an additional instrument enables policy-makers to solve the dilemma identified in section 2. Section 3.2 examines the effectiveness of exchange rate changes within the framework of MAB, obtaining results which are this time rather closer to those of recent Keynesian developments. The common element in these results is then stated more formally in section 3.3.

3.1. *Exchange rate changes in the Keynesian tradition*

Within the Keynesian tradition there have been two main approaches to evaluating the effectiveness of exchange rate changes as an instrument to correct balance of payments, or rather balance of trade, disequilibria.

The first approach is the 'elasticities approach' which focuses on the conditions for the various elasticities of demand and supply for imports and exports which need to be fulfilled if a devaluation is to improve the balance of trade. But why should there be any doubt about this? Is it not just another example of the workings of the price mechanism? Consider for example figure 8.1, which depicts the market for foreign exchange, with the supply of and demand for foreign currency plotted against its price, the exchange rate er (defined here as the home currency value of a unit of foreign exchange, as for example $er = 0.50$ when \$1 = 50p). Assume for the moment that there are no capital flows in either direction. The S_{FX} schedule which represents the realized proceeds of exports – a quantity of foreign currency whose holders want to exchange it for domestic currency – is drawn sloping upwards on the assumption that as the exchange rate is depreciated (er is increased) a country's exports become more competitive, demand increases and their total value rises. The D_{FX} schedule which represents the value of imports – a quantity of domestic currency whose holders want to exchange it for foreign currency – is drawn downwards-sloping on the assumption that at higher values of er imports are less competitive, demand for them falls and their total value decreases. A devaluation of the exchange rate, which in terms of the definition used here means an increase in the rate, will tend to raise the supply of and reduce the demand for foreign currency in figure 8.1, thus unequivocally improving the balance of trade. In figure 8.2 the S_{FX} schedule slopes not upwards but downwards, and more gently than the D_{FX} schedule; and here a devaluation will reduce the supply of foreign currency by more than it reduces the demand, so that the balance of trade deteriorates: at er_0 for example the balance of trade deficit is $q_0 q_1$, but at er_1 it is $q_2 q_3 > q_0 q_1$. Thus if the S_{FX} schedule is like that in figure 8.2 devaluation will worsen the balance of payments, whereas if the schedule is as in figure 8.1 it will improve it; changing the exchange rate will be a useful policy instrument only in the latter case. However the S_{FX} schedule of figure 8.2 is perfectly possible: it plots the proceeds of, or the revenue from, exports; that is the price times quantity, which can increase or decrease as the price falls (exports become cheaper in foreign currency as the exchange rate is increased or depreciated) depending on the size of the elasticity of demand.

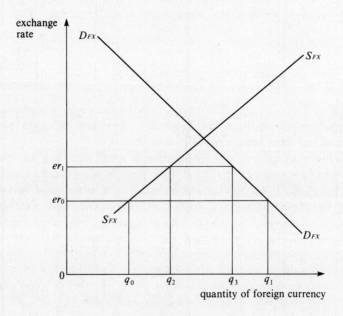

Figure 8.1

In principle a balance of payments deficit could be cured by a revaluation in the figure 8.2 case, but in practice this is likely to be a very awkward policy to carry through since the natural workings of the foreign exchange market would almost certainly tend to *raise* the price of the currency which is scarce relative to demand, in this case the price of foreign currency – that is to raise the exchange rate on the present definition.

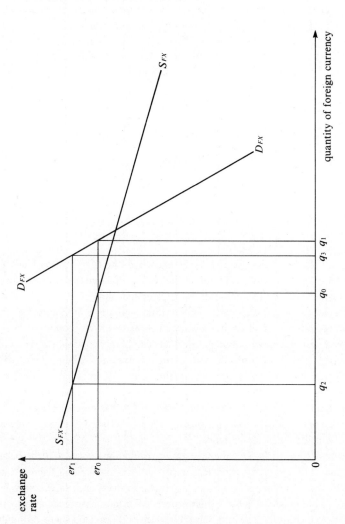

Figure 8.2

The elasticities approach which is developed on this basis is an attempt to relate the effect of devaluation on the balance of trade to these underlying elasticities of demand and supply. The full analysis is mathematically complex and the full result, known as the Robinson–Metzler equation, is difficult to interpret. However a useful simplification of that result is presented in the Marshall–Lerner equation. This is derived on the basis of two simplifying assumptions:

(a) that the elasticities of supply of exports in both the devaluing country and the rest of the world are infinite, that is exporters are prepared to supply any amount of their exports for the same price in terms of their domestic currency; and
(b) the original balance of trade deficit is zero – an admittedly odd assumptions, since a country whose deficit was zero would not usually be contemplating devaluation, but one which simplifies the mathematics.

On this basis attention is concentrated entirely on the domestic and foreign elasticities of demand for imports and the Marshall–Lerner equation can be derived, as follows:

$$10 \qquad \frac{\Delta B}{\Delta er} = (\eta_b + n_f - 1)$$

This implies that for a devaluation of the exchange rate ($\Delta er < 0$) the balance of trade will improve ($\Delta B > 0$) if and only if the sum of the domestic (η_b) and foreign (η_f) elasticities of demand for imports is greater than one.

The development of this approach led not unnaturally to a number of empirical investigations into the actual size of the relevant elasticities, with economists dividing into 'elasticity optimists' who thought the Marshall–Lerner condition was probably fulfilled, and 'elasticity pessimists' who thought it was not. The evidence which has accumulated seems now to have swung the balance of opinion firmly in favour of the first group when the effect of devaluation over any period other than the short run of say 3-6 months is being considered. For example Artus' (1975) analysis of the effects of the 1967 sterling devaluation reported elasticities of demand which sum to about 2.8, well above unity.

For the short run, however, there is still a strongly held view that the balance of trade may be worsened rather than improved by devaluation. There are two reasons for this. The first is that exporting firms, in many industrial countries at least, tend to quote, and to invoice their exports in, domestic currency prices: given the existence of contracts covering several months this implies a sharp drop in the foreign currency value of exports in the period immediately after devaluation, but no change in the foreign currency value of imports; only as new contracts are entered into and implemented will there be volume changes which work in the opposite direction. The second, more general, reason is that the responses of economic agents may take time to develop as a result of some intrinsic inertia in the underlying economic behaviour rather than of institutional factors such as the currency of invoicing. This difference between the short-run and medium-run effects of devaluation is often expressed in the concept of the J-curve, which is illustrated in figure 8.3: following a devaluation at time t_0 the balance of trade initially deteriorates up to time t_1, and then improves, thus tracing out something like a 'j' when plotting on a graph against time.

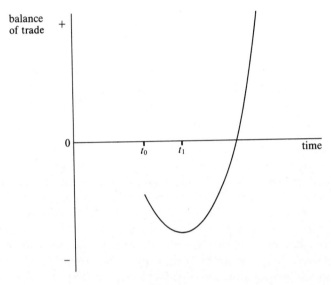

Figure 8.3

However the elasticities approach came under critical attack shortly after it was first developed, and this criticism stimulated the development of an alternative analysis of the effect of devaluation on the balance of trade which was more closely related to the conventional Keynesian macroeconomic model. The main criticism of the elasticity approach was that it was strictly a *partial equilibrium* approach; in particular it concentrated exclusively on the effects of price changes caused by the devaluation, and it ignored the effect of changes in income caused, for example, by the increased output of export goods and/or import substitutes. The 'absorption approach', the second approach in Keynesian analysis, was designed precisely to take account of such factors and to get away from what was seen by some economists at that time (the early 1950s) as a tedious and unresolvable empirical debate about the size of the relevant elasticities. In the standard national income accounting identity.

$$Y = C + I + G + X - H,$$

the first three terms on the right-hand side are defined as 'absorption' (A), that is goods and services absorbed within the domestic economy; the equation can then be rearranged to obtain the balance of trade as the difference between output and absorption:

11 $$B = X - H = Y - A.$$

The absorption approach involves analysing the effect of a devaluation on the balance of trade by assessing (a) direct effects on output, Y; (b) direct effects on absorption, A; (c) indirect effects on A resulting from changes in Y (for example, via the marginal propensity to consume); and (d) indirect effects on Y resulting from changes in A. Various specific direct effects have been identified; here only the two most important are mentioned. One is the 'idle resources effect', in which by improving the competitiveness of domestic goods devaluation stimulates the demand for, and therefore the output of, such goods: there is therefore a direct increase in Y. However it is important to note that the size of this increase will depend on the very elasticities that Alexander (1952), the originator of the absorption approach, was trying to get rid of. A second direct effect, this time on A, is the 'cash balance effect' in which devaluation raises the domestic price level (by raising the price of imports in domestic currency) and therefore *ceteris paribus* reduces the real value of the money balances held by the residents of the devaluing country. The latter, it is argued, will try to restore the previous relationship between their real incomes and their real cash balances by various means, all of which involve a reduction in absorption: individuals may directly increase their savings by reducing their consumption and firms may similarly reduce their investment; or either of these may sell off existing financial assets such as bonds, which would have the effect of lowering bond prices and therefore raising interest rates, thus indirectly discouraging consumption and investment.

To apply the absorption approach in a particular case it is necessary to assess all the various effects, direct and indirect, and then add them up to find out whether $\Delta B = \Delta Y - \Delta A \gtreqless 0$. However, as stated above, information on the size of the elasticities is still required, and a considerable amount of other information as well. Thus although the absorption approach has heavily influenced popular debates on economic policy (as in 'we as a country cannot consume more than we produce') it has not superseded the elasticities approach within the Keynesian tradition in the way that Alexander expected. Its most important contribution has probably been to highlight the question of what policies should accompany devaluation. In particular, if devaluation takes place when the economy is at full employment, then Y *cannot* increase (i.e. there can be no idle resources effect) so that for the balance of trade to improve A must fall. This could be allowed to happen automatically and gradually via the cash balance effect, but it could also be brought about more rapidly by policies of fiscal and monetary deflation accompanying the devaluation. This argument suggests a distinction between expenditure- (absorption-)*switching* policies such as devaluation, which are designed to switch domestic and foreign expenditure onto domestic output and thus bring about an increase in domestic output, Y; and expenditure-*reducing* policies such as increases in tax and interest rates, which are designed to reduce domestic expenditure and thus reduce A.

So far, then, it appears that within the Keynesian tradition there are two competing approaches (though some attempts have been made to synthesize them), which do not provide unambiguous general answers to the question of whether devaluation improves the balance of trade but provide a framework within which that question can in principle be answered for specific cases. During the 1950s and 1960s, although there were some heated debates, notably in the UK around the time of the 1967 sterling devaluation, a majority of economists would probably have answered that question for the typical case in the affirmative, and expositions of the conflict between internal and external balance in Keynesian models often assumed an affirmative answer. More recently, however, with the experience of sharp exchange rate changes since the breakdown of the Bretton Woods system, opinion has shifted strongly against devaluation as an effective instrument for controlling the balance of trade.

Economists had always been aware of the inflationary implications of devaluation, though this awareness had sometimes been submerged in textbook expositions, but recent experience, together with criticisms from exponents of MAB, has greatly strengthened this awareness. Instead of assuming, as they used to do, that an increase in import prices proportional do the devaluation is reflected in the general price level in relation to the proportion of imports to the national income, a majority of Keynesian economists would now assume that money wages increase in response to the initial inflation, increasing the inflation and generalizing it throughout the economy: thus a 10 per cent devaluation would now be expected to result in something approaches a 10 per cent increase in the price level (relative to what it would otherwise have been), rather than say 3 per cent for an economy whose imports were 30 per cent of its GDP. This shift of opinion can be related to changing Keynesian views on the workings of the labour market: whereas in the 1950s and 1960s most Keynesian economists would have argued that workers suffer from money illusion, that is they are concerned with and respond to money wages rather than real wages, since the mid-1970s Keynesians have tended to support some sort of 'real wage resistance' hypothesis in which workers react to cuts in their real wages caused by price increases and try to restore their real wages to the previous level by pushing up their money wages. Thus although they have arrived at the point via a different route Keynesian economists would now tend to agree with monetarists that in the medium run there is no money illusion and that general increases in prices will feed through *ceteris paribus* into money wages (in the monetarist model this occurs through inflation expectations shifting the short-run Phillips curve – see chapter 6).

The effect of this argument on analyses of the effects of devaluation on the balance of trade is to cut the ground from under the feet of the elasticity approach – since the improvement in the competitiveness of domestic output is now expected to be strictly short-term only – and, though to a lesser extent, the absorption approach, where no lasting idle resources effect can now be expected but where the cash balance effect may still operate and indeed be strengthened (by the larger inflationary effect of devaluation). It suggests that the primary effect of devaluation is to raise the domestic price level, so that even if a significant and lasting improvement in the balance of trade could be expected there would be substantial costs involved in using exchange rate changes as a policy instrument. Finally it should be noted that this theoretical argument is confirmed by empirical estimates from most of the major econometric models of the UK economy: although quite different mechanisms are involved in the way devaluation affects the price level in these models, when the response of wages to prices is taken account of they all predict price increases near to the proportion of the exchange rate change.

The conclusion of this discussion, then, is that because of factors rather different from those to which most importance was attached in the earlier stages of the debate, exchange rate changes must be regarded as an ineffective and costly (in terms of inflation) means of correcting balance of trade disequilibria: exchange rate manipulation cannot therefore solve the Keynesian policy-maker's dilemma.

3.2. *Exchange rate changes within the MAB framework*

After this relatively lengthy discussion of the Keynesian approaches to devaluation it is possible to deal more briefly with the effect of exchange rate changes within the MAB framework, since the results can be derived without difficulty from the model developed in section 2.2 above. Devaluation will affect the balance of payments only in so far as it affects either the growth of the demand for money or DCE. There is no obvious reason why DCE should be affected, but ΔM^D certainly will be. Under the extreme assumptions made in developing the very small, very open economy model of section 2.2 the domestic price level is always equal to the world price level converted into domestic currency by multiplying by the exchange rate. This means that when the exchange rate changes the domestic price level will also change to maintain the Law of One Price. In the case of devaluation the increase in the exchange rate will lead to an immediate equiproportional increase in the domestic price level. This increase will cause an increase in M^D and thereby an improvement in the balance of payments (ΔFA), since the latter is the mechanism by which the supply of money increases to come into line with the increased demand. However once the price level and M^D have increased, and the supply of money has adjusted via a balance of payments surplus, ΔM^D returns to its previous level and ΔFA is no longer affected by the devaluation. In a more 'realistic' model even of a very small, very open economy the adjustment of the price level would take at the very least several months, and ΔM^D would therefore be higher (though by a smaller amount) than it would have been otherwise throughout that period, so that the balance of payments improvement would be similarly spread out in time. However the essential point remains, that devaluation improves the balance of payments because it induces a rise in the domestic price level, but once domestic prices have come back into line with world prices the balance of payments improvement disappears.

The same basic result also emerges from the more 'moderate' version of MAB for a medium-sized open economy discussed informally in section 2.2, though it could be argued that a somewhat more extended period of adjustment, say 2–4 years, would be appropriate. Thus within the MAB framework the effects of exchange rate changes fall primarily, and in the long run only, on the domestic price level, and there is only a passing improvement in the balance of payments.

3.3. Conclusion

This section started from the apparent dilemma for policy-makers which arises in the Keynesian analysis from the conflict between internal and external balance under fixed exchange rates, and proceeded to examine the possibility that exchange rate changes would provide policy-makers with an 'extra degree of freedom' – that is, increase the number of policy instruments relative to the number of policy objectives, and thereby enable the dilemma to be solved (see also chapter 1).

What has emerged from the discussion, however, is that in both modern Keynesian thinking which incorporates some kind of wage–price feedback, and in the MAB analysis, the primary effect of exchange rate changes is to alter the domestic price level. A further conclusion from this discussion, which has not been specifically emphasized so far, is that the Keynesian concept of internal balance conflates two policy objectives – full employment and price stability – which in modern Keynesian thinking, and also to a large extent in monetarist thinking, are separate and independent of each other. This means that there are *three* objectives of policy – full employment, price stability and external balance. It might seem that with three objectives, rather than two, it is even more important for governments to be able to use the exchange rate as an extra policy instrument. However 'freeing' the exchange rate from a permanently fixed parity, in the form either of discrete changes in an otherwise fixed parity or of continuous flexibility, does not increase the number of instruments available to policy-makers, rather it changes the objective to which the exchange rate is 'assigned': with fixed exchange rates the exchange rate is in effect being used to peg the domestic price level to the world price level, whereas changing that rate involves using it to control the balance of payments instead. Over-expansionary policies which produce balance of payments deficits under fixed exchange rates produce high inflation instead under flexible rates.

The ability to change the exchange rate does not then give policy-makers an extra degree of freedom, it does not increase the number of instruments relative to the number of objectives, and it does not make the process of macro-policy design necessarily any easier. However this does not mean that exchange rates should always be fixed, for there are a number of other points that will be considered in the next section before any conclusion can be reached on that question.

4. The Flexible Exchange Rate Alternative

Section 3 concentrated on discrete exchange rate changes within the context of a fixed parity system; this section turns to the alternative to that system, a regime of flexible exchange rates. It starts by taking a look at what has happened to exchange rates since the Bretton Woods system of fixed but adjustable parities broke down in the early 1970s. Section 4.2 examines one particular aspect of international monetary relationships, that of international capital movements which have increased dramatically since the late 1950s (when most European currencies became fully convertible) and which, it is argued, contribute substantially to the exchange rate volatility discussed in section 4.1. Section 4.3 then takes a brief look at the arguments for and against fixed and flexible exchange rates.

4.1. *Exchange rates since the end of Bretton Woods*

The Bretton Woods system of fixed but adjustable exchange rates, which had been in operation since the Second World War (though in full operation only since the late 1950s), broke down in the early 1970s. As a gold exchange standard its demise can be located in August 1971 when the US authorities ended the gold convertibility of the dollar, while as an adjustable peg system its demise is better located in March 1973 when the European currencies linked together in the 'Snake' (most of the EEC currencies other than sterling, plus the currencies of some other small West European countries) began to float against the dollar. For 3½ years from the summer of 1972 there were a series of more or less intensive negotiations over the design of a successor system to Bretton Woods, but the necessary agreement was never reached. Instead the 'non-system' which had developed since 1973 was in effect legalized by the decisions of the Interim Committee of the IMF in Jamaica in January 1976, and has continued in existence ever since.

It is called a 'non-system' because, unlike the Bretton Woods system or the gold standard before the First World War, there is no agreed set of rights, responsibilities and obligations laid upon IMF member countries, no order imposed on international monetary relationships: countries can float their currencies or peg (fix) them; they can peg them to anything they like other than gold; they can hold reserves in any form they like; and they can adjust to balance of payments disequilibria in any way they like. In practice most of the smaller countries have chosen to peg to one of the major currencies; and there have been repeated efforts within the EEC to limit the fluctuations between member countries' currencies. At the time of writing (early 1986) there were four major currency blocks floating more or less freely against each other: the US dollar, the Japanese yen, the eight members of the EEC other than the UK whose currencies were linked in the European Monetary System (EMS), and the pound sterling. Even between these major blocks there has been considerable central bank intervention in the foreign exchange market, and the kind of flexibility which has existed for most of the period is often referred to as 'managed flexibility' or 'dirty floating' to distinguish it from the 'perfect flexibility' (zero central bank intervention) usually intended by advocates of flexible exchange rates.

Figure 8.4 shows the movement in the exchange rates of sterling since 1970, (a) against the dollar and (b) against a basket of currencies in the form of the 'effective exchange rate' (where the weights on the various currencies are determined by their importance for UK trade, including that to third countries). The figure is based on annual data, which in effect average the fluctuations in the rates within the calendar year and therefore present a picture of much smoother movements than would be given by weekly, monthly or even quarterly data. Nevertheless it is clear from the figure that strong fluctuations in the rates have occurred.

From 1969 to 1971 the UK balance of payments had shown large surpluses, following the 1967 sterling devaluation. In the general realignment of exchange rates which took place in the Smithsonian Institute in Washington in December 1971, as one of the final attempts to patch up the Bretton Woods system, sterling was revalued slightly against the dollar and marginally against all currencies together. In March 1972 the UK government, which had negotiated the UK's entry into the EEC as from January 1973, agreed to join the EEC countries' 'snake in the tunnel' – an arrangement by which fluctuations between member countries' currencies would be limited to a narrower band of 2¼ per cent (the snake) within the wider band of 2¼ per cent margins either side of parity agreed at the Smithsonian conference (the latter replacing the 1 per cent margins of the original Bretton Woods arrangements).

However by June 1972 the government was forced by strong capital outflows to float sterling, allowing it to depreciate out of the snake, a development which is generally interpreted as the result of the government's own highly expansionary macro- and monetary policies at this time. Sterling has been floating ever since, with the government intervening to varying degrees in the foreign exchange market at different times. It depreciated intermittently through the rest of 1972 and 1973, reaching $2.32 at the end of 1973 as against $2.55 at the end of 1971 (the effective

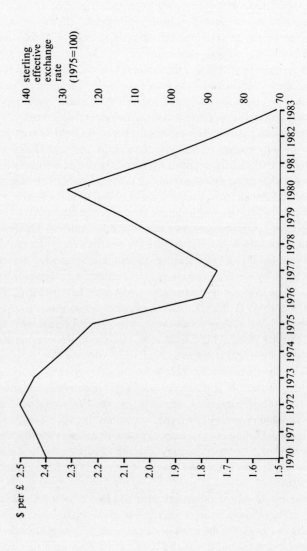

Figure 8.4. Sterling exchange rate. *Sources: International Financial Statistics Yearbook*, 1982, *and Bank of England Quarterly Bulletin*, June 1984.

depreciation was roughly twice as large – comparable in size to the devaluation of November 1967 – since the dollar was also depreciating in effective terms from February 1973).

During 1974 and 1975 the depreciation was rather slower; some economists would ascribe this to the tightening of macro-policy in general and of monetary policy in particular, while others tend to stress the large inflows of money from the OPEC countries during 1974, when they were unwilling to risk the confiscation of their assets by investing their balance of payments surpluses (the result of the 1973-4 oil price rise) in the US.

In 1976 there was a prolonged sterling crisis from March through to November with the sterling exchange rate (both effective and against the dollar) reaching a trough in October, some 20 per cent below the level of March. This crisis came to an end in November 1976 with a significant tightening of monetary policy and the opening of negotiations with the IMF. However before long sterling began to move strongly in the opposite direction, despite substantial purchases of foreign currency by the Bank of England: the government was forced to choose in the autumn of 1977 between its monetary target and an implicit exchange rate target designed to maintain the competitiveness of the UK economy.

Over 1978 as a whole the sterling effective rate was unchanged but sterling appreciated against the dollar, which suffered something of sterling's 1976 experience. From early 1979 to early 1981, partly because of the tightness of monetary policy in this period, sterling underwent a substantial appreciation, particularly in effective rate terms, while the dollar itself began to strengthen in late 1980. Finally since early 1981 the exchange rate (on both measures) has depreciated, but by much less in effective terms than the 1979-80 appreciation despite the fact that the UK's inflation was well above that of most other industrialized countries between 1978 and 1982.

It appears then that the UK has experienced considerable exchange rate fluctuations in the period since sterling was floated in 1972, many of them not predicted by the government or by outside observers. At the very least these sharp movements in the rate can be said to have created problems for policy-makers and to have complicated the process of designing macro-policy. Three examples will suffice. First the 1972-3 depreciation did much to undermine the government's prices policy, since it caused the prices of imported raw materials and other industrial inputs to rise, and such rises were defined as 'allowable costs' which companies could pass on to their customers. Secondly at the time of the 1976 collapse of sterling UK inflation was falling strongly, but under the impact of the depreciation it rose again in the fourth quarter of 1976 and the first half of 1977: if sterling had not depreciated in 1976 it seems likely that UK inflation would have continued to fall throughout 1976 and 1977 and would have gone into single figures perhaps a year earlier than it did (the first quarter of 1978). Thirdly the effect of the 1979-80 appreciation of sterling was to concentrate the impact of the government's deflationary policies heavily on the traded goods sector; this may have increased the cost of reducing inflation by adversely affecting manufacturing capacity over the longer term.

On the other hand it can be argued that exchange rate movements are primarily the effect of government policies, so that if unexpected movements occur, and cause the economy to diverge from the path the government had expected it to follow, then that is a result of the government taking inadequate account of the openness of the economy in its policy-making rather than a fault of flexible exchange rates as such. Of the three examples above this argument can be plausibly maintained for 1972–3, though perhaps less clearly for 1976 and 1979–80.

How does this experience compare with the UK's experience with fixed exchange rates before 1972? The 1950s and 1960s witnessed substantial fluctuations and recurring crises in the balance of payments, which was widely regarded as the major problem of macro-policy and a key constraint on economic growth generally through the pressure it brought upon the government at intervals to pursue deflationary policies. The year-to-year fluctuations in the balance of payments over this period are often described in terms of 'stop-go' – the process by which, it is alleged, government policy alternately expanded the economy when the balance of payments was in surplus in order to reduce unemployment, and contracted it to cure the balance of payments deficit which subsequently developed, after which it would again expand to reduce the unemployment which had now risen. At the same time the trend balance of payments (its average over the cycle) deteriorated, particularly with the highly expansionary policies of 1963–4. The Labour government which took office in October 1964 spent 3 years trying to avoid devaluation, but was finally compelled to accept it by the balance of payments crisis of November 1967. There was then a considerable lag before the balance of payments improved significantly, but 1969–71 were years of record balance of payments surpluses.

Since sterling was floated, however, the balance of payments has been replaced by inflation as the major perceived problem for macro-policy (see chapter 1). Comparison between the two periods is of course complicated by the fact that many things were 'not equal' as between them: in particular for all the major countries economic growth has been much slower and inflation higher in the 1970s and early 1980s than in the 1950s and 1960s. Nevertheless the replacement of the balance of payments by inflation in public concern provides striking confirmation of the argument of section 3.3, that exchange rate flexibility does not solve the problem facing policy-makers but merely changes its nature. In terms of past UK experience at least, then there is no obvious conclusion as to whether fixed or flexible exchange rates are preferable.

What about the experience of other countries since 1973? Over the period there have been a number of major trends in the movements of individual currencies: as can be seen from figure 8.5, the US dollar has fluctuated considerably since 1970 but returned roughly to its original level in 1982; the Deutschmark has undergone a strong and consistent appreciation; the French franc has oscillated but

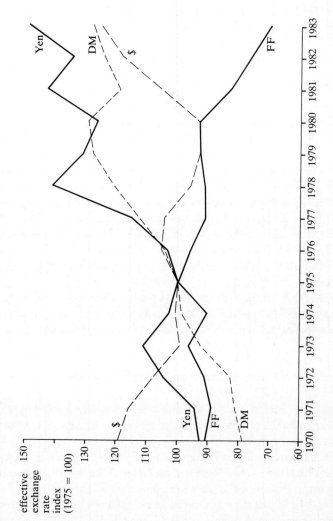

Figure 8.5.   Effective exchange rates of the US dollar, Deutschmark, French franc and Japanese yen. *Sources: International Financial Statistics Yearbook*, 1982, and *Bank of England Quarterly Bulletin*, June 1984

depreciated significantly since 1980; and the Japanese yen has appreciated, though rather less consistently than the Deutschmark. For the present discussion, however, what matters is not so much the trends but the short-term fluctuations around them, which are widely regarded as having been substantial if not actually excessive. For example, a recent article by Zis (1983) examined the fluctuations in the dollar/French franc, dollar/Deutschmark, dollar/yen and dollar/sterling rates (using monthly data for 1973–82) and concluded, 'In summary, the experience of the last decade has not matched the expectations of those who advocated exchange-rate flexibility prior to 1973. Exchange-rate changes have been large, volatile and unpredictable.' Similar comments have been made by many other economists, for example Williamson (1983, p. 242): 'The evidence since the adoption of widespread floating in 1973 is that floating rates are volatile. Instead of the smooth and moderate adjustments that most economists had expected would prevail . . . rates have often jumped around wildly.' Furthermore this volatility has imposed certain costs, since price levels have not adjusted as quickly as exchange rates and therefore countries' competitiveness has been affected. As Williamson continues, 'Countries suffering exaggerated appreciations have had their tradeable goods sectors threatened with serious damage (for example, Switzerland in late 1978, Britain in 1980 to 1982), while exaggerated depreciations have imposed severe inflationary pressures (Britain in late 1976, the United States in late 1978, Germany in mid-1981).' Of course the fixed rate Bretton Woods system was not without its problems either (it is unlikely that it would have broken down if there had not been problems), and the overall context of macro-policy was different between the fixed and flexible rate periods.

It is clear that something should be said about the basic arguments for and against fixed and flexible exchange rates. First, however, it is necessary to consider international capital movements and the determinants of (flexible) exchange rates.

4.2.   *Capital mobility and the determination of exchange rates*

The original Bretton Woods agreement laid considerable importance on the advantages of a multilateral payments system involving convertibility of national currencies for current account transactions, but it was assumed at that time (1944) that capital transactions would continue to be controlled more or less strictly. In the event while the post-war liberalization of trade took longer than the transactional period originally expected, it was also accompanied by a liberalization of exchange controls. By 1958 all the major industrialized countries had abolished restrictions on capital transactions by non-residents, although they continued to maintain a variety of controls, which were increasingly thought to be ineffective, on residents' transfers of capital in or out of their currencies and borders. These controls were primarily designed to protect countries' balances of payments; in some countries they have been relaxed or even eliminated (e.g. in the UK from 1979) since the adoption of flexible rates.

Between 1958 and 1973 there was an enormous increase in capital mobility, that is in both the amount of short-term capital available to move between currencies and countries in pursuit of higher interest rates and/or capital gains from currency realignments and in the speed with which such movements could take place (as a result of improvements in communications technology). Capital mobility in this sense is difficult to measure; one way is to examine the short-term changes in the foreign exchange reserves of countries which experienced substantial inflows or outflows. For example Williamson (1977) quotes figures which suggest a 20-fold increase in the largest weekly inflow into West Germany, as between the late 1950s and the early 1970s, both of these being periods of speculation on a revaluation of the Deutschmark (while German trade increased over the period by less than five times).

There is no doubt that this increase in capital mobility contributed to the breakdown of the Bretton Woods system. Under that system the fact that parities *could* be adjusted, together with a general reluctance on the part of governments to adjust them unless adjustment was clearly necessary and widely agreed to be so, meant that when a parity change was likely speculators – which means here multi-national corporations and traders as well as financial institutions – faced a one-way bet: either there would be a parity change, in which case they stood to make substantial capital gains; or there would not, in which case they would neither gain nor lose. Thus revaluations of the Deutschmark, for example, took place in 1961 and 1969 under the pressure of massive speculative inflows, while the week preceding the sterling devaluation of 1967 was one of a number of periods of intense speculative outflows which threatened to exhaust the UK's foreign exchange reserves.

It is generally agreed that capital mobility on the definition above has increased since the adoption of flexible rates in 1973, although it is difficult to measure this, partly because central banks are no longer committed to intervene in the foreign exchange market to maintain fixed parities. Furthermore it is also generally thought that capital mobility is an important factor in the exchange rate volatility which has been observed over this period. To explain this view it is necessary to say something about what determines exchange rates when they are flexible.

In principle the Keynesian theories of the balance of trade discussed in sections 3 and 4 could be transformed into theories of the determination of the exchange rate, for example by assuming that the exchange rate tends towards the equilibrium rate given by the intersection of the S_{FX} and D_{FX} curves in figure 8.1; thus anything which shifts either of the curves (e.g. monetary of fiscal policy at home or abroad) will now change the exchange rate. Similarly it is possible to turn the MAB round into a theory of exchange rate determination, in which different rates of monetary growth in different countries generate differing rates of inflation, and the exchange rate adjusts to maintaining the Law of One Price. However the

Keynesian theories have no place for capital movements of the kind discussed above, while strong evidence has accumulated since 1973 that the Law of One Price does not hold in the short run. Thus neither the Keynesian nor the MAB analyses can explain the fluctuations in exchange rates since 1973.

Instead, economists have recently developed what is known as the 'asset market approach to exchange rate determination'. In this approach the exchange rate is regarded as simply the price of a financial asset (foreign currency), which is determined in a financial market comparable to those for other financial assets such as bonds, rather than as the outcome of balance of payments flows. The key factor is people's *expectations* of future exchange rates: exchange rate changes involve capital gains or losses for those holding the currencies concerned, so people will buy or sell the currency now if they expect the rate to be different in the future, and such sales and purchases will themselves bring about actual changes in the exchange rate now.

Of course the analysis is more complicated than this – how, for example, do people form their expectations about the exchange rate? – but there is not the space to go into these complexities here. What should be noted from this brief discussion, however, is the point that at a general level the volatility of exchange rates which the world has experienced since 1973 can be understood in terms of approaches to exchange rate determination which emphasize *capital movements in response to expectations of exchange rate changes*.

4.3. *Fixed versus flexible exchange rates*

The debate between supporters and opponents of fixed and flexible exchange rates has been both long-running and many-sided. Here it is possible only to indicate the principal arguments on each side.

The most important argument in favour of fixed, and against flexible, exchange rates is that fixed exchange rates make for less uncertainty and therefore encourage international trade and investment, the efficient allocation of resources and the appropriate international division of labour. Now it is true that fixed rates reduce uncertainty about the exchange rate, but in so far as the factors which cause a flexible rate to change still exist, then under fixed rates they may cause balance of payments disequilibria. There will therefore be a different sort of uncertainty relating to how governments faced with these disequilibria may respond, for example by deflationary fiscal and/or monetary policies or the tightening of capital controls.

The argument is often put forward by way of an analogy with the regions of a country which share a common currency and are able to take full advantage of the possibilities of specialization. If countries fixed their currencies, it is argued, they would be able to reap the advantages of specialization in a similar way. However this analogy is defective, since governments frequently erect various sorts of barriers to the free movement of labour, capital, goods and services between countries, such as do not exist between the regions of a single country, and such barriers impede the efficient international allocation of resources just as much as uncertainty about exchange rates. Furthermore such policies may well be justified in so far as there is no international mechanism of redistribution comparable to that which can be provided by regional policy within a country.

On the other hand the most important argument in favour of flexible, and against fixed, exchange rates is that flexible exchange rates allow countries to choose their own rate of inflation. It used to be thought that flexible rates acted to insulate a country from both 'real' and 'nominal' shocks in the rest of the world – that is, shocks to real variables such as income and trade flows, and shocks to the price level. But it has now been established that in a world of capital mobility flexible rates cannot insulate a country against real or nominal shocks in the short run or against real shocks in the long run. However it is undoubtedly the case that in the long run flexible rates allow countries to inflate at their own chosen speeds; in so far as that choice is made at the level of individual countries, there may be something to be said for flexibility of exchange rates between countries. How much there is to be said for it, however, will depend on the value attached to the rate of inflation itself.

Neither of these arguments is completely convincing. Indeed, despite a long-running debate it seems clear that *at a general level* none of the arguments involved in the fixed versus flexible exchange rates controversy is both decisive and significant. On the other hand a number of the arguments would point strongly in one direction or another *in specific circumstances*. Take as an example the question of whether the UK should participate in the exchange rate mechanism of the European Monetary System (EMS). If it did, this would be tantamount to fixing the exchange rate of sterling against the other EMS currencies and letting it float against other currencies such as the dollar and the yen in line with the EMS currencies. Now there are a number of more or less complex technical issues involved here relating to the precise operation of this mechanism, but there are at least three major considerations relating to the preceding discussion. First, UK participation in the mechanism would imply an acceptance by the UK over the long run of the inflation rate of the country that dominates the EMS, namely West Germany: whether that is considered desirable or not depends largely on judgments as to what sort of macroeconomic policies the German government is likely to pursue in the future, and how important the level of inflation is in any case. Secondly it is likely that the exchange rate uncertainty engendered by the UK's current (Spring 1986) non-participation acts to inhibit the UK's integration into the European Community: again whether that is thought desirable or not depends on answers to a number of other questions such as the desirability of integration in general and the probable political direction of the European Community in the future. Thirdly, while this cannot be demonstrated conclusively, many economists would argue that if the

UK had been participating in the EMS exchange rate mechanism since 1979, then sterling would not have appreciated by so much in the period up to early 1981 and would not subsequently have depreciated by so much: participation would, in other words, have inhibited the formation of the exchange rate expectations which contributed so much to the fluctuations of sterling over this period. At the same time, however, participation would probably have obliged the government to deflate more moderately than it did – and whether that is thought desirable depends on a range of other factors and judgments.

4.4. *Conclusions*

What conclusions, if any, can be drawn from this section on flexible exchange rates? First exchange rates have fluctuated considerably since the early 1970s when the Bretton Woods system broke down, more than had been expected and in ways that have undoubtedly contributed at times to the problems of designing and implementing macroeconomic policy. Secondly the volatility of exchange rates is particularly connected to the greatly increased capital mobility, and in this situation the determination of exchange rates is heavily influenced by expectations. Finally the arguments on either side of the fixed versus flexible exchange rates controversy do not provide an unequivocal recommendation in favour of either exchange rate regime; they may, however, point strongly in one direction or another in *specific cases*.

5. Review and Conclusion

The main points made in this chapter can be summarized as follows. First, the openness of an economy on a fixed exchange rate imposes some sort of constraint in domestic policies of reflation – a strong constraint according to the Keynesian analysis and a weaker one according to the 'moderate' version of the MAB; moreover this constraint cannot easily be avoided by the use of import controls. Secondly, devaluing a fixed exchange rate may shift the constraint temporarily but in the long run it simply creates inflation. Thirdly, floating the exchange rate is not a general panacea either, because of its possible inflationary implications and because of the additional problem of possible exchange rate volatility; nevertheless in some circumstances it may well be the best alternative available.

Policy-makers in an open economy, as opposed to a closed one, are likely to have one more policy objective: balance of payments equilibrium under fixed exchange rates, exchange rate stability (not constancy) under flexible exchange rates. But they will also have one more policy instrument: the exchange rate itself under fixed rates, and the amount of intervention in the foreign exchange market under flexible rates. Thus no simple conclusion can be drawn as to the balance of advantages of openness for macro-policy; it is not necessarily either more or less difficult to achieve the ultimate objectives of macro-policy such as high and growing living standards in an open rather than a closed economy. However, the policy issues are certainly more complicated in an open economy, and it would be foolish for the policy-makers of an open economy to act as if they were operating in a closed economy.

References

Alexander, S. S. (1952) 'Effects of a devaluation on a trade balance', *IMF Staff Papers*, 2, 263-78.

Artus, J. R. (1975) 'The 1967 devaluation of the pound sterling', *IMF Staff Papers*, 22, 595-640.

Williamson, J. (1977) *The Failure of World Monetary Reform, 1971-74*. Nelson, London.

Williamson, J. (1983) *The Open Economy and the World Economy*. Basic Books, New York.

Zis, G. (1983) 'Exchange-rate fluctuations: 1973-82', *National Westminster Bank Quarterly Review*, August, pp. 2-13.

9

The Supply Side
and Industrial Policy

GRAHAME THOMPSON

1. Introduction

In the USA a new body of literature emerged in the late 1970s, referred to as 'supply-side economics', which developed a range of policy suggestions associated with the withdrawal of government from intervention in the market. In broad terms this concern with the supply side has by no means been confined to the United States. It also became a policy issue in the UK (and, one might add, in much of Western Europe as well). Margaret Thatcher's government was elected in 1979 and again in 1983 on a platform that involved, among other things, a strong commitment to the withdrawal of a range of government-financed and promoted interventionist programmes in the industrial field. Mrs Thatcher's policy was based upon the stimulation of the industrial structure through the privatization of nationalized industries and other 'free market' policies, and a strong commitment to the 'reform' of the labour market. All these add up to a sustained focus on the conditions of supply of inputs in the economy.

Thus any discussion of the supply side involves issues of *inputs* to economic activity and how effectively these inputs are combined to provide a supply of output. This chapter begins by looking at the conditions and circumstances of the supply of inputs and their organization, and at the consequences associated with that supply, at a macro-level. However, it should become clear as the analysis proceeds that it will of necessity entail a move into a more disaggregated and micro-framework. An emphasis on the supply side must straddle both macro- and micro-dimensions to the economy.

Although the supply of inputs is based upon both labour markets and the structure of production, this chapter concentrates upon the latter of these. Questions of incentives to work and the importance of wage and salary levels as inputs into firms' cost functions have already been dealt with at length in other chapters. Despite the fact that most supply-side policy emphasis in recent years has been directed at labour market conditions other aspects of production, such as the character of the industrial structure; the size and composition of the capital stock; the role of technology; the levels, quality and types of investments; and managerial competence and effectiveness are also legitimate supply-side concerns. It is these, along with the associated issue of factor productivity, that form the focus for the investigation below. Clearly something has already been said about these issues in previous chapters, particularly in chapters 4 and 5. These issues are also sometimes summed up in a policy context under the term 'industrial policy'.

2. Positioning the Aggregate Supply Curve

An interest in the supply side of the economy is not something confined to one particular economic theory or position, although by and large it has tended to become focused on the position that stresses 'market' organized responses to the economic depression of the 1970s and 1980s. It is this position that has seized the initiative on the supply sides as part of its general critique of Keynesian methods of demand management. It is linked to the emergence of pro-market monetarism and a re-stimulated neo-classical theoretical tradition. However, 'supply-side economics' should not be confused with an all-embracing monetarism. It forms a distinct area of inquiry, both theoretically and policy-wise, and can be at serious odds with monetarism on a number of counts (Thompson, 1986, chapter 4).

It is the shape of the aggregate supply (AS) function which is usually used to differentiate monetarist and Keynesian assumptions, and analyses the economy. But this chapter is more concerned with the *position* of the AS function and how that position can be *changed*. A policy focus emerges here, since it is policy initiatives that are designed to shift the AS function into a more appropriate position with respect to aggregate output and price consequences. In chapter 2 it was pointed out that the following remain constant along an upward-sloping aggregate supply curve: the money wage rate, the stock of capital, the state of technology, the price of raw materials, the size of the population of working age, the preferences between work and leisure, the replacement ratio, and the organizational procedures of production. Thus if we are concerned with a shift in the supply curve rather than movement along it, it is these features that will change. Some of these will be more open to policy initiatives than others. For instance, the money wage rate, the replacement ratio, the state of technology and the capital stock have come to the fore as objects of policy at one time or another over the post-war period.

On the other hand, the prices of raw materials, particularly those emanating from overseas, have been less open to domestic policy initiatives, and have rather been exogenously determined in the UK context. For instance, as we shall see, the oil price shock of the mid-1970s had a considerably detrimental impact on the UK supply-side position. Of course, the domestic cost of foreign-produced raw materials can be influenced by exchange rate changes, which have been subject to government policy. Also domestic raw material prices are clearly subject to policy initiatives.

With respect to the size of the population of working age, this is a variable that is likely to change only slowly and be determined somewhat exogenously of government policy. Similar considerations are likely to typify the preferences between work and leisure, although trade union organization can influence these since it affects the terms on which labour is supplied. There is also likely to be some interrelationship between the money wage rate variable and the preferences between work and leisure. Finally, by and large the organization of the production process has been left to individual firms to supervise, and has not appeared as an explicit policy area for governments.

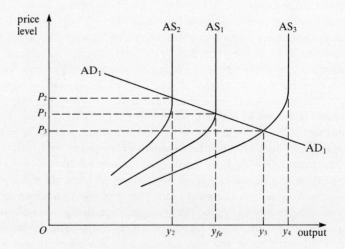

Figure 9.1. Changing the aggregate supply schedule

Figure 9.1 can be used to sum up these points. It shows the usual upward-sloping aggregate supply curve. The curve AS_1 is upward-sloping to the point of full employment output, at which point it becomes vertical in a normal Keynesian fashion. Any change in the variables held constant along this curve will shift it either to the left or to the right of AS_1, i.e. to AS_2 or AS_3. Supposing we have a given aggregate demand schedule AD_1, then in the initial situation output is at its full employment level yf_e and the price level is at P_1. If the aggregate supply curve moves inwards to position AS_2 the price level will rise to P_2 and output will fall to a new full employment level y_2. If however, policy initiatives or changes in economic conditions were to push the aggregate supply curve out to position AS_3, the price level would fall to P_3 and output would expand to y_3. This is the kind of result those emphasizing supply-side initiatives would clearly like to achieve: an increase in aggregate output and a reduction in the general price level without having to alter the aggregate demand schedule. Indeed, under the conditions shown in figure 9.1 it would be possible to stimulate additional output up to the new full employment level y_4 associated with AS_3 by generating additional aggregate demand, but this would increase the price level.

In the analysis that follows we shall not formally consider shifts in the aggregate demand schedule, rather we concentrate upon the weakness in the supply side and on policies proposed to remedy this. However, any specifically Keynesian approach to aggregate supply-side policies would also be likely to be accompanied by positive demand policies (chapter 4). The argument here is that significant supply-side adjustments are best achieved when producers can have some confidence and optimism about sales and demand prospects. Thus supply adjustments are less likely to be successful during periods of deflation and recession in Keynesian terms. This emphasizes the interdependencies between aggregate supply and aggregate demand (see also chapter 10). However, for the purposes here we concentrate specifically upon the supply side and leave out of account any possible accommodating demand adjustments.

3.   What is the Problem?

3.1.   *Introduction*

Those who emphasize the supply side of the economy have suggested that Keynesianism underestimates or even ignores the question of the need for structural change in the economy. The Keynesian emphasis on the manipulation of aggregate demand gives the impression that economies can be regulated and managed adequately simply by altering the size and composition of the government budget.

There are basically two kinds of response to this perceived failure. On the one hand a 'hands-off' approach is suggested. A withdrawal of government intervention and the suspension of fiscal policy initiatives to try to steer the economy is advocated. On the other hand there are those who see this as requiring a much more active interventionary stance to restructure economic processes, institutions and the like which cannot be sufficiently influenced simply by government subsidy or taxation measures. In both of these cases, Keynesianism is relatively discredited as the main mechanism for dealing with supply-side macro-management problems.

This dissatisfaction with the emphasis on Keynesian demand management macroeconomic regulation also stems from the experience of actually trying to manage the UK economy over the post-war period. One of the continually re-occurring problems has been that with demand stimulation the expansion of the economy soon came up against supply-side bottlenecks and constraints. The failure of domestic supply to adapt quickly enough resulted in a sudden upsurge in imports to fill the gaps in supply so created, and this engendered a subsequent balance of payments disequilibrium. The expansion then had to be halted to correct the balance of payments position. This sluggishness of supply adjustment is a further reason for concern with it in a policy context.

In addition, the relative decline of the UK economy and its lack of international competitiveness in manufacturing contributed to a sense of severe unease, particularly as the recessions of the mid and late 1970s and early 1980s developed. The UK economy suffered worse than its main rivals during this period, demonstrating its particularly weak international position (chapters 1 and 3). This led to a great emphasis on the necessity to make the economy more cost-competitive and to put strong downward pressure on prices as a prelude to renewed economic growth.

3.2.   Declining competitiveness

One important measure of the relative competitive position of the economy can be seen from figure 9.2. This shows an index of the changes in relative unit labour costs for the UK over the period 1962–82. This measures the ratio of average hourly earnings to productivity (output per hour) in the UK relative to a weighted average of competitors' unit labour costs. It is thus a standardized measure, for manufacturing activity only, which in figure 9.2 has also been adjusted to take account of exchange rate movements. The exchange rate-adjusted series steadily declined from the mid-1960s until around 1977 (though with some cyclical fluctuations) and thereafter experienced a very sharp rise over the next 3 years. Since 1981 UK relative labour

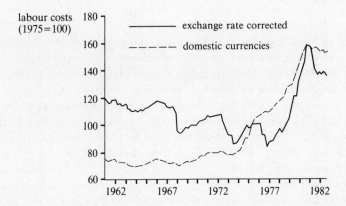

Figure 9.2.   Relative unit labour costs, UK, 1962–82. *Source: Economic Progress Report*, No. 158, July 1983, HM Treasury.

costs have fallen once more. This fall was continued in 1983 and 1984 (not shown on the figures).

A declining relative labour cost implies a movement of the AS curve in figure 9.1 out to the right, while an increasing relative labour cost implies a shift of this curve to the left. An interesting point to be drawn from this figure is that the UK has by no means experienced continually *rising* unit labour costs, even though it has tended to experience a continually worsening manufacturing export performance and failed to stem the tide of imports. In figure 9.3 a measure of import penetration of manufacturing goods is plotted which shows a rising trend from just over 5 per cent in 1955 to 22 per cent in 1980. (According to some estimates this had risen to 28 per cent by 1982 – see Bredenkamp, 1984, table 2.)

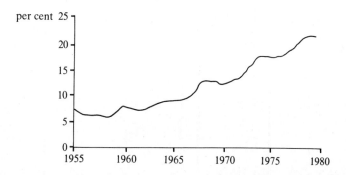

Figure 9.3. Import penetration ratio for products of manufacturing industry in the UK. *Source:* Williams *et al.*, 1983, graph 1, p. 8. *Notes:* Imports are calculated as percentage of home demand and exports. The ratio therefore registers UK manufacturers' commitment to exports and rising exports to sales ratios which partly offset increasing import penetration.

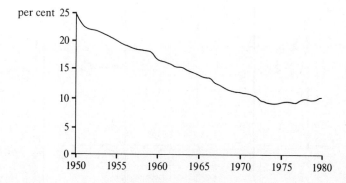

Figure 9.4. Britain's share of world trade in manufactures. *Source:* Williams *et al.*, 1983, graph 2, p. 10.

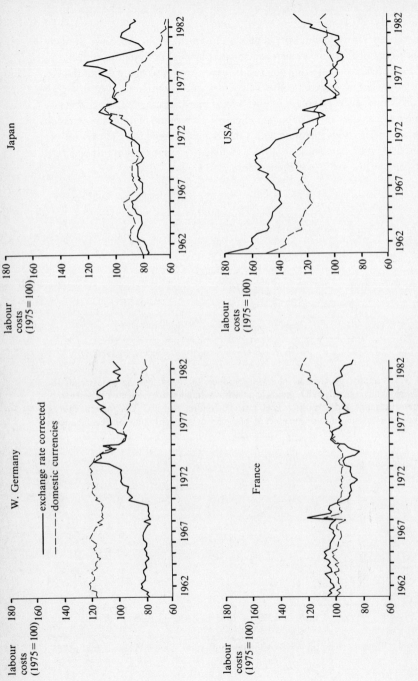

Figure 9.5. Relative unit labour costs: West Germany, Japan, France and the United States. *Source: Economic Progress Report*, No. 158, July 1983, HM Treasury.

Figure 9.4 shows what has happened to the UK's share of manufacturing exports. Throughout the period of the long boom in world trade – between the early 1950s and the early 1970s the volume of developed country exports grew by 8 per cent per annum – the UK's share declined steadily. The slide was halted in about 1973 when Britain's share stabilized at around 9 per cent of world trade, though more recently it has begun to deteriorate again (to 7 per cent in 1984).

Returning now to the data plotted in figure 9.2, we can compare the figures given there for the UK with similarly constructed figures for our main economic rivals, Germany, Japan, France and the USA. These are shown in figure 9.5. For Germany and Japan their adjusted unit labour costs were in fact *rising* over the period between 1960 and 1977 – Germany from 79 to 111, Japan from 90 to 140. While they were increasing or maintaining their shares of world manufacturing trade – Germany steady at 18 per cent, Japan increasing from 5.4 per cent to 14.1 per cent – their unit labour costs were on the increase. For France unit labour costs over a similar period were more or less steady, and for the USA – another country experiencing difficulties over its comparative trading position – labour costs were falling rather like the UK's (Fetherstone *et al.*, 1979).

Some of these longer-term trends were upset after the mid-1970s oil shock. But before we move on to review this development let us just look at what determines cost competitiveness measured in the manner discussed so far (see also chapter 3).

In practice changes in cost competitiveness can come about via three main separate influences. These are:

(a) Changes in the *exchange rate:* a fall in the exchange rate improves cost-competitiveness, providing that domestic costs do not rise to offset it; a rise in the exchange rate produces the reverse effect, again provided that domestic goods do not change to offset it.
(b) A change in the *growth of earnings* relative to those abroad: a relative fall in these will lower domestic unit labour costs relatively and enable firms to compete better at home and abroad.
(c) A change in the *growth of productivity* relative to that abroad. If productivity in the UK grows less quickly than that abroad UK unit labour costs will increase relative to those abroad and make British firms less competitive.

The latter two influences determine domestic unit labour costs while adding in the first of these determines overall international competitiveness.

A word of warning is in order at this stage concerning labour productivity (item (c) above). Labour productivity measures the quantity of output produced for a given input of labour. An increase in labour productivity does not simply mean an increase in 'work effort' in some unproblematical way (although it may involve this in part as discussed below). Rather it predominantly reflects changes in output relative to labour input. Thus an increase in labour productivity will mean that

Table 9.1.   Comparative unit labour costs, 1975–82; total increases (%)

	UK	USA	France	W. Germany	Japan
Earnings	182	86	161	70	56
Productivity	22	11	38	28	51
Unit labour cost	131	68	90	32	3

Source: Economic Progress Report, No. 158, July 1983, table 1, p. 3.

output per unit of labour input (somehow measured) will increase. The cyclical pattern reflected in figure 9.2 results largely from the cyclical pattern of economic activity. In the upswing and boom, output increases faster than labour input as any excess capacity is reduced; this is measured as an increase in labour productivity. Conversely, in the downswing output is generally reduced faster than workers are laid off (and overtime reduced); this is measured as a fall in productivity. As we shall see below, however, this usual pattern was disrupted slightly after 1979 when there was an increase in productivity as output declined.

If we look at figure 9.2 again it is clear that domestic unit labour costs, shown by the line marked 'domestic currencies', were fairly steady over the major part of the period to the mid-1970s (though will some cyclical fluctuations). Thus the main reason for the decline in overall unit labour costs must have been the relative depreciation of the exchange rate. This is shown in figure 9.6. However, around 1975–77 domestic labour costs escalated, the exchange rate appreciated after 1977 and overall relative costs increased dramatically as a result of both these adverse tendencies.

In table 9.1 the position of the UK economy compared to its main rivals is given for the period 1975–82. This table also decomposes the comparative change in unit labour costs into the two domestic influences discussed above. The UK's relative position deteriorated sharply over these 7 years (although it improved

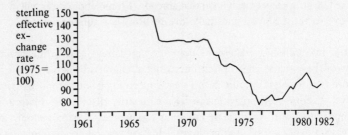

Figure 9.6.   Sterling's effective exchange rate. *Source: Economic Progress Report*, No. 146, June 1982, graph 3, p. 7.

somewhat between 1980 and 1982). Earnings increases in the UK were the highest among the countries shown. Productivity increases were the lowest, except for the USA.

An influential argument advanced by Forsyth and Kay (1980) used to explain this rapid deterioration in the relative manufacturing performance of the UK economy in this period invoked the impact of North Sea oil production on the structure of the economy. Forsyth and Kay suggested that while oil added considerably to the growth of the economy it did so in a highly unbalanced manner because it arose in a single sector. In particular, North Sea oil involves a large expansion of the traded sector of the economy, but as the oil part of the traded goods sector increases, the other part of this sector is squeezed. Thus manufacturing, which makes up a disproportionate part of the non-oil sector, will contract. The mechanism which brings about this structural change is a rise in the exchange rate because of the increased balance of payments surplus due to a decline in the import of oil and an increase in its export. This reduces the competitiveness of British manufactured goods and increases the attractiveness of imports. The decline in manufactured exports and increase in imports restores balance of payments to equilibrium.

Thus the fact that the UK became a net exporter of oil in the early 1980s implied an appreciation in the exchange rate and a decline in the competitiveness of UK manufacturing industry. Forsyth and Kay argue that the manufacturing sector would have to contract as a result. A look back at figure 9.6 and then at figure 9.2 suggests that the exchange rate rose and the exchange-rate-adjusted unit labour cost curve did move up sharply in the period 1979–81. But it was anticipated by an increase in domestic unit labour costs by about five years. The increases here can be attributed partly to the way the domestic economy reacted to the first and second oil price shocks beginning in 1973. This induced an energy price push in domestic costs which was compounded by active trade union agitation and success on the wages front. Hence the rise in earnings figure of 182 per cent shown in table 9.1 for the UK.

An explanation for the rather more long-term trend in the decline of the UK's manufacturing capability, experienced in the period prior to the late 1970s, could also be made in terms of the *sources* of cost competitiveness. As we have seen, the increasing cost competitiveness of the UK economy in the period of the 1960s and early 1970s was mainly attributed to the depreciation of the exchange rate. This may have been a *weakness* of the economy. Perhaps exchange rate depreciation is a much less effective means of achieving a sustained improvement in cost competitiveness than faster productivity growth and lower relative domestic costs would have been. Faster growth in productivity, for instance, quite apart from making higher real incomes possible, would almost certainly have produced a faster growing economy which in turn would have fed favourably into the factors that go to make up 'non-price' competitiveness.

At this point we reach a crucial stage in the analysis; the issue of 'non-price competitiveness'. Overall competitiveness will depend in part on the cost-based measures of competitiveness discussed so far, but it will also depend upon a host of less tangible factors. With respect to manufactures, *quality* and *design* matter to purchases, as well as price. For capital and other durable goods, *delivery dates* and *after-sales service* will be important; for non-durable goods and services it may be *reliability* and *continuity of supply*. Effective marketing may also have a significant influence on performance. It is these other aspects of competitiveness that are termed 'non-price competitiveness', and unlike relative costs and prices they are not readily quantifiable. Favourable non-price competitiveness also tends to be associated with favourable productivity growth.

Clearly the figures discussed so far ignore the aspect of non-price competitiveness. It may well be that the main reasons for the decline in the UK's share of manufacturing exports and the increasing import penetration of its economy is due to these factors rather than to cost competitiveness, although the unquantifiable nature of the non-price features makes this proposition difficult to test. However, a strategy which exclusively focuses on cost competitiveness and ignores these other non-price elements may completely miss the point of the real reasons for the economy's decline.

Another problem with the figures quoted above is that they relate to *labour* costs and not *total* costs. This mainly reflects the availability of suitable data and the difficulty of measuring capital costs. But in practice this may not matter too much. There are good reasons for believing that non-labour costs will vary much less between countries than labour costs. For instance, capital costs have tended to be equalized between countries as the international integration of capital and money markets has advanced. There are still important differences between countries here, notably arising because of balance of payments problems that have resulted in differential interest rates as a mechanism for correting these. But with flexible exchange rates this is now more likely to be a short-period phenomenon. As far as raw materials are concerned these are generally homogeneous and tend to be traded internationally, such that comparable exchange rate adjusted prices exist in different countries. However, in individual industries – where raw materials comprise a large proportion of overall factor inputs and where domestically produced raw material inputs have been supplied at a lower than world price – significant cost advantages have been gained. This has been true of a number of the NICs.

A further point to note is that the data are related to manufacturing activity only. Again, this is partly the result of a lack of any more comprehensive data on the service sector, for instance. But while manufacturing output is only about a quarter of total output in the economy, it still accounts for about half of all exports and imports. Thus manufacturing continues to be a vital element in the UK's domestic and trading environment, even though it has contracted over the last twenty years or so. It is still a central element in the determination of living standards in the UK and cannot be ignored in a policy context.

Despite a number of important reservations, then, labour costs in manufacturing still appear as the main input into firms' cost functions, and hence the relative differences between these is a good indicator of overall international cost competitiveness.

3.3. Cost competitiveness and output changes

While we are dealing with cost competitiveness it is worth standing back a little to ask why it is so important and why it receives so much attention in economic policy debates. The basic idea can be summed up in figure 9.7, which shows very simply the relationship between lower costs and output. We might call this a 'black box' theory of the relationship between inputs with a lower cost and the favourable output consequences. The firm in this case is a 'black box' that transforms the inputs into an output. Because this kind of a conception informs a good deal of popular political debate it is worth looking at its possible implications.

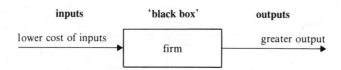

Figure 9.7.   Inputs and outputs

Clearly, the conception that lies behind this simple formulation would assume the firm to be an uncomplicated profit-maximizer. Thus with lower input costs the firm's cost function is reduced. With a given demand curve the equilibrium price would fall and the amount demanded would increase (involving a movement along the given demand curve) such that an increased quantity was produced and sold.

However, suppose we now consider the firm not to be a profit-maximizer but instead, assume for convenience that it is a 'satisficing' firm, broadly speaking. This enables us to open up the 'black box' a little to see what strategies management might pursue under the circumstances of reduced factor input costs. In figure 9.8 some of the possible output consequences of reduced input costs are shown. In this case the outcome depends upon decision made within the firm itself.

For instance, any potential cost advantage offered by a decrease in input costs could be eaten away by the increased provision of bonuses and better non-pecuniary benefits (fringe benefits and 'perks') and the like for managers (this could even be extended to the shop-floor as well). In effect this would be equivalent to increasing wages and salaries by indirect means from the point of view of the individual firm. Secondly, the potential advantage of lower costs could be taken in the form of

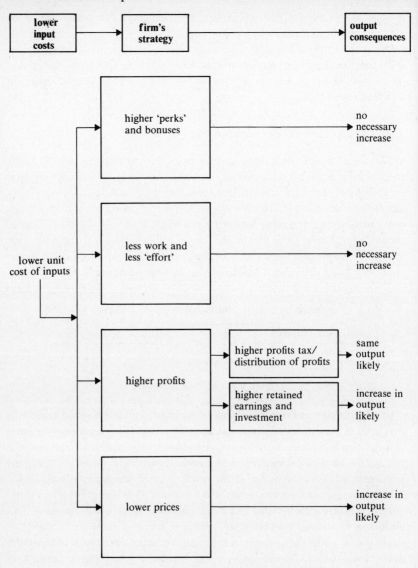

Figure 9.8.   Lower input cost and firm's response

greater 'leisure'. The managers and workers could work fewer hours, put less effort into their work, take longer holidays, etc. In both of these cases there would be no necessary increase in output. However, there may be some increase in that not all the potential benefit need be 'internally' distributed in this way. These two cases are instances of the increase in X-inefficiency.

Thirdly, lower input costs might simply be converted into higher profits. If these are 'externally' distributed either in the form of higher company taxation or to shareholders as dividends, then again no output increase would be necessary. In fact this is likely to result in similar output levels. In this case of higher profits, only if retained earnings are increased which are then converted into new investment would we expect an increase in output to result. This could be part of a strategy that eventually lowered prices, particularly if economies of scale could be reaped with increased investment.

Finally, we have the strategy of reflecting the lower input costs immediately in lower prices, which in turn would lead to some increase in output. Exactly how much output increases clearly depends upon the level of price reduction and the elasticity of demand for the product in question.

From this analysis we can see that what precisely goes on at the level of the firm is vitally important in any strategy that has as its objective an increase in output by reducing the costs of inputs.

The analysis so far has focused on the likely effects of reducing the costs of inputs in the context of individual firms. But if we take the overall macroeconomic effects of some of the possible consequences mentioned above, then a slightly different result might emerge. For instance, at the level of the economy overall the distribution of profits as dividends will appear as income to some agent and hence nominal national income will have increased. If nominal national income increases, yet an output to accommodate it is not forthcoming, then this would suggest that the price level will rise.

In practice, then, any reduction in input costs need not necessarily result in an increase in price competitiveness and output. As we have seen, international cost/price competitiveness can decline while input costs are increasing and 'output' from the economy in terms of its relative export and import performance is also declining. In addition non-price competitiveness is likely to be important. Therefore the emphasis on lower input costs as a necessary prerequisite for output increases and a gain in price or cost competitiveness may be misplaced.

However, it is usual to assume that as input costs decline then relative prices will change and/or profit margins will increase. Thus if UK exporters are faced with a lower growth of domestic costs they will either reduce their selling prices abroad to secure relative price advantage and increase volume sales or maintain their prices in order to improve profit margins; or they will do both of these to some extent. But as we have seen, neither of these two 'options' is necessary, and even the increase in profit margins might be distributed away from the firm to the government (via taxation) or to shareholders (via dividends). There is no necessary reason why domestic output should expand, particularly if this increase in the income of the government and of shareholders were spent abroad.

3.4. *The question of investment*

In this sub-section we look at the issue of investment in relationship to Britain's economic problems. This can be developed in terms of the production functions shown in figure 9.9. The initial production function is represented by $q_1 = f_1 (l, \bar{k}, \bar{t})$ and with labour input l_1 output q_1 is produced. If we were to increase the capital input *or* to change the state of technology (t) such that increased productivity ensued, or if we were to adopt a policy that changed both of these, via investment, then the production function would shift upwards in Figure 9. Production function $q_2 = f_2 (l, \bar{k}^*, \bar{t}^*)$ is drawn such that both k and t have changed (this is denoted by the asterisk). Under these circumstances, with the same input of labour l_1, investment has enabled a greater output to be produced, increasing from q_1 to q_2.

In terms of the aggregate supply function shown in figure 9.1 the capital stock was one of the economic features kept constant along this curve; thus investment, which adds to the capital stock, will tend to push the schedule out to the right (to AS_3 in figure 9.1). Of course, any scrapping of plant and machinery will tend to reduce the capital stock, which will in turn have the opposite effect on the aggregate supply schedule by shifting it to the left (to AS_2 in Figure 1). In this section, however we shall be concentrating on net new investment, i.e. on *increases* in the capital stock. New investment could also be linked to lower unit labour costs if such investment increased the productivity of labour by increasing the output per unit of labour input. We shall come to these productivity changes in the context of the UK economy later in this section.

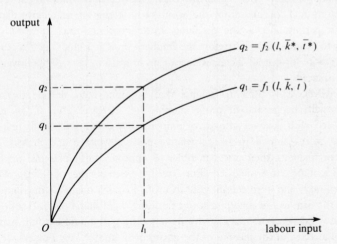

Figure 9.9. Investment and the production function

It is often suggested that the main reason for the decline in the manufacturing sector, and of the economy more generally, is that the UK has failed to maintain sufficient levels of investment. In chapter 1 it was pointed out that the UK has invested a lower proportion of its GDP than most other comparable countries through the post-war period (although they were close to the US ratios) and that its record on manufacturing investment alone, at least in the 1970s, was little better (chapter 1, tables 1.3 and 1.4).

We can now look at the trends and composition of investment in more detail (see also chapter 4). The share of total investment in nominal GDP in the UK rose steadily from about 12 per cent in 1948 to about 18 per cent in the mid-1960s; it reached a peak of just over 20 per cent in 1974, since when it has shown an overall decline to around 17 per cent.

Figure 9.10 shows the trends in investment as between the manufacturing and service sectors of the economy, net of leasing on both counts. The published figures on investment essentially classify fixed investment by ownership rather than by end use. Investment in assets which are then leased is thereby classified as expenditure by the service sector (including banks which have been heavily involved in the leasing business), while these assets are actually used in the production industries. Leasing comprised some 20 per cent of the total fixed investment in manufacturing by 1982.

The main point to be drawn from figure 9.10 is the way investment in the distributive and service industries has been steadily growing since 1965, and how in manufacturing, despite cyclical variation, it remained reasonably stable up to 1979 but then fell away rapidly, with a hint of an upturn in 1983. Investment in the service industries was double that in manufacturing by 1980. Thus the relative demise of the manufacturing sector, at least as one to which investment has been directed, began well before the 'oil economy' came on stream in the late 1970s, but this coincided almost exactly with the absolute fall in manufacturing investment. Presumably the rapid appreciation in the exchange rate adversely affected the expectations of businessmen, who reacted accordingly by cutting investment. As of 1983–4 business investment seems to be recovering with a 12 per cent increase in manufacturing and an 8 per cent increase in service industries (chapter 4).

3.5. *Investment and productivity*

We can now turn to the issue of the productivity of the investment that has taken place. One thing that has continually puzzled economists is the apparent lack of any general and clear-cut relationship between levels of investment, productivity and growth in the UK economy. Although the UK has not been investing as much as most other advanced economies, its record is not very different from these; it

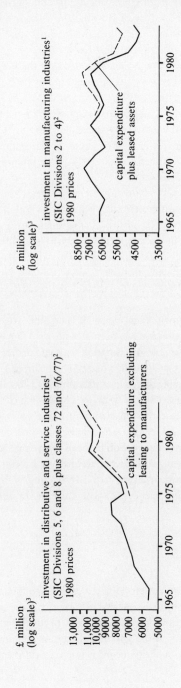

Figure 9.10. Investment in service and manufacturing industries (net of the leasing element)

Notes:
[1] Figures from the third quarter of 1983 are forecasts.
[2] SIC refers to the relevant Standard Industrial Classifications used to categorize different economic activities.
[3] The log scale on the vertical axis simply converts the raw data into a logarithm. This compresses the upper values of the scale and enables rates of change to be more easily identified.
Source: Economic Progress Report, No. 164, January 1984, p. 2, HM Treasury.

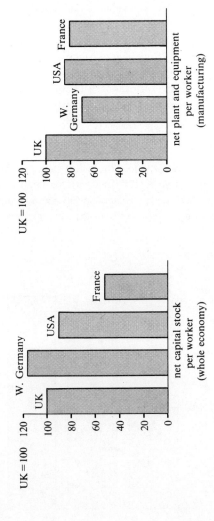

Figure 9.11. Index of capital per worker, 1980 (UK = 100). *Source:* Kaletsky, 1983.

only differs by a few percentage points from its rivals. This is also confirmed if we look at the stock of capital per worker as shown in figure 9.11.

The UK is better placed than the other economies in terms of plant and equipment per worker in manufacturing. What does differ considerably, however, is the output gained from that investment or use of capital stock. Figure 9.12 shows that in 1980 the UK produced half the output per unit of capital employed in manufacturing industries compared with West Germany and the USA, and under two-thirds that of France. If we now look at the incremental capital–output ratio, i.e. the increase in output per increment in capital used adjusted for labour use, the position of the UK is somewhat worse. In Figure 9.13 this is shown averaged over the years 1964–73 and 1973–9 for a number of countries. The UK began in a disadvantaged position which became relatively much worse in the late 1970s.

There are a number of explanations that have been advanced to account for these conditions. The age structure and technological mix of the UK capital stock may be inferior to its competitors. However, there seems little evidence to suggest that the UK has a grossly older capital stock in the manufacturing sector than its competitors, although on the issue of technological characteristics of any *new* investment (which obviously affects the incremental capital output ratios in particular) things are less settled. Katrak (1982) suggests, for instance, that the UK's investment and exports have become less technologically intensive in recent years. A further explanation could be in terms of management strategies involving the allocation

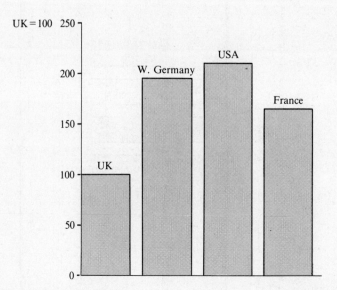

Figure 9.12.   Index of output per unit of capital in manufacturing, 1980 (UK = 100). *Source: Economic Progress Report*, No. 167, May 1984, p. 2 and OECD.

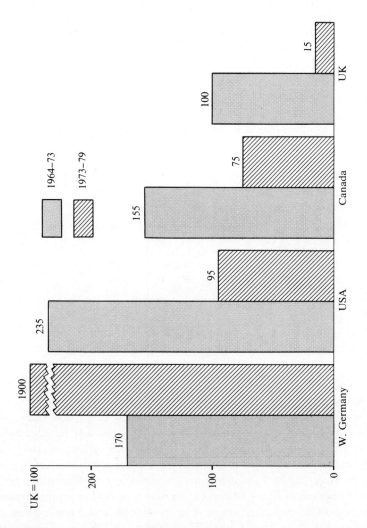

Figure 9.13. Comparative incremental capital–output ratios in manufacturing (adjusted for labour use), 1964–79 (UK = 100). *Source: Economic Progress Report*, No. 167, May 1984, p. 2.

of investment to particular product sectors, though Williams *et al.* (1983) provide evidence that the UK's export sectoral profile is not substantially different from other comparable countries. The way the actual processes of production have been organized and arranged in UK industry may lead to lower productivity. This connects to the idea that UK labour and trade union restrictive practices have been the main reason preventing comparable capital productivity. Finally we can point to the comparative role of taxation and subsidies to investment incentives as offering an explanation. The UK might over-subsidize investment such that its quality is impaired. This is an issue that the Conservative government highlighted as an area for reform in 1984, and we concentrate on this in the discussion immediately below because it also raises some more general issues.

Table 9.2 shows the taxes and subsidies to investment, 1973 and 1978, for a number of industrialized economies. The UK had the highest overall tax relief in 1978. Thus one of the reasons for low productivity might be that such relatively high subsidies to investment in the UK have encouraged firms to invest simply for tax reasons.

Table 9.2.   Taxes (+) and subsidies (−) to investment (as percentage of asset price)

	1973	1978
UK	− 2.4	− 4.4
Belgium	+ 0.6	+ 5.9
France	+ 1.0	+ 7.6
Germany	+ 5.9	+ 4.0
Italy	+ 12.8	+ 18.4
Japan	+ 1.4	+ 1.4
Netherlands	+ 5.0	+ 7.7
USA	− 3.0	− 0.6

Source: Treasury and Civil Service Committee, 1984.

If subsidies make the cost of investment lower or even negative, firms will be encouraged to invest in projects with lower returns than they would otherwise have done (or even with negative returns). Further the way these subsidies have been organized in the UK may have encouraged firms to invest more on the basis of financial dealing than on real productive potential. For instance tax allowances against investment, taking the form of lower corporation tax, were the main reason for the development of leasing. Manufacturing firms were not in a position to take full advantage of these subsidies because of low profit levels, but commercial banks, enjoying much healthier profits, were. They developed the leasing business as a result. Leasing effectively enables tax concessions to be switched to the lessor (such as a bank), the legal owner of the assets involved. By deferring the lessor's tax payments it was possible for the lessor to make the asset available to the lessee

Table 9.3. Relative tax subsidies to different kinds of physical investment, 1980

	UK	W. Germany	Sweden	USA
(a) Plant and machinery	13.7	5.5	10.0	8.2
Buildings	6.1	5.7	6.3	5.9
Difference	+ 7.6	− 0.2	+ 3.7	+ 2.3
(b) Manufacturing	11.0	5.2	7.3	4.7
Commerce	6.4	5.6	6.1	6.2
Difference	+ 4.6	− 0.4	+ 1.2	− 1.5

Source: Treasury and Civil Service Committee, 1984, Appendix 10, Annex 1.

on more favourable terms than could be achieved through direct purchase. In either of these cases, investment overall could be of a poorer quality than otherwise, although it may be more extensive than otherwise, i.e. the subsidies may have encouraged more investment than would have otherwise have been the case.

The UK has also subsidized plant and machinery to a greater extent than other economies. Assuming a 10 per cent pre-tax real rate of return, table 9.3 shows the post-tax returns to plant and machinery compared to buildings in the UK, Germany, Sweden and the USA. There is thus a discrimination against service sectors, the Treasury has argued; in 1980, for example, 50 per cent of manufacturing capital stock was in plant and machinery as against 30 per cent in the service industries. When these calculations are repeated on the basis of the relative weights of the different kinds of investment in manufacturing and commerce, the figures shown in section (b) of table 9.3 emerge, again demonstrating the highly discriminatory nature of subsidies to the manufacturing sector.

In the context of trying to increase employment potential the Treasury argued in 1984 that this discrimination against the service sector should be halted. Service industries are generally thought to be more labour-intensive than manufacturing industries, so encouraging investment here (or rather not discouraging it so much relative to manufacturing) is a way of increasing employment possibilities. This demonstrates the way in which 'industrial policy' and 'employment policy' have been interlinked.

However, there may be an anomaly in this argument about the effects on investment of discriminatory tax incentives. It was pointed out with reference to figure 9.10 that investment in the service sectors has been on a strongly growing trend, while investment in manufacturing has been static or declining. Thus even though there seems to have been a tax advantage in investing in the manufacturing sector, actual investment has been growing in just that sector which is supposedly discriminated against. This should make us sceptical of the argument that these tax advantages and disadvantages are the main reason for the distribution of investment, and indeed its quality. Thus a policy directed at altering this aspect may have missed the point.

As a response to the discrimination in investment allowances the Conservative government announced a package of measures in its 1984 budget to 'reform' company taxation. These included a progressive reduction of. the mainstream corporation tax rate from 52 per cent to 35 per cent and the phasing out of various investment reliefs, including stock relief, the first year investment allowance for plant and machinery and initial allowances for industrial buildings.

Clearly, the reduction of the corporation tax rate is likely to increase companies' potential investment funds since it will enable them to generate larger retained earnings. On the other hand the reduction in investment allowances and stock relief is likely to reduce the incentive to invest. Thus the exact impact on companies is likely to vary depending upon the mix of tax liabilities and reliefs they face. As corporation tax is reduced, and as tax liability increases with lower investment allowances, companies in different sectors will be differently affected. Some estimates made at the time suggested that more companies would be brought into a positive tax position, so that the overall tax burden on companies would increase, i.e. post-tax company profitability would decline, and with it possibly investment (Devereux and Mayer, 1984). The measures could certainly put a stop to the expansion of leasing, and even undermine it altogether. Tax liabilities would become effective on investment that had previously escaped it through leasing arrangements. The commercial banks estimated that they would be faced with an increased tax bill of £2 billion at 1984 prices.

From this discussion of the comparative failure of the UK economy to generate investment of the right quality, and use it to produce productivity levels that other economies have achieved, it should not be thought that productivity gains have altogether failed to emerge in the UK. One measure of productivity – output per person employed in manufacturing – is shown in figure 9.14 for the UK over the period 1962 to 1983. It is clear that on the basis of this measure there have been some important, if modest, gains in productivity over the period up to at least the early 1970s. The pattern shown here is mirrored quite closely if we were to take another measure of productivity over the period, output per man hour in manufacturing. It is generally agreed that a series for output per man-hour is a better approximation of the trend in productivity than crude output per worker figures, because it contains a partial correction for changes in labour utilization rates. This question of corrections for what are in fact cyclical changes in labour utilization rates (as mentioned above in connection with cost-competitive changes) becomes extremely important if we are to isolate the underlying trends in productivity of the economy. To illustrate this we will take the period of the early 1980s as an example, when it was widely claimed that there had been a real breakthrough in the productivity potential of the economy, due largely to government policy and the recession. This is reflected in figure 9.14 with the significant increase in output per person during the early 1980s.

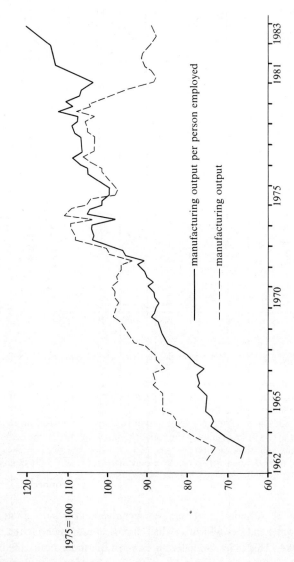

Figure 9.14. Output per person employed, manufacturing (1975 = 100). *Source: Economic Progress Report*, No. 142, February 1982, HM Treasury, p. 6, and *Employment Gazette*, September 1983, p. 518.

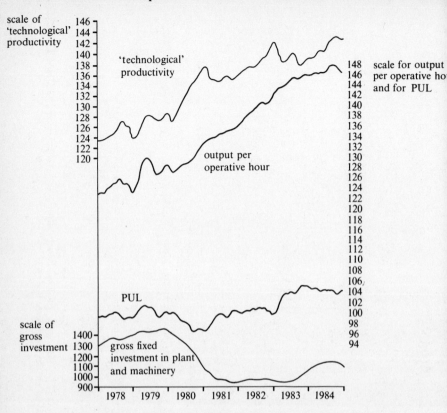

scale of 'technological' productivity

'technological' productivity

output per operative hour

scale for output per operative ho and for PUL

PUL

scale of gross investment

gross fixed investment in plant and machinery

Figure 9.15. Measures of productivity and investment, 1978–84

Notes

1 The scales for all indicies are based upon three-month moving averages, seasonally adjusted.

2 For 'technological' productivity, PUL and output per man hour, 1971 = 100. For gross fixed investment 1981 = 1300.

3 The PUL index and the 'technological' productivity index are based on returns from a sample of 131,500 operatives drawn from some 171 firms reporting to the authors stratified by product mix and other factors.

4 Definitions of PUL and 'technological' productivity are given in the main text.

Source: adapted from Bennett and Smith-Gavine, 1985, chart 11, p. 9.

In figure 9.15 an index of output per operative hour is plotted (along with a number of other indexes which we shall discuss in a moment), over the period 1978 to 1984. This index provides an estimate of labour hours used including overtime, but it does not account for what might be termed 'undertime' (Buiter and Miller, 1983, p. 355). This is time that is paid for but which is not worked to produce an output. Such 'undertime' could arise in the context of labour 'hoarding' during recessions and/or simply increased idle time or 'oddjobing' around the factory when demand is slack. To try and account for this the PUL index (percentage utilization of labour) is constructed, and this is shown in figure 9.15. This measures the varying intensity with which a given hour is worked. It is based upon long-established work measurement techniques which accurately record minute-by-minute tasks – 'standard psycho-physiological quanta of human effort', or work units, measured by 'standard' seconds and minutes. This PUL index can account for the changing intensity of effort at the workplace. It can be seen that this was on a rising trend between 1981 and 1983, although it seems to have peaked at the end of 1983. In fact a cyclical pattern of this kind has been observed over the 1970s and 1980s, and indeed is to be expected, given that there is a physical limit to the effort that can be expended in this manner (theoretically equal to 100 per cent utilization of labour, but administratively somewhat less than this).

If the PUL index is subtracted from the index of output per operative hour, then the resulting adjusted series accounts for the 'real' productivity increases. In figure 9.15 this series is termed 'technological' productivity. In effect this means the sort of productivity growth that arises from improvements in equipment and production methods that go with it – or more occasionally in improved methods without enhancing the equipment available. It represents the genuine growth in output productivity – the thing that economic progress in this field is measured by.

Looking at this 'technological' productivity index demonstrates that there was some genuine growth during 1980, but that this faded away somewhat in 1981, picked up to peak again at the end of 1982–early 1983, and then steadied out again. The trend in the overall post-1980 period has in fact been modest by the historical standards of the index, and even the rather dramatic increase in 1980 was paralleled by a similarly rapid increase in 1971 and in the later 1974 to late 1975 period (Bennett and Smith Gavine, 1985, p. 9). Thus far from the post-1979 period demonstrating a qualitative change in the productivity potential of the economy, its effects were probably confined to the year 1980 only, at least as of 1984.

These findings have been confirmed by an independent econometric analysis conducted for a similar period (Mendis and Meulbauer, 1983 and 1984). These authors have constructed their own measure of 'utilization corrected' productivity and again stress the necessity to adjust the cyclical changes in labour (and capital utilization) before longer term trends can be discerned. Over the longer post-war period they estimate annual productivity growth of 3.4 per cent for 1955 to 1973. This fell significantly between 1973 and 1979, largely because of the oil price shock, to 1.4 per cent. It was negative for 1979–80 (–0.3 per cent), and 2.9 per cent for 1980–3 (Mendis and Muelbauer, 1984). Thus the annual growth for 1980–3 was lower than for 1955–73. The year 1980 was also picked out as showing a particularly rapid growth in utilization adjusted productivity, gaining over 11 per cent between the first quarter and the second quarter 1981 (Mendis and Muelbauer, 1983) and accounting for the bulk of the post-1980 increase.

Thus the post-1980 growth in productivity was not without its precedents in the post-war period. But what was striking about it was the way such productivity increases were gaining at a time of sharply falling manufacturing output. Looking back to figure 9.14 it can be seen that output fell from mid-1979. Between the end of 1979 and the end of 1980 it fell by an unprecedented 16.2 per cent. Such a rapid collapse was not even experienced during the Great Depression of the 1930s. For the first time in the post-war period the trend in manufacturing output and in manufacturing productivity diverged considerably.

One of the main reasons put forward to account for this situation was the rationalization of capacity and labour brought on by the recession in the economy. UK manufacturing output fell as the recession deepened, demand fell and import penetration gathered pace. This implies that some of the existing capital stock was either scrapped or made idle. One measure of the utilization of the capital stock is given by the CBI's capacity utilization index plotted in figure 9.16 for the years 1972 to 1984. This is an indication of capital idleness, and it increased significantly between 1979 and 1981 just as output was falling. In 1980 over 80 per cent of firms said that they had idle capacity on their hands. What this measure does not indicate, however, is the capacity that was actually scrapped during the period. Capacity simply made idle could be reintroduced into production quickly if economic circumstances changed, but capacity scrapped no longer exists, and implies an unambiguous shift in the aggregate supply function to the left.

Two time series measures of the capital stock are published by the Central Statistical Office, but these are known to be the most unreliable of all official statistics. The *gross stock* simply measures accumulated investment each year minus any capital that has come to the end of its life in that year. During the period of its life, which is quite long, the average life of capital assets in 1980 being taken as thirty years, capital is assumed to yield equal capital services per year. The *net capital stock* subtracts accumulated depreciation each year from the gross capital stock and this assumes that the flow of capital services declines geometrically over the life of the asset.

Both of these capital stock measures depend crucially on assumptions made about asset lives. These are probably particularly unreliable during periods of marked structural change or prolonged underutilization of capacity. The increase in energy prices could shorten the life of many capital goods and underutilization might lead to a more rapid decay. Rapid technological advance could also shorten asset lives. As a result of all these influences, which were thought to be particularly strong in the depression of the late 1980s, the extent of scrapping could have been much greater than suggested by the conventional methods used by the CSO in calculating retirements (NIESR, 1983, p. 23; and LBS, 1985, chart 5, p. 84). Thus although the offical measure of net capital stock fell slightly in the early 1980s, this was probably a significant underestimate.

Given that some capital was actually scrapped, the usual *a priori* suggestion would be that this was the least efficient. If this was the case, the average level of

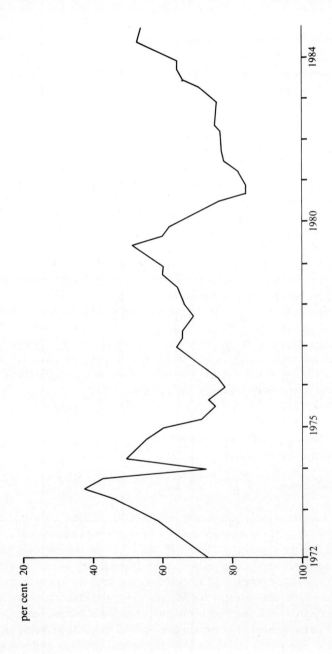

Figure 9.16. Capacity utilization 1972–84 (per cent of firms in CBI survey working below capacity, inverted scale). *Source*: reported in Rosewell, 1984.

productivity of the surviving capacity would increase. This result would hold even if there were no better productive use made of that surviving capacity. Similar results would hold in the short run, if production units were simply shut down and made idle rather than scrapped. As can be seen from figure 9.16 there seemed to have been something of this latter effect in the early 1980s. Thus at least some part of the productivity increase referred to above may have been the result of the elimination of capacity by either scrapping or forced idleness. At the same time this would contribute to the decline in output. Thus productivity increased, partly as an effect of a statistical anomaly which did not imply better use being made of the remaining capital equipment, and partly because of a real increase in 'technological' productivity, as discussed above.

However, there is another complication here. In the above discussion it was accepted that the least efficient capital or firms were the ones that were the first to be eliminated. But this need not necessarily be the case. A very important consideration in questions of bankruptcy is the liquidity position of firms. This liquidity position depends upon such financial features as the firm's cash flow situation, its debt profile, is demand characteristics, etc., and these need not be directly linked to its economic productive efficiency. Thus firms could go into liquidation that were efficient but did not have a sufficiently buoyant liquidity position to buttress them in the short term.

One final point is that all the authors discussed above stress the necessity of an increase in capital investment as a prerequisite for a real increase in trend productivity in the economy. As can be seen from figure 9.15, and as was reported earlier (p. 269), investment actually fell considerably in 1980, with only a small recovery as of the early part of 1984. It is this issue of increased investment that is crucial to the long-term productivity growth of the economy.

4. Recent Approaches to Industrial Policy and the Supply Side

4.1. *Introduction*

As was mentioned in the introductory remarks to this chapter, dissatisfaction with the performance of the economy came to the forefront of political and economic discussion as the recession of the late 1970s set in. The type of policies pursued in the post-war period came under increasing critical scrutiny and new ways of trying to orientate policy were proposed. In this section we look at two polar examples of this. These are stated rather boldly here to contrast their main features. No attempt at a full-scale critical evaluation of their possible consequences is made, other than to mention one or two more obvious points or problems associated with each. Any proper evaluation of these proposals could not avoid introducing explicit political criteria of assessment, something forced upon economic analysis by the increasing polarization of opinion in contemporary Britain.

4.2. *A question of competition and incentives?*

There is no general agreement on how best to engender a better supply condition for the economy, but the dominant set of arguments in the post-1970s period has been typified by a position that has stressed the virtues of greater market-organized competition and the regeneration of personal economic incentives. (This section relies heavily upon Thompson, 1986, chapter 4.)

When the Conservative government gained office in May 1979, it inherited the set of problems discussed above in terms of the relative performance of the UK economy. As figure 9.14 has shown, more or less immediately UK manufacturing production took a dramatic downward trend. What was the government to do? In fact in embarked upon a radical course, at least as far as intentions were concerned. The government argued that the economic decline of Britain was a result of the undermining and erosion of the elementary principles of free market capitalism through the growth of the welfare state, egalitarianism and a militant trade union movement. These were the end-products of decades of domination by social-democratic ideology over all the mainstream political and economic tendencies during the post-war period. The problem was to displace a paternalistic, bureaucratic state apparatus that had grown up around these tendencies and replace it with the renewed vigour of individual initiatives. This required a withdrawal of state involvement from the regulation and management of much economic activity, in the wake of which private economic initiative would grow and thrive. The re-defined role of the government was to provide the conditions in which incentives for both workers and employers or entrepreneurs could flourish. To do this required a two-pronged attack, aimed at the two main areas of economic activity outlined earlier in this chapter which go to make up the conditions of supply in the economy, i.e. the labour market and the structure of production, broadly speaking. In both cases the emphasis was to be on reducing the cost of inputs into the production process.

As far as the labour market was concerned, a range of issues were involved. While some economists who argued along these lines recognized that wage demands by trade unions did not of themselves raise or lower the rate of inflation, they still insisted on strong resistance to excessive wage demands that outstripped productivity growth. Trade unions were directly responsible for the level of unemployment if they insisted on a level of real wages which firms could not pay. Trade unions were also responsible for stagnation and a slow rate of growth, to the extent that they were capable of resisting rationalization, the introduction of new machinery and the reorganization of production and the labour process aimed at raising productivity. Thus these kinds of arguments were used to justify both a reduction in the 'monopoly power' of trade unions in the context of labour market adjustments and a resistance to higher money and real wages in the economy. Legislation was introduced in 1980, 1982 and 1984 in an attempt to make trade union activity more difficult to organize and sustain. The resulting downward pressure on the money wage rate that might evolve from these policies could at least prevent the aggregate supply curve shifting as fast to the *left* in figure 9.1 as might otherwise have been the case. (An increase in money wages moves the curve to the left while a reduction moves it to the right.)

Of course, the effects of high unemployment and stagnant or falling living standards might create pressures for an expansion of government expenditure and hence, it was argued, of the money supply. If the government were to give way to these pressures, higher rates of inflation would result. This, then, would be another indirect result of trade union activity. The use of 'demand management' in this way, however, is likely to result in failure, from the point of view of this perspective, because government efforts to realize a higher level of employment or a faster rate of growth by expanding demand falter in the face of a 'natural' rate of growth and a 'natural' rate of unemployment (chapter 3). These are themselves determined by the institutional organization of markets and other underlying conditions of the economy, and an expansion of demand beyond a point dictated by these would simply lead to inflation. This implicity brought in the idea of a vertical long-run aggregate supply curve. However, there might be some temporary trade-off between unemployment and inflation (chapter 6).

An additional element in this set of arguments against 'demand management' and for improving labour market supply incentives revolves around taxation. Pressures for demand-managed reflation under conditions of monetary stringency can lead to taxation increases to raise the necessary finance. This is to be avoided at all costs. Indeed, the idea here was quite the reverse. Part of the pulling back of state involvement is to pull back on the taxation front as well. This is one of the main planks on which supply-side economics was built. Here it is sufficient to point out that reductions in the levels of taxation – whether corporate or individual – is again seen in the context of incentives to the supply and demand for labour. Put simply, a reduction in corporate taxation increases the demand for labour, while a reduction in personal taxation rates gives incentives to work harder. In both cases gains in real output would result, it was argued.

Associated with these arguments about tax reductions were others focusing on the replacement ratio, i.e. the ratio of income out of employment to income in employment. Supposing a policy were introduced to lower this replacement ratio, say by cutting various welfare benefits; this would stimulate the supply of labour, it was argued, which in turn would shift the aggregate supply function to the right. In chapters 3 and 4 this contentious claim was debated in terms of the possible incentive effects of lowering the replacement ratio.

Table 9.5. The privatization programme

	Amount (£m)
1979/80	
5 per cent of BP	276
25 per cent of ICL	38
Shares in Suez Finance Company and miscellaneous	57
1980/1	
50 per cent of Ferranti	54
100 per cent of Fairey	22
North Sea oil licences	195
51 per cent of British Aerospace	43
Miscellaneous and small NEB interests	91
1981/2	
24 per cent of British Sugar	44
55 per cent of Cable and Wireless	224
100 per cent of Amersham International	64
Miscellaneous plus Crown Agent and Forestry Commission land and property sales	204
1982/3	
51 per cent of Britoil (first cash call)	256
49 per cent of Associated British Ports	46
BR hotels	34
Sale of BA subsidiary, International Aeradio	60
Sale of oil licences, oil stockpiles and miscellaneous	108
1983/4	
Second cash call for Britoil	293
7 per cent of BP	565
25 per cent of Cable and Wireless	260
Miscellaneous (estimate)	132
1984/5	
100 per cent of Enterprise Oil	392
50 per cent of Wytch Farm	215
48.5 per cent of Associated British Ports	52
76 per cent of Inmos	95
100 per cent Jaguar	297
100 per cent of Sealink	66
British Telecom (first cash call)	1,506
Sale of oil licences and miscellaneous (estimate)	160

(continued)

Table 9.5. *(continued)*

Planned Sales	Estimated value (£m)
1985/6 and beyond	
48 per cent of British Aerospace	350
British Airways	800
British Telecom (second cash call)	1,205
British Airports Authority	300
British Shipbuilders warship yards	200
Cable and Wireless	640
Royal Ordnance	200
National Bus	200
Rolls-Royce aero engines	300
Short Brothers	100
Thames Water	500
Other water authorities	500
Remaining minority holdings	500
	£bn
British Gas	6–8
British Telecom 49.8%	6.7
British Petroleum 31.4%	3.2

Source: Midland Bank Review, Spring 1985, p. 19 and *The Economist*, 16 November 1985), p.88.

So much for the labour market arguments. What about the area of supply involving production characteristics and conditions more directly? Here there was also a number of issues. One of the most important and controversial of these in the UK was the programme of privatization a number of the nationalized industries and other publicly owned corporate entities like parts of British Leyland and British Petroleum. The early results of this policy for the UK are shown in table 9.5.

The argument here was that these organizations are basically inefficient in terms of their cost and productivity records compared to private industry equivalents (Pryke, 1982; Beesley and Littlechild, 1983). The conversion of these activities to private businesses would provide the necessary incentives for costs to be kept down and profitable organizations to ensue. No longer would government subsidies be available. In the case of organizations like British Telecom and British Airways, the aim is both to convert them to privately owned commercial operations and to open up a more competitive environment in which they could work by allowing competitors to enter the market (Mercury in the case of British Telecom) and deregulating markets in others (allowing British Midland Airways or British Caledonian to compete with British Airways on a range of domestic and international routes, for instance). In these cases the objective is to put downward pressures on costs by re-organizing the capital stock in the first instance rather than by increasing that stock overall. However, it is confidently expected that this in itself will stimulate new investment in new technological fields, thus increasing the capital stock overall.

The controversial nature of the privatization programme concerned the relative importance within the strategy attributable to increased competition, on the one hand, as opposed to raising finance to offset the PSBR and allow tax cuts, on the other. In effect the government was creating a set of very large *private* monopolies by denationalizing the industries (or duopolies in some cases). These were then to be subject to regulation by agencies such as OFTEL (British Telecom and Mercury), the CAA (British Airways and competitors, and the British Airports Authority), and a proposed gas regulatory body. Thus the implication of this part of the strategy, even if 'competition' is accepted as one of its main motives, was to change the *form* of intervention in the economy rather than to abandon it all together.

Added to these kinds of proposed measures can be a range of fiscal incentives. For instance, special allowances and subsidies have been granted to firms who want to invest in new technological equipment of the 'robotic' and information technology type. Fundamental research into advance software is to be subsidized from government sources. Also in the British context a range of fiscal and other incentives has been granted to firms who are prepared to set up in designated 'enterprise zones', mainly in rundown industrial and urban areas. Again the intention here is that if normal constraints and regulations can be lifted on private firms, they will seize the opportunity and stimulate real output.

Thus the new technologies of robotics, information technology, bio-technology, acoustic, optic and ceramic technologies were to be given a high priority. The rejuvenation and the renewal of the capital stock and its more efficient cost-effective organization would require the replacement of old, inefficient and rundown stock. As a prelude to this there would be a 'shake-out' of the existing productive capacity. The idea was that a leaner and fitter economy was a precondition for the new technology to take hold.

One noteworthy feature associated with these latter policy measures has been to emphasize very limited and specific assistance to firms, particularly in the context of regional-based subsidies. Highly discriminatory targets are set for companies who are to receive grants, and their achievements are monitored. But this requires detailed scrutiny of the firms involved and once again demonstrates the change in *form* of the intervention implied rather than a simple withdrawal from it. What the approach does not do, however, is to intervene against what is seen as a benign market-dictated efficiency and profitability. It also avoids the large-scale restructuring interventions which typified government action in the mid-1960s to late 1970s on the industrial front. By and large it also avoids any attempted reorganization of internal managerial practices. Rather the problem has been the labour market and the general incentive structure of grants to investment. Foreign 'best practice' firms are to be encouraged to set up in the UK, but they will only act as 'models' to which (it is hoped) indigenous firms will look and learn.

4.3.   *An alternative economic strategy?*

While the set of arguments outlined in section 4.2 comprised the main thrust of the post-1979 Conservative government's economic policy towards industry, the particular measures suggested were not the only ones on offer as far as the supply side was concerned. A different approach at the time was offered by the so-called 'alternative economic strategy' (AES), which more or less suggested the opposite course to the incentives approach. This argued for a *more* active role for the state and greater planning of economic activity than even that typical of the 1960s and 1970s experience (CSE, 1980; Currie and Smith, 1981; and Desai, 1983).

This strategy begins from a position of particular concern over the levels of unemployment in the economy. The explicit objective was to return to a position of 'full employment' within a span of three to five years (if not sooner). To achieve this a range of policies was proposed:

(a) A reflationary package through increased public expenditure and/or devaluation of the national currency.
(b) The expansion of public ownership and the extension of control over the industrial sector via a system of 'planning agreements'. These latter would involve trade unions' and employers' agreement with respect to firms' investment levels, manning practices, sales effort, pricing policy, training practices and the like, i.e. an extension of worker control over both the conditions of production and the longer term trajectory of the firm itself.
(c) Import controls and restrictions on capital exports.
(d) Policies for job creation, work sharing, early retirement and a shorter working week.
(e) Price controls (though in most versions not incomes or pay controls).
(f) A state finance investment bank (of the NEB variety) to pick 'possible winners' and stimulate weak or strategically important sectors of the economy.

Here, then is a comprehensive package of policies that is aimed at most of the structural weaknesses outlined in the early part of the chapter. This could be said to be as wide in its scope as the 'incentives approach' outline in section 4.2, although involving a different type of proposed action.

The AES was an 'umbrella' strategy. Under it a range of debates could take place about exactly which parts were desirable and feasible, and to what extent, so there was no single and definite accepted programme. In this way it was rather similar to the incentives strategy, where a range of particular policy suggestions could also be generated and pursued. Both of these offer a framework for debate and examination of the possible specific policies. Clearly the AES also has a strong 'demand management' component built into it, but this is positively avoided and quite out of the scope of the discussion in section 4.2.

The AES also begins from a different assumption about the labour market. It is concerned with the way in which the conditions of supply and demand for labour are presumed to have altered in the 1970s, a consequence of which was the dramatic rise in unemployment already discussed in previous chapters. Essentially the AES sees this as resulting from a lack of adequate demand. The aggregate demand curve has been shifted down from its interaction with the aggregate supply curve at a presumed full-employment level, to a position where this interaction now leads to a rise in unemployment.

There is an added implication embodied in the AES, however; namely that the supply and demand schedules for labour itself have shifted during the 1970s. In particular, there has been both a negative shift in the demand for labour curve and a negative shift in the supply of labour, such that as a result these interact below the 'previous' full employment levels. The demand for labour schedule has shifted because the recession has physically eliminated a large section of the economy's productive capacity (capacity has been scrapped – see above) and the supply schedule has shifted because a section of the workforce is no longer seriously in the labour market (it has deregistered as being employable). Some of these points have been made in the context of chapters 4's discussion of Keynesian policies.

Clearly, the AES type approach begins with the assumption that the economy is very seriously depressed in terms of both aggregate demand and aggregate supply conditions. There is a potential here, but it would require a radical and widescale structural reorganization of the economy if anything like full employment is to be realized. The idea is that changing incentives is insufficient to elicit this response in the economy. Even to shift the schedules 'back' to their 'original' positions would require an enormous effort aided and led by the state.

The AES relies on three main areas to generate these desired movements. One is on the investment front. Here the state is to play the major role in co-ordinating and stimulating investment. The object is to shift the position of the production function by both reorganizing the structure of production and increasing the level and quality of investment and technique. Secondly, the AES proposes import controls, with the intention of stimulating *internal supply*. The increase in aggregate demand will not result simply in an increase in imports but will generate internal mechanisms of supply stimulating further investment and employment. Capital controls will prevent the 'export' of potential investment finance as well. Finally, the AES is relying upon an increased measure of industrial democracy and price controls to encourage productivity increases and prevent inflationary consequences. The idea here is that these will put downward pressure on the money wage rate. In fact this is probably one of the weakest parts of the AES: the absence of some firm policy proposals to control the possible inflationary wage and income consequences resulting from increased demand would probably undermine these attempts to stimulate the long-term supply side of the economy (see also the discussion of incomes policies in chapter 3). The expenditure involved with the AES would also need to be financed by the government and this could in turn lead to inflationary pressures. In addition, the other proposals made with respect to the labour market, i.e. early retirement, a shorter working week and work sharing (however desirable in their own right) are likely to hold back the increase in supply. The result of this set of policies could be less real output than might otherwise have been the case. As it stands, however, the AES proposals represent something of a return to the instruments of economic policy that typified the industrial field in the 1960s and 1970s, if in a bolder and more extended form. They could even be compared with the instruments designed for the management of industry during the Second World War.

5.   Conclusion

This chapter has concentrated on the problems of the UK economy from the supply or input side. It had looked at possible ways of shifting the aggregate supply curve out to the right in an aggregate price output space. In this context of economic growth and change a somewhat different set of economic problems and issues arise than those associated with either managing aggregate demand or with the possible inflation and unemployment trade-off. In particular, these are issues of structural change in the economy and its underlying cost structure. Indeed, the main emphasis in the early part of the chapter was to look at the constituent elements that make up an economy's 'cost-competitiveness'. There it was pointed out that the overall international competitive performance of an economy may be less determined by its input cost competitiveness than by its non-price competitiveness, the decisions made by its firms, and exchange rate changes. Strategies that over-emphasize reducing the cost of inputs to the exclusion of these other important considerations may thus prove unsuccessful in stimulating the supply side as a result. However, experiments to stimulate the economy by putting downward pressure on costs and rearranging the productive structure are now well under way. Changes in the aggregate demand side are being underemphasized with this approach, and it marks a major turnround in post-war economic policy-making.

In contrast to the approach which emphasizes greater market-organized competition, less regulation and a general withdrawal of government interference, there has been a set of policy responses that have wished at least to maintain the extent of intervention, if not to increase it. Within this position there is also an element that sees the necessity to promote a more radical 'planning' of the economy, as a response to the critical state of the supply side. However, perhaps we should end this chapter by reference to figure 9.17. This shows the familiar dramatic fall in output between 1979 and 1981, its stagnation through to 1983, but a gradual

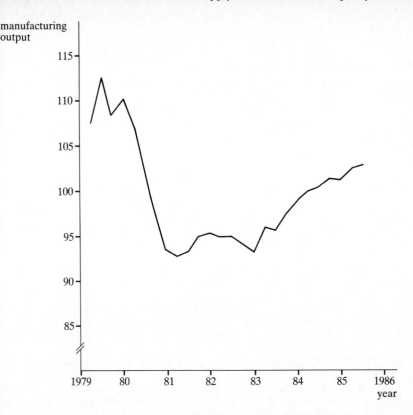

manufacturing output

Figure 9.17. UK manufacturing output, 1979–86 (1980 = 100)

growth over 1984 and 1985. Thus, despite what one may feel about the supply side strategies outlined above, it must be recognized that something of a 'recovery' was already under way by the mid-1980s.

References

Beesley, M. and Littlechild, S. (1983) 'Privatization: principles, problems and priorities; *Lloyds Bank Review*, No. 149, July.

Bennett, A. J. and Smith-Gavine, S. A. N. (1985) 'The index of percentage utilization of labour', *Bulletin to Co-operating Firms*, No. 48, May.

Bredenkamp, H. (1984) 'Measuring import-penetration in the UK', *Treasury Working Paper*, No. 30, June.

Buiter, W. H. and Miller, M. H. (1983) 'Changing the rules; economic consequences of the Thatcher regime', *Brookings Institution Papers on Economic Activity*, No. 2, Washington, The Brookings Institution.

CSE (Conference of Socialist Economists) (1980) *The Alternative Economic Strategy*, CSE Books, London.

Currie, D. and Smith, E. (eds) (1981) *Socialist Economic Review*. Merlin Press, London.

Desai, M. (1983) 'Economic alternatives for labour, 1984-9, in Atkinson, A., *et al. Socialism in a Cold Climate*. Unwin, London.

Devereux, M. and Mayer, C. (1984) *Corporation Tax: the impact of the 1984 budget*. Institute for Fiscal Studies, London.

Fetherstone, M. *et al.* (1979) 'Manufacturing export shares and cost competitiveness of advanced industrial countries', *Economic Policy Review*, No. 3. Department of Applied Economics, Cambridge.

Forsyth, P. J. and Kay, J. A. (1980) 'The economic implications of North Sea oil revenues', *Fiscal Studies*, 1(3), 1-28.

Kaletsky, A. (1983) 'The heresies of Mr. Lawson', *Financial Times*, 11 April.

Katrak, H. (1982) 'Labour skills, R&D and capital requirements in the international trade and investment of the United Kingdom 1968-78', *NIER*, 101, 38-47.

King, M. A. and Fullerton, D. (1984) 'The taxation of income from capital: a comparative study of the UK, USA, Sweden and Germany'. In King, M. A. and Fullerton, D. (eds) *The Taxation of Income from Capital*. Chicago University Press, Chicago.

LBS (1985), *Economic Outlook*, 10(1).

Mendis, L. and Muellbauer, J. (1983) 'Has there been a British productivity breakthrough?' Centre for Labour Economics, Discussion paper No. 170, August. LSE, London.

Mendis, L. and Meulbauer, J. (1984) 'British manufacturing productivity 1955-1983: measurement problems, oil shocks and Thatcher effects', Centre for Economic Policy Research, Discussion Paper No. 32, November, London.

NIESR (National Institute of Economic and Social Research) (1983), *National Institute Economic Review*, Appendix B, pp. 23-5, November.

Pryke, R. (1982) 'The comparative performance of public and private enterprise', *Fiscal Studies* 3(2), 68-81.

Rosewell, B. C. (1984) 'The CBI industrial trends survey and capacity working'. Paper presented to the IER/EPSG conference on the Theory and Measurement of Capacity Utilization, Warwick University, February.

Thompson, G. F. (1986) *The Conservatives' Economic Policy*. Croom Helm, London.

Treasury and Civil Service Committee (1984) *The 1984 Budget*, 4th Report, HCP 341, April.

Williams, K., Williams, J. and Thomas, D. (1983) *Why are the British Bad at Manufacturing?*, Routledge and Kegan Paul, London.

10

Some Reflections
on the AD/AS Model

VIVIENNE BROWN

Throughout this book we have been using the AD/AS model in order to examine aspects of the UK economy and the controversies that have been engulfing discussions of macrotheory and policy. The AD/AS model was outlined in chapter 2, and later chapters have put this model to work in various ways, perhaps even extending it, in following through a particular piece of analysis. But one thing we have not done yet is turn our attention to the model itself.

So far we have accepted the AD/AS model in a rather unproblematic way without considering how this particular model developed, or how its adoption has reflected and influenced the course of the theoretical and policy debates between Keynesians and monetarists over the years. Nor have we considered other contributions to the debate on the economy which are not easily articulated in terms of the AD/AS model. In this concluding chapter, therefore, I shall examine the way that the adoption of the AD/AS model by orthodox Keynesianism has helped to orientate macroeconomic debates in a specific direction, and has had the effect of foreclosing debates which are conducted within other theoretical frameworks. This chapter, then, has rather more of a theoretical slant than some of the earlier chapters as I try to examine some of the implications of focusing the book's discussions around the simple textbook AD/AS model.

For the early Keynesians the basic message of the *General Theory* was that there was an absence of reliable self-adjusting mechanisms in a monetary economy. Whereas the classical economists, according to Keynes, relied on changes in relative prices – the wage rate and the rate of interest – to correct any departures from full employment, Keynes argued that these changes were inadequate and inappropriate to the task of providing mechanisms of self-adjustment at a time of large-scale unemployment. Keynes's argument was that the cause of the unemployment was a deficiency in aggregate demand, and that the appropriate policy solution was to increase effective demand. Thus the early simple versions of the *General Theory* based on the 45° diagram were able to concentrate exclusively on the goods market in determining the level of income and employment, as in this model relative prices and monetary variables were excluded from affecting output and employment. In addition, the model presupposed that increases in aggregate demand could secure increases in real output up to the full employment level without any repercussions on the price level.

But this was clearly too simple. The 45° diagram was based almost entirely on the consumption function and did not do credit to the lengthy discussions in the *General Theory* either on the marginal efficiency of investment or on the role of monetary factors. Hicks (1937) interpreted the *General Theory* in terms of the interaction between the goods market and the money market where Keynes's discussion of liquidity preference and of the marginal efficiency of investment could be accommodated. This then became the standard textbook treatment of orthodox Keynesianism. The IS curve shows the combinations of rates of interest and real income levels which satisfy equilibrium in the goods market, and the LM curve shows the combinations of interest rates and real income levels when the money market is in equilibrium. Together the two schedules determine a unique equilibrium $r:y$ combination.

But although the domain of the money market had been included within the orbit of standard macroeconomic theory, Keynesians continued to deny it any role in determining the level of real output. In this the IS–LM framework of analysis proved to be very useful in facilitating the debate between Keynesians and monetarists which centred on the slopes, positions and stability of the IS and LM curves. Keynesians tended to argue that the level of investment was determined exogenously (or by changes in the level of aggregate demand) and was not very responsive to changes in the rate of interest. This meant that the IS curve was very steep, if not vertical, and was subject to sudden shifts. Keynesians also argued that there tended to be a floor rate of interest below which the rate of interest did not fall – this meant that the LM curve was horizontal over a part of its range. This Keynesian view of the IS–LM diagram is shown in figure 10.1a. Here we can see

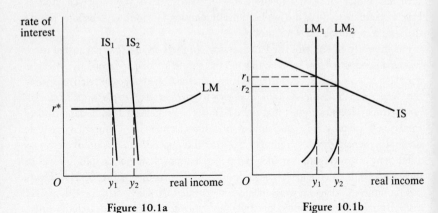

Figure 10.1a   Figure 10.1b

that the level of output is still determined by the goods market while the level of interest is determined by the money market.

In policy terms this means that priority is accorded to fiscal policy rather than monetary policy; in figure 10.1a this means that the IS curve shifts to the right from IS_1 to IS_2. This point of view was advanced in para. 511 of the Radcliffe Report in 1959: 'we envisage the use of monetary measures as not in ordinary times playing other than a subordinate part in guiding the development of the economy'. In reviewing fiscal policy the Radcliffe Report emphasized the primary importance of the Budget balance in affecting the total pressure of demand and in the economy (see chapter 4's discussion of fiscal stance) and attached only a secondary significance to the selective Budget measures which aimed to influence private sector decision-making, such as investment allowances and individual tax changes (paras. 516–17). The Report's criticisms of the effectiveness of monetary policy centred on the difficulty of controlling demand pressures by influencing either the availability of bank credit (by restrictions on the rate of interest or by direct controls) or the 'supply of money' in the economy (para. 514) (see chapter 7's discussion of monetary policy).

The monetarist view of the IS–LM diagram was largely the reverse of the Keynesian one: investment was highly interest-elastic and so the IS curve tended to be rather flat, whilst the demand for money was interest-inelastic and so the LM curve tended to be rather steep. This view of the IS–LM diagram is shown in figure 10.1b. Here we can see that the order of determination is reversed: the level of output is determined by monetary factors, whilst the rate of interest is determined by the goods market, by the condition that savings must equal investment. In this case an expansionary monetary policy would be represented by a rightwards shift of the LM curve from LM_1 to LM_2. During the 1950s and 1960s this emphasis on monetary policy was mainly an emphasis on using the rate of interest to affect expenditure decisions – investment and consumption decisions – by changing Bank Rate and by adjusting hire purchase terms. In the later post-war period the emphasis of monetary policy shifted to controlling the money supply as the most effective way of controlling aggregate demand.

Although there was a tendency to polarize the issue into these two opposing interpretations of the IS–LM diagram, the two positions were drawing closer together. Orthodox Keynesians came to recognize the impact of the money market on the level of real output together with the interest-elasticity of the marginal efficiency of investment. Thus, it became easy to draw a 'compromise' IS–LM diagram such as figure 10.2 (also shown as figure 2.14 in chapter 2) where the IS curve takes the conventional negative slope and the LM curve takes the conventional positive slope. But this meant that the Keynesians acknowledged that monetary policy did have some influence on real output; an increase in the money supply (accepted as exogenously determined – some Keynesians would deny this) would lower the rate of interest which would lead to an increase in investment

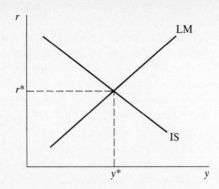

and consumption too. The effectiveness of monetary policy is illustrated in such a diagram by the extent of the rightward shift of the LM curve together with the slope of the IS curve (the steeper the IS curve, the less effective would the policy be). It also meant that the effectiveness of fiscal policy would be reduced by the extent to which the increased interest rates following demand expansion would curtail investment. The effectiveness of fiscal policy would be shown by the extent of the rightward shift of the IS curve together with the slope of the LM curve (the steeper the LM curve, the less effective the policy).

Thus the debate between orthodox Keynesians and monetarists over the relative effectiveness of fiscal and monetary policy reduced to one of establishing the relative interest-elasticities of the IS and LM curves. Certainly the two opposing groups seemed to be as much united by a common theoretical framework, as they were separated by their disagreements over the values of the various coefficients. As a result of this the orthodox Keynesian case could no longer be based on a separation of the determination of output from monetary factors.

In policy terms this meant that both fiscal and monetary policy were seen as important dimensions of the government's overall approach to controlling the level of aggregate demand in the economy. Keynesians and monetarists might attach different relative weights to the effectiveness and appropriateness of fiscal and monetary policy, but there was a certain amount of common ground shared by both sides. Indeed, in one respect it could be said that monetary policy had been absorbed into the prevailing package of Keynesian demand management policies. This period of relative agreement on the objectives and array of instruments of government policy may be seen during the Wilson and Heath periods of office in the 1960s and 1970s.

The other main area where Keynesianism had been on the defensive was in connection with the Pigou effect, whereby it was argued that wage reductions would cause a general reduction in the price level such that the increased value of real balances would provide a stimulus to aggregate demand via their stimulating effect on consumption. This attempt to offer a vehicle for the self-adjusting character of the economic system also posed the issue for Keynesianism of the relation between the price level and the level of real output. This relation had seemed not to be very relevant for simple Keynesian models which linked their analyses of demand deficiency with extensive under-utilization of capital equipment and where fiscal expansion could take place without promoting inflationary pressures. But as Keynesianism had taken on board the effects of integrating the money market into its analysis of aggregate demand, so with the increasingly inflationary 1960s and 1970s it had to confront the issue of the determination of the price level.

The orthodox Keynesian response was to examine the determination of the price level by the interaction of aggregate demand and aggregate supply. This had been implicit in the early expositions of Keynesian theory (e.g. Smith, 1956) but it was not until the formal elaboration of the aggregate demand and aggregate supply model that the determination of the price level became a central concern. Similarly, the incorporation of supply-side factors based on the aggregate production function and the labour market had been a part of those early standard Keynesian macro-models alongside the IS–LM analysis, but the development of the AD/AS model helped to emphasize the importance of supply-side factors in the determination of prices and output. Here then we see two more areas of common ground between the orthodox Keynesians and the monetarists: first, that the price level is determined by demand and supply in a conventional neo-classical manner; and second, that the supply side of the economy was based on a short-run neo-classical production function such that the marginal product of labour would fall as output increased, which implied that output could increase only if real wages fell.

Thus when orthodox Keynesianism accepted a downward-sloping aggregate demand schedule based on (1) the interest-elasticity of the marginal efficiency of investment and (2) the Pigou effect, it had substantially accepted the monetarist criticisms of its formulation of the demand side of the economy. It also accepted that the price level was determined by the interaction of demand and supply. The only area where disagreement could persist lay on the supply side of the economy. But here too we have seen that there was substantial agreement, as the *General Theory* had apparently not broken from the traditional Marshallian micro-underpinnings: perfectly competitive firms operated in a short-run regime of diminishing returns in the presence of the fixed factor capital. This meant that output could be increased only by moving along the existing production function, which implied that real wages must fall if profit-maximizing firms were to increase their rate of output. This, of course, implied that the AS curve would be vertical at existing real wages.

The only point of difference to remain between orthodox Keynesians and monetarists lay in the supply function of labour. Here there were two main points at issue. Firstly, in what sense could 'involuntary' unemployment of labour be said to exist when it was associated with a level of real wages above the market clearing level. This then raised the question of why the real wage did not fall in the presence of unemployment to the level that would clear the labour market. Keynesian responses here emphasized that workers were unable to influence the real wage simply by agreeing to a different money wage, while monetarist responses tended to emphasize the monopoly power of trade unions in demanding a real wage that was too high for market clearing. But this brings us to the second point at issue: whether the supply of labour depends on the real or money wage. In addition to the issue of the involuntariness of involuntary unemployment, this question is also significant, as it bears on the question whether workers could be cajoled or fooled into accepting the lower real wages that were necessary for output to expand. Would workers accept a permanent reduction in their real wages – as a result of money illusion, the fear of unemployment, or a rational emphasis on relativities rather than real take-home pay? Here we can see the vestigial traces of the earlier and simpler Keynesian emphasis on the separation of prices from output: if only one price, the money wage, could be held constant during a reflationary period of demand expansion, then there could be a sustainable increase in real output and in employment.

We can also see the crucial importance of the formulation of the supply of labour for the *policy implications* of the consensus AD/AS model that had emerged. Previously Keynesians and old-style monetarists had agreed that government policy *could* affect the level of output and employment; they differed only in their relative emphasis on fiscal and monetary policy. Now Keynesians and new-style monetarists were disagreeing on the more fundamental issue of whether government can have *any* impact on output and employment in the longer run.

This difference is illustrated by the sharp break in policy that is represented by Margaret Thatcher's two governments since 1979. The emphasis of these governments has consistently been that of the new monetarism, that neither fiscal nor monetary policy can affect output and employment even in the short term as they are determined instead by the individual supply factors of incentives and willingness to work. Government monetary policy, the Medium Term Financial Strategy, has been directed towards controlling inflation, not towards controlling the level of economic activity; and the government denies the Keynesian accusation that the tightening of fiscal stance and the high rates of interest and exchange rate that accompanied this policy, precipitated the recession of 1979–81 by severely reducing the level of aggregate demand. The only area of policy where Margaret Thatcher's government has acknowledged that policy can have any effect on employment is that of direct labour market policies. These policies have included the weakening of trade unions, the removal of some statutory protection for the low-paid, the tightening up of social security legislation, and some reductions in national insurance contributions, all of which have been directed towards reducing the real wages paid out.

But this stark difference between the policy conclusions of orthodox Keynesianism and the new monetarism masks the theoretical convergence that is reflected in their shared use of the AD/AS model, a convergence that some economists would characterize by describing orthodox Keynesianism as Keynesianism in the short run and monetarism in the long run. If this is so, then much depends on how long this short run is, and by how much output and employment can be increased before workers try to restore their real wages. This theoretical convergence between orthodox Keynesians and monetarists is also reflected in their shared acceptance of the notion of a natural rate of unemployment, which again illustrates the increased significance of the supply side of labour. All the econometric studies of the NRU by both Keynesian and monetarist economists have reported that the NRU has been increasing since the 1960s (Metcalfe, 1984), and this is put down to changes on the supply side of labour (i.e. a leftward shifting supply schedule of labour) such as the pursuit of real wage increases ahead of productivity gains and an increased reluctance to enter into low-paid employment because of high replacement ratios (see chapter 3). Thus, the widely quoted study by Layard and Nickell, 1985, published in the Keynesian *National Institute Economic Review*, can be used by monetarists as well as Keynesians to support their own arguments: whereas Keynesians can argue that this study shows that three-quarters of the increase in unemployment from 1975-9 to 1980-3 was the result of inadequate aggregate demand, monetarists can argue that the NRU has increased along with the actual rate of unemployment in recent years so that government macro-policy can only attempt to reduce unemployment by a few percentage points (by 3.68 per cent) if inflation is not to start increasing again (see chapter 4 for some criticisms of the NRU).

This chapter has underlined the theoretical similarities between orthodox Keynesianism and monetarism, similarities which are illustrated by the development of the AD/AS model which is itself the product of the absorption of orthodox Keynesianism into a mainstream macroeconomics that is based on the general principles of neo-classical economics. Thus, it is misleading to see the simple, textbook AD/AS model as a 'neutral' theoretical space on which various competing theories may be objectively compared. Rather, the AD/AS model is itself the product of the debate between orthodox Keynesianism and monetarism, a debate which has become more and more anchored in the neo-classical principles of resource allocation. Just as neo-classical (Walrasian) economics emphasizes the joint determination of prices and outputs given the exogenous factors of preferences, endowments and technology, so the AD/AS model is focused on the joint determination of the price level and real income, given preferences, resources (the labour force and the capital stock) and technology.

The problem, then, is that this simple AD/AS model is not well suited to representing other positions within Keynesianism apart from the orthodox Keynesian position; nor is it appropriate for discussing other positions that lie outside the orthodox Keynesian – monetarist controversy. As this book has rather been centred on the AD/AS model, this means that these other positions have taken on a more shadowy and marginalized presence within the general arguments of this book, whereas arguments that can be expressed in terms of the AD/AS model have been more easily accommodated within the book as a whole.

An example of the latter case can be found in chapter 4, which argued that one weakness of the AD/AS model is that it assumes a fixed level of capital in use, and that this prevents it from developing a coherent account of the unemployment of labour and capital during a recession. This lacuna is partly attributable to the Marshallian concept of the short run that underpins macroeconomics and that is shared both by orthodox Keynesianism and monetarism. But it is also the result of the underlying neo-classical emphasis which has pervaded the development of the AD/AS model, and which emphasizes the role of price adjustment within a market economy. This has meant that the issue of unemployment has been seen primarily in terms of the malfunctioning of the price system in failing to establish market clearing. This has resulted in an extremely narrow view of production and the way that the production process is organized in the short run, where output can expand only if real wages fall.

But this criticism can easily be accommodated within the simple AD/AS model. Recognizing the reduction in the capital stock in using during a recession means that aggregate demand and supply are not independent of each other: if the AD curve shifts to the left then so does the AS curve. The policy implication of this analysis is that policy-induced increases in aggregate demand will also increase aggregate supply and, indeed, that policy should be so directed to ensure that the corresponding increase in aggregate supply for a given increase in aggregate demand is as large as possible. This means that increases in aggregate demand *can* increase output and employment without stimulating inflationary pressure and without necessitating a fall in real wages, and it also suggests that significant improvements in the supply side of the economy cannot be expected to take place unless there is an accompanying increase in aggregate demand.

Another example can be found in chapter 9, which discusses both market-orientated and state interventionist approaches to improving the supply side of the economy. Here again the starting point of the analysis is the simple AD/AS model, but by emphasizing the issue of *shifts* in the AS curve it was able to move beyond the conventional Keynesian–monetarist short-run controversy by recognizing that such shifts are the result of a wide range of economic and social factors, and are not restricted to changes in the supply of labour and the nominal wage rate.

There are other positions within Keynesianism which are not so easily expressed in terms of the simple AD/AS model. This model emphasizes the joint determination of output and prices, and the importance of the impersonal, competitive market forces of demand and supply in effecting this. This is at odds with an approach to the macroeconomy which emphasizes the significance of imperfect competition, imperfect knowledge and increasing returns to scale in a real world dominated by large corporations and oligopolistic structures. In such a world, prices are not the competitive outcome of anonymous market forces, but are the result of specific pricing practices exercised by these large corporations. In this world, cost-plus pricing tends to dominate; this means that prices are raised if costs increase, if wages rise or if the price of imported raw materials or fuels increase, for example. In this case, therefore, the price level is not determined by the level of aggregate demand as affected by government fiscal and monetary policy, but by the reactions of the large corporations to changes in the cost variables, especially wages. In other words, the price level and output are independently determined. The policy implications of this model are different from those of the orthodox Keynesian/monetarist AD/AS model; in this case governments can pursue expansionary policies without inflationary consequences as long as there is an effective incomes policy in operation to keep wage increases in line with productivity increases.

Such results are not easily accommodated within the AD/AS model representing price–output space, and this means that organizing a discussion of macro-theory and macro-policy in terms of the AD/AS model will tend to marginalize or even exclude approaches which are not based on the static neo-classical model of competitive resource allocation. The radical Keynesian approach (e.g. Kaldor, 1983) is an example of this. It emphasizes imperfect competition and returns to scale, together with a cost-plus or structuralist approach to inflation, and stresses the independent determination of price (by supply-side factors) and output (by demand-side factors). If this approach is represented within the price–output space of the AD/AS model, this can only be done by presenting it as taking 'extreme' positions of the AS (horizontal) and AD (vertical) curves. But this is to try to represent it within a framework that it rejects, and so it appears to marginalize it in relation to what is presented as the main arena of debate.

This can also be seen in the radical Keynesian approach to the money supply which underlies their derivation of a vertical aggregate demand curve which is unresponsive to changes in the monetary aggregates (a classic statement of this is Kaldor, 1982; the post-Keynesians have also taken up this position, see Lavoie, 1984). The radical Keynesians (and post-Keynesians) reject the orthodox Keynesian/monetarist consensus that the money supply can be treated as an exogenous variable and, therefore, a possible policy instrument in determining the level of nominal aggregate demand. They emphasize that the supply of money is wrongly conceived as a stock rather than as the supply of loans which is a flow variable. This supply of loans is not exogenously given by the Central Bank but is endogenously determined; that is, it is demand-determined by entrepreneurs requiring credit money to finance their monetary outlays as part of an ongoing production process. In this 'monetized production economy' the money supply therefore has no independent causal status and determines neither demand, employment nor the rate of inflation.

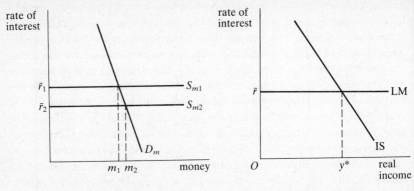

Figure 10.3a   Figure 10.3b

Using the IS–LM approach we could say that the supply of money curve is horizontal, not vertical. This is shown in figure 10.3a, which represents a conventional though fairly inelastic downward-sloping demand curve for money and a perfectly elastic money supply at the prevailing rate of interest set by the Central Bank. If the demand for money has some interest-elasticity, then changes in the rate of interest will indirectly affect the supply of money via the demand for money. In this case if monetary policy could reduce the rate of interest from $O\bar{r}_1$ to $O\bar{r}_2$, this would increase the supply of money from Om_1 to Om_2. If, however, the demand for money is not interest-elastic (i.e. the demand curve for money is vertical) as the monetarists have claimed, and with which radical and post-Keynesians tend to agree, a monetary policy focused on interest rate changes could be effective only at one remove further still; in so far as a reduction in interest rates increases income levels via the investment-multiplier process, this would increase the demand for money (i.e. the vertical demand curve would shift to the right) and so increase the supply of money.

Translated into the IS–LM diagram these results mean that the LM curve is horizontal, whatever the interest-elasticity of the demand for money. This is illustrated in figure 10.3b. In this case, as we saw above in connection with figure 10.1a, monetary policy is ineffective except in so far as direct control over the rate of interest is used to stimulate investment. Thus, the radical Keynesian criticism of the ineffectiveness of monetary policy in trying to use monetary aggregates to determine the level of income (or rate of inflation) endorses the earlier Keynesian position, but it does this by switching the focus of its attack from the demand side of the money market to the supply side. Far from seeing liquidity preference underlying the demand for money as the central element in the debate between Keynesians and monetarists, this has now become more or less irrelevant, and instead the radical Keynesians insist that it is the endogeneity of the money supply that renders monetary policy ineffective. As discussed earlier, in chapters 6 and 7, this particular policy debate became of heightened interest after 1979 when Margaret Thatcher's government came to power on a monetarist anti-inflation platfom in which control of the money supply was seen as the key to controlling inflation. Part of the radical Keynesian argument against this was that the money supply could not be controlled, and so could not function as a policy instrument in the manner proposed by the monetarists (see e.g. Kaldor's evidence to the Treasury and Civil Service Committee in 1980 in Kaldor (1982), Part II). As chapter 7 has outlined, in the event the financial targets of the Medium Term Financial Strategy were continually being overrun and the Chancellor of the Exchequer announced in October 1985 that the £M3 targets would be suspended for the time being.

In view of the problems involved in representing other Keynesian positions within the AD/AS model, some Keynesian approaches have eschewed this model altogether. Given the neo-classical emphasis on simultaneous price and quantity adjustment in reaching market-clearing equilibrium, Keynesian approaches that emphasizes quantity rationing and disequilibrium states where markets do not clear, have chosen not to use the AD/AS model, but to develop their own theoretical framework. Building on the original work by Clower (1965) and Barro and Grossman (1971) this school of Keynesian economists emphasizes a short-run fixed price model where quantity constraints form the basis of the important interactions between markets which do not clear.

A major focus of interest for this approach is the range of possible interactions between the goods market and the labour market. Here the demand for labour depends on whether the planned supply of goods is actually sold, and the demand for goods depends on whether the planned supply of labour is realized. Hence, a distinction is made between unconstrained, i.e. notional, demands, which pertain

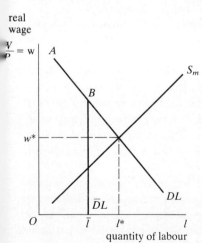

Figure 10.4a. The labour market

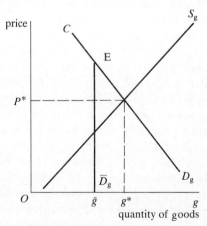

Figure 10.4b. The goods market

when plans are fulfilled in the other market, and constrained demands which pertain when supply plans in the other market are not fulfilled. Keynesian unemployment is characterized by excess supply in both the labour and the goods market; as firms are constrained in the goods market this means that the relevant demand for labour is the constrained demand and not the notional demand for labour. This is shown in figure 10.4a which illustrates the labour market and figure 10.4b which illustrates the goods market. The curve AD_l represents the notional demand curve for labour in figure 10.4a, whereas the constrained demand curve is shown by the kinked demand curve ABD_l. Thus, even with a real wage at the Walrasian market-clearing rate Ow^*, there will be an excess supply of labour equal to $\bar{ll}^*$. The goods market is shown in figure 10.4b. Here the constrained demand for goods is shown by the linked demand curve $CE\bar{D}g$: even with a price of OP^*, the market clearing price, there is a lack of effective demand such that the planned supplies exceed effective demand by $\bar{gg}^*$.

Clearly in this model the constrained demands are not independent. Thus any attempt to eliminate the excess supplies by changing the price of labour or of goods will be unsuccessful unless it succeeds in affecting the constrained demand in the *other* market and so lifting the constraint in the first market. Thus the effect of changing the real wage rate depends on the impact that this has on the demand for goods, and hence on the demand for labour; the problem here is that whilst increases in the real wage rate reduce the excess supply of goods by increasing demand in the goods market, they also cause an increase in the supply of labour such that, although employment will increase, it is just possible that unemployment may also increase. This problem would be overcome, however, by an increase in government expenditure which would operate directly on the demand for goods, increasing output and reducing unemployment (Malinvaud, 1985, pp. 58–65).

The opposite regime of classical unemployment pertains when there is excess supply in the labour market but excess demand in the goods market. In this case consumers are rationed in the goods market because firms' supply is constrained; workers are rationed in the labour market because firms' demand for labour is constrained. In this case, reducing real wages provides the incentive for firms to produce more and, hence, results in a reduction of unemployment; as firms switch to their notional supply of goods they also switch over to their notional demand for labour. To the extent, though, that the notional demand for goods would be reduced by the fall in real wages, the final market-clearing level of employment would be smaller than the original level.

Another school of Keynesian economists which have rejected the orthodox Keynesian–monetarist AD/AS model are the post-Keynesian writers. This is a more heterogeneous group of economists than the non-market-clearing group, and their interests are not restricted to macroeconomics and monetary theory but include classical political economy and Marxist theory (see Harcourt, 1985 for a brief survey of the heterogeneous interests of the post-Keynesians). We have already seen that this group argues that the endogeneity of the money supply vitiates the monetarist policy of attempting to control the supply of money. This group also argues that the AD/AS model conventionally used in textbooks is not that of Keynes's *General Theory*. Instead they use an alternative aggregate demand and supply model purportedly derived from the *General Theory* which directly determines the level of *employment* (rather than the level of real national income). Given this equilibrium level of employment, the schedule of the marginal product of labour shows the corresponding level of the real wage rate. This is shown in figures 10.5 and 10.6 (see Davidson and Smolensky, 1964; Davidson, 1983a,b).

The basic aggregate demand and supply model is shown in figure 10.5. The aggregate supply schedule, Z, relates expected scales proceeds to employment (given techniques, the stock of capital, the degree of competition and the money wage rate). Its positive slope shows that employment increases as sales proceeds increase. The aggregate demand schedule, D, shows that aggregate demand also increases as

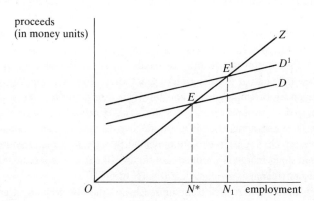

Figure 10.5.

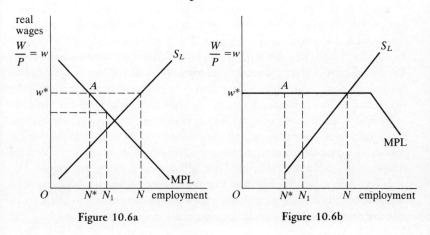

Figure 10.6a   Figure 10.6b

employment increases (given the propensity to consume and the rate of investment). The point of intersection of these two curves at E is defined following Keynes as the point of effective demand, and it is this that determines the equilibrium level of employment, ON^*. Thus, in this model, employment is determined by the level of effective demand; conditions in the labour market simply determine the level of real wages and the extent of unemployment. The production theory underlying the post-Keynesian approach is basically the same as the neo-classical theory; a short-run production function is used but this may show diminishing (as in figure 10.6a), or a constant (as in figure 10.6b), marginal product of labour (MPL). The marginal product of labour curve shows the real wage received by workers for any level of equilibrium employment. Thus, at point A in either figure 10.6a or 10.6b the real wage is shown as Ow^*, and the horizontal distance between the marginal product of labour curve (sometimes called the market equilibrium curve) and the supply of labour at this real wage rate, gives the amount of unemployment, N^*N.

This approach emphasizes that the marginal product of labour curve is not the demand curve for labour. Hence the amount of employment is not increased by reductions in the money wage unless the level of effective demand is increased. According to this view it would be wrong to think of movements taking place *along* the MPL curve as the quantity demanded of labour responds to changes in the real wage rate; rather, the direction of causation is reversed as effective demand fixes the quantity of employment, and this then determines the real wage. The only way to reduce unemployment is to shift the aggregate demand function upwards from D to D^1 with an increased level of effective demand, E^1, and a higher level of employment, ON^1. This level of employment then requires a reduced real wage in the diminishing marginal product case (figure 10.6a) or a constant real wage in the constant marginal product case (figure 10.6b).

Although the non-market-clearing approach and the post-Keynesian approach use different theoretical frameworks, they do show the same theoretical objective of trying to provide a more rigorous underpinning for the basic Keynesian proposition that it is the level of aggregate demand that determines the level of employment and output in the economy. From different standpoints they both criticize the notion that a fall in money wages is sufficient to increase employment. The non-market-clearing approach argues that the 'notional' demand for labour becomes irrelevant when there is Keynesian unemployment, and it emphasizes the significance of the 'constrained' demand function for labour for which the level of demand for goods is one of its arguments. In this case Keynesian unemployment is compatible with the market-clearing wage rate Ow^*, which means that government policies to increase demand, and switch the economy back from the constrained regime to the notional regime, need not be based on reducing real wages. The post-Keynesian approach emphasizes that the aggregate marginal product curve of labour is not the demand for labour; employment is determined by the level of effective demand and the marginal product curve simply shows the resulting real wage rate. In this case, government policies to increase demand would involve a reduced real wage in the diminishing product case (figure 10.6a) but not in the constant marginal product case (figure 10.6b). In this respect the post-Keynesian policy conclusion is more akin to the traditional Keynesian argument that, in the presence of diminishing returns, real wages must fall if employment is to increase.

The non-market-clearing approach emphasizes the importance of a rigorous choice-theoretic foundation that is very much in the tradition of Walrasian general equilibrium analysis, whilst the post-Keynesians turn to a strict exegesis of Keynes's *General Theory* in an attempt to uncover its original meaning. But in spite of their different approaches to modelling the macroeconomy, the theoretical and policy conclusions of their work are similar: as (Keynesian) unemployment is caused by a deficiency of aggregate demand, governments should attempt to maintain an adequate level of aggregate demand in the economy. Neither approach gives any support to the new monetarist position that unemployment can be resolved by allowing market forces more freedom to determine labour market outcomes.

We have seen that there are a number of arguments that can be broadly designated as Keynesian which cannot easily be represented within the AD/AS model. These arguments suggest a more active role for short-term government economic policy in maintaining an adequate level of aggregate demand. These arguments also connect up with a range of other government initiatives in economic policy-making in addition to the more traditional areas of fiscal and monetary policy. Some would welcome a more positive attitude to an incomes policy, for example, in order to prevent real wages from rising in excess of productivity increases. Others would welcome a more active stance on the issue of industrial policy in facilitating much-needed structural changes within the UK economy.

This brings us to a major weakness of the AD/AS model for policy assessment purposes: its fundamentally short-term nature. The problem is that policy decisions and assessments have to take into account an evaluation of the medium-term (and long-term) changes in the economy, as well as the purely short-term ones, and here of course the AD/AS model is silent. These longer-term changes are modelled within the AD/AS approach as exogenous changes, on the side of demand or supply or both, and may have their origin within the domestic economy or in the international economy. Though the AD/AS model provides a framework for analysing the *effects* of these exogenous changes, it does not provide a model for analysing the *causes* of these exogenous changes, and here there are very different views expressed by different economists.

As an example of this, we can take the well-publicized slow-down in the rate of economic growth in the industrialized countries since the early 1970s; between 1973 and 1981 the rate of growth of labour productivity slowed down in comparison with 1960–73 (see Matthews, 1982 for the proceedings of a conference which discussed this slow-down; and see chapter 1 above). In table 10.1 we can see a decline in rates of growth in output (Q) and in labour productivity (Q/N) during the

Table 10.1.   Changes in GDP (*Q*) and GDP per person employed (*Q/N*)*: annual average increase per cent

	1960-73	of which: 1967-73	1973-9	of which: 1973-5	1975-9	1979-81
France						
Q	5.6	5.6	3.1	1.7	3.9	0.8^a
Q/N	4.7^a	4.7	2.9	1.9	3.4	1.1^a
Germany						
Q	4.5	5.3	2.4	−0.6	4.0	0.8^a
Q/N	4.4	4.8	3.2	2.1	3.7	0.8^a
Japan						
Q	9.9	9.5	3.7	0.7	5.3	3.7^a
Q/N	8.5	8.3	3.0	0.9	4.0	2.8^a
UK						
Q	3.1	3.4	1.3^b	−0.8	2.4	1.5^b
Q/N	2.8^a	3.3	1.2	−0.7	2.2	2.1
US						
Q	4.1	3.6	2.7	−0.8	4.5	1.0
Q/N	2.2	1.4	0.4	−1.0	1.1	0.3

^{a} Estimated or partly estimated.
^{b} If oil and natural gas are excluded, it is estimated that GDP grew by 0.8 per cent annually from 1973 to 1979 and fell by 1.8 per cent annually from 1979 to 1981.
*GDP refers to GDP at constant market prices, employment to civilian employment.
Source: Morgan (1982), p. 21.

1960-81 period as a whole, the one exception being the UK case in 1979-81 where the fall in output was accompanied by an increase in labour productivity. (This increase was discussed in chapter 9, where it was suggested that there are doubts as to whether it will continue). In terms of the AD/AS model this fall in the rate of growth of labour productivity could be represented by a leftwards shift in the AS curve signifying a structural shift in the production function. But what has caused this shift? On this the AD/AS model has no answer, as it does not include any specification of the determinants of the long-run growth rate in the economy such as population, skills, capital stock and technology. Further, we can see that the rate of growth is declining at different rates in different countries; this means that the production function is shifting differently for different countries.

Thus the structure of relative international competitiveness is changing, reflecting these shifts in supply, and these changes are also affecting the structure of relative demands in the world economy. Here we can see the significance of the changing international division of labour with countries such as Japan and the newly industrializing countries effectively outcompeting Western European countries in the production and aggressive exporting of manufactured goods. This then raises more fundamental questions about the capacity of countries such as the UK to adjust to modern competitive conditions, investing in modern technology with viable industrial relations, in order to facilitate much-needed structural change.

Economists have put forward a number of different explanations in trying to account for this slow-down in productivity, but we can roughly separate them out into two different groups. One of these groups sees the slow-down in productivity as largely the result of exogenous shocks to the system in the sense that not only are the causes exogenous to the short-run model of output determination, but they must of necessity be exogenous to *any* model of economic behaviour. These exogenous shocks would include such things as natural disasters (e.g. harvest failures), wars, government interventions and, of course, the OPEC oil price increases.

Certainly the oil price rises in 1973/4 and 1979 have had a considerable impact on reducing growth, and this may be modelled in terms of their effect on the demand and supply sides of the economy. On the demand side – and this tends to be a Keynesian interpretation – it is said that the OPEC oil prices rises caused aggregate world demand for goods and services to fall as the change in the terms of trade caused a massive switch in purchasing power from the oil-importing countries to the oil-rich countries. Keynesians would emphasize here the effects of governments' failure to maintain an adequate level of demand in order to counteract this, a failure which was largely prompted by balance of payments problems and the inflationary pressures generated by the commodity boom and the oil price rise itself.

On the supply side – and this tends to be a monetarist interpretation – it is argued that the increase in raw energy costs for oil-importing countries caused a leftwards shift in the demand curve for labour and, hence, in the aggregate supply schedule. This meant that the feasible rate of growth of real wages would have to fall, reflecting the reduction in per capita income caused by the determination in the terms of trade. Apart from the effects of the OPEC price rises, monetarist supply-side explanations of declining productivity also emphasize the deleterious effect of the (to them) excessive government intervention in the economy which fuelled inflation, feather-bedded inefficient firms and facilitated excessive wage increases.

These explanations framed in terms of exogenous shocks operating on the demand and/or supply sides of the economy – where the exogenous shocks may be government interventions or OPEC oil price rises – are easily accommodated within the AD/AS model, even though the model is not used to explain them. These types of explanations have frequently been referred to in the course of this book. But there is another group of explanations for the productivity slow-down that focuses instead on seeing the slow-down as itself a part of the regular, cyclical functioning of the economy. According to this approach, apparently exogenous events such as the productivity slow-down should be explained endogenously within the economic model. Theories which fall into this class of explanation explicitly attempt to take a more dynamic view of the working of the economy in attempting to trace out the causes of structural shifts. I will just mention a few examples of such theories here – theories that have been referred to in a rather more oblique way in parts of this book, or else have not been included in the book at all.

One such approach relates to the work of Kondratieff in his attempt to identify long waves in economic life lasting about 50 years. Kondratieff's original project lay in identifying long waves in various price and output series that were then available to him, but his work developed in various ways in response to criticisms and discussions of his major paper on the subject (Kondratieff, 1935). Kondratieff identified two long waves lasting 40 to 60 years, from 1790 (approx.) to 1844–51, and from 1844–51 to 1890–6; a third unfinished wave he identified as starting 1890–6 with the downswing starting 1914–20. Kondratieff's work has been taken up recently by some economists because, in addition to identifying these long waves in the nineteenth and early twentieth century, this approach has been used to suggest that the post-war boom lasting until 1973 and the subsequent reduction in growth rates may be part of a fourth Kondratieff cycle starting with the post-war boom. Certainly the advanced industrialized countries have experienced considerable variations in their rates of growth over time, but the question is whether these variations are systematic and endemic. A statistical demonstration of the regularity of such 'long waves' in economic life has not been securely established by the available data (see e.g. Maddison, 1982 for a critical review of this), but various possible explanations have been proffered to account for them.

One type of explanation has focused on the role of cycles in innovation activity which form the basis of these long waves. According to the scheme proposed by Schumpeter, the first Kondratieff cycle was based on cotton textiles, iron and steam power, the second Kondratieff was based on the development of the railroads, and the third Kondratieff was based on electricity and the development of the car industry (see e.g. Duijn, 1983 for a discussion of this and other approaches). If this scheme is extended to the post-war period, then it is suggested that the fourth Kondratieff has been based on computers and electronics, and that if an upturn occurs in the 1990s this will be based on new industries such as biotechnology and new communication and transport systems. It is argued that each upswing in the cycle is associated with a new 'technological revolution'; those sectors with the greatest innovative activity in the new technology of the day are also those sectors with the highest growth performance and become the industrial leaders of their time. Thus, it is the product and process innovations in the technologically advanced sectors that lead the economy out of the depression period and into the new upswing, though different interpretations stress different time-profiles for the major technological advances. Some writers stress the innovative imperative of deep crises and low profits, others stress the uncertainty of the depression period which inhibits innovative activity which becomes significant only in the upswing phase, whilst others emphasize the importance of the role of the gifted and far-sighted entrepreneur in introducing innovations ahead of the market.

Another approach to accounting for these long waves has come from a Marxist writer, Ernest Mandel (1975), but he emphasizes a number of underlying causes of the long waves and does not prioritize technological change. Mandel's theory tries to combine Marxist theory and long wave theory in order to account for the successive periods of boom and slump that characterize capitalist economies, and in doing this he points to a number of exogenous factors that interact with the process of capitalist accumulation in causing the long waves. Other Marxist approaches to the cyclical nature of capitalist development have played down the uniform periodicity that characterizes the long wave approach, and have emphasized the importance of internal factors in causing crises and depressions.

As with Mandel, the starting point for these approaches is the importance of the rate of profit in driving the economic system forward. The primary internal driving force in capitalism is the pursuit of profit and the need to accumulate capital, i.e. to reinvest in further production in an attempt to increase profits. This pursuit of profit is based on a class system of ownership of the means of production. The working class do not own the means of production – the factories, machinery and raw materials – that are needed in the production process, but it is their work, their unpaid labour, that produces the profits upon which the accumulation process depends.

These Marxist writers stress that the rate of profit began to decline *before* the OPEC oil price rise of 1973. Pre-tax rates of return on the trading assets of industrial and commercial companies fell from the 1950s, the early 1970s and again from 1974. In addition, the share of profits as a percentage of domestic income also fell from the late 1960s and again after 1974. This suggests that although UK profitability did fall substantially at the time of the OPEC price rise, this was not the only factor affecting it, and that other factors were at work prior to the OPEC price rise which were reducing profitability (see e.g. Aaronovitch and Smith, 1981; Glyn and Harrison, 1980; Mandel, 1975).

The question that needs to be answered then is – why was profitability falling during this period? Debate here has centred on the interpretation of Marx's 'tendency of the rate of profit to fall' (*Capital*, vol. III, part III) as to why the process of accumulation inevitably goes into reverse at some stage and over-accumulation reduces the rate of profit. Two main arguments have been put forward here: first, that the capital: output ratio will eventually rise as new investments become less efficient; and second, that the share of income paid out as wages to workers will rise as real wages increase. (In terms of the theory advanced by Marx in *Capital*, this may be loosely construed as saying that the organic composition of capital will rise, or the rate of exploitation will fall.) Empirical estimates of these two possibilities raise a number of conceptual and statistical difficulties, but some support is claimed for both these propositions, especially the latter.

This emphasis on the rising share of wages in national income has led to a view of the recession of the 1970s and 1980s as the result of the over-accumulation of capital in relation to the supply of labour (see Glyn and Harrison, 1980; Glyn, 1982). According to this approach the barriers to the further profitable accumulation of capital were caused by the fact that labour supply was not increasing at a comparable rate with capital accumulation. Although labour immigration into the advanced capitalist countries, together with the increase in married women going out to work, had eased this, the reserve army of labour necessary to keep down wages and enforce labour discipline was gradually eroded, and with it one of the necessary prerequisites for continued profitable accumulation was disappearing. Thus, according to this view, the increased unemployment since the 1970s, and especially since 1979–81, is a part of the reconstitution of this reserve army of labour and the disciplining of the working class.

Not all Marxist writers agree with this conclusion. Fine and Harris (1985), for example, argue that the profitability of capital cannot be measured simply by the weakness of organized labour, and they stress that one of the problems of the British economy is that labour has been too *weak*. Instead of a high-wage, high-productivity economy, the British economy has increasingly become one where real wages are low compared with other Western European countries, and where manufacturing industry has become less productive and less able to compete internationally.

This then brings us to the analysis of class relations in these approaches. One axis of class relations is that between capital and labour, both in the sphere of distribution with the struggle over pay and in the sphere of production with the struggle over the intensity of work and control over work practices. Another axis of class relations is that between different segments or fractions of the capitalist class, between industrial capital and finance capital. Here many Marxist accounts of the relatively poor performance of the UK economy point to the special role of the City and the international orientation of UK capital (Aaronovitch and Smith, 1981; Fine and Harris, 1985; Leys, 1985). They stress the dominance of financial interests over industrial interests as represented by the power of the City, the official defence of the pound against the interests of domestic industry, the liberalization of exchange regulations and the pursuit of monetarist policies which have maintained high rates of interest.

Thus, long wave accounts and Marxist accounts (and those such as Mandel's that try to combine the two) draw attention in various ways to the essentially dynamic nature of capitalism. Here the longer-term fluctuations in profitability and growth derive basically from these internal dynamic forces even though the timing, severity and character of these longer-term changes are necessarily conditioned by a range of political, social and technological factors. But what implications does this approach have for economic policy, for smoothing out the fluctuations in economic activity and maintaining profitability and growth?

In some respects the implication for economic policy is simpler; instead of attempting to forecast or react to a series of exogenous shocks, policy would primarily need to be directed to the essential dynamic element that is itself the cause of the fluctuations, and this would then enable the economic system to withstand the exogenous shocks in a more robust manner. But this simplicity also carries with it a much more complicated and intractable policy stance. In the case of long waves based on changing technology it requires the government to be actively involved in anticipating and directing new programmes of technological research, and organizing a long-term industrial strategy based on this research. In the case of Marxist approaches to the process of capitalist accumulation this requires an active government policy to counteract the depressing influences on the rate of profit so as to ensure a smooth process of capitalist accumulation.

This approach therefore suggests a larger-scale and more interventionist character for state policies towards the economy, a character which would represent a considerable break-away from conventional models of state economic intervention in the UK although more in tune with traditions in Japan and some West European countries. It also poses the problem of the extent to which any institution such as the state can actually intervene in the economy to fundamentally change the dynamic laws of its operation. In this sense the state has to be both above the economy and also a part of it. For the Marxist approach this raises the additional problem of the class allegiance of the state; to what extent can the state run a capitalist economy in the interests of both capital and labour where the fundamental laws of capitalist accumulation are based on a conflict of interest between these two classes.

Thus, the policy implications of these dynamic approaches to economic development are not altogether clear-cut, but they do raise a rather different set of policy issues from those derived from the use of the short-run AD/AS model. By raising larger questions about the long-run determinants of growth and prosperity, they also pose more complex questions about social relations, technological change, and the role of the state in economic activity. This perhaps helps to explain why the AD/AS model has been found so convenient for policy discussions, in that it abstracts from some of these wider issues and focuses attention on a restricted number of economic variables. The aim of this chapter has simply been to remind you that the focus of this book on the AD/AS model has predetermined, to some extent, the kind of economic analysis and policy debate that could be covered.

References

Aaronovitch, S. and Smith, R. (1981) *The Political Economy of British Capitalism*. McGraw-Hill, London.

Arestis, P. and Skouras, T. (eds) (1985) *Post Keynesian Economic Theory: A challenge to Neo Classical Economics*. Wheatsheaf, Sussex.

Barro, R. J. and Grossman, H. I. (1971) 'A general disequilibrium model of income and employment', *American Economic Review*, 61, 82–93.

Clower, R. (1965) 'The Keynesian counter-revolution: a theoretical appraisal'. In *The Theory of Interest Rates*. Macmillan, London, ch. 5, pp. 103–25; reprinted in Clower, R. W. (ed.) (1969) *Monetary Theory*, Penguin, Harmondsworth, pp. 270–97.

Davidson, P. (1983a) 'The dubious labour market analysis in Meltzer's restatement', *Journal of Economic Literature*, 21, 52–56.

Davidson, P. (1983b) 'The marginal product curve is not the demand curve for labour . . .', *Journal of Post Keynesian Economics*, VI(1), 105–17.

Davidson, P. and Smolensky, E. (1964) *Aggregate Supply and Demand Analysis*, Harper and Row, New York.

Duijn, J. J. van (1983) *The Long Wave in Economic Life*. George Allen & Unwin, London.

Fine, B. and Harris, L. (1985) *The Peculiarities of the British Economy*. Lawrence & Wishart, London.

Glyn, A. (1982) 'The productivity slow-down: a marxist view', In Matthews (1982), pp. 148–66.

Glyn, A. and Harrison, J. (1980) *The British Economic Disaster*. Pluto Press, London.

Harcourt, G. C. (1985) 'Post Keynesianism: quite wrong or nothing new'. In Arestis and Skouras (1985), pp. 125–145.

Hicks, J. R. (1937) 'Mr Keynes and the 'classics': a suggested interpretation', *Econometrica*, 5, 147–59.

Kaldor, N. (1982) *The Scourge of Monetarism*, Oxford University Press, Oxford.

Kaldor, N. (1983) 'Keynesian economics after fifty years'. In Worswick, D. and Trevithick, J. (eds) *Keynes and the Modern World*. Cambridge University Press, Cambridge, pp. 1–44.

Kondratieff, N. (1935) 'The long wave in economic life', *Review of Economic Statistics*, 17, 105–15.

Lavoie, M. (1984) 'The endogenous flow of credit and the post Keynesian theory of money', *Journal of Economic Issues*, XVIII(3), 771–97.

Layard, R. and Nickell, S. (1985) 'The causes of British unemployment', *National Institute Economic Review*, 111, 62–85.

Leys, C. (1985) 'Thatcherism and British manufacturing: a question of hegemony', *New Left Review*, 151, 5–25.

Maddison, A. (1982) *Phases of Capitalist Development*, Oxford University Press, Oxford.

Malinvaud, E. (1985) *The Theory of Unemployment Reconsidered*, 2nd edn (1st edn, 1977), Basil Blackwell, Oxford.

Mandel, E. (1975) *Late Capitalism*. New Left Books, London.

Marx, K. (1972) *Capital*, vol. III. Lawrence & Wishart, London.

Matthews, R. C. O. (ed.) (1982) *Slower Growth in the Western World*. Heinemann, London.

Metcalfe, D. (1984) 'On the measurement of employment and unemployment', *National Institute Economic Review*, 109, 59–67.

Morgan, A. D. (1982) 'Productivity in the 1960s and 1970s', In Matthews (1982), pp. 17–28.

Radcliffe Report (1959) *Report of the Committee on the Working of the Monetary System*. Cmnd. 827. HMSO, London.

Smith, W. L. (1956) 'A graphical exposition of the complete Keynesian system', *The Southern Economic Journal*, 23, 115–25; reprinted in Mueller, M. G. (ed.) (1969) *Readings in Macroeconomics*. Holt, Rinehart & Winston, London, pp. 37–45.

Index